Writing for Accountants

Aletha S. Hendrickson
University of Maryland

COLLEGE DIVISION South-Western Publishing Co.
Cincinnati Ohio

Publisher: Mark Hubble
Developmental Editor: Minta Berry
Production Editor: Shelley Brewer
Production House: Matrix Productions
Cover and Interior Designer: Craig LaGesse Ramsdell
Photo/Art Editor: Jennifer Mayhall
Marketing Manager: James Sheibley Enders

AB85AB

ISBN: 0-538-83040-9

Library of Congress Catalog Card Number: 92-082624

1 2 3 4 5 6 7 8 9 DH 0 9 8 7 6 5 4 3 2

Printed in the United States of America

Preface

Writing for Accountants is a student-oriented text devoted to accounting communication. The text teaches accounting students and professionals alike the importance and the art of effective written and oral communication. Effective communication applies the best of classical and modern rhetorical theory to actual writing and speaking situations. *Writing for Accountants* stresses the modes of communication, issues, resources, types of argument, methodologies, and real-world situations encountered by accountants on the job.

Purpose of *Writing for Accountants*

Writing for Accountants is designed to close the communication gap often experienced by accountants and users of their communications. Designed for both preprofessional and professional accountants, *Writing for Accountants* addresses those patterns of thought generated within accountancy, prompted within its discipline, interpreted and sanctioned within its academic and professional institutions, and finally translated for the public by means of diverse modes of prescribed accounting communication. By working with proven rhetorical and composition practices, numerous real-world examples, and practical exercises, students and professionals apply sound rhetorical principles to accounting communications.

Writing for Accountants covers the basics of rhetorical appeals and composition practices. Because it is geared to the communication needs of accountants, it helps the preprofessional and the practitioner understand

- *What* is involved in the complicated arena of accountancy, including complex subject matter, hostile audiences, self-promotion, and self-preservation;

- *Why* communicating in the workplace makes or breaks accounting careers, attracts or repels clients, helps or hinders a writer's or speaker's intentions, aids or thwarts a reader's or hearer's comprehension;
- *Where* capitalizing on accounting methodologies and resources pays off in planning, composing, and reviewing accounting communications;
- *When* to use devices such as ambiguity, hedges, and passive voice—often cautioned against in ordinary business writing, but sometimes mandated by special circumstances faced by accountants in a litigious society;
- *How* to select from a virtual arsenal of weapons containing rhetorical strategies, proven composition practices, linguistic devices, and design approaches for effective presentation and communication.

Who Should Use Writing for Accountants

In Academia

Writing for Accountants is comprehensive enough to stand alone as the writing text for university and college writing courses and seminars. The text also supplements the writing component in writing-across-the-curriculum programs. With its varied content, case studies, and real-world examples, accounting professors can choose among its topics to augment any accounting course: lower, upper, and graduate level.

In the Workplace

Writing for Accountants serves as the textual resource for in-house writing seminars, and functions as a useful desktop reference for professionals. It can be used profitably for self-study. The text is also suitable for paraprofessionals, nonaccountants, and secretaries who work with accountants.

How to Use Writing for Accountants

Students and Professionals

By referring to the subject index, students and professionals can concentrate on particulars of written and oral communication applied to workplace situations. Chapter 7 is the reference chapter for the particulars of macro- and micro-composition, stylistics, grammar, spelling, and punctuation.

Instructors

The *Instructor's Manual* contains helpful comments on sections of the student text, including the learning objectives, key terms, tear-out exercises (many with suggested responses), and figures geared to each chapter. In addition, a suggested syllabus and a topical bibliography are provided.

Chapter Goals

The learning objectives heading each chapter summarize the content and highlight its relation to accounting communication. The brief **overview**, chapter **goals**, and **key terms** preview the material and prepare the student and professional to acquire and improve the specific rhetorical and composition skills covered in the chapter.

Key Terms

So that readers can easily grasp the material, definitions of unfamiliar rhetorical and composition key terms are placed at the head of each chapter. The text also contains a complete glossary.

Accessible, Plain Style

Writing for Accountants is written in a plain English style for greater readability and to exemplify the type of prose required for today's accounting communication. The prose style stresses accommodation to the special requirements of writing for accountancy. Also, the text is structured, formatted, and headed to facilitate reader comprehension.

Illustrations

Drawings, diagrams, charts, cartoons, and other graphics illustrate important concepts covered in the text. In addition, the illustrations exemplify the principles of document and graphic design discussed in Chapter 6.

Case Studies and Real-World Examples

Real-world accounting situations, communications, and issues are used so that students can address writing tasks they are likely to encounter on the job. Three major case studies in Chapter 5 typify the real problems accountants face in difficult workplace situations, and numerous true examples throughout the text portray accountants coping with everyday writing, listening, and speaking situations.

Actual Accounting Communications

Although some student examples are included, the emphasis throughout the text is on actual accounting communication. Source material is taken from the workplace, the writings of accountancy, and such respected accounting publications as the *Journal of Accountancy*, *The Practical Accountant*, and *Management Accounting*. Modes of writing common to accountancy stimulate student interest as they illustrate rhetorical principles and accepted composition practices. Students and professionals alike learn from actual writing encountered on the job—from writing involving real contexts, people, problems, situations, and current issues of accountancy.

Tear-Out Exercises

Seventy-four classroom-tested exercises offer practice in accounting-related communications, and in honing analytical, composition, and rhetorical skills used by accountants in the workplace. Most of the practical exercises involve actual accounting texts and/or workplace situations, and are designed to reinforce chapter objectives. Convenient end-of-chapter tear-out exercises can be completed in the classroom, office, or home, and they fit standard typewriters and word processors.

Content of Writing for Accountants (For Students)

Part One

Part One introduces the communicating accountant and the user of accounting communications.

Chapter 1: Accountants are Writers

As professionals, accountants are responsible for communicating important financial information to diverse audiences. This chapter dispels myths about bean-counting accountants and introduces the accountant as communicator. Accounting-related material—including the accountant's personality and image, a lease-buy problem, GAAP, and Grammatik V—addresses these **topics**:

- Understanding the accountant's role in communication
- Acknowledging the accountant's writing task
- Coping with writing anxiety
- Capitalizing on writing strengths
- Compensating for writing weaknesses
- Adapting accounting methodologies to writing tasks
- Using GARP: Generally Accepted Rhetorical Principles

Chapter 2: Accountants Write for Users

Accountants communicate with a wide range of users. This chapter introduces audience awareness and focuses on the user of the writings of accountancy. Accounting-related material—including the expectation gap, decision makers, data analyzers, review reports, natural language processing, payroll taxes, and third-party litigation—covers these **topics**:

- Identifying and analyzing internal and external users
- Anticipating and satisfying user expectation
- Understanding, accommodating, and exploiting user reading habits and strategies
- Structuring documents for reader comprehension
- Writing defensively for risky users

An **exercise** helps the accounting student and the professional understand how users process text by using frames of reference.

Part Two

Part Two teaches accountants to cope with the issues, communication modes, writing situations, user requirements, and writing tasks in the workplace.

Chapter 3: What Accountants Write

As accountants communicate within diverse workplace situations, they generate ideas, conduct research, and document sources—just as other writing professionals do. This chapter focuses on the content of the writings of accountancy: how accountants convert ideas, theories, data, and professional opinions into information for users. Accounting-related material—including the 150-Hour Law, Management Advisory Services, IRS offers-in-compromise, letters of complaint, and U.S. Tax Court practice—treats these **topics**:

- Analyzing argument
- Making logical, supported points
- Using workable research strategies
- Consulting and documenting professional resources

Twelve **exercises** help the accounting student and the professional to

- Identify issues in dispute within accountancy
- Determine causes of problems
- Evaluate situations and solve problems
- Generate fruitful topics and proposals

- Make and defend assertions
- Document sources

Chapter 4: Why Accountants Write
Accountants write with mixed purposes in the interests of themselves, employers, and internal/external users. This chapter focuses on what motivates accountants to write. Accounting-related material—including resume and cover letters, "spring purges," paper trails, collection letters, letters to the IRS, IRS Notice of Deficiency, letters of reprimand, and letters of complaint—deals with these **topics**:

- Writing effectively to enter, advance, and survive in the workplace
- Communicating appropriately with superiors, peers, and subordinates
- Conveying information to users persuasively
- Controlling tone in communication

Twelve **exercises** help the accounting student and the professional to

- Write successful resumes and cover letters
- Critique resumes and cover letters
- Analyze and manipulate tone in workplace documents

Chapter 5: Where Accountants Write
Accountants practice in various workplace situations as sole practitioners, members of accounting firms, governmental employees, and workers in private industry and not-for-profit businesses. This chapter focuses on actual case studies that illustrate how the communication of accountants is affected by complex workplace realities. The workplace situations of an IRS agent, CPA firm partner, accounting department supervisor, sales representative, church treasurer, accounts payable manager, controller, audit manager, and sole practitioner incorporate these **topics**:

- Analyzing vertical/horizontal and external/internal communication
- Recognizing the complications of writing for multiple users in a litigious society
- Contending with interpersonal, organizational, professional, legal, political, and societal realities of the workplace
- Writing, editing, and revising alone and collaboratively
- Developing practical checklists geared to the writings of accountancy

Ten **exercises** help the accounting student and the professional to

- Analyze workplace situations
- Understand the writer's and the user's roles in communication
- Avoid sexist and prejudicial language
- Define terms for multiple audiences
- Locate professional resources
- Create writing checklists geared to accountancy

Chapter 6: When Accountants Write
Accountants use conventional modes of communication appropriate to the occasion, audience, purpose, and message. This chapter focuses on documents commonly used throughout business in general and accountancy in particular. Accounting-related material—including engagement letters, collection letters, resume documents, an OCBOA report, financial statement cover letters, management letters, compilation reports, office notices, tax return cover sheets, and accounting firm brochures—is used to consider these **topics**:

- Recognizing the conventional writing modes of business and accountancy
- Manipulating formats and graphics to assist user understanding

- Designing attractive, readable documents
- Chunking texts for reader accessibility

Ten **exercises** help the accounting student and the professional to

- Create informative headings
- Make dense text readable
- Guide readers through text
- Design professional documents
- Illustrate financial data
- Critique a workplace document

Chapter 7: How Accountants Write

Accountants often convey complex accounting information to uncomprehending audiences who nevertheless use the data to make important financial decisions. As financial experts, accountants are expected to communicate appropriately, clearly, and completely—while projecting a professional image. By cultivating a user-based attitude, by developing strategies to improve readability, and by writing and punctuating correctly, accountants ensure effective communication and avoid costly reader misunderstanding.

This double-length chapter focuses on the rhetorical, stylistic, grammatical, and punctuation choices available to the accountant-writer. Accounting-related material—including a CPA firm's code of conduct, an accounting software advertisement, Taxpayer's Bill of Rights, Total Quality Management, business ethics, recommendation report, letter to the IRS, encroachment on CPA practices—is used to cover these **topics**:

- Organizing and composing a coherent message
- Writing readable prose
- Guarding the English language by using correct grammar
- Spelling correctly
- Improving editing skills
- Using GAPP: Generally Accepted Punctuation Practices

Twenty-one **exercises** help the accounting student and the professional to

- Outline for reader understanding
- Paragraph for readability
- Order sentences into coherent paragraphs
- Incorporate transitional devices
- Combine sentences
- Simplify prose by judicious pruning
- Convert nominalizations to active verbs
- Agree in number
- Avoid sentence fragments
- Clarify referents
- Place modifiers sensibly
- Construct parallel sentences, phrases, and headings
- Spell accurately
- Punctuate correctly
- Proofread for comprehension and correctness
- Edit written communications

Part Three

Part Three helps accountants to improve speaking and listening skills.

Chapter 8: Accountants and Oral Communication
Accountants receive and convey oral as well as written messages. This chapter applies rhetorical principles to listening and speaking situations of accountancy. Accounting-related material—including job interviewing and oral presentations—is used to examine these **topics**:

- Analyzing the listener's and the speaker's situations
- Interviewing job applicants
- Asking appropriate questions
- Exploiting individual strengths
- Identifying and overcoming individual weaknesses
- Catering to an oral audience
- Adapting rhetorical strategies to oral discourse
- Designing and delivering dynamic oral presentations
- Critiquing oral reports
- Using GALP (Generally Accepted Listening Principles) and GASP (Generally Accepted Speaking Principles)

Eight **exercises** help the accounting student and the professional to

- Assess listener attitudes
- Analyze speakers and audiences
- Design oral report handouts
- Identify rhetorical devices
- Evaluate oral presentations

Acknowledgements

I would like to thank Mark Hubble, Acquisitions Editor of South-Western Publishing Co., for his interest in a writing text geared to the needs of accountants. I am especially indebted to Minta Berry, President of Berry Publications Services, for her unerring guidance in matters both large and small as the manuscript took shape. I am grateful to Shelley Brewer, Production Editor of South-Western Publishing Co., for her expert assistance in the final stages of production; to Barbara Milligan, copyeditor (Matrix Productions), for her recommendations and fine tuning of the manuscript; and to Merrill Peterson, production manager (Matrix Productions).

I also thank the following faculty reviewers for their insightful comments and helpful suggestions:

Penne Ainsworth
Kansas State University

Jim Gosline
University of Southern California

James W. Hartman
University of Kansas

Robert Ingram
University of Alabama

Joan S. Ryan
Lane Community College

Wanda Wallace
College of William and Mary

I am also grateful to the following advertisers, organizations, and publications for various contributions to the text:

Association of Professional Writing Consultants
Career Development Center (University of Maryland)
College for Financial Planning
Consulting Success
The Damirus Corporation
Electronic Data Systems Corporation
Institute of Management Accountants

Intensive Educational Development (University of Maryland)
Management Accounting
MicroMash
National Council of Teachers of English
National Public Accountant
National Society of Public Accountants
Pencil Pushers Tax Software
The Practical Accountant
Professional Writing Program (University of Maryland)
Quarterly Review of Doublespeak
Research Institute of America
Society for Technical Communication
South-Western Publishing Co.
Technical Communication: Journal of the Society for Technical Communication
Warren, Gorham & Lamont, Inc.
Writing Center (University of Maryland)

The following individuals contributed invaluable suggestions, material, and encouragement:

> Norman Barotz; Deborah Bryant (Career Development Center, University of Maryland); Susan Brown Cappitelli (Director of Publications, National Society of Public Accountants); Kim Carothers; Stanley Dambrowski (Intensive Educational Development, University of Maryland); Frank DeBernardo; Dr. Jeanne Fahnestock (Director, Professional Writing Program, University of Maryland); Steven A. Fisher; Gary B. Frank; Dr. Keith Grant-Davie (Utah State University); Ken Gray (Marketing Director, Pencil Pushers Tax Software); Dr. Eugene R. Hammond (Acting Chair, Department of English, University of Maryland); Shirley Hauch; Glenn M. Hendrickson, CPA, MSM; Larry D. Horner, CPA; Dr. Jean Johnson (Professional Writing Program, University of Maryland); Robert M. Kenny; Dr. Susan D. Kleimann (Editor, *Consulting Success*); Mindy Kopyta; Mary Kunstman; Dr. Shirley W. Logan; Susan Malone; Grant W. Newton; Bruce Odza; Louise Predoehl; Randy E. Rager, CPA; Robert F. Randall; Dr. Leigh Ryan (Writing Center Director, University of Maryland); M. H. Sarhan; Dr. Marie Secor (Penn State University); Howard J. Sobelman, EA; Joe Spitzig; Joonna Trapp (Instructor, Odessa College); Deborah B. Vieder; Becky Weir.

I acknowledge the contributions of my business and technical writing students at the University of Maryland who granted permission to use their writing:

> Leslie Anschutz, Ricardo Ashby, Audrey Beard, Dianne Bors, Chandra Burrows, Lance Chernow, David Goldsteen, William Green, Luke Ho, Brett Kleger, Daniel Krieger, Daniel Lambert, Wei-Chiun Lee, Andrea Levine, Catherine Maselka, David McNair, Lisa Moorehead, Joseph Papandrea, Michelle Partilla, Brian Roberts, Adam Salti, Lizel Spencer, Mark Tash, and Kristin Wunderlich.

A special thanks is due my indefatigable research assistants, Tamye Lyles and Don Vogel. I am particularly grateful to the directors and instructors of the Professional Writing Program at the University of Maryland for generously allowing me to plunder their files and for their unfailing support and encouragement. The founder of the program, Dr. Michael Marcuse, sparked my interest in workplace writing, and the current Director of Writing Programs, Dr. Jeanne Fahnestock, fanned the flames.

Finally, I am grateful to my husband, Glenn, for allowing me liberal access to his accounting library, for patiently answering 1,001 questions about the intricacies of accountancy, and for supporting this effort in every way imaginable. To commemorate his thirtieth anniversary as an accountant, I dedicate this book to Glenn M. Hendrickson, CPA.

Aletha Hendrickson
University of Maryland

Contents

LIST OF FIGURES

Part One

Accountants Communicate with Their Readers

CHAPTER 1

Accountants Are Writers

OVERVIEW Ineffective communication renders the accountant's expertise useless. This chapter focuses on the accountant as communicator of financial information. It teaches the accountant-writer to:

- Acknowledge the accountant's writing task;
- Understand the accountant's role in communication;
- Cope with writing anxiety.

GOALS

◆ Assess writing skills.
◆ Adapt accounting methodologies to writing tasks.
◆ Capitalize on writing strengths.
◆ Develop strategies to compensate for writing weaknesses.

KEY TERMS

Boilerplate Form letters and workplace documents, sometimes personalized.
Ethos The character of the writer as perceived by the reader.
Exigence That which spawns written or spoken discourse.
Genre A prescribed mode of communication (e.g., engagement letter, resume, or letter of complaint).
Logos A logical argument, providing evidence to satisfy the reader.
Overhearer An unintended reader or user of a text (a third party).
Pathos An appeal to the self-interest of the reader.
Rhetorical situation The exigence, audience, and constraints affecting the writer and audience.
User-centered Written with user needs in mind.
Users Readers of the writings of accountancy.
Writer-centered Written from the writer's point of view, and failing to consider the needs of users.

Writer's block The inability to start or continue a writing task.
Writing anxiety Dread of the writing task.

The Mythical Accountant

The image of the humorless, green–eye-shaded accountant seated on a high stool is so pervasive that *The Practical Accountant* carries a semiregular feature, "Accountant's Image," that tracks how accountants are portrayed in the media. Stereotypical representations gleaned from diverse print and nonprint media sources tend to characterize accountants by appearance, personality, and work, as shown in Figure 1-1.[1]

To dispel the myths of appearance, you need only to thumb through a typical issue of the *Journal of Accountancy*. Of the sixty-six male accountants depicted in the June 1991 issue, a scant eight are "follically challenged," and only fourteen are "bespectacled." Most of the males look physically fit, as do the twenty-five female accountants illustrated.

Dealing with the myths of personality is a little more complicated. "Bookishness" is hardly a negative quality, especially for those accountants facing the 150-hour educational requirement. And what reader wants figures generated according to the "unmeticulous" accounting procedures employed by ex-accountant Bob Newhart, who quipped, "if you got within two or three bucks of it, [it was O.K.]"?[2] The accountants' renowned independence might be misconstrued as "aloofness" by the uninformed. And accountants who deal with demanding bankers, cantankerous clients, and exasperating government officials are anything but "meek." Those who consider accountants "boring" are ignorant of the dynamic way they grapple with crucial people-oriented issues daily. And accountants who find creative ways to deal with the latest Governmental Accounting Standards Board pronouncements (GASB) or the IRS's passive income regulations can hardly be called "unimaginative." The myths of appearance and personality that irk some accountants will continue to fill the "Accountant's Image" column in *The Practical Accountant*. In reality, such myths probably help the accountant's professional image.

Myths about the *work* that accountants perform do more than perpetuate the stereotypical bean-counting image. Accountants tend to perpetuate the number-crunching myth by failing to perceive themselves as problem-solving professionals who are responsible for communicating information critical to knowledgeable and unknowledgeable **users**, or readers of the writings of accountancy. Accounting journals, exposure drafts, continuing professional education courses, academic accounting curricula, and other professional activity testify to the focus of modern accounting and the qualities accountants need for practicing their craft. Thus, describing accountants properly takes quite a different chart (Fig. 1-2) from the stereotypical one shown (Fig. 1-1).

FIGURE 1-1
Qualities of the Stereotypical Accountant

Appearance	*Personality*	*Work*
Bald	Aloof	Pencil pusher
Drab	Meek	Number cruncher
Out of shape	Bookish	Scorekeeper
Hunch-shouldered	Boring	Calculator
Bespectacled	Passionless	Bean counter
	Frugal	
	Conservative	
	Meticulous	
	Unimaginative	

FIGURE 1-2
Qualities of the Accounting Professional

Character Traits	*Technical/Personal Skills*	*Work*
Objectivity	Electronic spreadsheets	Analyst
Industriousness	Word processing	Adviser
Conscientiousness	Tax packages	Evaluator
Creativity	Auditing software	Forecaster
Adaptability	Forecasting software	Marketer
Independence	Programming	Monitor
Trustworthiness	Systems analysis	Auditor
	Management	Manager
	Interpersonal communication	Calculator
	Oral communication	Instructor
	Written communication	Organizer
		Examiner
		Planner

Important as number crunching is to the accountant's task, the profession involves far more analytical, managerial, people, and communication skills than nonaccountants—or even some accountants—imagine.

The Problem-Solving Accountant

Accountants spend much of their working lives solving problems, as exemplified in these situations:

1. The Small Business Administration paid for travel expenses incurred by its former administrator that were improperly authorized and justified.[3] How can the U.S. General Accounting Office determine the appropriateness of the trips?
2. Lyle Tool Company wants to overhaul its inadequate inventory system. Would the periodic system or the perpetual system be more advantageous?
3. Shannon Shoe Corporation needs to raise $500,000 for capital improvements. Should the corporation issue common or preferred stock, or issue bonds?
4. DeePendable Restaurant Supply sales personnel are being paid on the basis of total sales. What alternative payment method would reward sales success while maximizing profits?

Obviously, accounting involves critical business situations. Yet solving complex problems is only half the accounting task. The other half involves communicating the solutions.

Block Masonry Contracting's Problem

Block Masonry Contracting tells its accountant that it needs a $120,000 hoist. The problem is how to acquire the hoist: should the company purchase or lease the equipment? To illustrate what skills are involved in solving this problem, the accountant must consider the following factors when determining the best way to finance the hoist:

- The company's cash position
- The company's taxable profit position
- The status of the company's balance sheet
- The company's credit position
- The company's policy regarding leasing equipment
- The effective interest rates
- The lease terms regarding cancellation or subsequent purchase

Analyzing the situation and factoring in the preceding criteria require analytical skills and precise calculations common to accounting tasks. But what good is such expertise if Block Masonry mistakenly buys the hoist instead of leasing it *because the accountant fails to convey clearly the recommendation to lease*? Think of the hours, effort, and money wasted if the paying client makes the wrong decision because the accountant has failed to communicate the result of complex deliberations. What is at stake for the accountant who does not make the effort to communicate? In this case, it is the loss of a client who fires the uncommunicative accountant. In the competitive environment of the nineties, accountants cannot afford to sabotage their professional endeavors by incompetent communication.

The Communicating Accountant

Luttrell Distributing Company engaged an outside accounting firm, Tyme and Billin, P.A., for their year-end audit report. In due course, the financial statement was received by Andrew Quagmire, co-owner and vice-president of Luttrell. After grappling with four pages of notes (disclosure footnotes) to the financial statement, Mr. Quagmire stormed into the controller's office, complaining that he could hardly discuss the report with bankers the next day if he couldn't understand the notes himself. The controller, Ronald Tweedle, spent half an hour trying to figure out the footnotes, but they were so poorly written that he decided to "translate" them. The translation from Generally Accepted Accounting Principles (GAAP) to readable prose took Mr. Tweedle half a day. He found the footnoted information, including disclosures regarding capitalized leases, accurate but unreadable due to the excessive use of GAAP language. He sent the audit back to Tyme and Billin with his translation, asking them to rewrite the footnotes so that nonaccountant users could understand the report.

Accounting literature abounds with articles bemoaning the sorry state of writing by accountants:

"Would You Really Want to Read Your Own Writing?"[4]
"Improving Annual Reports by Improving the Readability of Footnotes"[5]
"Better Written Communication Improves Financial Management"[6]
"The Literate Accountant"[7]
"Don't Let Your Writing Cost You Clients"[8]

Why would technically competent accountants risk future audit business and their careers by garbling their findings? Because accountants as well as other professional writers forget that users do not always share the same knowledge they do. Because accountants are comfortable in using technical jargon that took them years to master. In short, because they tend to be **writer-centered** rather than **user-centered**.

Readers of *Writing for Accountants* are assumed to be accounting and finance students, accounting professors, and accounting professionals. Even though this text is an accounting-specific rhetoric and uses concepts appropriate to the writings of accountancy, jargon has been minimized wherever possible for readers who must master rhetorical principles and techniques to write effectively—yet who cannot be expected to have the knowledge of professional rhetoricians. Imagine the reader's confusion if none of the key terms of this textbook—such as *ethos*, *genre*, *schemata*, and *heuristic*—were previewed, explained, and applied.

To use another example, do you prefer user-friendly computer software? Most people do because they don't have the time or inclination to wade through reams of computer documentation to get a program to run. Consequently, software houses that fail to render their offerings user-friendly hamper their sales. Like accounting students who study writing and computer operators who run programs, readers who use accounting information prefer user-friendly texts. Accountants must recognize that their writings often land on the desks of users who do not understand the language of GAAP or Generally Accepted Auditing Standards (GAAS)—much less the concepts. Thus, to meet user needs, accountants must strive wherever possible to communicate in language that all users can understand—in plain English. Today's workplace demands that the working accountant be a communicating accountant.

Assessing Writing Skills

One reason accountants perceive themselves as number crunchers rather than word crunchers is that they do not consider themselves practiced, competent writers. You can correct that misperception by recognizing that the accounting task is basically a communication task. And the first step in remedying writing deficiency—real or imagined—is by conducting an inventory of writing skills. Rather than try to grapple with the writing task as a whole, try breaking the process into rhetorical, macro, and micro elements.

Rhetorical Elements of the Writing Task

Rhetorical elements include the three persuasive appeals—*ethos*, *logos*, and *pathos*. **Ethos**, the appeal to the character of the writer as perceived by the reader, is affected by the document's appearance (presentation) and by the credibility of the writer's sources. **Logos**, the appeal to logical argument, provides evidence to satisfy the reader. And **pathos**, the appeal to the self-interest of the reader, puts the reader into a receptive frame of mind. The three rhetorical appeals, basic to informative and persuasive writing, permeate *Writing for Accountants*.

Another rhetorical element involves the **rhetorical situation**—that is, the constraints on you as writer, on your reader (audience or user), and on **overhearers** (unintended readers). One important part of the communication task is to select the appropriate **genre** (modes of writing such as resumes, letters of complaint, memos, engagement letters, and training manuals) and to adhere to its usual content and format. Just as important is to analyze your audience and overhearers, adapt language to your audience, and adjust your tone—in short, shape and fulfill your purpose in writing. To help you develop your rhetorical skills, Chapter 2, "Accountants Write for Users," helps you identify various types and expectations of audiences and overhearers for the writings of accountancy; and Chapter 5, "Where Accountants Write," teaches you how to analyze the complex rhetorical situations relevant to accountancy. Looking carefully at the overall communication situation, then, is critical to understanding and executing the writing task.

Macro Elements of the Writing Task

After you understand the necessity of considering the rhetorical appeals and analyzing the rhetorical situation inherent in writing, it's time to assess your organizational skills by placing your ideas into a coherent framework. Chapter 7, "How Accountants Write," discusses what's involved in organizing your thoughts into structured, lucid communication by fashioning chunks of manageable, readable text with the help of paragraphing and transitional devices.

Micro Elements of the Writing Task

Although the rhetorical and macro elements of writing make or break communicative effort, many writers feel that they are poor writers simply because they can't spell or because they don't know what to do with commas. Chapter 7 also deals with these and other elements at the sentence level, including style, word choice and order, grammar, spelling, and punctuation.

Capitalizing on Writing Strengths

Contending with rhetorical, macro, and micro elements of writing seems like a formidable goal, but accountants have a considerable array of skills with which to master the writing task. Notice how accountants are particularly equipped to tackle each element:

The Rhetorical Appeals

ETHOS Accountants enjoy a reputation for accuracy, objectivity, and independence. Consequently, users come to accounting texts expecting credible information. That expectation can be met by a professionally presented, well-written document.

LOGOS The mandates of GAAP, GAAS, GASB, and other criteria applied by accountants to various accounting tasks ensure that appropriate facts and data are included in the writings of accountancy. Thus, by following these professional standards and principles, accountants routinely incorporate evidence that satisfies users. In addition, accountants take advantage of checklists geared to the writing genres of accountancy to be sure that no required information is overlooked.

PATHOS Unless the communication is an IRS Notice of Deficiency or an unfavorable audit report, users welcome and need accounting communications. Therefore, reader self-interest is built into most accounting texts.

The Rhetorical Situation

EXIGENCE For many students, selecting topics to write about is a worrisome, time-consuming task. But for the accountant in the workplace, the reason for writing (**exigence**) is never at issue. The what, why, where, when, and how of writing is driven by professional mandates as well as by marketplace exigencies. Hence, the problem of subject or topic disappears with the demands of the job at hand.

CONSTRAINTS Due to professional standards, a litigious practice environment, and user expectations, accountants are well aware of what they should and should not communicate. Again, professional criteria and genre checklists help the accountant to manage the scope of the message and the content of the writing.

AUDIENCE The demands of an IRS letter, a banker's need for an update of a company's receivables, and a contractor's request for a job cost analysis all require communication geared to user needs. To fulfill their professional mandates, accountants must identify and analyze the needs of their users and overhearers.

Macro Elements of Writing

Financial statements are structured into sequenced chunks of data. For example, on an income statement, income or sales is naturally followed by the cost of sales; then operating expenses are followed by the "bottom line" (net profit). In the same way, accountants approach reports and other accounting communications methodically, with an eye to logical organization of information. Topics are separated into paragraphs with transitions to help the reader keep track of the writer's train of thought. As with subject matter, checklists help accountants follow a predetermined pattern, allowing the accountant-writer to organize material so that users can follow and understand it.

Micro Elements of Writing

Accountants are computer-literate, which makes coping with writing at the sentence level easier. Computers come loaded with spell-checkers, thesauri, and grammar checkers. Such computerized "writer's helpers" not only help accountant-writers to correct stylistic, grammatical, and spelling errors, but the software actually helps them identify recurring errors. For example, Grammatik 5, adapted for the American Institute of Certified Public Accountants (AICPA), analyzes text for style flaws, grammatical errors, homonyms and other commonly confused terms, capitalization errors, and punctuation problems.[9] Despite the utility and speed of such software, accountants cannot rely on grammar and spell-checkers alone to catch there writing errors. For example, only the trained human eye will catch the correctly spelled but misused "there" in the previous sentence.

Compensating for Writing Weaknesses

To diagnose writing weaknesses, accountants need only run their writing through a grammar checker such as Grammatik V. The program checks for grammatical and stylistic problems, and flags such common errors as split infinitives, double negatives, and subject-verb agreement, as well as passive voice, overlong sentences, prepositional strings, and wordiness. If you run a five-page report through the checker and find several instances of subject-verb agreement errors, then you know you have that particular grammatical problem and you can take steps to correct that tendency in your writing. The same is true of many other recurring grammatical, stylistic, spelling, or punctuation errors.

Macro-level writing problems, which involve structure, paragraphing, and incoherence, aren't as easily caught with the use of software. Working with published or self-generated checklists for the genre involved or following some sort of organizational plan such as an outline will help you create coherent, organized text.

Another way that accountants can ensure the readability and appropriateness of their written communications is to employ the same review process used for tax returns, audit reports, and other accounting tasks. Accountants can use computer "reviewers" to flag mechanical errors, and human reviewers with good proofreading skills to catch macro-level errors, formatting errors, and micro-level errors that checkers cannot catch. Reviewers should also avail themselves of checklists for the genre involved to be sure they cover everything necessary for content. Because it's usually easier to spot errors in someone else's work, peer or supervisory review should be performed on every text generated by accountants, and especially on text destined for outside users.

Coping with Writing Anxiety

Many accounting students know English majors who claim they cannot balance their checkbooks, who consider algebra more painful than a root canal, who sink into a coma-like state at the thought of taking calculus. These self-proclaimed math illiterates readily confess to a condition known as *math anxiety*. Likewise, English majors know of accounting majors who equate a twenty-page research paper with paying taxes, who prefer answering one hundred multiple-choice questions to responding to one essay question. Unlike the English majors who admit to math anxiety, many accounting students deny their **writing anxiety** by avoiding writing courses and by ignoring written communication as a key component of the accounting task.

Symptoms of Writing Anxiety

How can you tell if you suffer from writing anxiety? Look at the symptoms listed in Figure 1-3—for students and for accountants on the job.

The Cure for Writing Anxiety

Being anxious about writing is hardly surprising if you consider what is involved in writing. In any written communication—from an interoffice memo to voluminous pages of complicated notes to financial statements—you must juggle the following:

thoughts	classification
analysis	research
punctuation	word choice (diction)
word order (syntax)	ideas
time constraints	audience (readers)
overhearers	style
tone	purpose
genre	professional criteria
presentation	organization
revision	topic
content	graphics
document design	format
planning	spelling
proofreading	word processing

Recognizing what is involved in any writing task is only part of coping with writing anxiety. Acknowledging the *emotional* component of writing also helps defuse the fear of writing. Writing instructors notice that writing anxiety manifests itself in two distinct populations: prideful individuals who deny it ("there's nothing wrong with *my* writing") and insecure people who only too willingly admit it ("my writing is lousy"). The bad news is that everyone suffers from writing anxiety at some time, especially when something important is at stake, like grades or a promotion. The good news is that writing anxiety is manageable and downright curable.

Writing anxiety is often equated with **writer's block**—that miserable time when you stare at a blank sheet of paper or a computer screen, waiting for words that do not appear. Perhaps you can't start the first sentence, or you can't finish the last one. Writer's

FIGURE 1-3
Symptoms of Writing Anxiety

Accounting Students	*Accountants at Work*
Procrastinate on writing assignments; put off topic selection, getting started, doing research.	Procrastinate on wrapping up a job; delay drafting cover letters and reports until 4:30 P.M. on a Friday.
Turn in papers late.	Deliver reports late to clients and supervisors.
Refuse help from the instructor or the Writing Center.	Ignore spell-checkers and grammar checkers; resist submitting written work for peer or supervisory review. Never take writing seminars.
Never revise written work.	Rely on a secretary or senior accountant to "fix" written work.
Plagiarize by submitting purchased or borrowed papers.	Use **boilerplate** inappropriately.
Dread the essay portion of the CPA exam.	Prefer Continuing Professional Education (CPE) courses with no written component.

block, however, is only an intermittent symptom of writing anxiety. Chapter 7 offers advice on what to do when faced with the temporary phenomenon of writer's block.

The cure to the larger problem of writing anxiety involves recognizing the importance and complexity of the writing task. You can also effect a cure if you realize that a fear of writing is really a *fear of criticism*. This fear manifests itself in students who equate a low grade on a writing assignment with a personal attack—"she doesn't like my writing (she doesn't like *me*)"—or in accounting professionals who prefer that no one review their written communication. You are well on your way to a cure if you understand that writing, like interpreting a financial statement or calculating MACRS (Modified Accelerated Cost Recovery System) depreciation, is a learned skill that takes training and practice. Therefore, avoiding the writing task only aggravates writing anxiety. Because you don't get the practice you need to hone your writing skills, you can't develop confidence in your writing—thereby further increasing your writing anxiety.

Fortunately for accountants on the job, the pesky topic problem that bedevils students disappears. Accountants encounter identifiable rhetorical situations with each accounting task, so the "topic" arises from the job at hand. Thus, accountants know the purpose, audience, and constraints that affect a particular communication. Literate accountants who take GARP (Generally Accepted Rhetorical Principles) as seriously as they take GAAP and GAAS satisfy user expectation and fulfill their professional purpose.

Notes

[1] Characterizations of accountants are gleaned from "Accountant's Image," *The Practical Accountant*, various issues, 1986–1991.

[2] Bob Newhart, "Retirement Party," *The Best of Bob Newhart*. New York: Warner Bros. Records, n.d.

[3] U.S. General Accounting Office, "Small Business: Improper Payments of Former Administrator's Expenses," *Reports and Testimony: August 1991*: 18.

[4] Peter F. Stone, "Would You Really Want to Read Your Own Writing?" *The Practical Accountant* (May 1990): 67–70.

[5] Nicholas Schroeder and Charles Gibson, "Improving Annual Reports by Improving the Readability of Footnotes," *The Woman CPA* (April 1988): 13–16.

[6] Warren Bartz, "Better Written Communication Improves Financial Management," *The Government Accountants Journal* (Winter 1986–1987): 51–54.

[7] Donald F. Silver, CPA, "The Literate Accountant," *The CPA Journal* (March 1990): 8.

[8] Pearl G. Aldrich, "Don't Let Your Writing Cost You Clients," *The National Public Accountant* (July 1987): 64.

[9] Ralph Estes, ed., Grammatik V (New York: AICPA, 1990).

CHAPTER 2

Accountants Write for Users

OVERVIEW The diverse audiences for accounting communications range from bureaucratic government agents to friendly co-workers, from skeptical bankers to the general public, from anxious stockholders to demanding clients. This chapter focuses on the user or audience of the writings of accountants. It teaches the accountant-writer to:

- Adopt a user-centered attitude;
- Identify and analyze internal and external users;
- Anticipate and meet user expectations;
- Understand and accommodate user reading habits and strategies.

GOAL ◆ Understand why and how users read.

KEY TERMS

Deduction The process of reasoning from the general to the specific.
Ethos The character of the writer as perceived by the user.
Expectation gap The difference between what was meant by the accountant and what was understood by the user.
Genre Mode of business communication, usually formatted (e.g., resume, personnel manual, engagement letter, cover letter to financial statement).
Induction The process of reasoning from the specific to the general.
Logos A logical argument, providing evidence to satisfy the user.
Metadiscourse User-centered devices that guide reader understanding.
Overhearer Unintended user or reader of a text.
Pathos An appeal to the self-interest of the reader.
Reader expectation That which the reader expects to learn from a document.
Schema Knowledge about a situation, concept, or procedure stored in long-term memory, the result of prior exposure. (*Schemata* is the plural form.)

Identifying Users of Accountants' Writing

Like other professionals in the workplace, accountants generate memos, letters, reports, and other modes of business writing (called *genres*). Such communications are used *within* companies (internally) or *outside* companies (externally).

Internal Communication

Audiences for accountants within a company can be described by their place in the company hierarchy relative to the writer: superior, peer, or subordinate. Internal audiences can also be characterized by what they know about accountancy (accountant or nonaccountant), or by what they do with accounting information: make decisions, implement directives, analyze data, and perform other tasks.

Whatever the type of audience for interoffice or intraoffice communication, accountants who are interested in conveying information to users incorporate the three rhetorical appeals to ensure clear, concise communication:

- *Logos*, which furnishes information needed by the user.
- *Ethos*, which reflects the competency and credibility of the writer.
- *Pathos*, which meets the user's needs.

External Communication

Although accountants are best known for "number crunching," they are also "word crunchers" because they must convey complex data to users who need the information. External audiences range from the state legislature to the general public, from a client's divorce attorney to a client's insurance agent, from a national accounting organization—such as the American Institute of Certified Public Accountants (AICPA)—to a local accounting society, from a salesperson to a prospective client.

Like internal audiences, external audiences can be classified hierarchically in relation to the accountant, and can also be characterized by what they know. Knowledgeable audiences include fellow accountants, bankers, insurers, government agents, and similar professionals involved in accountancy. But the accountant's primary challenge is to convey information to *unknowledgeable* audiences who nevertheless have a pressing need for the data, such as boards of directors, stockholders and investors, clients, the general public, legislators, businesspeople, and government officials.

Whatever these diverse audiences need to know, they must have information from accountants in a form they can use. Let's use the financial statement as an example. External audiences need to know what the financial statement is, what to do about its information, how to handle the data, when to act upon the statement, where to process it, and why the financial statement is significant. Figure 2-1 illustrates how a financial statement from an accountant might be processed.

However users act upon and utilize accounting information, they must first understand it. As Figure 2-1 indicates, failure to comprehend information prevents the user from doing anything with it. Even worse for the accountant, an unknowledgeable user might use accounting information inappropriately, which could lead to misguided decisions—and possible litigation.

The writer who composes with the user's point of view in mind is user-centered as opposed to writer-centered. Because user-centered writers are concerned with what the user needs to know, they identify audience need by asking the following questions:

- Who will use the document? Could there be other users (overhearers)? What is the user's and/or overhearer's knowledge of accountancy? What is the user's and/or overhearer's relation to the writer?
- Why would the user and/or overhearer read the document? What is the user's and/or overhearer's attitude toward the subject matter?

FIGURE 2-1
How Users Process Accounting Information

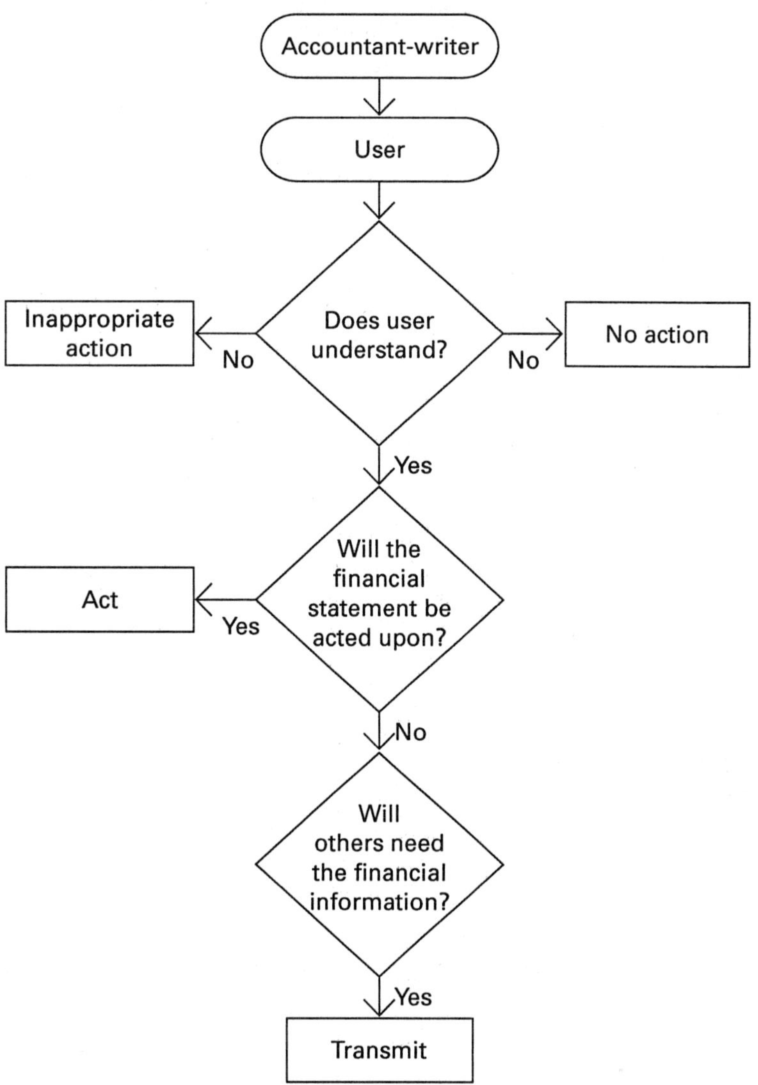

- What information would the user and/or overhearer expect to find in the communication?
- What should the user and/or overhearer know after reading it?
- How will the user and/or overhearer use its information?

Meeting User Expectations

Whatever their hierarchical relation to the writer, their level of expertise, or their need to know, users of financial information want clear, concise communication. An effective way to foster such communication is by setting up and meeting user expectation. Accommodating the user in this way paves the way for effective communication. Figure 2-2 shows some typical document factors and elements that trigger **reader expectation**.

The writing genre employed leads users to expect certain information. To illustrate, bankers expect much more from an audit report than from a compilation report. Prospective employees extract more information from an employee manual than from a job vacancy announcement. And taxpayers gain more knowledge on filing taxes from IRS instruction booklets than from tax forms. A particular genre also affects users'

FIGURE 2-2
Factors and Elements That Trigger Reader Expectation

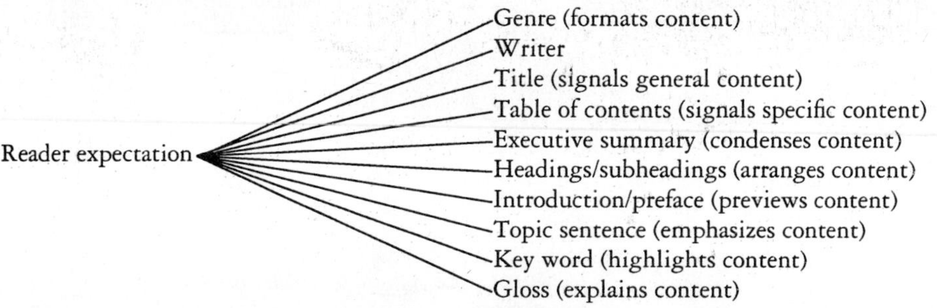

attitudes. Users approach an IRS Notice of Deficiency with hostility, for instance, whereas they receive a tax refund notice with unbridled joy.

Besides selecting the appropriate writing genre for the writing occasion and professional purpose, writers also incorporate elements that raise user expectation and that guide users to the meaning of the document. These elements are called **metadiscourse.**

Understanding the Reading Strategies of Users

To communicate effectively, accountants gear their messages to the needs of users as well as to the ability of users to understand. Arranging formats so that users can locate information easily, and using metadiscourse to assist understanding accommodates the way users (readers) process text. Readers process text for overall conclusions and recommendations (the bottom line) as well as for specific data and information (particulars).

Reading for the Bottom Line

Many users of accounting information—*decision makers*, for example—read for the bottom line and are interested in the financial health of a company so they can act prudently: stockholders make or fail to make sound investments; bank officers extend or withhold credit; bonders issue or deny performance bonds; production vice-presidents increase or decrease orders of raw materials. And they do these things all on the basis of accounting information. People who must make decisions are thus interested in the overall picture, conclusions, recommendations, consequences of acting or failing to act, and specifics to justify a decision. These **deductive**, bottom-line thinkers work from the general (the situation) to the particular (the recommendations), and benefit from metadiscourse that points out overviews and findings: informative titles, executive summaries, prefaces, headings, and the like.

Reading for Particulars

Other users of accounting information, such as *data analyzers*, look for particulars. Data analyzers are more detail oriented than decision makers. They tend to verify or modify accounting information, to process and assimilate data. They are interested in the data as well as the means used to produce the data. These readers **inductively** build from the particular (the specific facts) to the general (the conclusion). Like deductive readers, they too benefit from textual devices that enable them to find specific information quickly, such as titles, headings, tables of contents, key words, and glosses.

Processing Text through Schemata

Linguistic theorists hold that those who possess knowledge "about a subject do indeed find it easier to process new information about that subject than. . . readers without such prior familiarity: they comprehend the new information more quickly and thoroughly, and they recall more of it, in greater detail."[1] This knowledge, stored in long-term memory, is called a **schema**, or a frame of reference. It gives users an existing mental structure into which new information can be assimilated and later retrieved. Schema confirms that accountants, bankers, bonders, and others knowledgeable about accountancy process accounting information more easily and appropriately than those who do not share a rich set of schemata for accountancy.

An excerpt from a cover letter to a review report furnishes an example of schema theory at work:[2]

> A review consists principally of inquiries of Company personnel and analytical procedures applied to financial data. It is substantially less in scope than an audit in accordance with generally accepted auditing standards, the objective of which is the expression of an opinion regarding the financial statements taken as a whole. Accordingly, we do not express such an opinion.

A banker who reads the sentence, "A review consists principally of inquiries of Company personnel and analytical procedures applied to financial data," knows after reading the second word, "review," that the document is not to be trusted in the same way that an audit report is. In other words, the term "review" calls up a schema for something less in scope than an audit to the knowledgeable user. Conversely, "review" would fail to trigger the same schema for a first-semester accounting student.

Because of the schemata that readers may or may not bring to accounting texts, the accountant-writer must adjust his or her message to the potential understanding of the audience by modifying the vocabulary and depth of explanation. Accountants who share schemata for accountancy with an intended user will phrase accounting information differently from the way they would for those who do not share an accounting schema.

Accountants may efficiently and justifiably employ accounting jargon or buzzwords, then, to activate schemata in the knowledgeable audience. But because accounting jargon fails to trigger desired associations in unknowledgeable users, accountants should employ technical terms judiciously, lest users process the information inappropriately.

Test the effect of schemata on your comprehension by completing Exercise 2-1 at the end of this chapter.

Capitalizing on Reading Tactics

Thomas Huckin, a linguist, distinguishes between the "schemata [that] are stored in long-term memory and [that] thereafter guide the way [readers] perceive and remember things," and immediate understanding that depends on short-term memory.[3] Readers, especially those unfamiliar with the subject matter, are limited in the amount of new information they can grasp—as any student grappling with a 1,200-page cost accounting textbook knows. Cognitive psychologists report that readers absorb, store, and recall information because of "height in the text hierarchy, and recency of presentation."[4] Accordingly, accountant-writers format and word their texts to accommodate short-term memory. Important information is placed first in sentences and paragraphs, is placed prominently within texts, and is repeated to aid understanding and retention.

Previewing Material within Texts

Readers normally process text starting at the beginning of a document, availing themselves of textual cues that trigger specific schemata. Previewing aids include tables of contents, informative titles and headings, executive summaries, and prefaces—and enable the reader to "plug in" details that occur later in the text.

For example, notice in Figure 2-3 how the title and headings from the informative table of contents of an AICPA Practice Aid for Management Advisory Services, *An Introduction to Natural Language Processing*, trigger schemata (for knowledgeable users) and set up reader expectation by previewing the subject.[5]

Using Redundancy Effectively within Texts

Has an English instructor ever returned a paper to you with "redundant" marked in the margin? Your instructor probably wanted more than a rehashing or repeating of the same information, which contributed nothing to the reader's understanding of the material. There are, however, built-in redundancies that contribute to reader understanding; these deliberately placed repetitions are especially effective in imparting complex information to users who are unfamiliar with the material presented. Such strategically placed redundancies ensure that important information is presented in more than one way and/or place in a document.

Researchers in human memory note that only a few bits of data can be held simultaneously in short-term memory. Therefore, *repetition* is the key to overcoming a reader's tendency to lose information when short-term memory becomes overloaded. As readers process text in linear fashion, textual features such as headings,

FIGURE 2-3
Previewing Material by Using a Table of Contents

AN INTRODUCTION TO NATURAL LANGUAGE PROCESSING

CONTENTS

Heading previews content.

The topic sentence contains a boldfaced key term. The subject of the sentence is the key term.

The implication of payroll for employees and employers is stated.

The key term is repeated throughout the passage.

The last sentence previews the material to be discussed next.

PAYROLL AND PAYROLL TAXES

The term **payroll** is often used to refer to the total amount paid to employees for a certain period. Payroll expenditures are usually significant for several reasons. First, employees are sensitive to payroll errors or irregularities, and maintaining good employee morale requires that the payroll be paid on a timely, accurate basis. Second, payroll expenditures are subject to various federal and state regulations. Finally, the amount of these payroll expenditures and related payroll taxes has a significant effect on the net income of most business enterprises. Although the degree of importance of such expenses varies widely, it is not unusual for a business to expend nearly a third of its sales revenue for payroll and payroll-related expenses. These expenses and their related liabilities are discussed in the following sections.

FIGURE 2-4
Textual Cues That Aid Reader Comprehension

subheadings, topic sentences, subjects placed in emphatic positions in sentences, restatement, parenthetical definition, key words, glosses, and highlighting techniques aid the reader in grasping information. Such features organize material for readers, emphasizing the most important information. Repetition also helps the reader make connections with information stored in long-term memory. With enough effective redundancy, the reader can process text, add information to long-term memory, incorporate knowledge into schemata, or even develop new schemata. An excerpt from an accounting textbook in Figure 2-4 illustrates how textual cues move the reader along through the use of aids to both short- and long-term memory—and thus to understanding and retention.[6]

Accommodating Speed-Reading Techniques

Accountants, as well as other busy executives and professionals for whom time is money, strive to make the most of their reading time. For example, a rapid-reading course offered by AICPA for nine hours of Continuing Professional Education (CPE) credit, promises "skimming, scanning, previewing, and rapid reading techniques" that enable accountants to reach the upper limits of their reading power.[7] Audiences for professional communication routinely process text by using rapid-reading skills as well as other reading techniques, which include

SKIMMING Skipping over the text for general meaning.
SCANNING Perusing the text for specific information.
CLOSE READING Scrutinizing the text for comprehension.
REPETITIVE READING Studying the text for later recall of specific details.

Rapid-reading courses and books emphasize previewing techniques to allow hierarchical, deductive processing. The informative table of contents in Figure 2-3 allows readers to preview the material. Similarly, the heading and the boldfaced key term in Figure 2-4 direct the reader's attention to the material to be discussed.

Speed-reading experts advocate the following basic reading techniques:[8]

1. Skim for main ideas, using titles, headings, key words and other previewing helps.
2. Formulate questions about the previewed material that suit your purpose.
3. Scan for details that answer your questions.

Obviously, readers can apply speed-reading techniques only to well-organized material that signals its organization and hierarchy of ideas.

Chapters 6 and 7 cover the arranging of texts to meet user expectations and reading strategies—which ultimately improves the readability of the writings of accountancy.

Writing Defensively

The accountant-writer faces a formidable task. User-centered communication involves identifying the writer's purpose, analyzing the audience, accommodating user needs by using the appropriate genre, anticipating questions, and guiding users to meaning through user-centered devices (metadiscourse). Despite the accountants' best efforts to communicate clearly, however, users still misunderstand what accountants convey. The result is the infamous **expectation gap** that plagues accountancy. Much of this book is devoted to closing that gap—to helping accountants communicate clearly with users of accounting information.

The complexity of accountancy (and the difficulty that accountants experience in conveying financial data and findings) doubtless prompted one cartoonist to observe, "How can something be a generally accepted [accounting] principle if nobody understands it?"[9] The problem converts to a simple formula: GAAP = Gap.

It's difficult enough to communicate complex information to users, but when unintended recipients (overhearers) act on accounting advice, the writing task becomes more complicated—and risky. The user's need for information sometimes conflicts with the accountant's purpose in imparting it. In other words, the *user* creates the expectation gap. Because user expectation is unrealistic, and because accountants operate within a litigious society, accountants are forced to limit the information they transmit so that they reduce legal exposure. Indeed, they even attempt to limit the very audiences who read their documents, as this excerpt from a letter accompanying a compilation report illustrates:[10]

> A compilation is limited to presenting in the form of financial statements information that is the representation of management. We have not audited or reviewed the accompanying financial statements and, accordingly, do not express an opinion on them. Management has elected to omit substantially all of the disclosures required by generally accepted accounting principles. If the omitted disclosures were included in the financial statements, they might influence the user's conclusions about the company's financial position and results of operations. Accordingly, these financial statements are not designed for those who are not informed about such matters.

An attorney involved in accountants' liability issues, Katherine M. Mezzanotte, offers three reasons why accountants have to be careful about their composing strategies:[11]

> One of the major problems you, as accountants, face is that the professional service you provide is beyond the comprehension of the great majority of lay people, even those who are intelligent and relatively sophisticated. The other problem is that your findings on a review, audit or compiled financial statement greatly impact a company's ability to obtain financing, sell stock, etc. . . .

That leads to a third problem, and that is that you, as accountants, are subject to attack not only from the clients with whom you have contracted but also a secondary group of individuals with whom you have no direct contact or relationship who may rely on your findings in determining whether they should loan money to a particular company, invest in the company's stock, or even purchase the company. . . . Recent case law has. . . greatly expanded the scope of an accountant's liability to unknown and, quite likely, unintended recipients of their professional advice.

Although attorney John R. Gerstein advises accountants to "put their retainer agreements in writing (engagement letters), so that there is a clear record of the scope and limitations of any engagement," he cautions, in "Accountants—Be Careful What You Write:"

> Everything from a joking phrase, to an exaggeration, to an inartful expression of a concern written on a workpaper, a handwritten note, a letter, or an internal memorandum may be fodder for substantial cross-examination and later jury argument if the accountant becomes embroiled in litigation in the future.[12]

Gerstein advises the accountant-writer:

> Every time an accountant puts anything in writing, he or she should learn to visualize it being turned over years later to an adversary in a lawsuit against the accountant. The accountant should further picture being asked to explain or justify what he or she meant by the writing. Once you get in the habit of "monitoring" what you write, the task becomes easy. If anything, you become a better writer because you do not put reckless, careless, or inflammatory expressions of thought onto paper.[13]

Communicative accountants are user-centered in conveying information based on user need and capacity to understand. But the litigious situation forces accountants to be writer-centered as well, that is, to reduce legal exposure, to protect themselves from audiences who have the power to hurt them through lawsuits. This has changed the way that CPAs in particular write their reports, resulting in more defensive writing. A sole practitioner reveals the accountant's attitude toward users of accounting information: "I am trying to meet the needs of report users who bite."[14]

Notes

1 Thomas N. Huckin, "A Cognitive Approach to Readability," in *New Essays in Technical and Scientific Communication: Research, Theory, and Practice*, ed. Paul V. Anderson, R. John Brockmann, Carolyn R. Miller (Farmingdale, New York: Baywood, 1983): 92.

2 The text is excerpted from an actual letter accompanying a review report. Used by permission of the accounting firm.

3 Huckin, 94.

4 Huckin, 96.

5 Karl G. King et al., *An Introduction to Natural Language Processing* (New York: AICPA, 1990).

6 Philip E. Fess, CPA, and Carl S. Warren, CPA, *Accounting Principles*, 16th ed. (Cincinnati: South-Western, 1990), 426.

7 American Institute of Certified Public Accountants, "Reading Power: Getting the Most from What You Read," *AICPA Self-Study Curriculum Guide* (New York: AICPA, 1991), 47.

8 Material in this section is adapted from Nila Banton Smith, *Speed Reading Made Easy* (New York: Warner Books, 1987), 223–275.

9 Robert Meshnick, cartoon, *The Practical Accountant* (December 1987).

10 The text is excerpted from an actual letter accompanying a compilation report. Used by permission of the accounting firm.

11 Katherine M. Mezzanotte, "Errors in Judgment," *Accountants' Liability Newsletter* (Second Quarter 1991): 3.

[12] John R. Gerstein, "Accountants—Be Careful What You Write," *Accountants' Liability Newsletter* (First Quarter 1991): 6.

[13] Gerstein, 6.

[14] I am grateful to Prof. Keith Grant-Davie of Utah State University for reading this chapter and suggesting improvements.

NAME

EXERCISE 2-1: HOW SCHEMATA AFFECT UNDERSTANDING

Cover each passage with a piece of paper. Slowly uncover *one word at a time* to reveal the entire passage. Then answer the questions that follow each passage.

1. *High fat, salt, and sugar; fast, friendly service; arches; Ronald, Big Mac.*

   What word first triggered a schema for McDonald's? ______________________

2. *When the going gets tough, the tough get*

   Fill in the missing word. Why are you able to supply it? ______________________

   ____

3. *Is it wise for Linda to enter the engagement?*

   List the types of "engagement" that could be implied: ______________________

4. *We'd like to show appreciation for the gift of art.*

   What would "appreciation" mean to an accountant? ______________________

   To a nonaccountant? ______________________

5. *We have reviewed the accompanying statement of financial position of Bell Appliances, Inc. as of January 31, 1993 and 1992. . . .*

   What schemata does "reviewed" call up for an accountant? ______________________

   How might "reviewed" be interpreted by a nonaccountant? ______________________

6. *Thousands of multiple-choice questions; selected essay questions; CPA Exam; former CPA Exams, passing on the first try.*

   What schema does this passage trigger? ______________________

7. *Limited life; unlimited liability; material agency; articles of partnership.*

   What word first activated a schema for "partnership"? ______________________

8. *Allocating pass-through items to shareholders; applying passive activity loss rules; minimizing the built-in gains tax; taxable income allocated to shareholders.*

   What schema does this passage trigger? ______________________

Part Two

Accountants Convey Complex Information to Diverse Users

CHAPTER 3

What Accountants Write

OVERVIEW The writings of accountancy are as diverse as accountants' workplace situations. The accountant must generate ideas, conduct research, and document sources just as any other writer. This chapter focuses on how accountants convert ideas, theories, and professional opinions (often in accord with GAAP—generally accepted accounting principles) into useable information. It teaches the accountant-writer to:

- Analyze argument;
- Make logical, supported points;
- Use workable research strategies;
- Consult and document professional sources.

WRITING IN THE WORKPLACE

GOALS

- Adapt argumentative strategies to accountancy.
- Incorporate the six elements of Toulmin's Warrants in argument.

KEY TERMS

Ethos The character of the writer as perceived by the reader.
Invention The discovery of materials to develop an argument.
Logos A logical argument providing evidence to satisfy the reader.
Pathos An appeal to the self-interest of the reader.
Toulmin's Warrants A model for argument; an appeal to *logos*.

Making and Defending Assertions

Accountants spend their professional careers making assertions typified by these statements:

- Your state tax refund is $180.
- We should hire Violet Becker as our office manager.
- RealGood payroll software will solve our payroll problems.
- Your bill for the audit is $3,000.

Each of the foregoing statements has two things in common: (1) the accountant can furnish *evidence* to support the assertion, and (2) the statements are *arguable* (subject to a counterassertion), as shown in Figure 3-1.

To argue forcefully and persuasively in any writing in which you make and defend assertions—whether writing a bill, a letter to the editor, a letter of complaint, an article for a professional journal, or a letter of reprimand—requires techniques of argumentation. Two ways of ensuring that all possible means of arguing your points are employed are (1) Toulmin's Warrants and (2) questions prompted by the stases (the status of an argument, the issue in dispute, that will be discussed in the next section).

Toulmin's Warrants: A Template for Argument

Stephen Toulmin, in *The Uses of Argument*, discusses what enables a writer or speaker to commit "to the claims which any assertion necessarily involves."[1] His method, known as **Toulmin's Warrants**, involves six elements:

1. The *claim* (conclusion) is inferred from data and must be justified by data.
2. The explicit *data* (evidence, facts, or grounds) support the claim.
3. The implicit *warrant* authorizes (legitimizes) the claim or entitles a reader or hearer to draw a conclusion from the data.
4. The *qualifier* weakens the strength of the warrant and thus modifies the claim.
5. The *rebuttal* (exceptions to the rule) sets aside the warrant.
6. The *backing* or evidence supports the warrant.

FIGURE 3-1
Arguable Assertions

Evidence	*Assertion*	*Counterassertions*
The bottom line of the state tax return shows a refund of $180.	Your state tax refund is $180.	The $180 should be applied to next year's estimated tax.
		The tax return has not been prepared correctly.
Violet Becker has a B.A. in business; she managed an accounting office for 3 years.	We should hire Violet Becker as our office manager.	We don't need an office manager.
		We can't afford an office manager.
		Violet Becker may be incompetent.
RealGood payroll software processes payroll in half the time previously required.	RealGood payroll software will solve our payroll problems.	Our payroll problem lies not in processing data, but in getting the data to the payroll department on time.
The prepared invoice totals $3,000.	Your bill for the audit is $3,000.	The invoice includes services other than the audit.
		The audit engagement letter proposed an audit fee not to exceed $2,500.

Not every argument incorporates qualifiers, rebuttals, or backing, but sound arguments involve at least claims, data, and warrants. Figure 3-2 diagrams the three essential elements in Toulmin's scheme.

Now look at Figure 3-3, which illustrates how the first three elements of Toulmin's Warrants (data, warrant, claim) apply to the assertion, We should hire Violet Becker as our office manager.

By incorporating all six elements of Toulmin's Warrants, you strengthen your argument (through backing), and you also anticipate and prepare to counter possible objections to an assertion (with rebuttal and qualifier). Figure 3-4 shows all six elements of Toulmin's Warrants, and Figure 3-5 applies them to the assertion just discussed.

By looking at possible reasons that weaken or set aside the warrant, you can discover counterassertions. For example, someone opposed to hiring Violet Becker would look into her scholastic record as well as her performance record on the job. If her record in either area is weak, she wouldn't be hired—and the opposition would win the argument. If her record is strong, the opposition could pursue another line of argument, which could take the form of two assertions: (1) we don't need an office

FIGURE 3-2
Essential Elements of Toulmin's Warrants

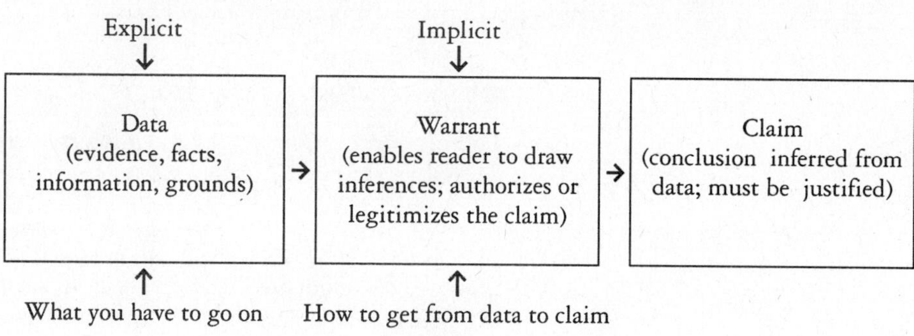

FIGURE 3-3
Application of Toulmin's Essential Warrants

Assertion: *We should hire Violet Becker as our office manager.*

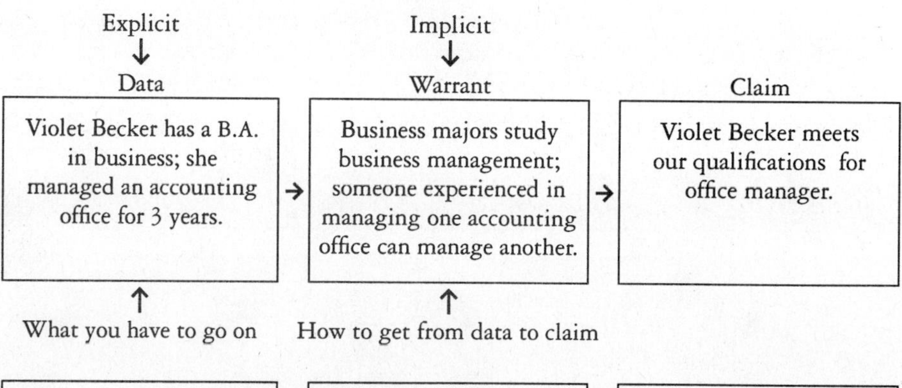

FIGURE 3-4
The Six Elements of Toulmin's Warrants

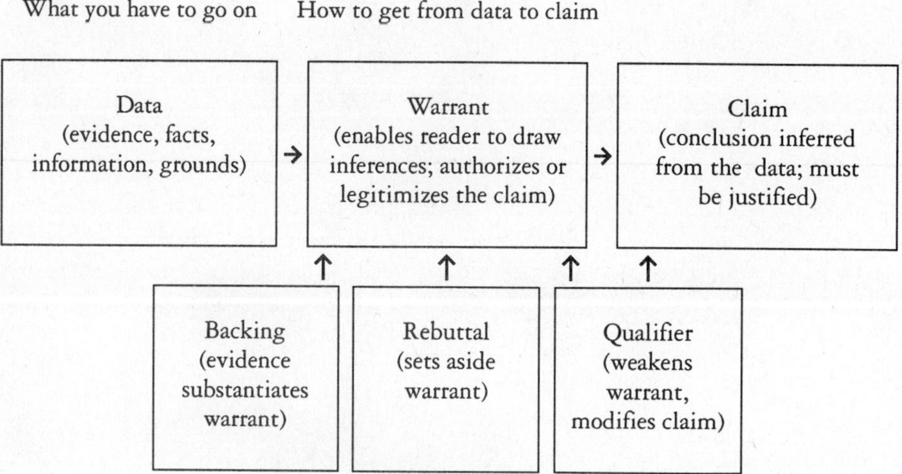

FIGURE 3-5
How Toulmin's Warrants Suggest Counterassertions

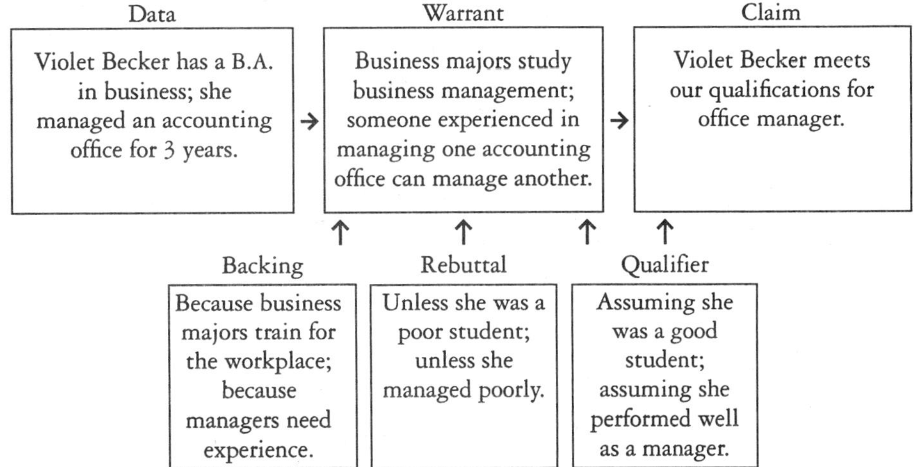

manager, and (2) we can't afford an office manager. Of course, these assertions would need to be supported by evidence. Solid arguments, then, spawn chains of counter-assertions and more assertions.

The foregoing diagrams of Toulmin's Warrants serve as a template that overlays all sound arguments. Making an assertion without evidence to support it, without warrants to enable the reader to draw a conclusion, and without the consideration of possible objections for counterassertions makes for shallow statements at best—and opens you to legal problems at worst. Any time you argue a point that could be challenged, consider the six elements of Toulmin's Warrants to construct a supportable, credible argument. Eugene Hammond, in *Critical Thinking, Thoughtful Writing*, encourages the use of Toulmin's Warrants by saying, "When you write with the care necessary to fill in all the boxes in this complex version of the Toulmin diagram, you are writing as responsibly as possible."[2]

Exercise 3-1 gives you practice in analyzing argument through the use of Toulmin's Warrants. Exercise 3-2 gives you practice in analyzing a sound argument.

USING THE STASES TO IDENTIFY ISSUES IN DISPUTE

GOAL ◆ Propose or challenge an action.

KEY TERMS
Exigence Events, audience, and situations that spawn discourse.
Invention The discovery and development of materials for argument.
Stasis The status of an argument, the issue in dispute (*stases* is the plural form).
Thesis statement The point of an argument, a supportable assertion.

The six elements of Toulmin's Warrants enable writers and speakers to make and defend supportable assertions by calling on explicit data (to support the claim) and implicit warrants (to authorize the mental leap required to draw a conclusion). When making claims, accountants must be prepared to use specific strategies to support those claims. Additional argumentative strategies are based on the classical **stases**—audience-centered ways of identifying and establishing an issue in dispute.

The classical stases were refined by a Greek rhetorician, Hermagoras, who "developed a complex four-part pattern for identifying the issue in dispute (i.e., the status of the argument)"... thus providing "key issues for use by the speaker. The issue in a given case is identified as that point at which an opponent takes an opposite view to one of the implied questions."[3] The stases prompt questions about four issues that are subject to dispute in certain types of arguments:

1. CONJECTURE Did something happen? Does something exist?
2. DEFINITION What is the situation, trend, or problem called? Who sanctions calling it that? Who would agree or disagree on its designation? What corroborating sources can be employed for agreeing or disagreeing with the designation?
3. QUALITY Is the situation, trend, or problem good or bad? From whose point of view?
4. OBJECTION Would anyone object to the issue? On what grounds? Are the grounds sanctioned? If so, are they sanctioned by a mutually recognized authority? Who raises the objection?

These questions prompted by the classical stases are implicit in broader questions that undergird argumentation, that permeate proposals for change. Modern rhetoricians Jeanne Fahnestock and Marie Secor, in *A Rhetoric of Argument*, contend that argumentation incorporates four basic questions answerable within four modes of argument:[4]

Question	*Mode of Argument*	*Argumentative Tactic*
What is it?	Classification	Identifying the characteristics of something.
How did it get that way?	Cause/effect	Determining the causes and effects of something.
Is it good or bad?	Evaluation	Assessing the usefulness of something.
What should we do about it?	Proposal	Deciding what action should be taken about something.

In this scheme, the numerous questions inherent in the classical stases translate into questions that are answered in thesis statements, as Figure 3-6 shows.

Using Argument to Modify Situations

Analyzing questions raised and answered in sound arguments enables accountants to make informed decisions about professional issues. It also empowers accountants to propose (or block) changes vital to the accounting profession, to their companies, and to their own self-interests.

If there is something an accountant can count on (besides taxes), it's *change*. No matter where an accountant is situated in the workplace, he or she is bombarded with ideas to modify workplace and professional situations (proposals) or recommendations

FIGURE 3-6
The Basic Questions of Argument

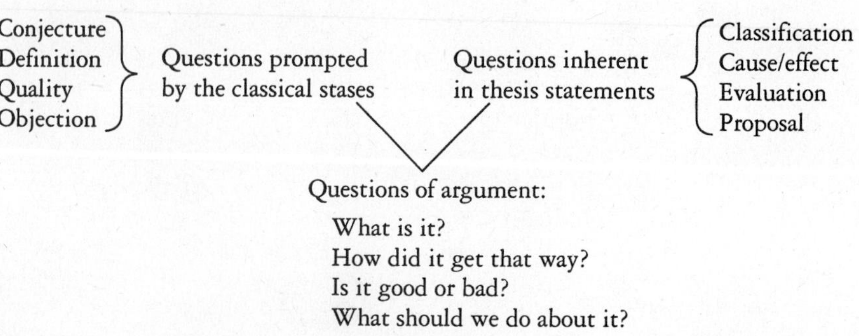

to block those ideas (counterproposals). A brief survey of recent accounting and related literature proves that the workplace is in a constant state of flux involving situations to be addressed, proposals and counterproposals to modify those situations, a public forum for discourse about the changes, and the probable means by which change can be effected (see Figure 3-7).

Covering the Bases of Writing Proposals

The examples given in Figure 3-7 illustrate that accountants are caught up in a whirlwind of recommendations for action or demands to oppose action. Workplace proposals run the gamut from the mundane (Should we purchase a color copier?) to something as far-reaching as company mergers. Regardless of the topic, all sound proposal ideas incorporate the previously discussed stases (ways of identifying issues in dispute) as well as elements and modes of argument.

According to Fahnestock and Secor, any argument or proposal worth defending has a **thesis statement** (What's the point?), an *audience* (Who has the power to act on the idea?), an *exigence* (Why now?), and *support* (Why should the idea be accepted?).[11] Before going to the bother of researching and writing a proposal or counterproposal, the busy accountant should employ a preliminary proposal checklist to ensure that the

FIGURE 3-7
Typical Proposals from Accountancy

Situation Addressed	*Proposal/Counterproposal from Published Literature*	*Forum for Discourse*	*Probable Means of Change*
Managers lack the qualities needed to cope with twenty-first-century realities.	To help students develop "leadership, ethics, cultural sensitivity, global perspective, entrepreneurial ability, interpersonal skills."[5]	Conference for business communication.	Business school curricula.
The Bank Insurance Fund is nearing bankruptcy.	*Immediate Measures That Can Be Taken to Strengthen the Bank Insurance Fund.*[6]	U.S. General Accounting Office report given before the Senate Committee on Banking, Housing and Urban Affairs.	U.S. Congress.
Small-business owners use the appeals process to fight the IRS or, alternatively, go out of business.	To "get lower-level collection personnel" to "use offers-in-compromise."[7]	"Inside the IRS," *The Practical Accountant.*	IRS agent training procedures.
Practitioners do not always consider what is involved in the use of confirmations.	To "provide practitioners with additional guidance about the use of confirmations."[8]	"Exposure Draft," AICPA Auditing Standards Board.	AICPA
The Management Advisory Services designation inadequately reflects consulting capabilities of its division members.	To "change the name of the [Management Advisory Services] division to the *Consulting Services* Division."[9]	*The CPA Management Advisor* newsletter	AICPA Division for Advisory Management Services.
Many states require 150 semester hours before a candidate can sit for the CPA exam.	To fight passage of the 150-Hour Law "in state legislatures across the country."[10]	Advertisement in *Accounting Week.*	State legislatures.

idea meets the minimum criteria for sound argument. The checklist shown in Figure 3-8 applies to a proposal from Figure 3-7 to change the name of the AICPA Division for Management Advisory Services to the Consulting Services Division.

To explore suitable topics for writing a proposal or counterproposal, complete Exercise 3-3.

What Is It?

Before you can propose or oppose something, you must identify and characterize what it is to ensure that your reader understands exactly what needs to be modified. Since your audience may not accept your representation of the situation, you must offer convincing proof or evidence to strengthen your assertion and to counter possible objections to your interpretation of it. Using Toulmin's Warrants enables you to "cover all the bases" in making a credible assertion about the situation you want to address. If you can get the audience to envision the situation the way you do, you pave the way for acceptance of your proposal idea. Using Toulmin's Warrants to formulate your assertion also helps you anticipate possible "holes" in your argument; in other words, if you cannot substantiate your assertion about the situation, you may not be able to defend your proposal idea. Figure 3-9 on page 32 applies the question, What is it?, to the situations already mentioned in Figure 3-7.

The chart in Figure 3-10 on page 32 illustrates how Toulmin's Warrants authorize the mental leap from a situation to the conclusion that something must be done (a tentative proposal to modify the situation).

Working out the warrants forces writers to consider not only the evidence that supports and suggests the claim, but to uncover possible evidence that would weaken or even destroy the claim. No proponent who wants to get an idea across can afford to be caught flatfooted because he or she has not carefully analyzed the situation involved from as many perspectives as possible.

Exercise 3-4 offers you practice in building well-thought-out arguments.

How Did It Get That Way?

Demonstrating that a situation exists and characterizing it shows *what* it is. If you have succeeded in suggesting that such a situation requires modification, your reader will want to know *why* it exists; in other words, how did it get the way it is? And asking *why* entails asking *who* or *what* caused the situation.

Investigating the causes of a situation often leads to unearthing clues to solutions to the problem. Correcting a situation might entail attacking the causes that produced it, which would in turn alter or eliminate its consequences (effects), as this diagram indicates:

The possible causes behind any situation include these types:[12]

CONDITION CAUSES Innate conditions, unavoidable influences, and contributing factors may pervade a circumstance—indeed, may be inseparable from it. For example, GAAS requires confirmations as part of outside verification procedures; therefore, GAAS imposes *unavoidable influence* affecting confirmations. Another example involves small-business owners and their obligation to pay taxes; dealing with the IRS is an *innate condition* of doing business in the United States. Condition causes are difficult to modify because they "go with the territory."

FIGURE 3-8
A Preliminary Proposal Checklist

1. What problem is addressed, or what situation will be improved?

   The MAS division name does not reflect the consulting capabilities of division members.

2. What is the purpose of the proposal?

   To change the name from Division for Management Advisory Services to the Consulting Services Division.

3. Who is in a position to take action on the idea (the primary audience)?

   The members of the AICPA Division for Management Advisory Services.

4. In what forum can you reach or influence the primary audience?

   The CPA Management Advisor.

5. Who will be involved in implementing the idea (the secondary audience)?

   The MAS Executive Committee.

6. Who will be directly affected by the idea (the tertiary audience)?

   MAS division members, members' clients, members' firms.

7. What evidence can be garnered to prove that the problem exists?

   Input from MAS division members and clients who are confused about what MAS entails.

8. What is bad about the current situation or problem?

   The current name focuses on management rather than on consulting, which connotes a wider area of expertise (computer, management, forecasting, etc.).

9. What probable causes of the problem or situation can be identified?

   MAS grew out of accountants' "advising management"; however, "consulting" in various areas of expertise reflects what accountants really do.

10. What solutions can improve the situation?

    A division name change followed by corresponding changes in accounting firm literature and in the accounting media, although taking time, will eventually educate the client about accountants' consulting functions.

11. What are possible benefits of the proposal to each audience?

    PRIMARY: The division name change would be in the members' best interests.

    SECONDARY: The name change would be consistent with the proposed Statement on Standards for Consulting Services.

    TERTIARY: The name change would result in less confusion for clients who desire certain consulting services from accountants.

12. How will the audience be adversely affected by the proposal?

    Reeducating clients requires time and expense.

13. Why is the writer in a position to address the topic?

    The MAS division sets standards for its members (i.e., the proposed Statement on Standards for Consulting Services). The name change is a natural outgrowth of the new standards.

14. How will the writer gather evidence to support the proposal?

    By looking at previous issues of *The CPA Management Advisor*, by interviewing members of the MAS Executive Committee, by interviewing MAS division members.

Situation Addressed	*Assertion (What is it?)*	*Preliminary Proposal Idea*
Managers lack the qualities needed to cope with twenty-first-century realities.	Managers are not equipped for today's workplace.	Help students develop leadership, ethics, cultural sensitivity, global perspective, entrepreneurial ability, interpersonal skills.
The Bank Insurance Fund is nearing bankruptcy.	The Bank Insurance Fund is undercapitalized.	Take measures to strengthen the Bank Insurance Fund.
Small-business owners use the appeals process to fight the IRS, or sometimes go out of business.	Offers-in-compromise provide a practical solution to small-business owners' tax problems.	Get lower-level collection personnel to use offers-in-compromise.
Practitioners do not always consider what is involved in the use of confirmations.	Confirmations are sometimes misused by practitioners.	Provide practitioners with additional guidance about the use of confirmations.
The Management Advisory Services designation inadequately reflects consulting capabilities of its division members.	The MAS division name is misleading.	Change the name of the Management Advisory Services division to the Consulting Services division.
Many states are requiring 150 semester hours before a candidate can sit for the CPA exam.	Requiring 150 semester hours to sit for the CPA exam is counterproductive.	Fight passage of the 150-Hour Law in state legislatures across the country.

FIGURE 3-9
Assertions That Identify and Characterize Situations

FIGURE 3-10
How Evidence Leads to a Conclusion

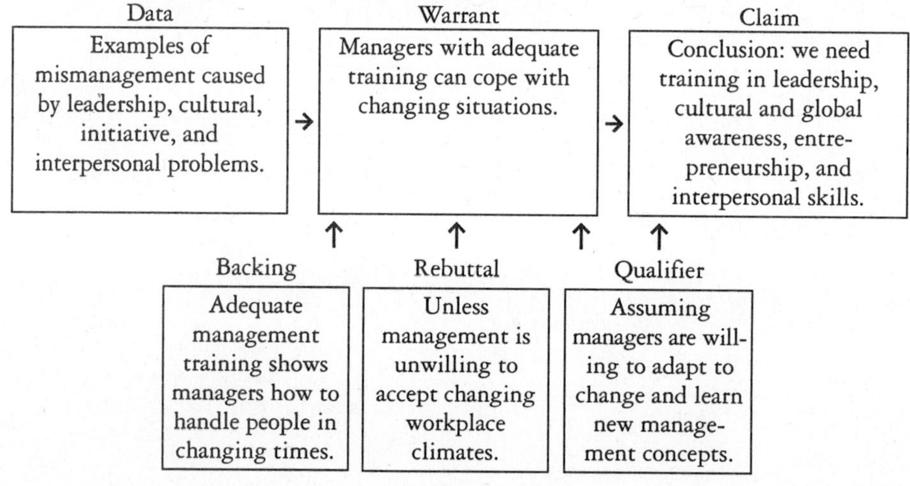
Assertion: Managers are not equipped for today's workplace.
Data
Examples of mismanagement caused by leadership, cultural, initiative, and interpersonal problems.
Warrant
Managers with adequate training can cope with changing situations.
Claim
Conclusion: we need training in leadership, cultural and global awareness, entrepreneurship, and interpersonal skills.
Backing
Adequate management training shows managers how to handle people in changing times.
Rebuttal
Unless management is unwilling to accept changing workplace climates.
Qualifier
Assuming managers are willing to adapt to change and learn new management concepts.

PRECIPITATING CAUSES If a group such as the Coalition Against Restrictive Entry is determined to fight passage of the 150-Hour Law in state legislatures, an immediate event triggers that action. For example, the introduction of a bill to mandate 150 hours of education before a candidate can sit for the CPA exam in a particular state legislature is a *precipitating cause* in the situation. As another example, if an accounting department wants a full-color copier, the *precipitating cause* to request one would be the breakdown of the old black-and-white copier.

CHAIN CAUSES In many situations, inherent conditions, unavoidable influences, or precipitating incidents cannot account for how a situation comes to be. Often there are "causes behind causes" or *chains of causes* that lead to a situation—over time. For instance, consider the following sequence of causes that led to the IRS efforts to promote offers-in-compromise as a tax-collection strategy:

The 1980s business boom ⟶ spawns small businesses.	Many small-business ⟶ owners are ill-equipped to cope with business realities and tax obligations.	The 1990 recession hits ⟶ many areas of the country.	Small businesses succumb to an ⟶ adverse business climate and to consequent tax troubles.	The IRS succeeds in putting many small businesses under, but taxes is costly; sees offers-in-compromise as an effective tax-collection tactic.

HUMAN CAUSES Accountants practicing in a litigious society know well how anxious most people are to assign blame. Professionals assume personal responsibility for their actions; thus, when something goes wrong, as it did in the savings-and-loan crisis, investigators look beyond the financial institution's officers to federal watchdogs and accountants who are charged with responsibility to monitor the institutions and to prevent such disasters. In the Bank Insurance Fund situation, who is to blame? The depositors who demand insured accounts and who file claims when banks fail? The legislators who proposed that personal accounts be insured? Bank officers who make unwise loans? Bank regulators who fail to spot banks heading for disaster? Accountants who give a "healthy" rating to sick banks? People tend to look for someone to blame. And if the human agents who actually cause the problem can be identified, pressure can be brought to bear on them, thus effecting a solution or modification of the situation.

RECIPROCAL CAUSES Some situations develop because of cause and effect or the so-called vicious circle. Something causes an effect that in turn triggers a similar effect, as this diagram illustrates:

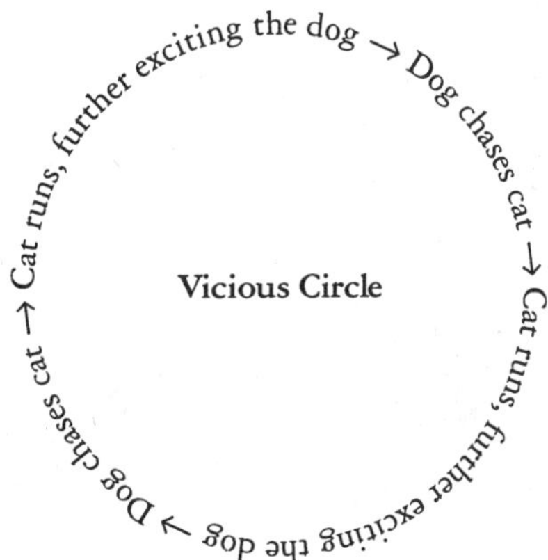

A beleaguered small-business owner might complain that the IRS tax code and costly recordkeeping requirements cause financial woes: the owner can't keep up with tax payments, which triggers even more costly IRS-related correspondence and expense, which causes more tax delinquency—and so on. Only a measure like offers-in-compromise can break the vicious circle.

ABSENCE CAUSES Accountants are supposed to spot trends and problems that indicate financial trouble for a company. An accountant's failure to report irregularities or other signals of financial mismanagement actually causes a situation. The *absence of interfering action* can cause a financial institution to fold, thus depleting the Bank Insurance Fund.

CHANCE CAUSES Fahnestock and Secor define *chance* as "the unexpected coming together of things that have their own causes."[13] The small-business owner who starts out at the peak of good economic times feels the tax bite during a subsequent recession. Taxes incurred at an economic peak must sometimes be paid in a valley. The owner usually can't predict a recession; for him or her, it is a *chance event*. The business failure will likely be blamed on chance, but in reality, the recession and the inability to survive it have distinct causes.

In addition, the kinds of causes just discussed—condition, precipitating, chain, human, reciprocal, absence, and chance—can be either *necessary* or *sufficient*.

NECESSARY CAUSES Without the cause, could the problem exist? Looking at the effect, you know you have a *necessary cause* if the cause is obvious, as these examples show:

Effect	*Necessary Cause*
1. The copier has no paper.	Somebody forgot to load the paper feed.
2. A fax transmission arrived.	Somebody faxed a message.
3. Dan is a CPA.	Dan studied for and passed the CPA exam.

SUFFICIENT CAUSE Could the cause explain the problem? When several causes could have produced an effect, you are considering *sufficient causes*; that is, any of them, given the necessary conditions, could be sufficient to cause the situation, as this illustration shows:[14]

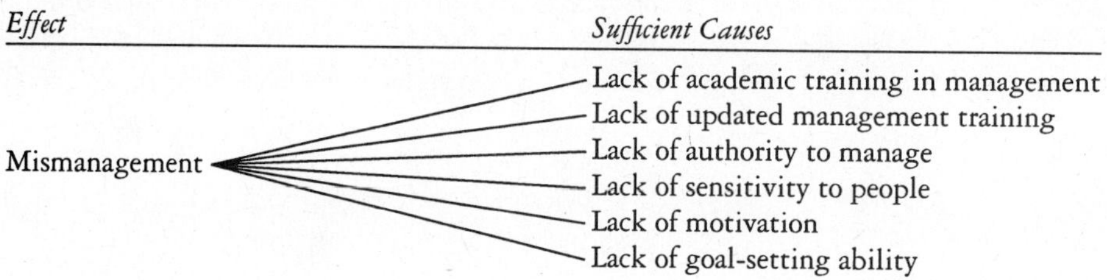

Distinguishing between necessary and sufficient causes is critical to appeal to your audience. They might accept your necessary causes, but you must use good judgment in offering sufficient causes. In fact, you might have to offer more than one possibility to prevent counterarguments. Whenever you assign a cause to a situation, ask yourself, How might this be challenged? and How would I refute the counterargument?

Analyze the causes of situations by completing Exercise 3-5.

Is It Good or Bad?

After detailing a situation and characterizing it, and then determining what caused it to get that way, you can *evaluate* it. By investigating whether it is good or bad, you consider the situation from your audience's point of view. It takes thoughtful analysis and inventive argument to persuade skeptical or antagonistic readers who disagree with your assessment of a situation. So, to reach a hostile audience, you should concentrate not only on *what* they might say against your views, but also on *why* they oppose them. Once you understand why they are antagonistic, you can look for ways to reach agreement, including appeals based on consequences, shared values, and authority.[15]

Appeal to Consequences

If the memory in your computer is so limited that you can't load the latest comprehensive tax package, you will have little trouble convincing even the most tight-fisted manager that expanded memory is necessary to do your job. Pointing out the undesirable *effect* of an inadequate computer system plants seeds in the mind of a manager that your assessment of the problem has merit. The present consequences ("this is the problem now") as well as future consequences ("this is what will happen if we do nothing") can be detailed to convince the audience that something must be done to modify the situation. For instance, the effects of mismanagement in a company can be demonstrated by examples. And you can speculate about the company's future if nothing is done. As another instance, the effects on MAS division members and clients can be spelled out if the Consulting Services division designation is not adopted. When appealing to consequences, concentrate on the interests of the audience (*pathos*). In other words, how do the consequences affect the reader, either directly or indirectly?

Appeal to Shared Values

All members of a firm may not agree on how to implement affirmative action, but all can agree on "fairness" as a basic principle. For this controversial topic, fairness becomes a *shared value* or a "bridge" between you and your opposition. Figure 3-11 suggests how overriding principles can be used to prepare the audience for your solutions; that is, the common goals implied by the bridge constitute areas of agreement between you and your audience.

Because not all values are equally important to an audience, writers establish a hierarchy of values, ranking their importance to them and to their readers. For example, a partner in an accounting firm argues against accepting an audit engagement involving a savings-and-loan association. Some partners favor the idea because it would net a lucrative client. But the partner *values* the potential risk to the firm in taking on a financial institution audit over the monetary value of the audit.

For another example, let's assume that ethical accountants operate from the following hierarchy of values:

The profession of accountancy
Professional standards (GAAP and GAAS)
Client interest
The firm, company, or agency interest
↓ Accountant self-interest

Let's suppose that an accountant proposes to the IRS that an offer-in-compromise might resolve a client's tax delinquency problem. He or she addresses an audience (an IRS agent) with quite another set of values:

A congressional mandate to collect taxes
IRS regulations and procedures
IRS regional and district policies
Departmental interests
↓ Agent self-interest

FIGURE 3-11
Proposals Based on Shared Values

Situation Addressed	*"Bridge" of Shared Values*	*Preliminary Proposal Idea*
Managers lack qualities needed to cope with twenty-first-century realities.	The company needs a productive working environment to stay competitive.	Help students develop leadership, ethics, cultural sensitivity, global perspective, entrepreneurial ability, interpersonal skills.
Small-business owners use the appeals process to fight the IRS, or sometimes go out of business.	Collecting partial taxes is better than collecting no taxes; enabling small businesses to stay alive is better than closing them down.	Get lower-level collection personnel to use offers-in-compromise.
Practitioners do not always consider what is involved in the use of confirmations.	Verification procedures protect the integrity of the audit and lessen legal exposure.	Provide practitioners with additional guidance about the use of confirmations.

Placing these two sets of values side by side shows the inherent conflict between professionals with differing mandates and goals. Even so, one area in which the accountant can appeal to shared values is apparent (shown by the dotted line):

The profession of accountancy	The congressional mandate to collect taxes
Professional standards (GAAP and GAAS)	IRS regulations and procedures
Client interest — — — — — — — —	IRS regional and district policies
The firm, company, or agency interest	Departmental interests
Accountant self-interest	Agent self-interest

Obviously, the more shared values that can be discovered and cited by a writer, the greater the appeal to the audience. Some areas in which shared values are found include morals, religion, the national interest, community interest, theories of academic disciplines, ethnic pride, traditions, precedents, regulations and procedures, cultural practices, family values, self-interest, and—for the accountant—the professional standards of accountancy.

Appeal to Authority

Any appeal is strengthened if a mutually recognized authority can be invoked. Like values, authority means different things to different people. Accountants, in particular, are subject to various levels of authority as suggested by the following chart:

A Certified Public Accountant	*A Noncertified Accountant*	*An Assistant Controller*
State Board of Accountancy	National accounting association	Board of Directors
AICPA	Local accounting association	VP of Finance
State accounting association	Local business licensing board	Treasurer
Partners in firm	Accounting manager	Controller
Tax partner		
Clients		

Arguments from authority are usually effective only when the audience is subject to or influenced by that authority. For example, AICPA's 150-hour mandate is taken seriously by its members and would-be members. Despite AICPA's considerable clout, however, noncertified accountants aren't likely to pay much attention.

Exercise 3-6 offers you practice in strengthening an argument by assessing a situation as good or bad.

What Should We Do About It?

Setting forth ideas to modify a situation—whether contained in an interoffice memo, a letter of complaint, a letter to the editor, a feasibility study, or a recommendation report—must accomplish the following tasks:

1. Demonstrate that a situation exists.
2. Characterize the situation as good or bad.
3. Explain the causes of the problem.
4. Point out undesirable consequences of the problem.
5. Suggest how the situation can be modified.

Exercise 3-7, Exercise 3-8, Exercise 3-9, and Exercise 3-10 give you a chance to analyze typical workplace and classroom proposals that call for change.

Identifying and Solving a Problem

From the aforementioned situations, you can see that finding problems to address in the workplace isn't difficult. In fact, problems that cry out for solutions abound; the trick is to generate workable solutions and to present them to the appropriate audience who has the power to sanction the proposal ideas. For the accounting student who has yet to take his or her position in the workplace, however, identifying and addressing a workplace problem isn't so easy. By carefully perusing articles, editorials, letters to the editor, news notes, announcements, and advertisements from *current* accounting literature, you can identify problems in the accounting profession and in the workplace, and you can explore solutions to them.

Exercise 3-11 will help you locate fruitful proposal topics. Apply the exercise to current issues of journals geared to accounting practitioners, such as the *Journal of Accountancy*, *The Practical Accountant*, *Management Accounting*, *National Public Accountant*, EA *The Journal of the National Association of Enrolled Agents*, and *Accounting Today*.

TO CITE OR NOT TO CITE

GOALS

- Acknowledge and document sources properly.
- Avoid plagiarism.

KEY TERMS

Bibliography A list of written and oral sources.
Citation An acknowledgement of a written or oral source.
Plagiarism The use of someone else's words or ideas without giving credit.

Plagiarism

Plagiarism has captured the headlines during the past few years. A U.S. legislator's speech was really someone else's; some students stand accused of using their professor's articles in master's theses and doctoral dissertations; and a college president stepped down after being charged with using someone else's ideas in a commencement speech without acknowledgment. Furthermore, plagiarism can haunt the writer or speaker decades after the fact.

Intentional Plagiarism

Plagiarism is knowingly or unknowingly using the words or ideas of someone else without giving proper credit. The most blatant kind of plagiarism—considered illegal in publishing circles (and unethical everywhere)—is deliberate plagiarism. You are guilty of intentional plagiarism if you

- Purchase or borrow a paper written by someone else and claim the work as your own.
- Use a portion of someone else's work without bothering to quote accurately.
- Paraphrase a passage without giving credit.

To plagiarize knowingly is to commit a dishonest act, one that carries serious consequences, depending on the forum involved:

1. As an *undergraduate student* in most colleges and universities, you could fail the course involved, you could be ordered to take a mandatory ethics course, you could be expelled from school, and you could have your degree subsequently revoked.
2. As a *graduate student*, you could be barred from admission to graduate school, you could be expelled, and you could lose your hard-earned degree.
3. As a *professional* in the workplace, you could damage your credibility (*ethos*), you could ruin your chances for advancement, you could lose your job, and you could face legal action.

Unintentional Plagiarism

Sometimes writers commit plagiarism without meaning to deceive their readers. Unfortunately, the results *look* like intentional plagiarism, and what reader is in a position to judge the writer's intent to deceive? Giving proper attribution by documenting sources is something every writer—student or professional—must master to avoid the appearance of plagiarism. Since all accountants are college-educated, claiming ignorance in how to document sources is hardly a valid claim. So whether plagiarism is deliberate or simply careless, the writer still faces the consequences of plagiarism.

The Plagiarizing Accountant

Accountants work with two kinds of documentation. In the "Importance of Documentation," Guy M. Hohmann, a CPA and attorney, advises accountants to include in their workpapers "engagement letters, management letters, representative letters and other documentation" to provide evidence of work performed should litigation arise.[16] Hohmann stresses that what is included in such documentation is as important as what is not. Understanding that this kind of documentation controls legal exposure is critical for the accountant to know.

Accountants encounter another kind of documentation that involves plagiarism: the **citation** of sources. Some ways that accountants avoid plagiarism involve these situations:

1. Just as accountants avoid rendering an opinion on work not performed, so they must assume credit for work performed. This principle controls situations in which "a predecessor accountant ceases operations," as shown in the following AICPA notice:

   AICPA NOTICE TO PRACTITIONERS FOR WHEN A PREDECESSOR ACCOUNTANT CEASES OPERATIONS. The notice states that whether or not the predecessor auditor has performed significant procedures, the successor auditor must perform any and all procedures necessary to form the basis of an opinion. The successor cannot assume responsibility for the work of the predecessor or issue a report with divided responsibility.[17]

2. Accountants refuse to publish financial statements not prepared by them on letterhead. To so publish is to deceive, and is thus a form of plagiarism.
3. Accountants who publish articles, letters to the editor, newsletters, or any writing cite sources carefully.
4. Accountants who give seminars or other oral presentations scrupulously credit their sources.
5. Accountants accurately cite the IRS code when advising clients on tax matters, as in this excerpt from a CPA firm's letter:

   Code Sec. 121(d) (9) provides a special rule for disabled taxpayers. If during the five year period preceding the sale, a taxpayer becomes physically or mentally incapable of self care and owns a residence that he has used as his principal residence for periods totaling at least one year during the five year period, the taxpayer will be treated as having used the property as his principal residence during that part of the five year period in which he owned the property and resided in any facility licensed to care for individuals in the taxpayer's condition.[18]

To sum up, accountants must acknowledge their sources for several reasons: to be accurate, to protect their reputation, to control legal exposure, and to provide information for readers who want a closer look at their sources, as this writer pointed out in a letter to the editor of *The National Public Accountant*:

[In "Tax Talk"], [while] there were some facts given, there was no explanation of the theory the court used to arrive at the decision. Neither was there a case number given so one could look it up. . . . Please give a citation so we can find the case if we want to look it up.[19]

Citation Styles

Plagiarizing in academia and in the workplace, then, implies dishonesty and carries severe penalties. So how can honest students and professionals ensure that they are citing sources correctly? The following tips will help:

1. Many professors prefer specific citation styles. Obtain the recommended style sheet or book.
2. Most publishers maintain citation style sheets. Write for one before submitting an article for publication. You can also infer citation preferences by studying articles in the publication itself.
3. Although bibliographic citation generators designed for computers contain numerous citation styles (WP*Citation* lists 107), all are derived from three basic methods: parenthetical, footnote, and endnote.

Documenting Parenthetically

Parenthetical documentation is common in scientific and social writing, and in writing about literature, as shown in this example:

> Some analysts, however, question if these changes constitute "improvements in 'communication' between auditor and the user" or "alter the purpose of the report by adding new messages," thus *increasing* liability (Elliott and Jacobson, 72–73).[20]

Advantages include not having to skip to the footnote or endnote to locate a source. The main disadvantage is that the reader is constantly interrupted by parenthetical matter. Also, citation styles that specify an author and year are imprecise. More precise are styles that call for page numbers (see Figure 3-12).

So that the reader knows in which publication the parenthetically cited author appears, a **bibliography** or list of works cited is necessary, as illustrated in Figure 3-13.

Documenting with Footnotes

Another common method of documentation (used by the *United States Master Tax Guide*, for example) is the footnote, as in this passage:

> (If B's basis for his interest in partnership property, other than unrealized receivables, were $9,000, he would recognize capital gain of $1,000. If his basis were $11,000, he would sustain a capital loss of $1,000) (Reg. § 1.751-1(g)).[3]
>
> ---
>
> Footnote references are to paragraphs of the 1991 Standard Federal Tax Reports.
> [3] ¶ 25,801[22]

Notice that the superscripted number refers the reader to the same number placed at the bottom or "foot" of the page for bibliographical or explanatory information. This method is less intrusive to the reader who is trying to concentrate on the subject matter.

Documenting with Endnotes

Endnotes are treated exactly like footnotes except that the documentation appears at the end of a chapter or article. *The Practical Accountant* uses endnotes. *Writing for*

FIGURE 3-12
Parenthetical References

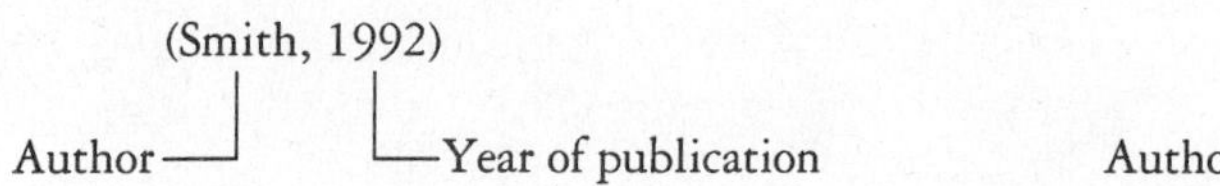

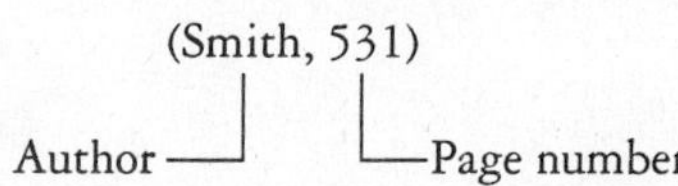

FIGURE 3-13
Parenthetical Documentation and Its Citation

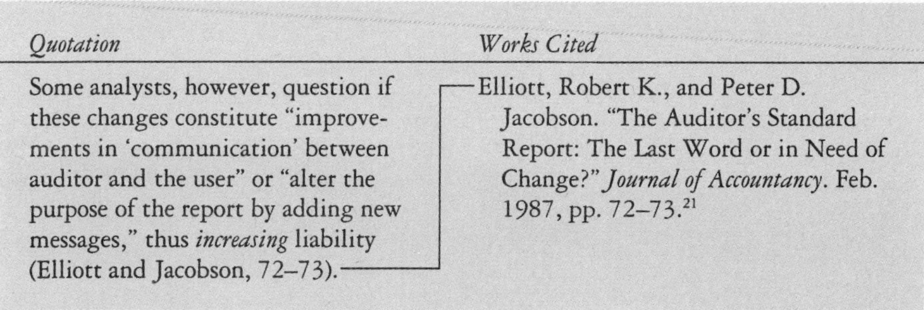

Accountants employs endnotes prepared according to *A Style Guide for Authors and Editors* and furnished by the editorial department of South-Western Publishing Co. Like footnotes, endnotes are less intrusive for the reader. Footnotes or endnotes may or may not contain a bibliography or a list of works cited, depending on the preferences of the editor or publisher. Both footnotes and endnotes contain the same elements as a bibliography, as this example shows:

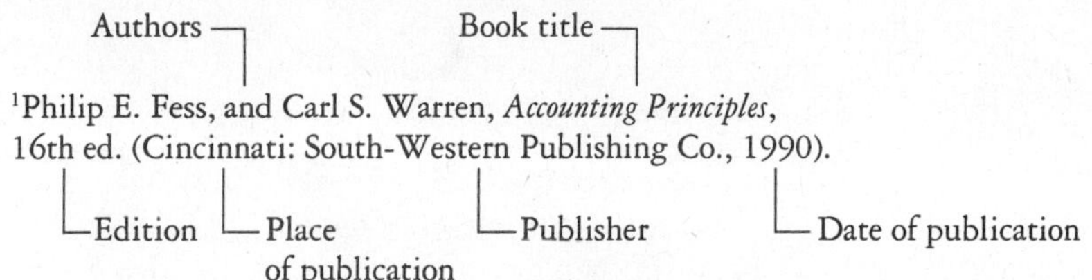

Like footnotes, endnotes may be explanatory, as this note illustrates:

> [1]An accountant was reprimanded by the IRS for failing to return an agent's phone calls, for failing to attend conferences, and for ignoring mail requests for information in connection with an audit. Reported in "IRS Slaps Practitioner for Neglecting Audit," *Accounting Today* (July 22, 1991): 7.

Whatever the citation method employed, be sure that each element is consistently placed within the citation, as shown in the following examples:

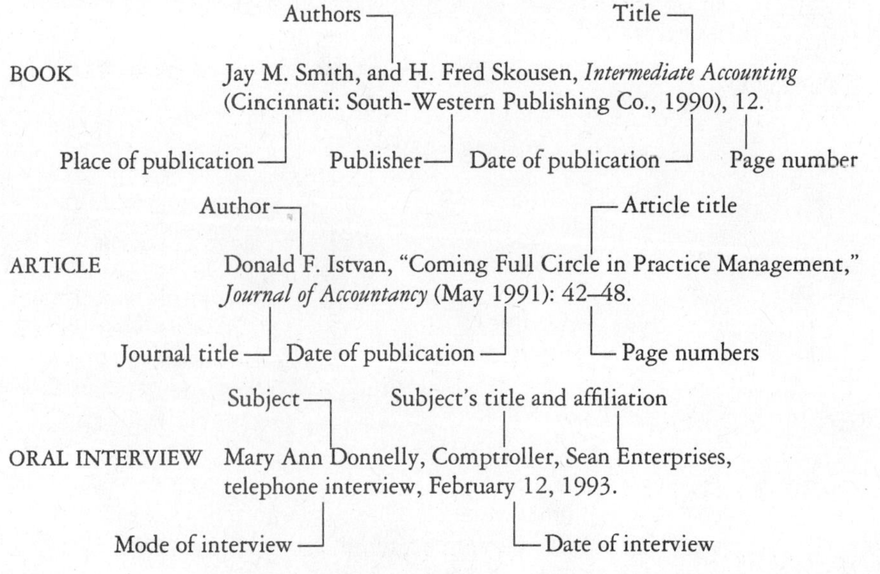

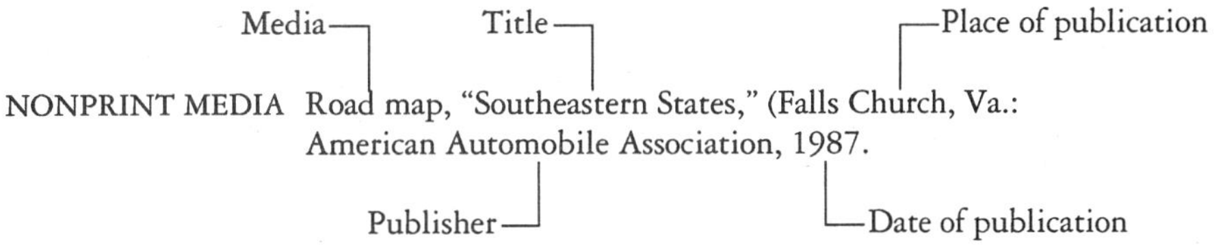

How to Quote

Writers use three types of quoted material: words or portions of sentences, a sentence, or chunks of text, as follows:

ORIGINAL TEXT

> . . . Do CPAs attempt to establish a hierarchy among audiences as they compose the [financial statement]? The answer varies. One Maryland/Pennsylvania senior partner establishes this hierarchy:
>
> - The client who pays our bill
> - The banker who uses the information
> - The lawyer who is a double-bladed axe due to a problem with understanding [the financial statement].
>
> Another District of Columbia sole practitioner makes no attempt to analyze audience, "I consider no audience whatsoever. I prefer to concentrate on my purpose." A partner in a Maryland regional firm concurs: "I don't think about my audience, only about the standards of my profession." A Maryland sole practitioner maintains that the client is the primary audience, but after that, his audience depends on client need: the bonding company if the client requires bonding; stockholders for a publicly held corporation; bankers if financing is sought.[23]

PORTIONS OF A SENTENCE

> Some CPAs "establish a hierarchy among audiences"; others concentrate on their purpose.

A SENTENCE

> One Maryland/Pennsylvania senior partner establishes this hierarchy:
>
> - The client who pays our bill
> - The banker who uses the information
> - The lawyer who is a double-bladed axe due to a problem with understanding [the financial statement].

CHUNK OF TEXT

> Another District of Columbia sole practitioner makes no attempt to analyze audience, "I consider no audience whatsoever. I prefer to concentrate on my purpose." A partner in a Maryland regional firm concurs: "I don't think about my audience, only about the standards of my profession." A Maryland sole practitioner maintains that the client is the primary audience, but after that, his audience depends on client need: the bonding company if the client requires bonding; stockholders for a publicly held corporation; bankers if financing is sought.

When quoting material—whether words, portions of a sentence, a sentence, or a chunk of text—what appears between quotation marks must be quoted *exactly*. Also, the quoted material must be worked grammatically and gracefully into the writer's text (without altering any portion of the quoted material).

The foregoing quotation can also be *paraphrased*, but care must be taken to preserve the meaning of the original text, as this paraphrase demonstrates:

PARAPHRASE When composing texts, CPAs have different conceptions of the audiences they address. Some establish a fixed hierarchy ranging from clients to bankers to attorneys. Others ignore audience to concentrate on their purpose or professional standards. Still others focus their attention on audience need.

Notes

[1] Stephen Toulmin, *The Uses of Argument* (Cambridge: Cambridge University Press, 1958, rpt. 1986), 97.

[2] Eugene R. Hammond, *Critical Thinking, Thoughtful Writing*, 2d ed. (New York: McGraw-Hill, 1989), 96.

[3] James J. Murphy, ed., *A Synoptic History of Classical Rhetoric* (Davis, Calif.: Hermagoras Press, 1983), 81.

[4] Jeanne Fahnestock and Marie Secor, *A Rhetoric of Argument*, 2d ed. (McGraw-Hill, 1990). The four basic questions and modes of argument are distilled from the work. Applications of the four questions are based on my interpretations, and I adapted them to argument as practiced by accountants in the workplace. I am indebted to Jeanne Fahnestock of The University of Maryland and to Marie Secor of The Pennsylvania State University for permission to use the questions. In addition, much of the material in this section is used in teaching workplace writing at the University of Maryland's Professional Writing Program. I am grateful to Professors Jeanne Fahnestock, Keith Grant-Davie, Jean Johnson, Shirley Logan, Michael Marcuse, Nancy Shapiro, and other past and current instructors in the program for generously sharing their expertise and material.

[5] "Call for Proposals," Eastern-Southeastern Regional Conference, Association for Business Communication, April 9–11, 1992: 1.

[6] U.S. General Accounting Office, *Index of Reports and Testimony: Fiscal Year 1990* (n.p., GAO, 1991): 151.

[7] "Inside the IRS," *The Practical Accountant* (July 1991): 29.

[8] AICPA Auditing Standards Board, "Exposure Draft, Proposed Statement on Auditing Standards," "The Confirmation Process," (New York: AICPA Auditing Standards Board, 1990), 2.

[9] "Proposed Consulting Standards," *The CPA Management Advisor* (Summer 1991): 1.

[10] Coalition Against Restrictive Entry advertisement, "Myths and Facts about the 150-Hour Law," *Accounting Week* (July 8, 1991): 31.

[11] Fahnestock and Secor, 22–26.

[12] Fahnestock and Secor, 147–173. The types of causes discussed are adapted from "The Kinds of Causes."

[13] Fahnestock and Secor, 161.

[14] Fahnestock and Secor, 155.

[15] Fahnestock and Secor, 225.

[16] Guy M. Hohmann, "The Importance of Documentation," *Accountants' Liability Newsletter* (First Quarter 1991): 3.

[17] Program summary, CPE cassette program, "Accounting & Tax Highlights," (June 1991): [1].

[18] Excerpt from a letter of a CPA firm to a client on income and tax issues for sale of real estate. Used by permission.

[19] Bill Fulcher, "Letters," *The National Public Accountant* (December 1990): 11.

[20] Aletha Hendrickson, "CPA Writing in Its Rhetorical Context," *Worlds of Writing: Teaching and Learning in Discourse Communities of Work*, Ed. Carolyn B. Matalene, (New York: Random House, 1989), 313.

[21] Hendrickson, 330.

[22] Commerce Clearing House, Inc., *U.S. Master Tax Guide* (Chicago: Commerce Clearing House, 1991), 126.

[23] Hendrickson, 324.

NAME

EXERCISE 3-1: FILLING OUT TOULMIN'S WARRANTS

The following items are three assertions with their counterassertions. For each, infer the missing elements of Toulmin's Warrants from the evidence given.

1. ASSERTION: RealGood payroll software will solve our payroll problems.

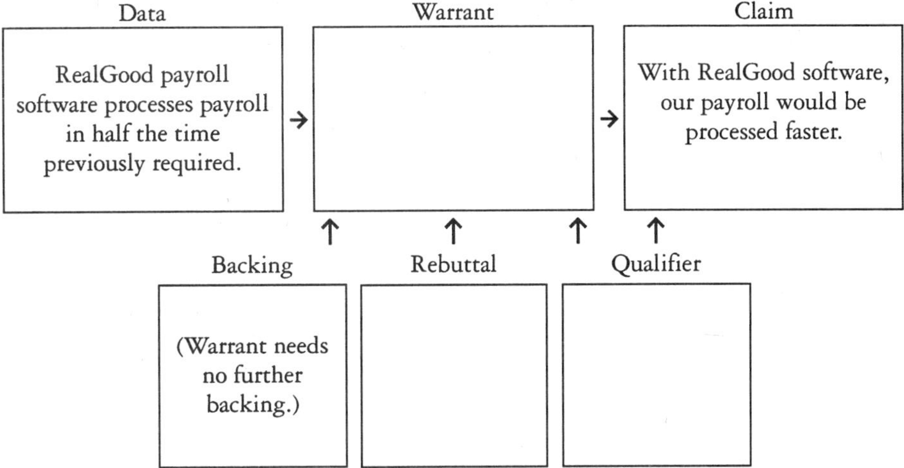

COUNTERASSERTION: Our payroll problem lies not in processing data, but in getting the data to the payroll department on time.

2. ASSERTION: Your state tax refund is $180.

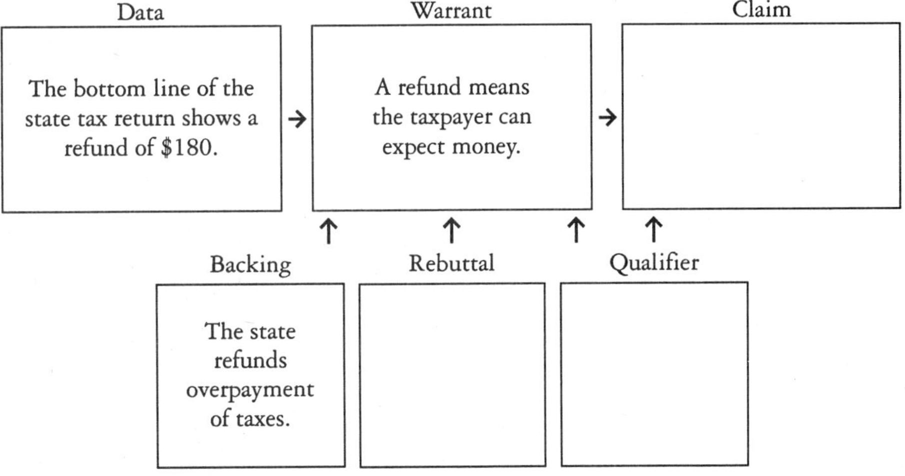

COUNTERASSERTION: The $180 should be applied to next year's estimated tax; the tax return has not been prepared correctly.

EXERCISE 3-1: FILLING OUT TOULMIN'S WARRANTS (CONTINUED)

3. ASSERTION: Your bill for the audit is $3,000.

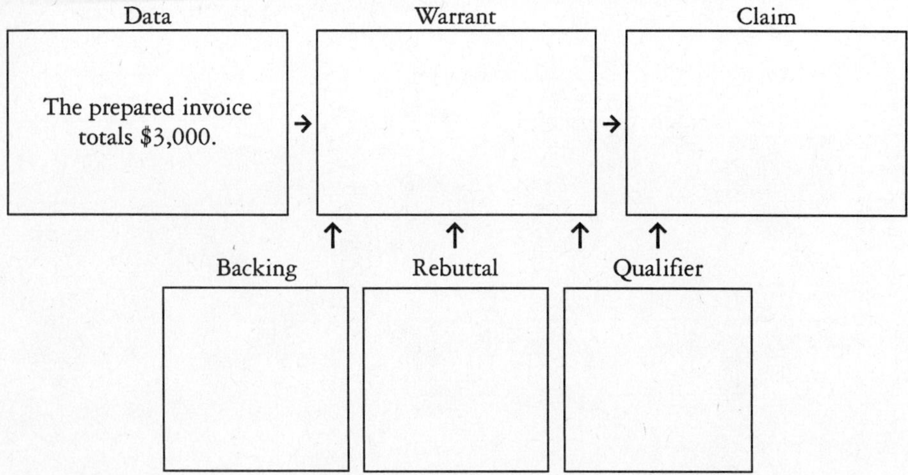

COUNTERASSERTION: The invoice includes services other than the audit; the audit engagement letter proposed an audit fee not to exceed $2,500.

NAME

EXERCISE 3-2: USING TOULMIN'S WARRANTS TO ANALYZE ARGUMENT

The following text is a letter to the editor from the August 1991 issue of *National Public Accountant.** Pick out *one* assertion of the several made, and write it where indicated. Then identify elements according to Toulmin's Warrants that strengthen or weaken that assertion, and place the elements in the appropriate boxes. Suggest counterassertions in the space provided.

"The ATA Designation"
By Norman Barotz

Regarding our not-for-profit professional membership association's recent agreements with the College for Financial Planning (specifically the licensing of the college's proprietary service mark "Accredited Tax Advisor[SM]"), I must speak out in opposition to this co-venture with the commercial (for profit) college.

The ATA designation is in conflict with the Constitution, Bylaws, Code of Ethics, Rules of Professional Conduct and Rules of Professional Conduct for Members in Tax Practice.

The Code of Ethics states: "Members of this Society shall not seek to obtain clients by advertising or other forms of solicitation in a manner that is false, misleading or deceptive." The use of proprietary designation even with the service mark ([SM]) is misleading unless accompanied by a statement to the effect that the designation is a proprietary service mark of the College for Financial Planning and is *not recognized* by any taxing authority.

The violation is evident in light of Rule 10, Interpretation 10-2, of the Rules of Professional Conduct which states: "Advertising or other forms of solicitation that are false, misleading or deceptive or contain any other representation that would be likely to cause a reasonable person to misunderstand or be deceived are not in the public interest and are prohibited." A reasonable person would expect that a person advertising himself as an accredited tax advisor was somehow licensed or regulated. In this industry, IRS licenses and regulates enrolled agents nationally, and each of the 50 states licenses and regulates certified public accountants and attorneys. Some states such as California have created licensed tax practitioners. The ATA[SM] would confuse and mislead a reasonable person into believing that the practitioner had some sort of license.

The ATA designation also violates Rules 1 and 9 of the Rules of Professional Conduct for Members in Tax Practice. Rule 1 mandates referring clients to persons admitted to practice before IRS—EAs, CPAs or attorneys. Rule 9 requires compliance with Circular 230 for members who are not enrolled. Section 10.50 of Circular 230 proscribes willfully and knowingly seeking to deceive or mislead the public.

This association by virtue of Article III of its Constitution has been specifically named by IRS in Circular 230. That very special position is jeopardized by backing a designation that competes with EAs, CPAs or attorneys.

Not only is the ATA designation a disservice to the public, it is a fraud upon the members who are not currently enrolled. The fees for the course work and accreditation exam are money poorly spent. The money could be used for an enrolled agent preparatory course. My guess would be that the IRS fee for the enrollment exam is only a fraction of what will be charged by the college to take the ATA exam. The course work may have value to improve skills or develop a specialization after IRS enrollment is achieved.

Until now, NSPA has been a force by encouraging any member in tax practice to become an EA. This new alliance is contrary to everything this association was formed to do some 45 years ago. Maintaining standards and increasing public confidence is achieved by promoting a national standard. The EA is licensed by the main tax administration agency, the IRS. We do not need another spoon of alphabet soup to attempt to sell to the public.

* Norman Barotz, "The ATA Designation," *National Public Accountant* (August 1991): 4, 13. Reprinted with permission of the *National Public Accountant.*

As a member of NSPA, I urge you to reject this crass commercialism. Keep the Society in compliance with our Constitution and Bylaws, Code of Ethics and various Rules of Professional Conduct. The public is best served and least confused by having only *true* designations, not "initials for sale" by private entities answerable only to their owners. I would fully support a designation if and only if it were an advanced certificate. In this context, one of the minimum requirements would have to be enrollment to practice before the IRS as an EA, CPA or attorney.

ASSERTION: ______________________________

____

Data → Warrant → Claim

Backing | Rebuttal | Qualifier

COUNTERASSERTION(S): ______________________________

____

____

____

____

NAME

EXERCISE 3-3: A PRELIMINARY PROPOSAL CHECKLIST

To ensure that an idea for a proposal or counterproposal meets the criteria for sound argument, apply the following questions to a specific workplace problem or to a situation within accountancy:

1. What problem are you interested in addressing, or what situation do you want to improve? ______

2. What is the purpose of your proposal? ______

3. Who is in a position to take action on your idea (the primary audience)? ______

4. Through what forum can you reach or influence the primary audience? ______

5. Who will be involved in implementing your idea (the secondary audience)? ______

6. Who will be directly affected by your idea (the tertiary audience)? ______

7. What evidence can you give to prove that the problem exists? ______

8. What is bad about the current situation or problem? ______

9. What probable causes of the problem or situation can you identify? ______

10. What solutions can you suggest to improve the situation? ______

11. What are the possible benefits of the proposal for each audience?

    Primary audience: ______

    Secondary audience: ______

    Tertiary audience: ______

EXERCISE 3-3: A PRELIMINARY PROPOSAL CHECKLIST (CONTINUED)

12. How will any part of the audience be adversely affected by your proposal? ____________________

13. What is your interest in the topic? Why are you in a position to propose the topic? ____________________

14. How will you gather evidence to support the proposal? ____________________

NAME

EXERCISE 3-4: USING TOULMIN'S WARRANTS TO AUTHORIZE PROPOSAL IDEAS

The following is an assertion from Figure 3-9. Using Toulmin's Warrants, indicate how the assertion might be supported. For example, the data could include concrete examples, personal anecdotes, the testimony of others, published facts, and/or statistics. Supply information prompted by the elements of Toulmin's Warrants, and also furnish counterassertions.

ASSERTION: The Management Advisory Services division name is misleading.

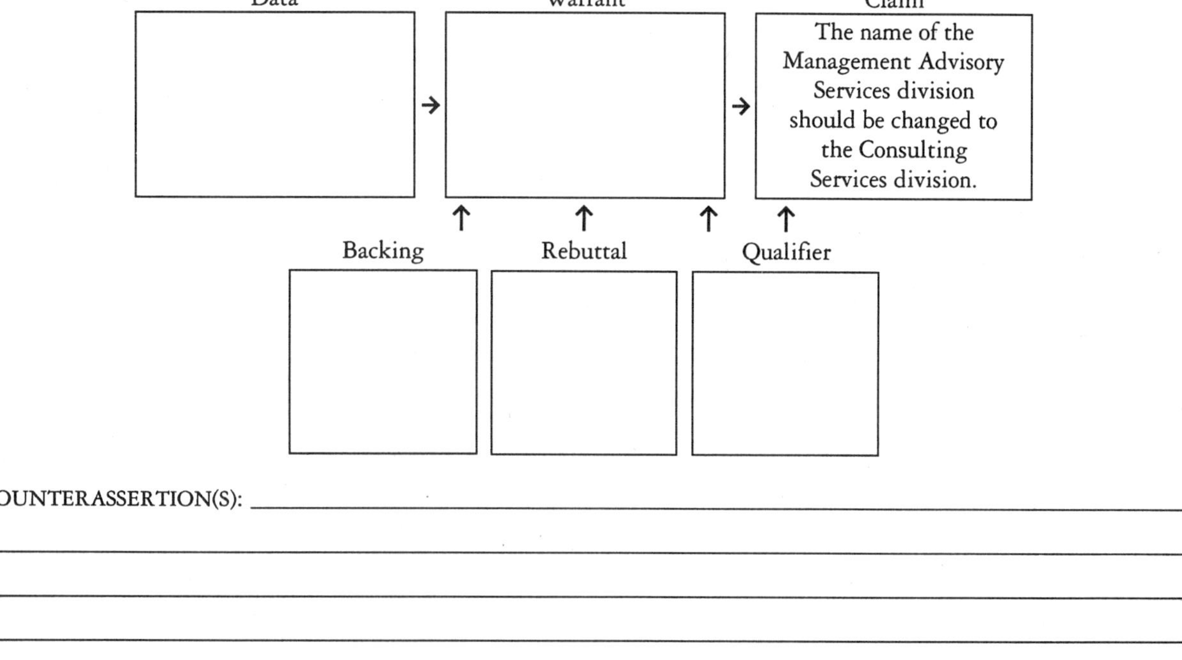

COUNTERASSERTION(S): ____________________

____

____

____

____

NAME

EXERCISE 3-5: A CHECKLIST OF CAUSES FOR SITUATIONS

Using "The ATA Designation" (Exercise 3-2), or one of the examples from Figure 3-7, or a *current* situation from accountancy or your place of work, answer the following questions. Then list possible causes in the categories given. Include evidence for each cause and possible objections to the cause. Lastly, check (✓) whether the cause is *necessary* or *sufficient*. Of course, not all situations will involve all the causes listed.

Summarize the *situation* you are analyzing: ______________________

____

____

____

____

What *effects* of the situation need modification? ______________________

____

____

____

____

Types of Causes	Necessary?	Sufficient?
Condition: ______________________	____	____
______________________	____	____
______________________	____	____
______________________	____	____
______________________	____	____
______________________	____	____
______________________	____	____
______________________	____	____
______________________	____	____
______________________	____	____
______________________	____	____
______________________	____	____
Precipitating: ______________________	____	____
______________________	____	____
______________________	____	____
______________________	____	____
______________________	____	____
______________________	____	____
______________________	____	____
______________________	____	____
______________________	____	____

EXERCISE 3-5: A CHECKLIST OF CAUSES FOR SITUATIONS (CONTINUED)

Types of Causes	Necessary?	Sufficient?
Chain:		
Human:		
Reciprocal:		
Absence:		

Types of Causes	Necessary?	Sufficient?
Chance:		

NAME

EXERCISE 3-6: EVALUATING A SITUATION

Using the situation implied by "The ATA Designation" (Exercise 3-2) or another current situation from accountancy or the workplace, answer the following questions.

1. Describe the audience addressed. ____________________

2. Is there enough credible evidence to convince the audience that the situation really does exist? What sort of evidence is available? Would the audience believe the evidence? Does the evidence suggest that something must be done to improve the situation? ____________________

3. What kinds of causes led to the situation? ____________________

4. Describe how the effects or consequences of the situation might be portrayed realistically. How do they affect the audience either directly or indirectly? ____________________

5. What shared values can be invoked to establish common ground with the audience? ______________________

6. What authority bears on the proposal writer? On the audience? What authority would the audience respect? ______

NAME

EXERCISE 3-7: ANALYZING A PROPOSAL—A LETTER OF COMPLAINT

HACKERS UNLIMITED
P. O. Box 201
New Orleans, LA 70803

March 1, 1993

Oswald Sucz, Customer Representative
Page Lifter Copiers
1024 University Avenue
New Orleans, LA 70806

Dear Mr. Sucz:

On October 1, 1992, we signed a one-year agreement to lease your top-of-the-line copier, Super Page Lifter. A copy of the lease agreement is attached. Over the four months we have had the copier, we have averaged 2,000 copies a month, well under the 4,000-per-month advertised capability. Even with this lighter-than-usual use, the copier has malfunctioned repeatedly, causing us to call in your repair technician on eleven different occasions. Problems included jammed paper feed, streaked copies, and a defective "off" switch. Attached are copies of the repair reports.

In short, your copier has caused us much wasted time, ruined paper, and frustration. Because the Super Page Lifter has not met our expectations for the "reliable, efficient office helper" you describe in your promotional literature, we request a replacement that will deliver trouble-free copies for the duration of the lease, *or* a release from the lease. If we discontinue the lease, we are willing to pay 4 cents per copy ($.04 x 8,000 = $320.00).

Because the copier is again inoperable (the paper feed still jams), we need to hear from you now. Thank you.

Sincerely,

Marge Sheltama

Marge Sheltama
Office Manager

Enclosures

EXERCISE 3-7: ANALYZING A PROPOSAL—A LETTER OF COMPLAINT (CONTINUED)

1. What is Sheltama's assertion? ______________________________

2. What evidence does Sheltama furnish that a problem exists? ______________________________

3. What are the consequences of the problem to Hackers Unlimited? To Page Lifters? ______________________________

4. Defend Sheltama's proposed solutions as reasonable and feasible from her point of view and from Page Lifter's point of view: ______________________________

5. What would happen if Sheltama had taken no action? If Page Lifter takes no action? ______________________________

NAME

EXERCISE 3-8: ANALYZING A PROPOSAL—A LETTER TO THE EDITOR*

To the editor,

I read with interest the article in the October 1990 issue of the NPA [*National Public Accountant*] entitled "Territorial Conflicts in the Licensing of Accountants" [by William Sager]. I would suggest that "Political Conflicts" might have been added to the title.

The Massachusetts' affiliate of NSPA [*National Society of Public Accountants*], MAPA, is one of those state organizations that protects the current licensed public accountants, most of whom are getting toward the end of their careers, while allowing NSPA members who are not CPAs or RPAs only associate membership in the state organization. The end result is that NSPA members who care about the issues mentioned in the article have no forum or power to lobby for the changes suggested by Mr. Sager.

At some point, NSPA may need to legislate criteria for its state affiliate's membership. In the case of Massachusetts, NSPA members who are not CPAs or RPAs are truly second class NSPA citizens since we are unable to be elected to an office statewide (or even serve on a committee) and thus have no way to become active nationally.

There are many NSPA members who are not qualified to be members of MAPA. If we truly believe there is a place in the future for a second level in the accounting profession, perhaps it is time for a new affiliate in Massachusetts.

Mary Kunstman
Natick, MA

1. What are Kunstman's assertions? ____________________

____

2. What problem does Kunstman address? ____________________

____

____

3. What evidence does Kunstman offer to prove the problem? ____________________

____

____

____

____

4. What kinds of accountants might see the problem as she does? ____________________

____

____

5. What caused the problem? ____________________

____

____

____

* Mary Kunstman, "Letters," *National Public Accountant* (December 1990): 4. Reprinted with permission from the *National Public Accountant*.

EXERCISE 3-8: ANALYZING A PROPOSAL—A LETTER TO THE EDITOR (CONTINUED)

6. What are the consequences of the problem? For noncertified accountants? For certified public accountants? ________

7. What solutions to the problem does Kunstman propose? ________

8. How would her proposal ideas solve the problem? ________

9. Who would be likely to accept her ideas? ________

10. In her forum (*National Public Accountant*), does Kunstman address a predominantly sympathetic or hostile audience? Which parts of her argument would appeal to which segments of the audience? ________

NAME

*EXERCISE 3-9: ANALYZING A PROPOSAL—A STUDENT REPORT**

Body of the letter of transmittal to the primary audience, the Maryland Association of CPAs:

Please accept the accompanying report entitled "The 150-Hour Requirement for Future CPAs," which asks MACPA to increase their current educational standards. The report discusses the advantages and disadvantages of raising educational requirements beyond the bachelor's degree. It advises MACPA to adopt the AICPA 150-hour program to meet the high demands of the modern business environment.

[The student proposal]:

The 150-Hour Requirement for Future CPAs

EXECUTIVE SUMMARY

By the year 2000, an accountant will need 150 hours of college education to be a member of the American Institute of Certified Public Accountants. AICPA is advising the states to adopt a similar requirement to become a CPA. Their feeling is that the undergraduate accountant does not have the analytical thinking, problem-solving skills, and written and oral communication skills needed to succeed in the business world today. If Maryland mandates the 150-hour requirement, brighter students will be attracted to the profession. The passing rate of the CPA exam would increase. Accounting firms' operating expenses would decrease because less in-house training would be needed, and the personnel turnover rate would decrease.

INTRODUCTION

A common question facing the accounting profession today is whether the current educational standards meet the high demands and constant change of the business world. The AICPA does not think so:

> The financial arena is becoming more complex with each passing day. Men and women at all levels of business, commerce, industry and government must deal with these complexities. They are turning to certified public accountants for assistance in handling these new challenges and in making critical business decisions. But prospective CPAs need more education to master the growing scope of knowledge needed to practice tomorrow's accounting (Beckman 6).

In an effort to restructure the accounting profession, the AICPA passed a bylaw amendment that states, after the year 2000, 150 college-level credit hours are required to become a member. It then becomes each state's decision whether or not to implement the requirement. As states begin adopting the 150-hour requirement, an additional 30 hours of education beyond the bachelor's degree will be required to sit for the CPA examination. Florida will be used as an example to show successful implementation of the 150-hour requirement.

MACPA should review their current educational standards and should consider upgrading them to meet the high demands of the changing business world.

AICPA'S INCENTIVE FOR INCREASING EDUCATIONAL STANDARDS

The reason AICPA feels accountants need more education is to meet the demands of the business environment. "`Significant changes both in accounting and in the services demanded of CPAs have created a body of knowledge that can't be assimilated in the normal undergraduate program,' said AICPA president Philip B. Chenok" (CPA Education

* The paper is adapted from a 1991 Business Writing course student proposal. Names of interviewees have been changed.

Requirements 22). Another reason is to attract high-achieving students to the accounting profession (Collins 55).

THE 150-HOUR PROGRAM

AICPA does not suggest that the added 30 hours of education be in additional accounting courses. Instead, their objective is to offer a broad education and to prepare graduates for success in the complex business environment (Collins 56). Because accounting undergraduates lack analytical thinking and problem-solving skills, and written and oral communication skills, the additional 30 credits are not strictly accounting credits. A model of the proposed curriculum follows:

60-80 semester hours, general education
35-50 semester hours, business administration
25-40 semester hours, accounting education

Deborah MacGill, a 1991 accounting graduate of the University of Maryland, states "there are so many things you need to know in accounting that you don't learn in the classroom. You need more of an understanding of the business world" (MacGill). Another accounting major, Barron Oliver, adds that "there is definitely not enough emphasis on the use of computers in teaching accounting." Both students plan to attend graduate school whether Maryland requires it or not.

The AICPA membership voted in January 1988 by an 82% majority in favor of requiring 150 semester hours and a bachelor's degree for AICPA membership (CPA Education Requirements 22). According to Nancy Tang in "A Dilemma in the Profession: Should Additional Education Requirements Beyond the Baccalaureate Degree Be Required?" (Tang 21), proponents of the 150-hour program argue:

1. The requirement will advise states to adopt similar programs.
2. Education beyond the bachelor's degree should be required as in other professions such as law or medicine.
3. More analytical thinking, problem-solving, ethics and logic, and oral and written communication skills are needed for entry into the profession.
4. A broader education is needed because of the expansion of accounting theory, the increased complexity of business issues, the scope of services offered within the profession, and the increased numbers of specific standards.
5. Students who have a bachelor's degree realize that the minimum hours for graduation are not sufficient.

According to Tang (21-22), opponents of the 150-hour program argue:

1. There is no guarantee that all states would require additional education.
2. AICPA's requirement does not specifically indicate the details of the program. Thus, states may require additional accounting hours rather than general education hours.
3. The requirement does not indicate when additional education is more appropriate and effective.
4. Since the requirement is aimed at those preparing to be CPAs, those accountants in industry and government will also be affected.

Vincent Shelby, a CPA with a Big Six accounting firm, feels that the 150-hour program is a "waste of time." He says that the cost of education is getting too high to require another 30 hours, that "salaries better go way up if a master's degree is required" (Shelby). He also thinks that the 150-hour program is a way AICPA can control the number of CPAs entering the profession.

Leigh Ratliff, Assistant Vice-President of Cold Water National Bank, also disagrees with the 150-hour requirement. She states, "there is a big difference between public and industry accounting. It would be beneficial for accountants in public practice to have 150 hours of education because they hold themselves out to the public as experts, but in industry, it is not necessary" (Ratliff).

ADVANTAGES OF THE 150-HOUR PROGRAM

As the 150-hour requirement is adopted by more and more states, the profession of accountancy, society, and accounting students will benefit in many ways. Most important, the profession will attract brighter students. Florida discovered that the "fifth year requirement adds a new level of screening for entry to the profession and increases rigor of the educational experience; this in turn attracts a higher caliber of student" (Anderson 57).

A broader education will enable young accountants to respond quickly to a complex, changing business environment. The accountants will have developed better analytical thinking, problem-solving skills, and written and oral communication skills, thus making it easier to survive in the profession. Students will improve their performance on the CPA examination with an extra year of education. Ever since Florida adopted the 150-hour requirement, the passage rate of first-time takers of the CPA exam has increased significantly (Anderson 59).

Accounting firms would benefit because their new employees would be productive earlier. Exposure to broad education and computer tools would prepare students to meet the demands of business quickly. As a result, firms will lower their training expenses.

DISADVANTAGES OF THE 150-HOUR PROGRAM

While additional education benefits the accounting profession, it also can create some problems. Because accounting is a service-oriented profession, the increased education requirement will drive up the price of accounting services, which in turn may cause businesses to seek less expensive alternatives for services usually performed by accountants (Beckman 6). Thus, people less qualified than CPAs will perform the needed services.

In addition, accounting firms will be faced with paying higher starting salaries to graduate students. However, Wilber Van Skoik of Harper, Van Skoik & Co. believes, "[t]he people coming out of these programs are staying in public accounting, so our turnover rate has dropped significantly. I don't have to spend money training three people to get one" (Beckman 6).

Colleges and universities will experience increased costs in establishing graduate programs to accommodate more students remaining in school for an extra year (Beckman 6). They may have to hire more faculty, provide more classroom space, or add additional sections of courses. Some colleges and universities may have to develop an accounting graduate program.

The additional year of education may cause a decrease in the supply of accounting graduates because of the cost of graduate school. However, the student must remember that his or her starting salary may be higher with an additional year of school.

A PERSONAL OPINION

I am a junior at Penn State University majoring in accounting. Within the next three years, I plan to take the CPA examination and pursue a career in public accounting. I support the 150-hour requirement because I feel the undergraduate program does not prepare a student to succeed in the business world. Accounting professors place a strong emphasis on the theories of accounting instead of relating these theories to the challenging issues faced by practitioners in the accounting profession.

CONCLUSIONS

By the year 2000, the AICPA hopes that each state will adopt the 150-hour program. Since the licensing of accountants is controlled by the states, a uniform program needs to be developed so reciprocity is not a problem. Currently, eight states require 150 semester hours to sit for the CPA examination. Adopting these requirements has been difficult for these states, but at the same time it has been rewarding. Some of these difficulties include the high cost of education and the cost incurred by universities and colleges to provide the required curriculum. However, AICPA is attempting to combat the high cost of continuing education for both students and college officials. A. Tom Nelson, chairperson of the AICPA postbaccalaureate education requirement committee, pointed out (AAA 104):

1. "The costs are already being incurred by students who elect graduate study."
2. "Many schools now have excess capacity in graduate programs, so there should be low incremental costs."
3. "Undergraduate requirements at many schools have been increasing; some schools currently require 145 hours for a bachelor's degree."
4. "The trend toward decreasing undergraduate enrollments frees resources that can be shifted to the graduate level."

Because AICPA cannot demand that states adopt this proposal, they feel the reluctant states are hindering the accounting profession more than they are trying to improve the credibility of accountants. Therefore, as more states mandate this needed education, other states will follow suit.

RECOMMENDATIONS

The Maryland Association of CPAs should consider adopting the 150-hour requirement. Adopting it will enhance the overall quality of the accounting profession and will attract brighter, more qualified students.

Firms should consider providing assistance to their entry-level employees to meet the 150-hour requirement. For example, firms could establish programs allowing students unpaid leaves for full-time or part-time study. Students could work during the busy season of accounting and return to school during the slow season. In addition, scholarships could be made available to ease the student's financial burden.

NOTES

"AAA Supports AICPA 150-Hour Requirement." *Journal of Accountancy* 166 (November 1988): 102, 104, 106.

Anderson, Henry. "The 150-Hour Requirement: Florida's Experience." *CPA Journal* 58 (July 1988): 56-62.

Beckman, Ronald. "The 150-Hour Requirement for Accounting Students." *South Dakota Business Review* 48 (December 1989): 1, 6-7.

Collins, Stephen H. "Meeting the New 150-Hour Standard." *Journal of Accountancy* 168 (August 1989): 55-57.

"CPA Education Requirements: A New Report Issued." *Journal of Accountancy* (October 1988): 22, 96.

MacGill, Deborah, 1991 accounting graduate of the University of Maryland. Telephone interview, College Park, Maryland, June 28, 1991.

Oliver, Barron, 1991 accounting graduate of the University of Maryland. Personal interview, Rockville, Maryland, June 26, 1991.

Ratliff, Leigh, CPA. Personal interview, Olney, Maryland, June 28, 1991.

Shelby, Vincent, CPA. Telephone interview, Olney, Maryland, July 2, 1991.

Tang, Nancy O'Rourke. "A Dilemma in the Profession: Should Additional Education Beyond the Baccalaureate Degree Be Required?" *The Woman CPA* 49 (October 1987): 21-22.

EXERCISE 3-9: ANALYZING A PROPOSAL—A STUDENT REPORT (CONTINUED)

1. What is the student's main assertion? ______

2. Why is her choice of audience appropriate? ______

3. What problem does the student address? ______

4. What evidence does she offer to prove the problem? ______

5. What kinds of evidence does the student employ to support her assertion? ______

6. Would the evidence be considered credible by her audience? ______
   Why or why not? ______

7. How could the student strengthen her evidence? ______

8. How does the student incorporate points of view other than her own? ______

9. Does she cover opposing arguments with credible evidence? ______

10. Do her opposing arguments help or hurt her case? ______
    Why? ______

11. What caused the situation that the student describes? ______

EXERCISE 3-9: ANALYZING A PROPOSAL—A STUDENT REPORT (CONTINUED)

12. Is the situation good or bad? ______

    Why? ______

13. What will happen if nothing is done to modify the situation? ______

14. What are the consequences of the problem for CPAs? ______

    For accounting students? ______

    For employers? ______

    For the profession of accountancy? ______

15. What solutions does the student propose? ______

16. Are the solutions feasible? Why or why not? ______

17. Would her solutions solve the problem? Or create other problems? ______

    Specify. ______

18. Who would be likely to accept the student's ideas? ______

    To reject them? ______

19. What common ground or values does the student invoke? ______

20. Is her audience potentially sympathetic or hostile? ______

21. Is her proposal effective? Why or why not? ______

NAME

EXERCISE 3-10: ANALYZING A PROPOSAL—AN OPEN MEMO

"Tax Court Small Case Practice by EA's--It's About Time!*

By Howard J. Sobelman, EA
[President of the National Association of Enrolled Agents]

On March 14, 1991, legislation was introduced in the House of Representatives by Congressman Leon Panetta (D-CA) to permit Certified Public Accountants and Enrolled Agents to represent taxpayers in the U.S. Tax Court in disputes involving $10,000 in tax or less.

Current rules allow attorneys to practice in Tax Court without demonstrating any particular knowledge of tax law, and their qualifying for practice at Tax Court is a relatively simple procedure. However, non-attorneys are required to take a difficult written examination which covers court procedures as well as tax law. This test is so difficult that few pass.

The procedure for small tax cases is very different from that of "regular" Tax Court cases. They are conducted in an informal manner and normal court procedures are not followed. Indeed, it is structured so that a taxpayer may represent himself.

Enrolled Agents, who have demonstrated knowledge of tax law, and are required by the Director of Practice to remain current in tax law by taking the necessary amount of continuing education hours, are eminently qualified to represent taxpayers in these proceedings, and in many cases would be the same persons who prepared the taxpayer's return.

Certified Public Accountants, as well as Enrolled Agents, are authorized to practice before the Internal Revenue Service, and are governed by the strict rules and ethics set forth in IRS Circular 230, and in many cases also would be the same persons who prepared the taxpayer's return, thereby being totally familiar with the facts and circumstances of the issues at hand.

Much time and expense would be saved for the taxpayer by employing a CPA or EA to represent him in these cases, and the use of these representatives would greatly aid the Tax Court in arriving at a fair and proper disposition.

This measure had previously been adopted as part of the House of Representatives tax bills passed in 1984 and 1986, but was removed from both final bills by the House-Senate Conference Committee.

As Congressman Panetta points out in his statement accompanying the bill, "This legislation is needed to provide fairness to taxpayers who have disputes with the Internal Revenue Service in cases involving $10,000 or less. Current law denies them an opportunity for the least expensive, most effective possible representation before the Tax Court in these cases."

I urge all Enrolled Agents to write their congressmen, requesting them to vote in favor of this bill.

1. What is Sobelman's assertion? ______________________________

____

____

2. Why is his choice of audience appropriate? ______________________________

____

____

3. Are Enrolled Agents likely to be sympathetic or hostile to his ideas? ______________________________

* Howard J. Sobelman, "Tax Court Small Case Practice by EA's—It's About Time!" *EA The Journal of the National Association of Enrolled Agents* (Summer 1991): 2.

EXERCISE 3-10: ANALYZING A PROPOSAL—AN OPEN MEMO (CONTINUED)

4. What situation does Sobelman address? ______________________________

5. What caused it? ______________________________

6. Is the situation good or bad? ______________________________
   Why? ______________________________

7. What evidence does he offer to prove the problem? ______________________________

8. How does he invoke common ground or values? ______________________________

9. Why doesn't Sobelman present opposing arguments? ______________________________

10. What is his proposal? ______________________________

11. Who would benefit from his idea? ______________________________

12. Is the idea feasible? Why or why not? ______________________________

13. What are the likely consequences of his proposal to Enrolled Agents? ______________________________
    To CPAs? ______________________________
    To noncertified accountants? ______________________________
    To attorneys? ______________________________
    To taxpayers? ______________________________

EXERCISE 3-10: ANALYZING A PROPOSAL—AN OPEN MEMO (CONTINUED)

14. Who would oppose his proposal? ______________________________

    Why? ______________________________

15. Why is Sobelman's "urge to action" critical? ______________________________

    ____

    ____

    ____

    ____

NAME

EXERCISE 3-11: IDENTIFYING ISSUES IN ACCOUNTANCY

From your reading in practitioners' journals, answer the following questions. Concentrate on *problems* that need to be solved. As you complete this form, don't worry about the solutions; they will surface as you analyze and investigate a particular situation.

What does analyzing RECENT periodicals (articles, ads, news notes, letters to the editor) tell you about the following:

1. Current issues discussed? ______________________________

2. Professional controversies? ______________________________

3. Environmental concerns? ______________________________

4. Safety concerns? ______________________________

5. Legal concerns? ______________________________

6. Women's issues? ______________________________

7. Minority issues? ______________________________

8. New government/tax regulations? ______________________________

9. Management problems? ______________________________

10. Employee problems? ______________________________

11. Capitalizations, funding, bonding problems? ______________________________

12. Ethical concerns? ______________________________

13. Competency, literacy, retraining, continuing professional education concerns? ______________________________

14. Recent medical concerns? ______________________________

15. Recent technological impact? ______________________________

16. Current theoretical issues? ______________________________

17. The focus of block/full-page ads? ______________________________

EXERCISE 3-11: IDENTIFYING ISSUES IN ACCOUNTANCY (CONTINUED)

18. The focus of classified ads? ______

19. Values reflected in the literature and ads? ______

20. New software? ______

21. Encroachment/competition? ______

22. Can you speculate about what the accountancy profession will be like in the next twenty years? ______

From your reading, list topics that you would like to investigate, or identify situations that you think need modifying:

______

NAME

EXERCISE 3-12: QUOTING MATERIAL

The following is a letter from an accounting firm to the president of an industrial park management office.* Quote or paraphrase portions of the letter as directed:

Quigley, Cumquat & Quorum, Chartered
Certified Public Accountants
100 Main Street
Ithaca, New York 14850
(607) 555-3972

March 26, 1993

Ethelbert McGarey, President
Foursquare Industrial Center Corp.
Ithaca, NY 14851

Dear Mr. McGarey:

We are pleased to have this opportunity to submit the following proposal for the audit of the financial statements of Foursquare Industrial Center Corp.

Our audit will be made in accordance with generally accepted auditing standards, and accordingly, will include such tests of the accounting records and such other auditing procedures as we consider necessary in the circumstances to express an unqualified opinion that the financial statements are fairly presented in conformity with generally accepted accounting principles. If we find that we cannot render such an opinion, we will discuss the reasons with you in advance and the alternative report that could be rendered.

We are the auditors of more than a dozen authorities including industrial development authorities. In addition to traditional accounting, auditing, and tax functions, our broad-based and diversified practice also offers management advisory services.

We would expect our audit to begin in late April 1993. Upon completion, we will deliver our report to the Board of Directors of Foursquare Industrial Center Corporation and would be pleased to have a meeting with the members to answer any questions about the financial statements that they might have.

Fees for our services are based on the time required to complete our audit, plus out-of-pocket expenses. As you have requested, we have computed a blended hourly rate of $75.00 per hour. This rate averages all staff levels necessary to complete the audit. You will be billed monthly as the audit progresses, and invoices will be due when rendered. If the foregoing is acceptable to you, please sign the copy of this letter in the space provided and return it to us.

Thank you for considering Quigley, Cumquat & Quorum, Chartered for your audit. We look forward to working with your organization. If you have any questions, please call.

Sincerely,

By: ______________________________
Accepted this _______ day of _________.

* The text is adapted from a letter of an accounting firm. Used by permission.

EXERCISE 3-12: QUOTING MATERIAL (CONTINUED)

1. Mr. McGarey writes a memo to his Board of Directors commenting on the cost of the audit. Compose a paragraph explaining what "blended" hourly rates mean. Work in one or more direct quotes from the letter.

____

____

____

____

____

____

2. You are a graduate accounting student researching how accountants promote their services within letters (as opposed to promotional materials such as brochures and newsletters). Quote from the letter (using endnote form) to make your point, and furnish the citation for "Works Cited."

Endnote: ______________________________

____

____

____

____

____

Works Cited: ______________________________

____

____

3. You are an accounting student explaining to another accounting student what engagement letters entail. Paraphrase all paragraphs except the third one. Be careful to convey the meaning of the text.

____

____

____

____

____

____

CHAPTER 4
Why Accountants Write

OVERVIEW Accountants simultaneously write out of self-interest, in the interests of employers, and in the interests of internal and external users. This chapter focuses on what motivates accountants to write. It teaches the accountant-writer to:

- Write effectively to enter, advance, and survive in the workplace;
- Communicate appropriately with superiors, peers, and subordinates;
- Convey information to internal and external users despite conflictive personal, employer, and professional constraints;
- Employ practical strategies to fulfill the accountant-writer's own purposes.

WRITING TO ENTER THE WORKPLACE

GOALS

- ◆ Write an effective resume and cover letter.
- ◆ Evaluate resumes and cover letters.

KEY TERMS

Logos A logical argument providing evidence to satisfy the reader.
Ethos The character of the writer as perceived by the reader.
Nominalizations Nouns formed from active verbs.
Pathos An appeal to the self-interest of the reader.
Presentation A display aimed at influencing the reader.
Telling facts Relevant details from which the reader draws inferences.
Telling verbs Active verbs from which the reader draws inferences.

Introduction: Resumes and the Accountant

The days of remaining with the same company for decades seems to have gone the way of the abacus. American companies increasingly shuttle employees through revolving doors. *Outplacement*, *golden handshake*, and *downsizing* are terms workers are learning in the nineties—the hard way; just ask the 265 KPMG Peat Marwick partners, dismissed as part of a "streamlining" operation in February 1991. Since job changes (forced or voluntary) rarely come at a convenient time, the prudent, farsighted accountant will update his or her resume periodically as a hedge against unforeseen job upheavals, against the notorious post–tax season "spring purges" feared in many accounting firms. Obviously, writing a resume is harder when the writer is unemployed, financially and emotionally spent.

Accountants both write and evaluate resumes; in other words, accountants present themselves to a prospective employer, and they also evaluate prospective employees, through the use of the resume. Accountants need sound rhetorical principles for writing effective resumes and cover letters, and they also need to develop critical eyes for evaluating resumes. This chapter includes resume and cover letter criteria and checklists, as well as exercises for editing practice.

The Resume Reader

The heavily formatted resume comprises a long-standing and easily recognized business genre. The user expects a neat, uncluttered **presentation** with standard information conveniently placed and concisely worded. Because the busy resume evaluator sometimes spends as little as thirty seconds assessing a resume, the prospective employee can hardly afford to waste the reader's time by indulging in rambling, wordy prose. And because first impressions tend to be lasting, the resume writer can ill afford a sloppy presentation, hard-to-find data, and mistake-laden, ungrammatical writing. The purpose of most resumes is to gain an interview; therefore, the initial impression conveyed by the resume's presentation is *everything*. *Ethos* (the credibility of the writer) eclipses even *logos* (the content of the resume), as well as *pathos* (an appeal to the employer's self-interest), although all three appeals are critical to an effective resume.

The audience for resumes varies with the type and size of businesses. A reader may be:

- A personnel officer in a large corporation, with no technical knowledge of the job offered;
- The entrepreneur of a small company;
- A supervisor with expertise in the position advertised;
- An outside CPA asked to "whittle down 200 resumes to the best twenty."

Most job seekers have no idea who will actually read their resume. Obviously, designing a resume to please such diverse readers takes ingenuity and expertise. But tried-and-true rhetorical principles enable the resume writer to provide proof of capability; to enhance a professional, competent image; and to appeal to the self-interest of the employer. To incorporate all three rhetorical appeals (*logos*, *ethos*, and *pathos*) into a resume is to write a persuasive document—to convince a reader that the writer is worth interviewing.

Logos: Providing Evidence to Satisfy Reader Wants

One of the challenges of resume writing is selecting the qualifications that suit an applicant to the skills required by a particular job, while limiting the presentation to one page each for the resume and for the letter of application. A longer resume is warranted only for positions requiring extensive experience and for an academic resume (known as a *curriculum vitae*). You need to write a "first cut" resume—that is, a resume designed to survive the first round of evaluations. Many large companies advertise (usually in large block ads carried in major papers), hoping to draw several hundred responses. No resume is read until the desired number arrive. Then reviewers scan the resumes for the select few candidates to be interviewed. For such resumes that are read quickly with specific criteria in mind, a second page for either the resume or the letter slows down the evaluator and thus is not advised. In addition, the reader wants to find information fast. Deviation from ordinary resume conventions in accounting-related jobs will likely cause the reader to turn to another resume that satisfies his or her wants.

Resume formats vary somewhat, but the following are standard resume elements in four categories: required, advised, optional, and ill-advised.[1] As Robert Half, CPA, Chairperson of Robert Half, International, Inc.—a personnel recruitment firm specializing in financial personnel—observes, "The best indicator of successful future performance is successful past performance."[2] Thus, the successful job applicant will select appropriately from the list of required, advised, optional, and ill-advised items to present his or her achievements, qualifications, and work experiences in ways that convince the employer that he or she deserves an interview.

Required

NAME, ADDRESS, AND PHONE NUMBER Place these on the resume and the letter of application, as well as on any supplemental pages (if required); such as a salary history page, a reference page, portfolio samples, and writing samples. Some resume writers center "Resume" as a heading above their names, but why take valuable vertical space to state the obvious? Better to highlight your name; it constitutes the heading.

EDUCATION List before "Work Experience" unless your experience is relevant and extensive. Omit high school, since it is assumed for college graduates. List degrees in reverse chronological order, starting with a degree in progress, or a degree just completed. Furnish degree, major and minor fields, graduation date or date expected, university, and location of university. List grade point average (GPA) if distinguished, geared to a specific scale (for example, 3.5 on a 4.0 scale). List academic honors and awards. *A plus*: If you financed over fifty percent of your education/living expenses, say so. (It shows initiative.)

WORK EXPERIENCE Experience can be paid or unpaid (don't overlook internships and volunteer work), full- or part-time. In reverse chronological order, list title, organization, location, and dates of employment. Describe duties by using action verbs in parallel form (see Fig. 4-1). Do not mention why you left a company. *Pluses*: The handling of money, people skills, effective written and oral communication, managerial experience, a high-pressure environment, and promotions.

Advised

RELEVANT COURSEWORK Don't fill limited resume space by listing courses assumed in your major (for example, Intermediate Accounting for accounting majors). Do, however, list allied coursework such as Business Writing, Business Law, Business Communication, and Statistics.

MILITARY SERVICE List service branch, rank, and dates of service. Describe duties as you would Work Experience. *Pluses*: Promotions, leadership, security clearances.

COMPUTER SKILLS List languages, hardware, and software in order of importance to employer. Place the skills in a separate category if the job announcement emphasizes computer expertise; otherwise, list under Work Experience or Education.

PROFESSIONAL AND SOCIAL ORGANIZATIONS List memberships. *A plus*: Offices held.

LICENSES List licenses or certificates held, or include the date you expect to sit for professional exams (e.g., the CPA exam or the IRS Enrollment Examination).

HONORS AND AWARDS Academic honors go under Education; work-related awards go under Work Experience.

LANGUAGE SKILLS List foreign-language proficiency: fluent, reading, or conversational.

CITIZENSHIP List if ad calls for U.S. citizenship (many government-related jobs require it).

ACTIVITIES List community, social, fraternal, or other organizational activities. *A plus*: Volunteer service involving finances and people skills.

PERSONAL INTERESTS This item can supply an "ice breaker" for the interview, but limit it to one line. Avoid overinflating (i.e., don't state that you read Plato and Aristotle for pleasure unless you actually do). Omit dangerous pursuits, such as skydiving, which tend to scare off insurance-minded employers.

REFERENCES If the advertisement calls for references, list these on a separate page. Otherwise, state "References available upon request."*A plus*: Mention that writing samples or other portfolios are available, if appropriate.

Optional

CAREER OBJECTIVE Objectives tend to be windy (lacking substance) and ambiguous. Precise objectives can be stated in the letter of application. Avoid using "entry-level position" as your career goal.

TECHNICAL SKILLS These should exclude computer skills.

PLACE OF BIRTH This is usually irrelevant unless U.S. citizenship is an issue.

The following items could be included on a resume, but are better addressed in the letter of application:

NONSMOKER A plus if the employer maintains a nonsmoking environment.

AVAILABILITY

WILLINGNESS TO RELOCATE

WILLINGNESS TO TRAVEL Important for many accounting-related jobs.

Ill-Advised

Why take the space to summarize a resume, which should be a summary in itself?

Because inquiring into the following is illegal in many states, why reveal your ignorance of the law by furnishing such personal details?

Date of birth	Ethnic background
Marital status	Religious affiliation
Name and occupation of spouse	Political affiliation
Names and ages of children	Health
Sexual orientation	Height and weight

Writing Persuasive Job Descriptions

Having selected from your education, work experience, and accomplishments, you next want to present your qualifications in the best possible light. Relevant detail, action verbs, and parallel construction help.

Telling Facts. Robert Half maintains that "the less specific candidates are when they are describing what they did, the more likely they are trying to inflate the importance of what was actually accomplished."[3] Employers want to know *how many* people you supervised or trained, *what kinds* of computer hardware and software you have worked with, *percentages* of increases in sales or productivity for which you were responsible, and *amounts* of money you handled. Entry-level applicants may feel hampered in providing such specifics, due to lack of experience. By the use of **telling facts**, readers can draw inferences and conclusions.[4] However, the applicant can *suggest* trustworthiness, reliability, initiative, profit-mindedness, stability, written and oral communication skills, leadership, detail-orientation, and rapport with people (people skills)—qualities desired by every employer. Exercise 4-1 gives you practice in drawing inferences and in implying desirable qualities in a job description.

Telling Verbs. Employers are more likely to interview candidates with hands-on experience and relevant skills. Rather than fill job descriptions with weak verbs that do little to enhance the applicant's expertise, select from active or **telling verbs** to characterize duties and responsibilities. Telling verbs relate to people, things, and ideas. The action verbs listed in Figure 4-1 are in the past tense (for past jobs); use present tense for present jobs.

Often accompanying weak verbs in resumes, **nominalizations** (nouns formed from active verbs) seem to add impressive detail to an applicant's qualifications. Instead, nominalizations tend to add unneeded words, slowing the resume reader down. Converting nominalizations to active verbs creates a more telling, less ponderous reading, as in the following pairs of nominalizations and active verb revisions:

Original | Conducted investigations of account discrepancies.
Revision | Investigated account discrepancies.

Original | Performed interpersonal conflict assessments.
Revision | Assessed interpersonal conflicts.

Original | Did analyses of general ledger coding problems.
Revision | Analyzed general ledger coding.

Writing Parallel Job Descriptions

Persuasive applicants use expressive action verbs that tell about the applicant's accomplishments; they convert noun forms to verbal forms when possible. But using

FIGURE 4-1
Telling Resume Verbs[5]

People		*Things*		*Ideas*	
Activated	Effected	Audited	Expedited	Adapted	Invented
Adapted	Explained	Built	Facilitated	Analyzed	Investigated
Adjusted	Managed	Calculated	Familiarized	Coordinated	Maintained
Administered	Motivated	Changed	Formulated	Created	Manipulated
Advertised	Organized	Compiled	Generated	Defined	Marketed
Advised	Programmed	Completed	Governed	Devised	Modified
Analyzed	Promoted	Constructed	Guided	Educated	Monitored
Arranged	Stimulated	Created	Improved	Established	Negotiated
Assembled	Supervised	Designed	Increased	Explained	Obtained
Calculated	Taught	Drafted	Invented	Illustrated	Persuaded
Catalogued		Edited	Prepared	Implemented	Presented
Collaborated		Enlarged	Programmed	Initiated	Presided
Conducted		Established	Revised	Innovated	Proposed
Consulted		Evaluated	Specified	Integrated	Reviewed
Coordinated		Examined	Verified	Interviewed	Synthesized
Directed		Expanded		Introduced	Wrote

verbal forms can create grammatical and stylistic problems when verb forms are not parallel, as in this example:

Original

- Recorded expense receipts.
- Converting written records using Multiplan.
- Enter daily business receipts into journal.

Revision

- Record expense receipts.
- Convert written records using Multiplan.
- Enter daily business receipts into journal.

Notice how the revised versions convert all verbs to the appropriate tense in parallel form. Exercise 4-2 offers you practice in converting cumbersome noun forms to active verb forms and in revising job descriptions with faulty parallelism.

Ethos: Building a Professional Image

Whether intended or not, resumes convey to the reader a favorable or unfavorable impression of the writer. Consider the following excerpted job descriptions from an actual two-page resume:[6]

Delores Martin Resume

Streets of New York $3.50 an hr.
3120 E. Cactus Rd. Scottsdale, Az. 5-23-84 to 6-8-84
salads, waitress and dishes.
Waitressing is not for me.

N.A.C.O.G. (northern Arizona council of governments) $3.35 an hr.
Prescott, Az. 6-10-85 to 8-1-85

deckwork, drywall hanging and finishing, painting and cleaning and let's not forget insulation. (AAAGGHH!) TEMPORARY

Dart Drug $3.40 an hr.
chantilly, Va. 11-10-85 to 2-3-86

cashier, stocking shelves, putting customer rejects back and collecting carts.
Quit to work for Sunshine for more money.

Sunshine Trucking $6.00 an hr.
Chantilly, Va. 2-6-86 to 2-26-86

Freaked the boss out. He thought I was incompetent and that may very well be. I was also on 3 hrs. sleep.

Would you want to interview this applicant for a position with your company? If you opted to interview this candidate, how would it reflect on your credibility? Using resume conventions and the rhetorical appeals (*logos*, *ethos*, and *pathos*) as guides, critique Delores Martin's resume excerpts in Exercise 4-3.

Pathos: Appealing to the Reader's Self-Interest

By incorporating telling facts and verbs into every section of your resume, you suggest to the employer that you have specific skills and training for the job (a logical appeal), and just as important, you have desirable characteristics no employer can resist (an ethical appeal). Ideally, you would tailor each resume sent out to the particular job. However, many applicants find customizing each resume too time-consuming. Even so, the successful job applicant carefully tailors the resume cover letter (letter of application) to each job because critical to job hunting at any stage in a career is the pathetic appeal—that is, appealing to the employer's self-interest. Although the resume affords ample opportunity to convince employers that it would be in their best interest to interview you, the letter of application allows you to send an "all-purpose" resume, accompanied by a painstakingly crafted letter geared to stated job criteria.

When perusing job announcements and advertisements, read carefully, looking for "telling details" to which you can appeal. For example, if the ad mentions a "nonsmoking atmosphere," you would want to state that you are a nonsmoker. If the ad lists "effective communication skills" as a job requirement, you would mention your publishing, editing, or speaking experience. In other words, you should draw inferences from the ad's text about what would appeal to the employer's self-interest, as shown in Figure 4-2. Notice that inferences prompt you to examine what in your background, training, and experience would interest the employer. Exercise 4-4 offers you practice in selecting details to exploit in your letter of application.

FIGURE 4-2
Employment Advertisement Inferences

ADVERTISEMENT

FINANCE/ACCOUNTING ASSISTANT

Fast-Go, an employee-owned company and a dynamic leader in the travel industry, has an excellent opportunity for a recent college graduate for an entry-level accounting/finance position. The successful candidate will have a degree in Finance or Accounting, be self-motivated, have good organizational ability, have good communication skills, like to take on responsibility, work in a high-pressured fast-paced environment, and like to work with computers. We offer an excellent benefits plan. For consideration, please send resume and letter to: 301 E. 20th St., Alexandria, VA 22301.

Attn: PD

INFERENCES (Of Interest to the Employer)

TRAVEL INDUSTRY: Any travel agency experience?

ACCOUNTING/FINANCE MAJOR: Accounting/finance courses? Internships? Work experience? Held treasurership in organization? Member of professional associations? Studying for professional exam?

SELF-MOTIVATED: Financed own education? Worked without supervision? Paid on commission basis? Entrepreneur?

WELL-ORGANIZED: Overhauled filing, computer, or accounting system? Officer in organization? Headed any projects? Did you carry unusual course or work load?

COMMUNICATOR: Ever published? Spoken to groups? Any telemarketing experience? Did you write or edit any work-related communications? Have you tutored or taught? Any writing awards? Sales experience? Any writing, speech, or communication courses or seminars?

RESPONSIBLE: Ever handled cash on the job or in organizations? Trained or supervised others? If you worked summers, were you asked back? In charge of any projects? Any work or organization awards? Worked with children or youth?

HANDLE PRESSURE: Did you open or close a fast-food restaurant? Work in high-pressure environment such as post office at Christmas, advertising, or college registrations desk? Work unusual hours, or carry heavy course load? Handle customer complaints?

COMPUTER LITERATE: Any computer languages, programming, hardware or software experience? Familiar with accounting packages? Spreadsheets? Databases? Do you own a computer?

Writing the Resume Cover Letter

Perhaps no workplace letter poses more difficulties for the writer than the one-page letter of application for a job. The reason? You know your purpose (to secure an interview), but you usually don't know your reader personally. This could account for the uninformative, pretentious, and clumsy letters that often accompany resumes.

Since most employers screen resumes quickly, what purpose does a cover letter serve? First, a business document is usually accompanied by a transmittal or cover letter. Second, and more important to the resume evaluator, a letter of application is a true indicator of the applicant's ability to communicate. After all, if you are hired, you will doubtless represent the company by writing on the job. The cover letter, then, previews what the employer can expect of your communication skills. Because application letters are a convention in applying for a job, why not take full advantage of the opportunity to persuade an employer that you deserve an interview.

Logos: Telling Evidence. The employer pays dearly to advertise for the exact qualities desired in an applicant. And people skills, reliability, trustworthiness, and effective communication are valuable to all employers. The successful applicant will, therefore, incorporate evidence of his or her capability, geared to the ad criteria, as well as to criteria assumed for any job. Obviously, the key to effective resume cover-letter writing is to match your skills, education, and experience to the stated job criteria. The failure to provide relevant, telling facts and evidence wastes an employer's time and ruins your chance to be summoned for an interview. The following sample is the entire body of an ineffective resume letter.[7]

> I am enclosing my resume in response to your advertisement in the *Times-Gazette* of Tuesday, April 23. I would appreciate an opportunity to discuss this position and my credentials in a personal interview.
> I can be contacted anytime at 203-261-7111 (business) or 203-767-1988 (home).

What in this letter would compel a resume evaluator to read the resume or to call for an interview? By changing the date and newspaper reference, you could use this letter for any ad, but to do so is to pass up opportunities to highlight qualifications that uniquely suit you to the position.

Ethos: Establishing Credibility. The crisp feel of quality letterhead, embarrassing typographical errors, and an unsigned resume cover letter, all tell something about you and contribute to a positive or negative impression in the mind of the reader. The detail-oriented accountant can hardly afford to misspell the prospective employer's name in the salutation, or to let typos stand, or to write a garbled sentence. The cover letter must therefore be carefully crafted for attractive and consistent layout, correct spelling and grammar, and confident voice—in short, anything that would contribute to competence. Just as you would not show up at a job interview with your shoelaces untied or with ketchup slopped over your jacket front, so you cannot send a sloppy cover letter.

Pathos: Interesting the Employer. Effective resume cover letters incorporate telling evidence, not only to highlight capabilities, relevant experience, and education, but to convince the reader that taking a further look would benefit the company. By scrutinizing each word in a job advertisement or announcement and thereby drawing inferences about qualities the employer seeks, you can customize your presentation to meet the expectation or self-interest of the reader. While avoiding the extremes of bragging ("You can stop searching; I'm the staff accountant you've been looking for") and timidity ("I really need the entry-level staff accountant job and would be very grateful for any time you could spare to grant me an interview"), write your cover letter, trusting your qualifications and knowing that you have exhausted all possible avenues of appeal. If you incorporate sound rhetorical strategies, you can write to prospective employers with full confidence.

Resume Cover-Letter Elements

The resume letter is not as bound to formatting and conventions as are resumes. Because the letter is a business genre, and because the reader expects to find information in certain locations, the successful applicant observes business writing conventions. The following elements apply to resume cover letters:

STATIONERY Use quality white, off white, or light gray (exceeding 20# cotton rag content) stationery for both the letter and resume. Recycled stationery is a good option, especially if the employer is environmentally conscious. Mail your presentation in a 9" x 12" envelope to avoid folding it, or use a matching long business envelope. Type your address labels.

LETTERHEAD Never use another company's stationery. You can use personal stationery, if it is businesslike. Or you can create your own on a laser printer, as shown in the following two examples. Include your name, address, and phone number:

John M. Smith

---

13 South Street, Birmingham, AL 35201 (205) 555-1234

Example 1

Alicia T. Johnson
Post Office 401
Snyder, TX 79549
(W) 915-555-3456 (H) 915-555-6789

Example 2

DATE This belongs in the upper-left corner. Spell out the month (e.g., February 4, 1993).

INSIDE ADDRESS This should be single-spaced, flush with left margin. Double-check the address with the advertisement or announcement. Use U.S. Post Office designations for states and zip codes: "Roswell, NM 88201," not "Roswell, N.M." Use this sequence:

Name
Title
Firm name
Street address or post office box
City, state, zip code

SALUTATION Avoid gender-specifics unless you know the reader. Say "Dear Sir or Madam" rather than "Dear Sir." "Hello!," "Hi," and "Dear Judy" are far too casual for a resume cover letter. Avoid "To whom it may concern." If possible, obtain the name of the resume evaluator. Punctuate with a colon (:), which is more formal than a comma (,).

BODY Use single spacing with double spacing between paragraphs. Set right margins for "ragged" to avoid unsightly spaces between words caused by justified right margins. In the opening paragraph state that you are applying for a specific position or type of job. Mention how you learned of the opening: an advertisement, a job announcement, a certain agency, or a certain person. In the second paragraph, outline your interest in the position, field, or company. Briefly explain how your experience, education, and skills suit you to the job. Emphasize what you can contribute to the company. Do not rehearse what you've stated in your resume; instead, highlight your qualifications, mentioning additional details you couldn't fit into your resume. Whet your reader's appetite by furnishing tidbits to interest him or her in your qualifications. Avoid dense text, however. If your paragraphs are too long, or your letter too crowded, the reader will move along to a more accessible document.

An optional third paragraph would continue to appeal to ad criteria such as nonsmoking environment, own transportation, or willingness to travel or relocate. Avoid slipping into a philosophical mode. Like the words in your resume, each word in your letter should contribute to your purpose: to convince your reader that you are worth talking with.

Many job applicants find difficulty extricating themselves from the last paragraph. Take a tip from Richard D. Altick, who advises, "Say what you have to say, and when you've said it, quit."[8] Invite your reader to call you for an interview (restate your phone number for his or her convenience). Avoid being overly aggressive ("I will call your secretary next week to set up an appointment") or being overly timid ("I hope you can find time in your busy schedule to see me for an interview at a mutually convenient time"). Omit the phrase "a mutually convenient time." The employer isn't really interested if the interview time suits you; be prepared to accommodate his or her schedule.

COMPLIMENTARY CLOSE Choose from the formal to the less formal: "Very truly yours," "Yours truly," "Sincerely yours," and "Sincerely." Place at the left margin.

SIGNATURE There should be quadruple spacing between the complimentary close and your typed name, which should also be placed at the left margin. Sign above your typed name in black or dark blue ink, as shown in the following example. Remember that sending an unsigned letter is like going to an interview barefoot.

Very truly yours,

Janet C. Duncan

Janet C. Duncan

REFERENCE INITIALS These notations such as ("JCD:mwc") indicate that your secretary typed the letter. Depending on where you are in your career, the notation could be considered pretentious. Also, having your secretary type your resume cover letter might inform the office grapevine of your job search.

ENCLOSURE An enclosure notation signifies that documents are enclosed, such as the resume, writing samples, salary history, list of references, or job application forms. Example:

Encl: Resume
Salary History

FORMATTING Be consistent in vertical and horizontal spacing, and create one-inch margins for the top and bottom and the right and left sides.

For editing practice in revising and writing opening and closing paragraphs, complete Exercises 4-5 and 4-6.

Write to Enter the Workplace: The Resume/Cover-Letter Assignment

From a major newspaper, select a block advertisement featuring a job you qualify for (or will soon qualify for). If you choose an entry-level position, or if you are a recent college graduate (or will soon graduate), limit your resume and cover letter to one page each (to survive the "first cut"). If you have extensive, relevant work experience, confine your resume to two pages and your cover letter to one page.

Prepare an application "package" to include:

- resume
- cover letter
- envelope
- salary history (if called for in the ad)
- list of references (if called for in the ad)
- writing sample (if called for in the ad)
- portfolio (if called for in the ad)

Study the advertisement carefully, word by word. As a persuasive writer, you will want to appeal to every bit of detail mentioned by the employer. After you are satisfied with your drafts, critique your resume and cover letter, using the Resume Checklist and the Resume Cover Letter Checklist at the end of this chapter.

WRITING TO ADVANCE AND SURVIVE IN THE WORKPLACE

GOALS

- Recognize the role of tone in workplace writing.
- Control tone.
- Evaluate and edit for tone.

KEY TERMS

Attributor The source for a writer's ideas, facts, and information.
Emphatic Expression of confidence in an assertion.
Hedge To pull back from an assertion.
Paper trail Filed or circulating writing often forgotten by the writer.
Schema A frame of reference or associations that can be activated by language.
Tone The writer's attitude conveyed in the text, which affects reader reaction.
Voice The role, persona, or stance assumed by a writer.

Introduction: Tone and the Accountant

Any accountant who expects to stay in business and to interact effectively with others in the workplace needs to learn to control and adjust the **tone** of his or her communication. Merely distinguishing between the *formal* tone of a financial report cover letter to a client and the *informal* memo written to a close colleague is not enough. No matter what the genre, the tone can run the gamut of being

objective	to	subjective
personal	to	distant
user-centered	to	writer-centered
logical	to	emotional
polite	to	rude
tactful	to	crude
respectful	to	insolent
inviting	to	threatening
humble	to	arrogant
courteous	to	abrupt
appreciative	to	unappreciative
strengthening	to	patronizing
sincere	to	evasive
friendly	to	hostile
sensitive	to	callous
exuberant	to	depressing
diplomatic	to	cavalier

As you can see from the preceding list of tonal polarities, problems of tone are not confined to irate letters to the editor or desperate collection letters. Billing statements, letters announcing an increase in fees, letters of dismissal or letters of commendation, letters to the IRS, and promotional literature are just a few genres of the writing of accountancy that must consider tone. In fact, tone is critical to *all* workplace communication. Adjusting tone to suit your topic, purpose, and audience is critical to getting your point across, to retaining the goodwill of your reader, and to promoting an appropriate image.

Factors in Considering Tone

Handling tone in the writings of accountancy is not as simple as advocating a "you" attitude or formulating a positive message. You will have occasion to assert *your* position and to deliver negative messages. Tone is but one of the rhetorical strategies that effective writers manipulate to suit the occasion, purpose, and audience for a communication. The appropriate tone, therefore, requires analysis of the writer's purpose and audience—and much more. The accountant's writing task is so complex that the following factors must be considered in controlling tone (listed loosely under the three rhetorical appeals, *logos*, *pathos*, and *ethos*):

Logos

BUSINESS CONVENTIONS Even though accountancy is a highly specialized field with distinct writing genres, the tone of each communication must be consistent with ordinary business convention and practice. For example, a letter announcing an increase in fees would not be decorated by "smiley faces," or sent on a postal card, or printed in purple on burnt-orange stationery. Additionally, conventional letter, report, and memo formats would be followed.

LEGAL CONSTRAINTS In an effort to use a forceful tone in collection letters, some accountants like to imply legal action in a letter:

"We must now ask that payment be made within the next ten days or we will have no choice but to turn your account over to our attorneys for collection,"[9]

or in a photocopy notation:

"pc: Stockbridge Law Partnership."

Stanley Person, CPA, advises that invoking legal associations (activating a legal schema) can be risky. He reminds accountants, "Never intimidate or threaten a client unless you plan to follow through."[10] Accountants are cautioned against triggering law suits through aggressive collection efforts ("suits for fees"),[11] and "premium surcharges are sometimes assessed for firms which actively sue for collection of fees."[12] Accountants have to think twice about using such devices to strengthen collection efforts. Clients are likely to be annoyed by empty threats; or if they take the attempted intimidation seriously, they might respond with a dreaded, costly lawsuit.

OCCASION FOR WRITING An accountant who is hard up for cash to make additional tax season payroll might be more insistent in collection attempts than at other times of the year. A beleaguered accountant, writing the IRS for the tenth time about an uncorrected mechanical error, and pressed for results from a hassled client, might feel justified in writing a demanding letter. When they are caught up in the urgency of the moment, accountants must take particular care to adapt their tone to the *purpose* of the communication rather than to the *frustration* of the moment.

TIMING Timing of the communication can affect its tone. For example, if an accountant sends progressively assertive collection letters every three weeks, each must contain a mitigating statement such as "Please ignore this letter if your payment has already been sent" to cover the possibility of the payment crossing the letter in the mails.

Pathos

PROFESSIONAL STANDARDS Because of legal and professional constraints, the tone of certain genres within the writings of accountancy should be consistent with the subject matter. Your client would not expect to find a quip in the middle of an engagement letter, or a cartoon, like the one shown, within a financial forecast, to cite just two examples. To interject material that defies reader expectation is to prompt a reading (and reaction) other than that intended.

"I've completed your 10-year financial forecast, Mr. Jones. According to my projections, you have no future."

Conversely, writers and document designers often incorporate "eye catchers" to prompt desired readings. Notice in the following example that "Internal Revenue Service" is in boldface, and is larger than "Department of the Treasury," of which it is a part:

COLLECTION LETTER: "Confidential" or "Urgent" is stamped on the envelope. The following notices are at the top of the collection letter and also on the tear-off return portion:

PROTECT YOUR CREDIT RATING WITH OUR CLIENT

THE ACCOUNTANT'S PURPOSE Adjusting tone is necessary to achieve certain goals; for instance, a fourth attempt at collecting delinquent fees will not be written in the same conciliatory tone as the first attempt. Even the way accountants are fired during "spring purges" can be modulated to retain the goodwill of the terminated employee, according to James F. Fitzgerald, CPA, president of an executive outplacement firm. He observes that the "history of public accounting is rife with horrendous stories of people being fired in the most insensitive ways. . . . Rather than making [firing] such a terribly negative experience, why not make it a positive experience?" Fitzgerald concludes that "since these people may later become controllers or even CEOs of potential clients, it could hurt your firm to dismiss them in a negative or distasteful manner."[13] While few would accept being fired as a positive experience, Fitzgerald's point involves tone: *how* something is said or done can at least take the sting out of *what* is said or done. Fitzgerald advises the employer to "terminate the individual in a caring way that recognizes the person's dignity. Conduct the termination privately. State your decision as clinically as possible and allow the person to leave his or her self-image and self-esteem intact."[14]

READER'S STATUS The status of the reader relative to the writer determines the appropriate choice of tone. A job applicant must be more accommodating, more polite and more formal than an employee when writing an employer.

WRITER'S RELATION TO READER The accountant must analyze his or her relationship to the reader. Is the reader more prominent? How is the writer responsible to the reader? To a third party? To the client who pays the bill? How well does the writer know the reader? The accountant often writes on behalf of a client. Even if an Enrolled Agent knows a particular IRS agent well, a client may not appreciate a humorous letter to the IRS written on his or her behalf.

AUDIENCE ANALYSIS What is the reader's level of expertise compared to the writer's? The accountant must adjust his or her tone to avoid sounding patronizing or arrogant:

PROFESSIONALLY HELPFUL: Enclosed is your 1991 tax organizer to help you gather information needed for your 1991 income tax return.

PATRONIZING: I have formulated a *pro forma* that you should fill out. This will help me organize your 1991 tax information. The various categories may seem confusing, but just do the best you can.

STAKES FOR THE READER Part of accommodating the user is analyzing his or her situation. What is at issue or what are the stakes for the user? What does he or she stand to gain or lose? What is the likely reaction to the communication? Has the writer provided ways for the reader to "save face" or to avoid unpleasant consequences? If the accountant is interested in establishing cordial relations with the reader or in retaining goodwill, adjustments in tone are necessary for certain types of otherwise volatile communication involving "bad news" messages. The following lines allow the client to "save face" in a collection effort: "Enclosed is a copy of last month's bill for $300.00, which has not yet been paid. Perhaps the bill was overlooked."

RETAINING GOODWILL Despite a bad-news message, does the writer attempt to retain goodwill? Or if continuing the relationship is no longer desired (as in a "kiss-off" letter), is that evident as well?

GOODWILL: We cannot undertake an audit engagement because professional standards would require that we have expertise in the aircraft industry. We will be happy to continue to provide the tax planning and tax preparation services that we have provided in the past.

CLIENT DISCONTINUATION: We regret that we cannot continue to serve as your auditors because we are unable to reconcile full disclosure problems. We do wish you success in your business endeavors, and we appreciate the opportunity of having worked with you.

SCHEMA Difficulties arise when a writer fails to consider that a reader's frame of reference may differ from his or her own. Certain jargon, buzzwords, or even slang might activate a schema involving associations and meanings never intended by the writer. For example, today's accountant will be careful to avoid activating schemas (sexism, for instance) by being sensitive to gender-specific language or other language considered offensive by some readers: "I'll have my girl call you to reschedule the appointment." (See "Avoiding Sexist and Prejudicial Language" in Chapter 5.)

At times, the accountant will employ language that deliberately activates specific schemas to attain certain goals. For example, business collection letters as well as IRS instructions use words and phrases that trigger a legal schema:

COLLECTION LETTER "Before initiating further collection procedures, I feel obligated to make sure you understand the consequences of failure to pay this bill."[15]

IRS INSTRUCTIONS (preparer's statement): "Under penalties of perjury, I declare that I have examined this return, including accompanying schedules and statements, and to the best of my knowledge and belief, it is true, correct, and complete. Declaration of preparer (other than taxpayer) is based on all information of which preparer has any knowledge."[16]

COMPANY POLICY Some firms may practice a more formal or less formal style in their communications. To deviate from the norm might be incongruous with company practices.

THE ACCOUNTANT'S VOICE The **voice**, or "persona" of the typical accountant is like a role that he or she is expected to play (which, for the accountant, implies competence, professionalism, expertise, helpfulness, etc.). If the accountant's voice or tone suggests otherwise, it strikes a sour note in the "ear" of the reader just as surely as a dog's howling during a performance of Handel's *Messiah*.

WRITER'S STATUS An interoffice memo from a company controller is likely to carry more clout than that from a part-time accountant. The accountant who enjoys prominent status is in a position to write in a more forceful or authoritarian tone than someone who isn't in such a position. Likewise, a person occupying a lower rung in an organization must take that factor into consideration when writing to a superior.

STAKES FOR THE WRITER What is at issue or what are the stakes for the writer? What is to be gained or lost? Can the writer afford to back down or change a position? What prompts the communication? Securing goodwill for the profession, the company, or the writer? Professional standards? New or continued business? Increased accounting fees? Collections? Advancement? Demotion? Accountants write within complex situations involving clients, superiors, subordinates, peers, academics, and others, and must adjust their tone accordingly.

PAPER TRAIL Tone is critical to a writer's purpose and to audience compliance and goodwill—in short, to virtually all communication penned by an accountant. A factor critical to advancing and surviving in the workplace is the **paper trail** of letters, memos, reports, and other writing often forgotten by the author, but nevertheless lying dormant in some file—mute testimony to competence or ineptitude, to eloquence or crudity, to tact or poor judgment of its writers. Long after the accountant has left for greener pastures, interested parties can consult the historical record and draw conclusions about the accountant's professionalism. The accountant can never forget that paper trails exist, are consulted, and give evidence. The trails might even lead to offices other than a former employer's, because accountants often write for unknown third parties, stockholders, insurance bonders, bankers, vendors, colleagues, and others. Consequently, no accountant can afford to send an ill-considered letter or memo, hastily written in the pressure of the moment. As much attention must be given to *how* something is said as to *what* is said. (See Exercise 4-7 for practice in appraising and editing tone.)

Tone and the Reader

Tone often determines how a message intended by the writer ends up being perceived differently by the reader. Or to put it another way, tone can retain or break client goodwill. For example, look at the following two versions of a "kiss-off" letter—that is, a letter written by a fed-up accountant to a no-longer-desired client. The reasons may include failure to follow the accountant's advice, failure to pay bills in a timely manner, or failure to communicate concerns that affect the working relationship. Whatever the reasons, the accountant must notify the client that he or she must seek another accountant—that the relationship is severed. Because you never know where the letter will end up, it should be written so that goodwill is retained (i.e., the client must not suspect that he or she is being summarily dismissed); after all, the client may yet refer valuable contacts.

Version 1

Dear Mr. Sterling:

I see where IRS has again placed a lien against your property. Haven't I advised you repeatedly that you must file personal tax returns in a timely fashion? Calling me the morning that the return is due (in the worst part of tax season) is inconsiderate, and a sign that you continue to be irresponsible.

My reputation (and sanity) will be affected if you remain my client. Please find another accountant as soon as possible.

Very truly yours,

The preceding is what the accountant *wanted* to send. But thinking better of the ramifications of such a hostile message, the accountant sent the following letter instead:

Version 2

Dear Mr. Sterling:

To meet the time limitations of tax season, and to serve my year-round business clients properly, I find it necessary to restrict my tax season practice to year-round business clients.

I'm letting you know now, therefore, to give you time to find a tax preparer for this year's tax returns.I do appreciate your past business.

With best wishes,

The differences between the two versions can be categorized under the following heads:

Version 1: Oblivious to Tone

Negative connotations and assertions about client	IRS, lien I advised you repeatedly You must file Calling me. . . is inconsiderate You continue to be irresponsible

Version 2: Attention to Tone

Negative connotations and assertions about accountant	Time limitations To serve. . . clients properly Restrict my tax season practice I'm letting you know now. . . to give you time

Notice that both versions incorporate a "you" attitude, but Version 1 contains five assertions by the accountant against the client. He is blamed entirely. Version 2 assigns "blame" to the *accountant* for not being able to continue serving the client. In addition, Version 2 makes it seem as if the accountant is doing the client a favor. Both make it clear that the business relationship is severed, but Version 1 is likely to generate resentment, nonpayment of the bill (if one is outstanding), and negative referrals to business associates. Version 1 reflects negatively on the accountant as well as on the client. Version 2, conversely, accomplishes the desired result (the client becomes an ex-client), yet retains, or attempts to retain, the client's goodwill. Both versions tell the truth, but from different points of view. Version 1 accurately expresses the accountant's disgust and frustration. Version 2 tries to be considerate of the client's feelings, and tries to protect the reputation of the accountant.

Techniques for Controlling Tone

Because accountants write for a variety of occasions, purposes, and audiences, they must know how to manipulate language to control tone. Appropriate to all accounting communication are courtesy, accuracy, and professionalism. In contrast, inappropriate to the writings of accountancy are rudeness, threats, inaccuracy, biased language, sarcasm, and suggestive language. Some tips and examples on how to manipulate language to control tone are as follows:

To Foster Cooperation

1. Be polite.

   Rude: You failed to ship the copy machine toner. I need it *immediately*.
   Polite: The copy machine toner wasn't included in the shipment of January 20, 1991. Because we anticipate heavy copier use in February, March, and April, please ship the toner as soon as possible.

2. Promise only what you can fulfill.
3. Incorporate a "you" attitude.
4. Use "we" and "our" to suggest shared interests and goals.

   "I" emphasis: I anticipate ten registrants for the postretirement benefits presentation.

   "We" emphasis: We anticipate ten participants for our postretirement benefits seminar.

5. Show appreciation.

   Unappreciative: We received your resume. Call our office to to schedule an interview.

   Appreciative: Thank you for submitting your resume for our review. Please call our office to schedule an interview.

6. Include **attributors**.

   Nonattributed: Your personal property returns are due April 15. I'm lacking your inventory figures from January 1.

   Attributed: According to the State Department of Assessments and Taxation, your personal property returns must be filed by April 15. I will need your inventory figures of January 1.

7. Represent the situation and facts accurately.
8. Furnish needed information.

   Unhelpful: File Federal Form 966.
   Helpful: Because you are dissolving your corporation, you need to file Federal Form 966, "Corporate Dissolution or Liquidation" (enclosed), along with Form 1120S.

9. Specify what the reader should do.

   Vague: Enclosed are your completed tax returns, which should be filed on or before April 15, 1993.

Specific: Enclosed are your completed 1992 Federal and Rhode Island tax returns, which must be filed on or before April 15, 1993. Please review all forms for omissions or misstatements. Sign and date the originals, and mail the federal forms to:

Internal Revenue Service Center
Andover, MA 05501

Mail the Rhode Island forms to:

State of Rhode Island
Division of Taxation
One Capitol Hill
Providence, RI 02908-5801

10. Give reader-centered reasons for complying.

Writer-centered: Sign and return the enclosed engagement letter to me so that I can proceed with scheduling the audit.

Reader-centered: I've enclosed our current engagement letter, which explains our mutual responsibilities regarding the upcoming audit of your financial statements. Please review the letter, and call me if you have any questions. When I receive your signed copy, I will schedule the audit.

11. Request cooperation with a question.

Demanding: Pay your past due balance of $200 *now*.

Asking: Won't you please pay your past due balance of $200 today while you're thinking about it?

To Mitigate Unpleasant Messages

1. Be polite.

Rude: We found another candidate more qualified than you for the position of staff accountant.

Polite: Deciding among the final four candidates for staff accountant was difficult because all were well qualified. We have selected another candidate with extensive relevant experience, but we do appreciate your taking the time to meet with us. Because of your qualifications, we will keep your resume on file for three months and will contact you if a position opens up. Best wishes on your job search.

2. Show appreciation.

Unappreciative: We reviewed your proposal to purchase a full-color copier for the Personnel Department and decided we can't afford it.

Appreciative: Your proposal to purchase a full-color copier for the Personnel Department was well presented and carefully considered. Although the copier would be beneficial in some ways, it really isn't cost-effective. Considering our tight budget, we must decline the proposal at this time. We appreciate your efforts to upgrade Personnel's presentations.

3. Offer help.

Unhelpful: Personnel cutbacks force us to give you 30 days notice of termination of employment.

Helpful: We regret that budget cuts force us to reduce staff by giving you 30 days notice of termination of employment. We realize that personnel cutbacks can cause hardships. We hope, however, that the 30 days notice, four weeks severance pay, and outplacement assistance will help. We would, of course, be happy to provide you with suitable references.

4. Compliment or praise the reader when appropriate.

   Refusal: At present we cannot afford to implement your idea to order embossed letterhead, envelopes, and business cards.

   Positive refusal: While I agree that embossed letterhead, envelopes, and business cards would enhance the image of our firm, we cannot afford the extra expense just now. I can see that you are concerned about a professional presentation; when it's time to reorder our stationery, I'd be interested in your thoughts about color coordinating our stationery and our report covers and bindings.

5. Use tact.

   Tactless: Our nonsmoking policy has been in effect for six months. By now you should have been able to kick the habit.

   Tactful: As you know, our nonsmoking policy has been in effect for six months. We know how hard it is to break entrenched habits, but our closed ventilation system and newly passed county ordinance necessitate that smoking be banned inside our building. For the comfort and health of your co-workers, and to comply with county regulations, we ask that you refrain from smoking on the job.

6. Use the passive voice.

   Active: We are cutting the Accounting Department staff by 20 percent.

   Passive: The Accounting Department staff will be cut by 20 percent.

7. Be sincere.

   Insincere (kiss-off letter): You have been an esteemed client; I have valued our relationship.

   Sincere (kiss-off letter): We have appreciated your business.

8. Include an attributor:

   Non-attributed: We threw out the exemption for your wife's niece.

   Attributed: An exemption for your wife's niece cannot be claimed because she does not meet two of the five tests required for dependents. (Please see highlighted passages of ¶137 of the 1991 *United States Master Tax Guide*, copy enclosed.)

9. Use humor *sparingly*, and then only with selected readers. Never attempt humor when imparting bad financial news.

   Humorless: Our 386 computer processors do not require upgrading at this time.

   Good humor: Thank you for your offer to upgrade our five 386 computer processors to 486. The new 486 system would undoubtedly be faster and more efficient. Unfortunately, our staff accountants can barely keep up with the rapid screen changes of the 386. I fear that faster systems would cause severe brain overload.

10. Evidence regret.

    Matter-of-fact: Due to budget constraints, our department cannot afford color monitors at this time.

    Regretful: I regret that budget constraints prevent us from purchasing new color monitors just now.

11. Avoid blaming the reader.

Judgmental: Because you failed to divulge the source of the $100,000 funding to start your new business, we cannot accept the engagement to provide accounting services.

Nonjudgmental: Because of our firm's policy regarding knowledge of a client's source of financing, we regret that we cannot accept the engagement to provide accounting services.

12. Offer the reader alternatives.

No options: Unless we receive your payment in full ($1,200) within 30 days, we will be contacting our attorneys.

Options: If you find it impossible to pay the total amount due ($1,200) within 30 days, please contact us so we can work out a mutually agreeable payment schedule.

You will notice that taking the sting out of bad-news messages often takes more words. But when you consider the feelings of bad-news recipients, and when you want to prevent ramifications of bad news, the effort is well worth the extra time.

To Invoke Authority

1. Use official letterhead and logos.

Less authoritative: Acme Bookkeeping Service

More authoritative:

MEMBER
AMERICAN INSTITUTE OF
CERTIFIED PUBLIC ACCOUNTANTS
—
MARYLAND ASSOCIATION OF
CERITIFED PUBLIC ACCOUNTANTS

Very authoritative:

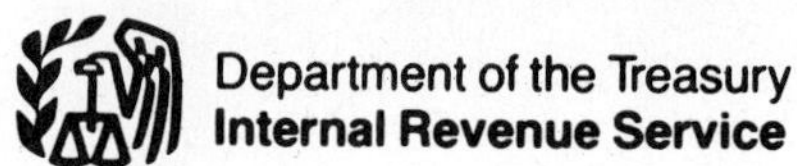

2. Use official titles.

Unofficial: John W. Harper

Official: John W. Harper, CPA, MBA

Official: Margaret T. Yindle, CPA, Managing Partner

3. Include attributors.

Nonattributed: We have decided not to issue interim financial statements to clients of nonpublic entities without first issuing a financial statement.

Attributed: In accordance with a recent pronouncement from the American Institute of Certified Public Accountants, we have decided not to issue interim financial statements to clients of nonpublic entities without first issuing a financial statement.[17]

4. Use formal language.

Informal: Dear Nancy,
Sincerely,
Bill

Formal: Dear Ms. Stein:
Very truly yours,
William H. Semies, Certified Financial Planner

To Be Assertive

1. Use personal pronouns (I, me, mine, my, myself).
2. Use "we" to imply institutional or organizational sanction.
3. Include attributors.
4. Use the active voice.
5. Be emphatic. Don't hedge.

   Hedged: I think Regulation 79 applies to your situation.
   Emphatic: Clearly, Regulation 79 applies to your situation.
   Hedged: The Problem Resolution Office may be able to help you.
   Emphatic: The Problem Resolution Office can certainly help you.

To Circumvent Liability

1. Avoid first-person pronouns.
2. Use the passive voice.
3. Include attributors.

   "Management has elected to omit substantially all of the disclosures required by generally accepted accounting principles."[18]

4. Use hedges.

   "The financial statements appear to be appropriate in form and free from obvious materials errors in application of accounting principles."[19]

To Intimidate

1. Invoke authority.
2. Activate a legal schema.

   If we do not receive payment in the amount of $3,000 within 30 days, we will have no choice but to institute legal proceedings against you.

3. Call attention to your superior position.

   As full professor of accounting at Ignatz University, I am in agreement with the recent move to require more essay-type questions in the CPA exam.

4. Use your official title.
5. Use your official letterhead.
6. Use threats.
7. Use "we" to imply institutional or organizational sanction.
8. Be patronizing.

   Our minimum fee for personal tax returns is $500; however, we will make an exception and process your return if you schedule an appointment early in February.

9. Use technical accounting jargon.

   Plain English: In preparing your tax returns, I used accelerated depreciation methods, and in preparing your financial statements, I used conventional straight line depreciation. This resulted in deferred taxes.

   Jargon: In preparation of your tax returns, MACRS and Section 179 were utilized, whereas in preparation of your financial statements, straight-line depreciation was used, resulting in a difference shown as deferred income taxes.

10. Write long, densely worded paragraphs.
11. Use all capital letters.

TO AVOID ADDITIONAL PENALTY AND/OR INTEREST, PLEASE ALLOW ENOUGH MAILING TIME SO THAT WE RECEIVE YOUR PAYMENT BY JUNE 30, 1991. MAKE YOUR CHECK OR MONEY ORDER PAYABLE TO THE INTERNAL REVENUE SERVICE. SHOW YOUR TAXPAYER IDENTIFICATION NUMBER ON YOUR PAYMENT AND MAIL IT WITH THE BOTTOM PART OF THIS NOTICE. IF YOU BELIEVE THIS NOTICE IS NOT CORRECT, PLEASE SEE THE INFORMATION ABOUT THE PAYMENTS YOU MADE ON THE FLAP OF THE ENCLOSED ENVELOPE.

PENALTY AND INTEREST CHARGES

$40.65 PAYING LATE - SEE ENCLOSED NOTICE, CODE 07

$63.89 INTEREST - SEE ENCLOSED NOTICE, CODE 09

(Excerpt from actual 1991 IRS Notice of Deficiency)

Addressing Difficult Situations: How Accountants Handle Tone

Being courteous and somewhat formal, avoiding offensive or charged language, giving the reader a chance to respond positively, incorporating a "you" attitude, evading responsibility by using the passive voice—these and other techniques help control tone. To see how accountants handle letters and memos arising from difficult circumstances, consider the following situations, accompanied by actual correspondence. Then analyze the correspondence in Exercises 4-8 through 4-12.

A Letter to the IRS

A valued client (worth 12 percent of a firm's annual revenues), irate over the accountant's seeming inability to halt unstoppable IRS notices of deficiency, demands a forceful reply to the IRS's latest computer-generated boilerplate letter. The problem: how to write a strong letter to the IRS that will achieve the desired results without antagonizing the agent, while placating the frustrated client. Using a "color analysis" technique, evaluate the accountant's letter to the IRS in Exercise 4-8. Highlight in *yellow* the figures and facts that support the accountant's claims, mark in *pink* the words or phrases designed to appease the IRS, accent in *blue* the words or phrases designed to appease the client, and *underline* the words or phrases that would put the IRS on the defensive.

A Letter from the IRS

Accountants write *for* the IRS as well as *to* the IRS. And they are good at it, because a letter from the IRS rattles its recipient as no other. In fact, accountants are often handed *unopened* IRS letters because many clients cannot bear the thought of reading IRS messages. Collection Division tactics and ensuing IRS notices are so effective that they are the envy of collection agencies: the IRS has collected 13 percent of business accounts and 43 percent of individual accounts that were deemed "uncollectible."[20] A 1986 study revealed that

> 978,390 of the 4.5 million taxpayers—almost one out of five—had signed installment agreements covering $1.2 billion in owed taxes. By early 1986, the same study discovered, 60 percent of the debt covered by these agreements, or $724 million, already had been paid.[21]

Examining an IRS boilerplate Notice of Deficiency will reveal why the IRS is considered a master of intimidating tone. Even though its mandate is clear—to exact taxes owed by often recalcitrant taxpayers—IRS officials write within a complex situation, and they address the most difficult of all audiences: a hostile public. Even so, you will see from Exercise 4-9 that not even the IRS can get away with unmitigated demands, with blatant intimidation, or with unsubstantiated assertions.

A Memo of Reprimand

Unfortunately, there are times when you must reprimand an employee in writing, usually for legal reasons. For Exercise 4-10, assume you are a supervisor in a state department of assessments. Paul Goodwin was hired three months ago as an accounting clerk. His performance has so far been unsatisfactory for the following reasons:

1. He has been absent three times (on Mondays).
2. He has arrived late to work seven times.
3. You have heard rumors about suspected substance abuse, but you have no proof.
4. Three days ago, you noticed an item in the local newspaper that Paul had been arrested on marijuana possession. Charges were dropped due to a technicality.
5. Paul spends much time on the telephone on personal calls.
6. Paul's latest computer entries for accounts payable contained five errors, and his total was one decimal point off.

Because of state civil service regulations, you cannot fire Paul without a lengthy procedure. You have talked with him twice about his absences and tardiness. Now, to put your concerns in writing (and to lay groundwork for dismissal), you feel it is time to write Paul a memo of reprimand. Write the memo in one page or less.

A Letter of Complaint

Dissatisfaction over faulty products and disappointing service is a fact of business life. You purchased a fax machine for $1,200 last November. You paid with your American Express card so that the one-year warranty is extended to two years. Shortly after the purchase, you noticed that the telephone receiver would not "hang up" properly, resulting in busy signals for clients trying to fax material. You returned the machine to the seller, who promptly replaced the machine with a new, identical model—without charge. Now you are in the worst part of tax season, and clients and colleagues are complaining that your fax machine seems always to be busy. You check it out and find that this machine also doesn't hang up properly. The seller can't seem to accommodate you this time, so you write a letter of complaint to the manufacturer.

For Exercise 4-11, write the letter in one page or less. Take care to incorporate all three rhetorical appeals: *logos*, *pathos*, and *ethos*.

A Memo for Two Audiences

Exercise 4-12 offers you practice in writing within another difficult office situation. You will write two memos, to two very different audiences.

You are the manager of the central office (with 35 employees) of Hardware Fair, a local hardware chain. The county has informed your company that two of the company's six executive parking spaces must be designated handicapped spaces to conform to a recently passed county law; thus two spaces reserved for executives will be lost.

A secretary, Ms. Alicia Trimble, age 64—or Allie, as she is affectionately called—was secretary to the deceased founder of the company. She plans to retire in one year.

As a courtesy, she has been allowed to park in one of the executive spaces for years, along with five executives. She suffers somewhat from arthritis, but is not eligible for a handicapped parking tag.

To make way for the handicapped spaces, the president of Hardware Fair has already decided to move Allie and also Richard Bowen, one of four department heads, from their executive parking spaces. Consequently, you have the thankless task of informing both Richard Bowen and Allie that they will henceforth have to park in the main parking lot.

For Exercise 4-12, write a memo to Mr. Bowen and to Allie, informing them that they must move to the main parking lot.

Notes

1. I am grateful to Dr. Leigh Ryan, Director of the University of Maryland's Writing Center, for suggestions for resume content.
2. Robert Half, CPA, "How to Evaluate a Resume," *The Practical Accountant* (February 1987): 24–25.
3. Half, 24.
4. Ken Macrorie, *Telling Writing*, 4th ed. (Portsmouth, N.H.: Boynton/Cook, 1985), 42-46.
5. Adapted from Becky Weir, et al., "Action Verbs," *Placement Manual* (College Park, Md.: University of Maryland, 1990), 11. Used by permission.
6. Other than the job applicant's name being altered, the excerpts from the resume are faithfully reproduced.
7. *The Accountant's Guide to Changing Jobs*, 3d ed. (Wickford, R.I.: Resource Publications, 1988), 30.
8. Richard D. Altick, "The Philosophy of Composition," in *The Art of Literary Research*, 3d ed. (New York: W. W. Norton, 1981), 210.
9. Mitchell Hakoun, CPA, and Gerald Tomlinson, "Urgent Request for Payment of Past Due Fees," in *Accountant's Complete Model Letter Book* (Englewood Cliffs, N.J.: Prentice Hall, 1987), 316.
10. Stanley Person, CPA, "A Cycle for Successful Billing and Collection," *Journal of Accountancy* (May 1989): 132.
11. Robert M. Parker and Michael J. Chovancak, "AICPA Accountants Professional Liability Plan: Premium Surcharges—Why They Exist and How They Affect Your Premium," *Accountant's Liability Newsletter* (August/September 1989): 1.
12. Terry Hothem, "Claim Report," *Accountant's Liability Newsletter*, (August/September 1989): 3.
13. James F. Fitzgerald, CPA, "How to Fire Future Business Developers," *The Practical Accountant* (February 1991): 65.
14. Fitzgerald, 65.
15. North Shore Agency, Inc., Great Neck, New York, collection letter for past-due magazine subscription, dated January 3, 1991.
16. Internal Revenue Service, "U.S. Corporation Short-Form Income Tax Return," Form 1120-A, 1990. [p. 1].
17. From the *AICPA NEWS* (September 1989): 1.
18. Dennis R. Meals, CPA, John R. Clay, CPA, and Dan M. Guy, CPA, *Guide to Compilation and Review Engagements*, Vol. 1, 12th ed. (Fort Worth: Practitioners, 1990), 6–57.
19. Meals, 3–83.
20. "IRS Collects on Many 'Uncollectible' Accounts," *The Practical Accountant* (September 1987): 48.
21. David Burnham, *A Law Unto Itself: Power, Politics and the IRS* (New York: Random House, 1989), 56.

Resume Checklist

Content

NAME Are your name, address, and phone number(s) on each page? Is your name appropriately highlighted?

OBJECTIVE Can you just as well mention your objective in your letter?

EDUCATION Have you provided degrees earned and dates, major and minor fields of study, university, and location? Is your GPA high enough to mention? Have you included honors or awards? Did you finance a major portion of your education? Have you indicated relevant coursework?

EXPERIENCE Have you considered all work experience, paid or unpaid, full-time or part-time? Have you included firm name, location, job title, dates of employment, promotions, and awards? Did you handle money? Did you supervise or train personnel? Did you write or edit on the job? Did you give oral presentations? Have you provided specific details of job responsibilities, and used action verbs in parallel form? Does your job description truthfully represent your contributions and accomplishments? If you served in the military, have you included leadership skills and security clearance?

AD CRITERIA Have you appealed to every detail mentioned in the ad? Have you incorporated ad language when appropriate?

SKILLS Have you listed your experience with computer languages, hardware, and software? Are you experienced in other technical equipment? Are you fluent in any foreign languages?

ORGANIZATIONS Have you listed memberships and offices held in professional and social organizations?

LICENSES Are certificates or licenses included? Or have you indicated dates you intend to sit for qualifying exams?

CITIZENSHIP Have you indicated U.S. citizenship (or alien status) if the ad calls for it?

ACTIVITIES Have you included community, social, or fraternal activities that highlight your people skills?

INTERESTS Have you limited your personal interests to less than one line?

REFERENCES Have you included "References available upon request"?

Format

SPACING Is your vertical and horizontal spacing consistent? Are your margins balanced? Does white space separate items attractively?

HIGHLIGHTING Have you employed typefaces, boldface, underlining, italics, and capitalization tastefully? Is the overall effect of your presentation too "busy" and cluttered?

HEADINGS Are headings informative and in parallel form? Do they enable the reader to find information easily?

ORDER Are your dates listed in reverse chronological order? Are your lists of relevant coursework, computer skills, activities, and interests listed in order of importance to the employer?

LANGUAGE Have you eliminated personal pronouns? Is your grammar correct? Is your syntax (word order) coherent and your diction (word choice) appropriate? Have you run your spell-checker, or have you proofread carefully for typos? Could your language be considered sexist or prejudicial?

Overall Impression

Would you consider a job applicant for an interview based on this resume? If you were responsible for evaluating resumes, could you use this resume to justify your choice of candidates to interview?

Resume Cover Letter Checklist

Content

DATE Is the letter currently dated?

INSIDE ADDRESS Is the employer's name and address spelled and ordered correctly?

SALUTATION Is the letter addressed to a person? Have you avoided unnecessary gender-specifics? Is the greeting too casual? Is it correctly punctuated?

BODY Does the letter "flow"? Does it sound choppy, stilted, or pompous? Do misspellings, bad grammar, incorrect punctuation, inappropriate words (diction), or garbled sentences (syntax) detract from your professionalism (ethos)? Do you employ active verbs where possible? Do you avoid nominalizations? Are any paragraphs over four or five lines long? In the opening paragraph, have you mentioned a particular job or occupation? Are the date and title of the ad cited? Is the title of the newspaper underlined or italicized? If a person told you about the job, have you indicated his or her name and title? Does the second paragraph highlight the strong points of your resume? Is the additional information tailored to the requirements stated in the ad? If you have included a third paragraph (which is optional), have you exhausted all possible appeals to the ad criteria? Does the letter close graciously? Is the reader invited to call for an interview, and do you furnish a phone number and the best times to call? Does the invitation to call sound too aggressive or too timid?

COMPLIMENTARY CLOSE AND SIGNATURE Is the close appropriate? Did you sign your letter?

INITIALS AND ENCLOSURE Do reference initials seem consistent with your status? Are your enclosures appropriately noted?

Format

STATIONERY/LETTERHEAD Is your stationery a conservative color, and of a quality texture? Does it match your resume? Is your letterhead businesslike? Is the envelope typed? Is your name highlighted? Is the typeface consistent with that of the resume?

SPACING/LAYOUT Is your vertical and horizontal spacing consistent? Are your margins balanced? Are your right margins unjustified (ragged)?

ORDER Are the elements in an order consistent with business letter conventions?

Is the letter tailored to the stated ad criteria? Does its overall appearance enhance a professional image? Does it sound as if it were written by a professional? Would *you* want to interview the writer?

NAME

EXERCISE 4-1: TELLING RESUME FACTS

In the space following each job description (excerpted from actual resumes), select the inferences below that could be drawn from each telling fact:

trustworthiness	stability	oral communication
reliability	profit-mindedness	leadership
initiative	written communication	detail-orientation
people skills		

Telling Facts	*Inferences*
1. Handled customer complaints and concerns.	______
2. Issued 5,000 checks per month.	______
3. Presently handle over $10,000 in cash daily.	______
4. Scout leader of fifty-member troop for two years.	______
5. Two years experience in accounts payable and receivable, general ledger, using Peachtree accounting package.	______
6. Use Lotus 1-2-3 to create liquidity calculations.	______
7. Financed 100% of education through telemarketing.	______
8. Coordinated summer archery program for 8 instructors and 500 campers.	______
9. Promoted to computer "first aider" after only one semester.	______
10. Edit correspondence for division personnel.	______
11. Firefighter for Kensington Volunteer Fire Department.	______
12. Developed sales policy manual.	______
13. Review and approve new customer applications.	______

From your work experience, write a job description incorporating telling facts. In the right-hand column, list the qualities you imply.

Job Description	*Implications*
______	______
______	______
______	______

NAME

EXERCISE 4-2: TELLING RESUME VERBS

In the space provided, change the following nominalizations, culled from actual resume job descriptions, to active verb forms (verbs that "tell"), in parallel form:

1. Responsible for the supervision of fifteen campers.

   ____

2. Performed the conversion of written records into computerized records.

   ____

3. Did reconciliation of check-control reports.

   ____

4. Duties included the verification and mailing of billing statements.

   ____

5. Facilitated the training and supervision of all new employees.

   ____

6. Responsibilities included processing of accounts payable.

   ____

7. Accomplished maintenance of accounting records.

   ____

8. Involved in the training and scheduling of waiter staff and trainees.

   ____

9. Controlled the sorting, distributing, and collecting of mail.

   ____

From your own work experience, write a job description incorporating telling verbs in parallel form. ______________

____

____

NAME

EXERCISE 4-3: RESUME CRITIQUE

In what ways does Delores Martin violate resume conventions in regard to the following:

Headings: ______________________________

Horizontal spacing: ______________________________

Parallel construction: ______________________________

Personal pronouns: ______________________________

Punctuation and capitalization: ______________________________

Salary: ______________________________

Sequence: ______________________________

Reasons for leaving jobs: ______________________________

Other: ______________________________

Ethos In what ways does Delores sabotage her own job-hunting efforts? How does her presentation affect her credibility?

____

____

Logos In what ways does Delores fail to provide evidence of expertise?

____

____

Pathos In what ways does Delores fail to appeal to the employer's self-interest? Does she reveal too much emotion?

____

____

Rewrite her "Dart Drug" job description:

____

____

____

NAME

EXERCISE 4-4: AD INFERENCES

To the right of each of the following typical ad excerpts, write inferences you draw from a close reading of the ad's text:

Advertisement Excerpts	*Inferences*
Responsibilities include performing routine and special financial reviews, examining accounting records and related documents, preparing formal written review reports.	
* * *	
Possess mature judgment and absolute integrity.	
* * *	
Attention to detail essential.	
* * *	
The successful applicant will possess a college degree with coursework in accounting and a desire to advance in a promotional track in the accounting field.	
* * *	
Applicant should be able to work overtime.	
* * *	
Ability to work under deadlines important.	
* * *	
Candidate should be willing to learn and participate in teamwork atmosphere.	

NAME

EXERCISE 4-5: RESUME COVER-LETTER OPENINGS

To the right of each opening paragraph from resume cover letters, characterize problems you notice from the following list. Then revise the paragraphs on the lines following each.

uninformative	timid	repetitive
windy	pretentious	vague
bragging	begging	irrelevant

Opening Paragraph	*Problems*

I noticed that you are running a large ad for staff accountants in the *Boston Globe*. Well, you can stop wasting money because you have found the ideal person—me!

Presently employed, I am seeking a connection with an accounting firm that will recognize and utilize my administrative abilities. I feel automatically thwarted from advancement in my present position because a son of one of the partners is slotted for the next junior partner opening. While I am assured of a permanent position here, obviously, further advancement is far down the line. Therefore, I am looking for a senior-level accounting position with your firm.

This letter is in response to your advertisement in the Thursday, July 2, 1993 edition of the *Baltimore Sun* for a general ledger specialist. I am very interested in applying for your opening for a general ledger specialist. Attached please find my resume, which I am taking the liberty of addressing to your attention.

I am writing in reference to the advertisement in the paper stating you had a position available for an accounting assistant. I am seeking this position to gain valuable on-the-job training that will augment my studies. I feel I could be an asset to your company because of my previous job experiences and the courses I have studied.

Opening Paragraph	*Problems*
It is my thought that you might be interested in my qualifications as set forth in the enclosed resume. I'm not exactly sure which position I want, but I am sure that once you read my resume, you will want to hire me for a responsible position.	

For the following ads, write opening paragraphs for letters of application:

ACCOUNTANT Accounting degree required with a minimum of 4 years experience in general ledger accounting and financial statement preparation. Self-starter and strong PC knowledge a must with emphasis in using QuattroPro, LOTUS 123, MAS 90.

* * *

SENIOR COST ACCOUNTANT (Activity-Based Costing) MDK Industries has an opportunity for a seasoned Senior Cost Accountant for their manufacturing facility. The successful candidate has

- 5 years cost accounting exp.
- "hands-on" track record in implementing Activity-Based Cost System
- interfacing with engineering, manufacturing, and materials team
- Lotus 1-2-3 and graphics
- Complete inventory evaluation
- Budgeting

NAME

EXERCISE 4-8: A LETTER TO THE IRS

Read the following letter to the IRS, and answer the questions in the right-hand column.

March 1, 1993

Department of the Treasury
Internal Revenue Service
Memphis, TN 37501

Re: Reference Number 12345678
Valued Client Charitable Foundation
Form 990T - May 4, 1989
Forms 941 - June 30, 1989 and
September 30, 1989

Enclosed is a copy of the above referenced communication dated December 20, 1990. Also enclosed is an IRS notice from your Philadelphia office dated November 21, 1989, which indicated:

1)--that there was an overpayment on a 990T return of $30,000.
2)--that these "overpaid taxes" of $30,000 were applied to unpaid amounts from Forms 941 for June 30, 1989 and September 30, 1989.

I called the IRS at 1-800-424-1040 on December 27, 1990, and spoke to agent Frost. I explained that first of all, an overpayment of $30,000 was utterly impossible (the 990T tax for that period was actually $1,000), and that there were no unpaid 941 taxes. Agent Frost could not explain the IRS errors, but she did promise to mail a transcription of transactions so that we might be able to see what had been done. As of today, over 60 days later, that transcription has not been received.

We would appreciate it very much if the Internal Revenue Service would:

1) remove the erroneous overpayment of $30,000;

2) correct the records to reflect that no 941 taxes are due for 1989. Further, inasmuch as the 941 deposits for 1989 were timely made, interest and penalties noted in the December 20, 1990 notice are improper. The IRS was notified by the taxpayer of the $30,000 IRS error on January 3, 1990.

Thank you.
Very truly yours,

Marcia S. Ensberg, CPA
Marcia S. Ensberg, CPA

(NOTE: The IRS eventually corrected the errors and rescinded the penalties and interest. The client complimented the CPA on a "well-written letter.")

List two assertions against the IRS by the CPA: ____________

____

____

____

____

____

How does the accountant incorporate *logos* (the logical appeal) in building her argument?

____

____

____

____

____

Using a yellow marker, highlight figures and facts that support the accountant's claims.

What do the figures and facts force the IRS to do? ____________

____

____

____

____

____

Using a pink marker, indicate the words or phrases designed to appease the IRS.

Using a blue marker, indicate the words or phrases designed to appease the client.

Underline the words or phrases that put the IRS on the defensive.

How would you characterize the tone of the letter? ____________

____

____

Does the letter contribute to or detract from a professional image? ____________

NAME

EXERCISE 4-9: A LETTER FROM THE IRS

Read the following letter from the IRS, and answer the questions in the right-hand column.

ALTHOUGH NOTICE AND DEMAND HAVE BEEN MADE FOR PAYMENT OF YOUR FEDERAL TAX LIABILITY SHOWN BELOW, WE HAVE NO RECORD OF RECEIVING THE AMOUNT DUE. THIS IS YOUR FINAL NOTICE BEFORE WE PROCEED WITH ENFORCEMENT ACTION. THE PURPOSE OF THIS NOTICE IS TO INFORM YOU OF OUR INTENTION TO LEVY UPON YOUR PROPERTY OR RIGHTS TO PROPERTY IN ACCORDANCE WITH SECTION 6331 OF THE INTERNAL REVENUE CODE.

TO PREVENT SUCH ACTION, SEND US, WITHIN 10 DAYS FROM THE DATE OF THIS NOTICE, YOUR CHECK OR MONEY ORDER FOR THE TOTAL AMOUNT DUE, PAYABLE TO THE INTERNAL REVENUE SERVICE. SHOW YOUR TAXPAYER IDENTIFYING NUMBER (SOCIAL SECURITY OR EMPLOYER IDENTIFICATION NUMBER) ON IT AND ENCLOSE THE BOTTOM PART OF THIS NOTICE TO ASSURE PROMPT AND ACCURATE CREDIT. AN ENVELOPE IS ENCLOSED FOR YOUR CONVENIENCE.

IF YOU HAVE RECENTLY PAID THE AMOUNT DUE BUT YOUR PAYMENT HAS NOT BEEN CREDITED TO YOUR ACCOUNT, OR IF YOU CANNOT PAY THIS AMOUNT IN FULL, CONTACT THE OFFICE SHOWN ABOVE WITHIN 10 DAYS FROM THE DATE OF THIS NOTICE. THE TELEPHONE NUMBER IS SHOWN ABOVE.

IF WE DO NOT RECEIVE YOUR PAYMENT OR IF YOU DO NOT CONTACT OUR OFFICE, ENFORCEMENT ACTION MAY BE TAKEN AT ANY TIME AFTER 10 DAYS FROM THE DATE OF THIS NOTICE WITHOUT ANY FURTHER NOTICE TO YOU. A NOTICE OF FEDERAL TAX LIEN MAY BE FILED WHICH CONSTITUTES PUBLIC NOTICE TO YOUR CREDITORS THAT A TAX LIEN EXISTS AGAINST YOUR PROPERTY. SALARY OR WAGES DUE YOU MAY BE LEVIED UPON, AS PROVIDED BY SECTION 6331 OF THE INTERNAL REVENUE CODE, BY SERVING A NOTICE OF LEVY ON YOUR EMPLOYER. BANK ACCOUNTS, RECEIVABLES, COMMISSIONS, OR OTHER KINDS OF INCOME YOU HAVE ARE ALSO SUBJECT TO LEVY. PROPERTY OR RIGHTS TO PROPERTY, SUCH AS AUTOMOBILES, MAY ALSO BE SEIZED AND SOLD TO SATISFY YOUR TAX LIABILITY.

[NOTE: The excavating contractor who received this notice ended up receiving a refund from the IRS.]

What is the IRS's assertion against the client? ________

____

____

____

What logical appeal does the IRS employ? ________

____

____

____

Circle the *hedges* in the Notice. Why does the IRS employ them?

____

____

____

What does the IRS want the reader to do? ________

____

____

____

Does the IRS offer any other options? ________

____

____

The IRS has been accused of utilizing intimidating tactics. Underline words or phrases that could seem scary to a taxpayer. What kinds of schemas are activated? ________

____

____

____

Highlight words or phrases that make the IRS seem helpful or courteous. Why would the IRS want to accommodate its reader? ________

____

____

____

Do you think this Notice gets results? Why or why not?

____

____

____

____

NAME

EXERCISE 4-10: A MEMO OF REPRIMAND

(See "A Memo of Reprimand" on page 95 for the situation relating to this memo.)

```
                         Interoffice Memo

                  State Department of Assessment

     To: Paul Goodwin
   From:
   Date:
Subject:
----------------------------------------------------------------------------------------
```

NAME

EXERCISE 4-11: A LETTER OF COMPLAINT

(See "A Letter of Complaint" on page 95 for the situation relating to this letter.)

Donald A. Vogelpohl, P.C.

Certified Public Accountant

CHAPTER 5

Where Accountants Write

OVERVIEW

Accountants work as sole practitioners; as members of small, mid-size, regional, or Big Six accounting firms; as Internal Revenue Service, Federal Bureau of Investigation, Government Accounting Office, and other governmental employees; as managers, controllers, or chief executive officers in private industry; and as employees for not-for-profit businesses. In short, accountants work wherever financial information is generated, analyzed, and conveyed to interested parties.

This chapter focuses on the diverse situations of accountants in the workplace. You will first look at the workplace situations of a controller, an audit manager, and a sole practitioner—and the writing and reviewing tasks caused by their various interactions with superiors, subordinates, colleagues, associates, clients, the public, and others. Then you will analyze the rhetorical situations of accountants, described in the case studies of three companies.

Contending with realities in the workplace forces the accountant who wants to communicate effectively to develop coping strategies. In later sections of this chapter you will find ways of avoiding sexist and prejudicial language; you will develop definitional strategies to gear technical language and concepts to the needs of nonaccountant users; and you will learn to develop and to employ writing and reviewing checklists geared to the special writing genres of accountancy.

This chapter teaches the accountant-writer to:

- Analyze accountant, employer, and internal and external user situations;
- Recognize the complications of writing for multiple users;
- Cope with interpersonal, organizational, professional, legal, political, and societal realities;
- Write, edit, and revise alone and collaboratively;
- Develop and use practical writing checklists geared to the writings of accountancy.

COPING WITH THE WORKPLACE SITUATIONS OF ACCOUNTANTS

GOALS
- ◆ Analyze a rhetorical situation.
- ◆ Analyze audiences for the writings of accountancy.

KEY TERM *Constraints* The components of a writer's or reader's situation that affect the writing or reading.

Between Rocks and Hard Places: Realities of the Workplace

Because of the complexities of their professional and workplace situations, accountants often find themselves in "lose-lose" situations, exemplified in the following scenarios:

- An *IRS agent* wants to relieve a widow of her tax obligations incurred by her irresponsible husband. Even though she had nothing to do with her husband's business, she did sign joint returns and she does have assets. Under congressional pressure to collect taxes due, the agent's supervisor won't budge on this one. Therefore, the agent sends a Notice of Deficiency.
- The *administrative partner* in a mid-size accounting firm pushes all junior partners, senior staff accountants, staff accountants, and newly hired accountants either to have or to be working on a master's degree. Facing resentment from senior partners who feel threatened by subordinates who advocate new theories, methods, and technologies—and from junior partners who want the senior partners also to earn master's degrees—he drafts a recommendation report for the next partners' meeting.
- The *accounting department supervisor* of a department store chain is under pressure from the new CEO to "restructure" her nonsupervisory accounting staff by retitling positions. The supervisor fights successfully to retain each employee's present salary level, but the new titles are, in effect, demotions. The "restructured" employees will no longer be eligible for their previous promotion tracks; thus, she expects to lose some of her best accounting clerks. Reluctantly, she writes a memo to her staff explaining the job restructuring.
- An accountant who is a *sales representative* for a software company has been asked to promote an accounting package that he expects will soon be replaced by a better version now in the beta stage of development. The office grapevine says that reduced price updates will not be made available for the current package; if that is true, his clients will have to purchase a completely new accounting package. He has to let his clients think that updates will be available as usual, but he fears the loss of future sales in his territory when clients are forced to purchase a new package. He spends considerable time drafting a memo to the sales manager, protesting a sales tactic that threatens his credibility and his client base.
- The newly elected volunteer *treasurer* for his church wants to change longstanding collection-counting procedures. Instead of having couples count the collections at the bank on the day following the services, the treasurer wants to have unrelated people count the money to avoid the appearance of impropriety. While he believes that none of the current counters are dishonest, he insists that proper internal control procedures should be followed to prevent theft in the future. He also realizes that his recommendations might be received by some of the counters as accusations. He carefully writes a memo to the church board, advocating the procedural change.

- The *accounts payable manager* of a national catalog sales company has been promised a computer system if she can subsequently trim her personnel costs by 20 percent. When she surveys the computer skills of her staff, she learns that most of the employees over age fifty lack the computer skills to handle the new system. Retraining would eat into the 20 percent she is supposed to cut, so she must fire some older employees. She writes letters of dismissal.

The agent, partner, supervisor, sales representative, treasurer, and manager are all caught in conflictive situations: they face undesirable consequences no matter what they do, and they all are forced to address their situations in writing. Hence, their situations can be termed *rhetorical*. Lloyd F. Bitzer, in "The Rhetorical Situation," identifies three components to any rhetorical situation:[1]

1. The exigence (what spawns the discourse)
2. The audience (the intended reader or the overhearer)
3. The **constraints** (the circumstances that affect the writing and reading of the discourse)

The aforementioned accountants were constrained to write because of circumstances related to their duties in the workplace. To refuse to act would be to neglect their professional responsibilities and to place themselves in jeopardy.

Accountants in the Workplace: The Controller of Aqua-Widget Company, Inc.

Figure 5-1 shows how a controller relates to people, companies, and agencies inside and outside Aqua-Widget, a national company.

The controller's relations among superiors, peers, and subordinates inside and outside the company are indicated by typical ongoing writing or reviewing situations in the chart on pages 116 and 117. Obviously, much of the controller's day is involved with writing and reviewing whole or partial texts, either alone or in collaboration with others. When writing collaboratively, the controller asks for macro-composition help from the Vice-President of Finance, reviews the wording of job descriptions from Human Resources as well as a draft to stockholders (micro-composition), and offers comments for a query from the State Board of Accountancy.

FIGURE 5-1
The Controller Situated within Aqua-Widget Co., Inc.

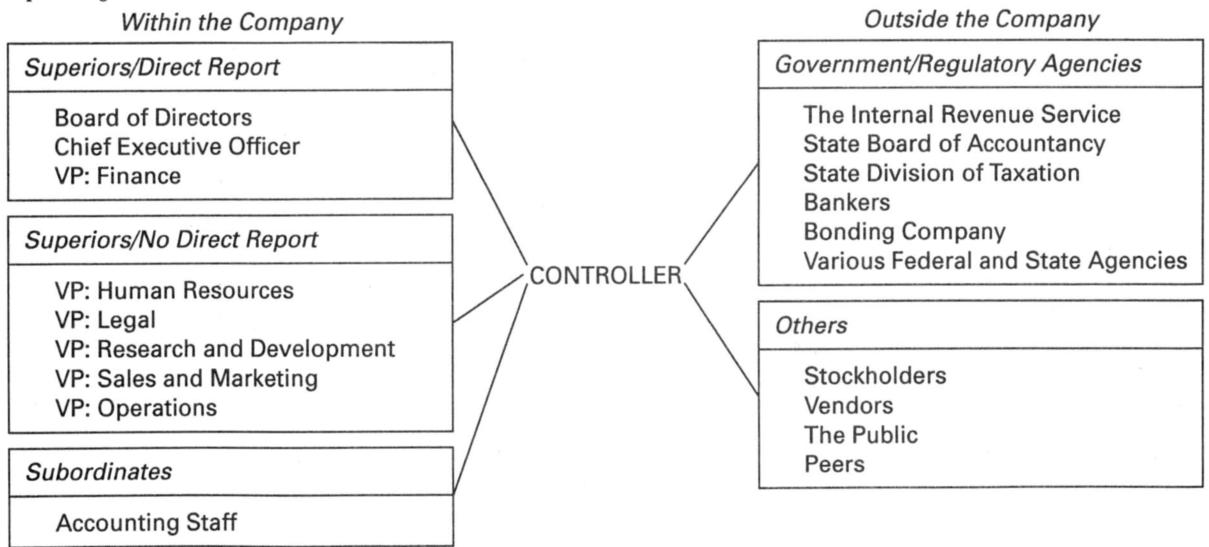

WITHIN THE COMPANY: SUPERIORS

Audience	*Writing*	*Exigence*
VP of Finance	Drafts semiannual planning document.	Controller needs approval of document's structural changes from previous document.
	Drafts complicated footnote describing a contingent liability in a financial statement for a bank.	GAAP requires disclosure.
VP of Human Resources	Writes memo requesting verification of status of three recently dismissed employees.	Department of Unemployment wants to know if the employees are eligible for unemployment benefits.
VP of Legal	Writes memo requesting review of lease agreement for warehouse space.	The lease requirements regarding insurance may not be appropriate.
VP of R & D	Writes memo asking R & D to justify its latest budget request.	Controller feels the budget request is not sufficiently documented.
VP of Sales and Marketing	Writes memo requesting updated sales forecasts and projections.	Controller needs the information for the financial planning document.
VP of Operations	Writes memo asking for current inventory levels.	Controller needs to know how much financing will be required for future purchases.

WITHIN THE COMPANY: SUBORDINATES

Audience	*Writing*	*Exigence*
Staff	Writes memo requesting vacation schedules.	Vacations need to be coordinated.
	Reviews job descriptions submitted by staff.	Human Resources needs updated job descriptions for recruiting and interviewing.
	Writes memo to the internal audit manager advising that his available sick leave is almost exhausted.	Controller suspects a major medical problem.

OUTSIDE THE COMPANY: GOVERNMENT AND REGULATORY AGENCIES

Audience	*Writing*	*Exigence*
Internal Revenue Service	Writes letter requesting a printout of IRS's record of the company's payroll tax deposits for the previous year.	Controller responds to a Notice of Deficiency.
State Division of Taxation	Writes a letter requesting a definition of sales tax requirements for sales of widgets to nonprofit organizations.	Controller needs to determine if sales to nonprofit organizations are taxable.
Department of Labor	Writes a letter requesting a ruling on the overtime requirements for salaried accounting staff.	Controller wants to offer lower-level accountants a specific payroll package.
State Board of Accountancy	Responds to a questionnaire on the proposed 150-hour requirement; appends a note favoring the new standards.	The 150-hour requirement is being hotly debated.
Bonding company	Faxes a request for a performance bond.	A large government contract requires bonding.
Bankers	Writes a letter requesting a proposal to finance ten delivery trucks.	The best financing terms are needed.

OUTSIDE THE COMPANY: OTHERS

Audience	*Writing*	*Exigence*
Stockholders	Reviews a draft of a preface paragraph for the budget forecast.	Controller wants to soften effects of heavy financing demands.
Vendors	Writes a letter to a supplier of widget components asking for better terms (60 vs. 30 days) in return for all company business.	Quality suppliers are readily available; controller is seeking more attractive terms.
The public	Writes letter agreeing to support a Civitan Christmas project.	The company wants to improve community relations.

Peers	Faxes committee (Members in Industry division of the state association of CPAs), notifying them of agenda for their upcoming meeting.	Members need agenda to prepare for the meeting.
	Writes notes to committee members, asking them to review an article on postretirement benefits to be discussed at next Members in Industry meeting.	Controller wants members to review material to be discussed.

Accountants in the Workplace: The Audit Manager of Bickerstaff and Flimnap, Chartered

Figure 5-2 shows an accountant situated as an audit manager in an accounting firm. Due to the nature of the job and size of the firm, interactions with diverse audiences aren't as extensive inside or outside the firm as those of the Controller in the preceding situation. The manager typically writes or reviews texts alone or in collaboration with others as indicated in the chart following Figure 5-2.

FIGURE 5-2
The Audit Manager Situated within Bickerstaff and Flimnap, Chartered

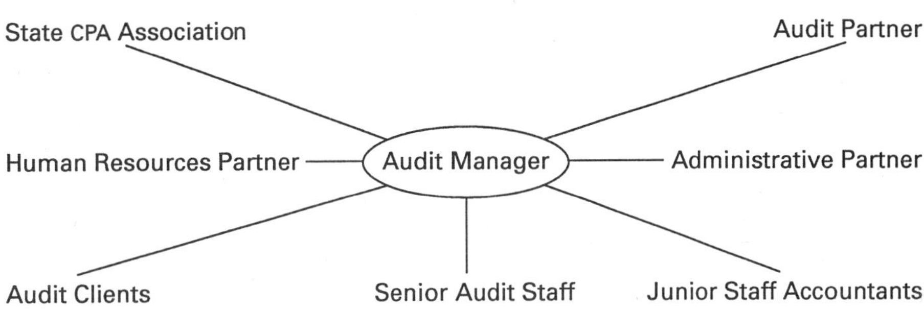

Audience	*Writing*	*Exigence*
Senior Auditor	Reviews reports on audits in progress.	Manager is responsible for progress of audits.
	Writes letters of recommendation to graduate schools for two staff accountants.	Firm requires a master's degree within 8 years of entering the firm.
Audit clients	Drafts management letter recommending changes in the accounts receivable department.	Errors in reconciling ledgers within the accounts receivable department are discovered.
	Writes engagement letter for regular audit client.	Firm policy requires precise engagement understanding.
	Writes letter to client justifying additional billing charges.	Client complains about higher audit costs.
Audit Partner	Writes memo advising status of audits in progress.	Partner requires weekly audit updates.
Human Resources Department	Writes memo detailing projected audit personnel needs.	Firm has landed a large audit client.
Administrative Partner	Writes monthly memo detailing projected audit fees.	Partner requires monthly audit fee update for financial planning.
Chair of Audit Committee, state association of CPAs	Drafts letter of opinion on Financial Accounting Standards Board (FASB) exposure draft (as committee member).	The Chair has requested written opinions on a FASB exposure draft to discuss at the next meeting.

Accountants in the Workplace: A Sole Practitioner, Francis U. Neely, CPA

Figure 5-3 shows a sole practitioner in relation to a wide array of correspondents, including governmental and professional organizations, clients and their associates, and professional contacts.

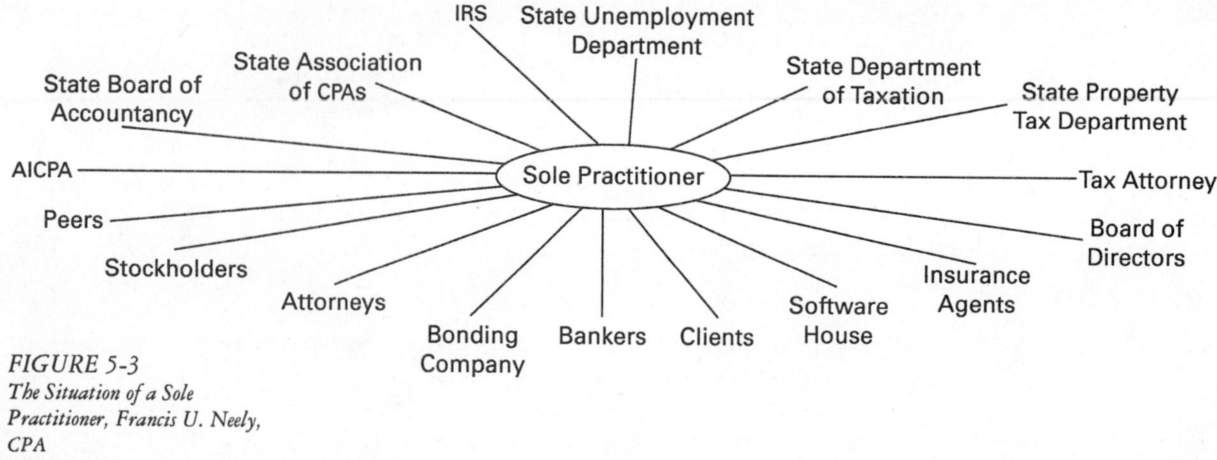

FIGURE 5-3
The Situation of a Sole Practitioner, Francis U. Neely, CPA

Audience	*Writing*	*Exigence*
AICPA	Writes letter seeking audit guides for the construction industry.	General contractor retains Neely's services.
State Board of Accountancy	Writes letter regarding reciprocity requirements for a neighboring state.	Substantial client plans to move to another state.
State Association of CPAs	Prepares description of his billing procedures for Management of an Accounting Practice (MAP) committee meeting.	MAP committee plans a seminar on billing procedures.
IRS	Writes letter asking that a client's audit be rescheduled.	The client is in Europe on a buying trip.
State Unemployment Department	Writes for quarterly report forms.	New client has not received initial reporting forms for quarterly payroll figures.
State Department of Taxation	Writes letter asking for the current status of a client's corporation.	Client may need to reactivate corporate charter.
State Property Tax Department	Writes letter seeking explanation of assessment values for client's personal property.	Assessed value did not agree with values reported on client's personal property tax return.
Peers	Faxes a request to a larger accounting firm to access their library.	Neely wants to check on IRS regulations regarding the dissolution of an S Corporation.
	Writes a letter requesting a client's depreciation schedule.	Neely needs the schedules from the client's former accountant.
Clients	Writes "kiss-off" letter to a tax client.	The client consistently fails to follow recommendations.
	Writes an article for his client newsletter about a tax law change.	Client newsletter is mailed monthly.
	Drafts an informational brochure about his services.	A targeted mailing to new area businesses is being considered.
Stockholders	Writes a proposal to a client's stockholders regarding corporate reorganization.	Fully depreciated assets of a recently acquired corporation could be revalued.
Attorneys	Writes a note to thank an attorney for referring a tax client.	About 40% of Neely's clients come through attorney referrals.
Bonding company	Writes a memo accompanying a financial statement, asking if additional information is required.	The client is trying to obtain a performance bond to bid on a contract.

Bankers	Writes a letter to introduce a new client, to describe the business, and to request an appointment to discuss a line of credit.	A new client needs a line of credit.
Software house	Writes a letter inquiring if scheduling software for a limousine service is available.	Limousine service client needs computer consulting services.
Insurance agents	Writes a letter asking if coverage is available for long-term risk of insecticide contamination.	Stockholders are pressing a client on safety issues of insecticide spraying.
Board of directors	Writes a letter advising the board to seek a larger accounting firm; recommends two.	Expansion of client into new financial enterprises is beyond Neely's expertise.
Tax attorney	Writes letter asking for an opinion on the best way to handle a complex sale of real property.	Client wants to minimize tax exposure.

Even though sole practitioners usually write alone, they still have occasion to write in collaboration with others. Neely furnishes a description of his billing practices for a seminar, and writes a proposal for a client's stockholders, which will be subject to review by others. This sole practitioner doesn't have the collaborative tasks typical of accountants in larger firms, in industry, and in government agencies, where he would have to cooperate in setting priorities and goals, dividing responsibility, and keeping to schedules. Nevertheless, he performs the tasks of collaborative writers in contributing specialized information, reviewing his own writing, and accommodating his writing to particular rhetorical situations.

Analyzing the Rhetorical Situations of Accountants: The MedWeCare Company Case Study[2]

The Principals

The MedWeCare Company, a regional medical supply distributor (partnership)
Mr. Schmidt, founder and partner of the MedWeCare Company
Mr. Acosta, partner of the MedWeCare Company
Ms. Theriault, controller of the MedWeCare Company

The MedWeCare Expansion

The MedWeCare Company, an East Coast medical supply distributor founded in 1978, rapidly expanded throughout the 1980s due to healthy demand, progressive product lines, and dependable service. Mr. Schmidt, its founder and dominant partner, was a hands-on administrator and managed the sales force and customer relations. The firm thrived due to his unerring sense of marketplace realities. He had taken Mr. Acosta into fifty-fifty partnership in 1981. Mr. Acosta contributed his expertise in medical supply product lines and extensive manufacturer contacts. They had managed financial matters adequately with the help of a full-time bookkeeper and an accounting firm for some years, but in 1988 decided to hire Ms. Karen Theriault, CPA, who left their accounting firm to become their controller.

A Partner's Proposal

In 1989 MedWeCare's sales increases caused a warehouse shortage. Mr. Schmidt wrote a proposal to his partner that the company purchase land and erect a building (with offices and adjoining warehouse facilities) in the industrial park in which they were currently leasing space. He felt that a building boom in the area would soon drive prices higher, so he proposed that bank financing be sought immediately.

The Controller's Recommendation

Concerned over the cost of permanently locating in the industrial park (which adjoined the small airport where Mr. Schmidt housed his Cessna), Mr. Acosta wrote a memo to Ms. Theriault, asking her to analyze the feasibility of the proposal. Her analysis yielded these findings:

1. The price of land was inflated due to its location near the airport.
2. Suitable land only twenty miles away could be purchased for 30 percent less.
3. Commercial space was only 70 percent leased in areas other than the industrial park. She felt that the commercial building boom had peaked.
4. Obtaining bank financing would be complicated by
   a. High interest rates
   b. Uncertainty of future profits
   c. Lack of outside capital
   d. The Company's cash requirement for continued expansion
5. She projected additional mortgage costs of $6,000 per month, compared with the current leasing cost of $2,500 per month.
6. She predicted severe cash-flow problems in future years.

Thus, Ms. Theriault favored purchasing land in a cheaper location, building later when the company was on better financial footing, and leasing warehouse space ten minutes away. After discussing the situation with a former colleague from the accounting firm (who concurred with her analysis), she presented her recommendations in a report to Mr. Acosta.

The Partners' Meeting

Even though Mr. Acosta had requested the analysis, Mr. Schmidt (the overhearer) had more clout in approving or rejecting Ms. Theriault's recommendations. Mr. Acosta generally agreed with the report, but Mr. Schmidt, who was anxious to build, disagreed with Ms. Theriault's conclusions. To placate Mr. Schmidt, Mr. Acosta suggested that an option be placed on suitable land *outside* the industrial park location. Mr. Schmidt resented the controller's intrusion into his expansion plans. They had, after all, hired a controller to perform accounting functions, not to make far-reaching executive decisions. Controllers come and go, but the firm was what mattered, and the partners *were* the firm. It was their money, their firm, their decision.

Mr. Acosta was surprised at the intensity of Mr. Schmidt's feeling. He thought that Ms. Theriault's cautious approach was sensible. How could waiting a couple of years hurt? But under Mr. Schmidt's leadership, MedWeCare had grown beyond expectations (and Mr. Acosta's income along with it), and competition for space at the industrial park was keen, so Mr. Acosta agreed (despite some nagging mental reservations) to at least look into buying land in the industrial park and to seek bank financing for the building. He wrote a memo to Ms. Theriault, directing her to look into bank financing.

The Outcome

Mr. Schmidt prevailed: two acres of land were purchased and a rather elaborate office/warehouse building (commensurate with others in the industrial park) was constructed. But because of the new mortgage payment ($3,500 above the previous monthly rent), MedWeCare soon found itself in a cash-flow bind. Mr. Acosta reminded his partner of Ms. Theriault's predictions. Mr. Schmidt blamed the company's financial straits on controllership problems, fired Ms. Theriault, and suggested that Mr. Acosta sell his interest to him at $500,000 to be paid out over ten years. Mr. Acosta accepted his offer and promptly opened a competing medical supply distributorship (in a location away from the industrial park), Ms. Theriault opened her own accounting practice, and Mr. Schmidt still pays $6,000 per month in mortgage payments at high interest rates even though rental values in the industrial park and elsewhere in the area have dropped.

Analysis

In Exercise 5-1, discuss the audiences, exigencies, and constraints affecting the MedWeCare documents.

Analyzing the Rhetorical Situations of Accountants: The Montana Electric Service, Inc. Case Study[3]

The Principals

Montana Electric Service, Inc., a large electrical contracting company
Mr. Sutherland, president of Montana Electric Service
Ms. Kerin, Mr. Sutherland's attorney
Mr. Luke, former accountant to Montana Electric Service
Mr. Michaels, current accountant to Montana Electric Service, and administrative partner (junior partner) of Flotsam and Jetsam.
Flotsam and Jetsam, P.A., mid-size accounting firm
Mr. Flotsam, co-founder and senior partner of Flotsam and Jetsam
Mr. Jetsam, co-founder and senior partner of Flotsam and Jetsam

Record of Relevant Correspondence

Mr. Sutherland writes a letter to Mr. Luke, dismissing him as the MES accountant.

The Lawsuit

Mr. Sutherland, president of Montana Electric Service, Inc. (MES), retained Ms. Kerin's services in a lawsuit against his accountant, Mr. Luke. In the past two years, Mr. Sutherland had incurred $17,500 in state and federal penalties and interest due to Mr. Luke's failure to prepare corporate tax returns in a timely manner. Ms. Kerin felt that Mr. Sutherland had a good chance to recover penalties and interest.

Ms. Kerin writes a note to Mr. Michaels, telling him she has recommended Flotsam and Jetsam to Mr. Sutherland.

A Recommendation

Because his taxes were so much in arrears, Mr. Sutherland asked Ms. Kerin to recommend a quality accounting firm. Ms. Kerin recommended Flotsam and Jetsam, P.A. because she had previously worked with the administrative partner, Mr. Michaels, who managed the local Helena branch office.

Mr. Sutherland writes to Mr. Luke, advising him that Flotsam and Jetsam is his new accounting firm and requesting that his financial records be returned immediately.

The Meeting

Mr. Sutherland met with Mr. Michaels to discuss the tax problems he was having with the state of Montana and the Internal Revenue Service, as well as his need for future accounting services. Mr. Sutherland agreed to ask Mr. Luke to turn over the MES records immediately.

The Problem

Mr. Luke failed to respond to Mr. Sutherland's request to either turn over the MES records to Mr. Michaels or to return the records to Mr. Sutherland. After two weeks,

Mr. Sutherland writes Mr. Michaels, advising him that he was unable to obtain the MES records. He asks Mr. Michaels to try to get them.

Mr. Sutherland asked Mr. Michaels's help in securing the records. Although Mr. Michaels wanted to obtain the records (MES was, after all, potentially a substantial client, and he hoped for more referrals from Ms. Kerin), he was uneasy about the propriety of a newly hired accountant requesting records from a previous accountant.

At the next partners' meeting, Mr. Michaels outlined the problem. He favored Ms. Kerin's taking legal measures to obtain the records, but Mr. Flotsam wanted Mr. Michaels to write a strong letter demanding the MES records. And Mr. Jetsam believed that his friend, the chair of the ethics committee of the Montana Association of Certified Public Accountants (MACPA), should be consulted. No consensus was reached by the partners, and still the MES records were not forthcoming.

The IRS sends Mr. Sutherland a Notice of Deficiency.

Mr. Sutherland faxes a message to Mr. Michaels to get the records and to proceed with his tax and accounting work as soon as possible.

Meanwhile, penalties and interest were piling up at MES. Mr. Sutherland pressed Mr. Michaels to secure the records and to get on with his accounting work. Mr. Michaels recounted the touchy ethical issues involved, but Mr. Sutherland insisted that Mr. Michaels take measures to secure the records. He also wanted Mr. Michaels to report Mr. Luke to the professional ethics committee, which would strengthen his case against Mr. Luke if the ethics committee ruled against him.

Mr. Michaels faxes a message to Mr. Sutherland to request an appointment to see him to discuss the situation.

Mr. Michaels writes a memo to his partners (with copies to Mr. Sutherland and Ms. Kerin), declining to secure the MES records personally and outlining his recommendations.

Mr. Michaels ascertained that Mr. Luke was a member of MACPA and AICPA, but felt that he, as the newly hired accountant, could not initiate proceedings against Mr. Luke with either group. He wrote a memo to his partners (with copies to Mr. Sutherland and Ms. Kerin), stating his recommendations:

1. Immediate arrangements should be made with the state of Montana and the IRS to suspend penalties and possible liens until the MES records could be secured.
2. Mr. Jetsam should call his friend on the ethics committee to help in securing the records, but to not report Mr. Luke officially.
3. If Mr. Jetsam's efforts were unsuccessful, Ms. Kerin's services should be sought to secure the records.
4. Mr. Sutherland should report Mr. Luke to the MACPA, and following their action, to the AICPA.

The Outcome

The state of Montana and the *IRS* agreed to suspend penalties and liens, but not interest, until the MES records could be obtained. Mr. Jetsam called the chair of the ethics committee (unofficially), who then called Mr. Luke. Mr. Luke returned the MES records to Mr. Sutherland within 48 hours. Mr. Michaels rectified the MES tax problems and has gained a satisfied client. Mr. Sutherland's lawsuit against Mr. Luke is pending.

Analysis

Analyze the rhetorical situation surrounding Mr. Michaels's memo to his partners, to Mr. Sutherland, and to Ms. Kerin. Use Exercise 5-2 to analyze Mr. Michaels's situation. Use Exercise 5-3 to analyze Mr. Flotsam's and Mr. Jetsam's situation. Both exercises can also be used to analyze any of the correspondence indicated by the preceding marginalia in the case study.

Analyzing the Rhetorical Situations of Accountants: The QRS Corporation Case Study[4]

The Principals

Mr. Carter, president of QRS Corporation
QRS Corporation, lessor of building to TUV Corporation

TUV Corporation, lessee of building from QRS

Mr. Mandel, junior partner of the mid-size accounting firm retained for the past four years by QRS.

Mr. Juntunen, senior partner in a small accounting firm, and Mr. Carter's personal tax accountant

The Problem

In 1990 the QRS Board of Directors met to discuss an offer made by TUV Corporation, the primary tenant of their building, to purchase the remaining 15 years of their lease. Under the terms of the lease, ownership of the building and assumption of the mortgage would go to TUV (the landowner) at the end of the lease. Because the Board was composed of nonaccountants, the directors decided to ask Mr. Mandel, their CPA, if the offer of $26,000 made by TUV for purchase of the lease was fair and reasonable.

The Calculation

Mr. Mandel considered these factors in his calculations:

1. The terms of the lease
2. The projected cash flow provided by the lease
3. The projected interest rates over the balance on the lease term

After completing his multipage, complex calculations, Mr. Mandel sent the cover letter shown in Figure 5-4, along with his figures.

The Board's Response

Mr. Mandel's cover letter and computations were not understood by the Board of Directors (all of whom were nonaccountants). Consequently, the Board took no action on TUV's $26,000 offer, and TUV continued to make lease payments.

The Lunch

Early in 1991 Mr. Carter invited his personal tax accountant, Mr. Juntunen, to lunch to discuss some individual tax matters. During the lunch, Mr. Carter told Mr. Juntunen about his Board's inability to come to a decision regarding the $26,000 offer made by TUV. Showing Mr. Juntunen the first accountant's calculations and cover letter, he said the main stumbling block was the meaning of the calculations presented as "net present value of future cash flows." The figures seemed meaningless without an explanation of that concept. Mr. Carter also wondered why Mr. Mandel did not hand the problem over to someone in the firm who had more expertise in handling similar situations. Mr. Juntunen agreed to review Mr. Mandel's calculations and to assess the fairness of TUV's offer. He concurred materially with Mr. Mandel's calculations and sent the letter shown in Figure 5-5 to Mr. Carter and the Board of Directors, confirming the calculations, explaining the significance of "present value" to the situation, and recommending that TUV's offer be rejected.

The Decision

The Board met again in 1992 with Mr. Juntunen's explanation of Mr. Mandel's calculations in hand. Now that they understood the "present value" concept of the lease, they rejected TUV's offer. Two months later, TUV made a new offer of $400,000, which QRS accepted.

FIGURE 5-4 Mr. Mandel's Letter

Wynken, Blynken & Knod, P.C.
21 Venture Way
Santa Barbara, CA 93107
(805) 555-4521 (805) 555-3954

May 3, 1990

Mr. James Carter, President
QRS Corporation
1121 Enterprise Street
Santa Barbara, CA 93106

Dear Jim,

As you requested, I have reviewed the information regarding the possible sale of your leasehold interest.

In order to give you a better view of TUV Corporation's offer to buy the lease at $26,000 and to assist you in your negotiations, I have made a more comprehensive analysis of the present value of the future cash flows available to you from your lease. Additionally, I have provided numbers translating the present values into equivalent sales prices reflecting three different interest rates.

Please review the enclosed calculations carefully and let me know should you have any corrections or questions. Once you have completed your review, please give me a call so that I can further explain my views. If it appears that you will be going forward with this transaction to sell your lease, I would like to bring someone else from my firm in on the transaction who has more experience in this particular area.

I look forward to hearing from you soon.

Very truly yours,

I.W. Mandel

I. W. Mandel, CPA
IWM:pwp
Enclosure: Present Value Calculations

FIGURE 5-5 Mr. Juntunen's Letter

Keljo and Juntunen, P.C.
130 Liberty Street
Santa Barbara, CA 93105
(805) 555-9205

March 4, 1991

James Carter, President
QRS Corporation
1121 Enterprise Street
Santa Barbara, CA 93106

Dear Jim,

I have enclosed an adjusted present-value computation of QRS Corporation's lease agreement with TUV Corporation.

I first computed the estimated cash flow for each of the remaining 15 years of the lease agreement. I then computed the current present value of the cash flow expected for each remaining year under the lease.

To understand the significance of these computations, you should understand that "present value" refers to the value in today's dollars of a sum of money to be received in the future.

In the computation, you will see that the present value of the cash flow for the year 2006 ($175,000) at a 9% discount rate is $50,000. This means that if you invested $50,000 in a savings account at 9% now, with interest compounded annually for 15 years, the balance in the savings account at the end of 2006 would be $175,000.

These computations are used to approximate the present value of future amounts. In reality, the savings interest would be compounded quarterly, monthly, or even daily. This example serves to demonstrate the relationship of the discount rate to the expected interest rate for the time period. If interest rates were higher, a lesser amount of initial investment would be necessary to arrive at 2006's cash flow of $175,000.

Therefore, if the interest rates for the 15-year period were expected to be 10% rather than the 9% considered above, the amount of initial investment (present value) required to accumulate a principal and interest total of $175,000 (2006's cash flow) would be $42,000. Restated, the present value of $175,000 to be received at the end of 2006 is $42,000.

If you add the present value of the 15 years remaining on the lease at 9%, you will arrive at a total present value of approximately $400,000. Therefore, TUV's offer of $26,000 should be rejected, and a copy of the enclosed calculation should be forwarded to them to show why the offer is grossly understated.

Please call me if I can be of further assistance.

Sincerely yours,

Melvin R. Juntunen

Melvin R. Juntunen
MRJ/msh
Enclosure: Present Value Calculations

Another Decision

Mr. Carter and the Board also decided to replace Mr. Mandel with Mr. Juntunen as their accountant.

Analysis

To analyze both accountants' rhetorical situations, do Exercise 5-4 and Exercise 5-5.

AVOIDING SEXIST AND PREJUDICIAL LANGUAGE

GOAL

◆ Avoid sexist and prejudicial language

KEY TERMS

Sexist language Gender-specific language that assumes a male or female bias.

Prejudicial language Language that calls inappropriate attention to a person's race, religion, national origin, disability, age, or sexual orientation.

Sexist Language[5]

Although accountants can't always control conflictive circumstances in the workplace, they can forestall possible volatile situations (and legal consequences) by adjusting themselves to workplace realities. One of those realities in the 1990s is the avoidance of language that offends particular segments of the workplace. With women comprising approximately half the American work force and nearly half the accounting majors, language that presumes a male bias (**sexist language**) is no longer acceptable. In fact, sexist language is prohibited in many companies, federal and state government agencies, local municipalities, and academia. You can no longer address an unknown reader as "Dear Sir," because chances are that the reader is a woman. You risk offending some readers if you indicate only one sex when both are involved ("mankind has come a long way in the past century"). And you present a situation unrealistically when you imply that only one sex is included (e.g., all secretaries are female; all CEOs are male). To be fair to all people in the workplace and to reduce legal exposure, use neutral terms when possible and gender-specific terms only when necessary. Notice the options in Figure 5-6.

A reader's perception of gender bias can be triggered by both visuals and text. For example, the March 1991 issue of the *Practical Accountant* contains visual depictions (photos and drawings accompanying both ads and text) of four men and no women. The same issue of the *Journal of Accountancy* depicts twenty-seven men and seven women. The implied message is that the profession of accountancy is comprised of at least 80 percent men when such is not the case. Judging from the March 1987 *Journal of Accountancy*, which indicates *five years earlier* that 75 percent of all accountants are men and 25 percent are women, male bias has remained more or less constant.

The American Institute of Certified Public Accountants sends a male-bias message every time one of its members encloses its leaflet "Please Check Your Account" with bank confirmation requests. The message implied in the following phrases is that all CPAs are men:

> This leaflet accompanies a statement of your account with a business firm and a request that you check the correctness of the statement for use by a CPA in his capacity as independent auditor.
>
> This request is not a means of urging you to make payment. The CPA is not a bill collector or a credit man.

FIGURE 5-6
Sexist, Neutral, and Gender-specific Terms

Sexist	*Neutral*	*Gender-specific*
businessman	executive manager business owner businessperson	businessman businesswoman
chairman	chair chairperson moderator coordinator head	chairman chairwoman
foreman	supervisor manager	foreman forewoman
man hours	hours	
mankind	people	men women
Dear Sir	Dear Sir or Madam Dear Personnel Officer Dear Manager	Dear Sir Dear Madam
salesman	sales representative salesperson sales clerk	salesman saleswoman
manpower	workers work force personnel human resources	
gal Friday	secretary assistant	male secretary

The CPA's job is to get at the facts—and in this he needs your help. Sometimes you are asked to advise him of whether the balance shown is correct.[6]

If you want to address the realities of the workplace and avoid offending readers, how do you get around the constant use of "he or she" or "him or her"? Look at these pairs in which sexist language is avoided:

1. Convert singular indefinite pronouns to plural forms:

Sexist Each manager must complete his eight hours of CPE management coursework by next December 31.

Neutral All managers must complete their eight hours of CPE management coursework by next December 31.

2. Eliminate the pronouns "he, him, his" and "she, her, hers":

Sexist Every secretary must submit her vacation schedule request by May 1.

Neutral Every secretary must submit a vacation schedule request by May 1.

3. Use neutral language:

Sexist Many businessmen appreciate having access to a Tax Resolution Officer.

Neutral Many business owners appreciate having access to a Tax Resolution Officer.

Offensive I'll have my girl fax the seminar schedule to you as soon as it is published.

Neutral I'll have my secretary fax the seminar schedule to you as soon as it is published.

Sexist	How many man-hours do you think our newly hired accountants worked this past tax season?
Neutral	How many hours do you think our newly hired accountants worked this past tax season?

Prejudicial Language

Just as sexist language offends readers, so does prejudicial language—that is, language that calls inappropriate attention to a person's race, religion, national origin, disability, age, or sexual orientation. While no professional deliberately engages in racist, prejudicial language, sometimes complimenting a minority perpetuates stereotypes:

Prejudicial	Nancy, who is wheelchair-bound, deserves credit for her dependability and dedication to her work.
Nonprejudicial	Nancy deserves credit for her dependability and dedication to her work.
Prejudicial	For someone on the high side of sixty, Robert's work record is exemplary.
Nonprejudicial	Robert's work record is exemplary.
Prejudicial	Xavier, an African-American, certainly eclipses all his colleagues in the Management Advisory Services department.
Nonprejudicial	Xavier certainly eclipses all his colleagues in the Management Advisory Services department.

To test your sensitivity to sexist and prejudicial language, complete Exercise 5-6.

DEFINING ACCOUNTING TERMS IN THE WORKPLACE

Because accountants explain complex accounting concepts and financial data for nonaccountants and fellow accountants alike, they often use specialized terms. Obviously, the following accounting terms would mean different things to an accounting professor and a first-year accounting student, to a company controller and a personnel officer, to a senior partner in an accounting firm and a client:

balance sheet
reserve
proceeds
retained earnings
value
work-in-process inventory

Miscommunication results when a term used by a writer is not understood by the audience.

During your career in accounting, you will communicate with fellow professionals within accounting (professional audiences) as well as with nonaccountant users (lay audiences) who need your expertise to make important decisions. Contrasting some characteristics of lay and professional audiences helps writers formulate suitable approaches when describing unfamiliar terms and concepts for each audience:

Lay Audience	*Professional Audience*
	Who
Generally unfamiliar with accountancy.	Familiar with most terms and concepts of accountancy.
Motivation for Reading	
Interested in financial information because of self-interest.	Reads to keep current in field, especially in areas of specialization.

1. Includes the use for information.	1. Includes the use for information.
2. Uses less jargon.	2. Incorporates more jargon.
3. Exhibits own credibility.	3. Refers to authoritative sources.
4. Utilizes several definitional techniques.	4. Uses some definitional techniques.
5. Uses shorter paragraphs and less complex sentences.	5. Employs sentences that are more complex.
6. Incorporates a "you" attitude.	6. Appeals to professional community; incorporates a "we" attitude.
7. Employs more restatement.	
8. Includes parenthetical definition.	
9. Supplies transitional words and phrases.	

Incorporating Definitional Techniques

Accountants who communicate clearly with both lay and professional audiences avail themselves of tried-and-true definitional techniques that include the following:

1. *Formal* (Aristotelian) definition assigns something to a *genus*, or a class, and then differentiates between the thing and other members of the class.

- Accounting (genus) encompasses various types of accounting, such as asset accounting, cost accounting, estate accounting, and financial accounting.
- Current Assets (genus) include cash, notes receivable, accounts receivable, and prepaid expenses.

2. An *explication* defines key words in a formal definition.

   Financial accounting is "activity associated with the development and communication of financial information for external users, primarily in the form of general purpose financial statements."[7]

3. An *operational* definition demonstrates where the term or concept might be observed.

   Manufacturers employ the cost-accounting system, which is "the perpetual system of inventory accounting for the three manufacturing inventories: direct materials, work in process, and finished goods."[8]

4. An *analysis* separates a whole into its component parts.

   Five classifications of accounts (assets, liabilities, owner's equity, revenue, and expenses) comprise a general ledger (a chart of accounts).

5. An *example* uses one member of a class to convey an impression of the entire class.

- Labor and materials are examples of costs of sales.
- "Deposits that are not immediately available due to withdrawal or other restrictions are sometimes referred to as *time deposits*. These deposits are often separately classified as 'restricted cash' or 'temporary investments.' Examples of time deposits include certificates of deposit (CDs) and money market savings certificates. CDs, for example, generally may be withdrawn without penalty only at specified maturity dates."[9]

6. *Graphics* illustrates a term or concept.

- The formula for computing simple interest is

  Principal x Rate x Time = Interest

  $$\$1{,}000 \times \frac{8}{100} \times \frac{90}{360} = \$20.00$$

- "The flow of accounting data from the time a transaction occurs to its recording in the ledger is diagrammed as follows:"[10]

Business TRANSACTION occurs	→	Business DOCUMENT prepared	→	Entry recorded in JOURNAL	→	Entry posted to LEDGER

7. *Comparisons* and *contrasts* suggest ways in which concepts are similar to or different from each other.

- A customer account receivable and a customer note receivable both represent money owed to a company by customers for goods and/or services; both may bear interest. However, the customer note receivable requires a legal document (a note), and the note itself may be bought or sold to anyone in or outside the company. The customer account receivable is owed only to the company.
- Bobby Bonilla of the Pittsburgh Pirates was recently offered a four-year contract worth $15.5 million. Wayne Gretzky of the Los Angeles Kings has a contract through the 1999 season. In sports it is common for 50 percent of a team to have multiyear contracts. This can promote loyalty to the employer. The same type of incentive can be offered to employees in a business. Multiyear profit-sharing plans are obtained through a 401(k) pension plan.[11]

8. An *analogy* compares two unlike things that have certain aspects in common. The idea is to describe something unfamiliar in terms of the familiar.

- Even in a place as innocent as the Tiny Tot Ballet Company, nepotism can be a problem. Consider the situation in which Mom, the ballet teacher, favors her daughter by awarding her the lead spot in the dance recital. Since the problem here is evident, it would not be hard to imagine the difficulties caused by a similar type of behavior in the workplace.[12]
- Integrated circuits (computer chips) have "gates" similar to the mechanical devices in an antique pinball machine. Each chip contains anywhere from 20 to 1,000 of these gates.[13]

9. A *metaphor* implies a comparison.

LMN company's filing system is a rat's nest.

10. A *simile* compares two things by using *like* and *as*.

An FASB pronouncement is like a legislative act.

11. An *elimination* indicates what something is not so as to clarify what it is.

- Although goodwill can't be spent, it is still considered a valuable business asset.
- Two or more people who join in a business venture, but do not incorporate, form a partnership.

12. An *etymology* details the origin of a word.

- *Depreciate* comes from the medieval Latin *depreciare*, a manuscript error for the late Latin *depretiare* (*de-* = down from + *pretium* = price.[14]
- *Modem*—"For two computer terminals to communicate, you need three things: data terminal equipment, a communication path (phone line), and data communication equipment. But computers talk in electric signals which are digital in make-up, and telephone lines operate in analog signals. Modems convert the digital signals to analog so they can travel across the phone line and then switch them back to digital so the computer can process them. This manipulation of data is called *mo*dulation and *dem*odulation, hence *modem*."[15]

13. A *history* traces the origins or development of something.

"Double-Entry System. The evolution of the system of record keeping which came to be called 'double entry' was strongly influenced by Venetian merchants. The first known description of the system was published in Italy in 1494. . . . Double entry provides for recording both aspects of a transaction in such a manner as to establish an equilibrium. . . . 'Double entry' provides for the recording of all business transactions in a systematic manner. . . . When the resources of a number of people were pooled to finance a single venture, such as a voyage of a merchant ship, the double-entry system provided records and reports of the income of the venture and the equity of the various participants. As single ventures were replaced by more permanent business organizations, the double-entry system was easily adapted to meet their needs. In spite of the tremendous development of business operations since 1494, and the ever increasing complexities of business and governmental organizations, the basic elements of the double-entry system have continued virtually unchanged."[16]

14. Projecting something into the *future* allows implications to be discussed.

AICPA's 150-hour education requirement for CPAs by the year 2000 has sparked lively discussion among professors, students, and practitioners alike. The move will be debated further as state associations of CPAs consider its adoption.

Parenthetical definitions help the reader to follow information, as does restatement. Simplifying a term parenthetically is a succinct way of ensuring that all readers will comprehend an accountant's message regardless of their accounting background. In their article, "How Management Accountants Can Communicate Better," the authors illustrate simplified terminology:

Allowance for depreciation (accumulated write-off of the original cost of equipment and buildings)
Retained earnings (profits reinvested in the business)
Marketable equity securities (short-term investments in stocks)
Trade accountants payable (amounts payable to vendors)
Unearned revenues (advance payments by customers)[17]

The following are other examples from the writings of accountancy that illustrate how accounting terminology is adapted to users who may have varying degrees of expertise in the field:

- "Pricing services based on the time and materials methodology means that the client agrees to pay the hourly rate for the efforts expended plus out-of-pocket expenses. Using this method should include an estimate (a cost estimate in the engagement letter for itemized services), a cap on charges (a clause in the engagement letter that states that the cost of the project will not exceed a certain amount), and a cap on regular rate charges (when the project reaches a certain cost level, the hourly rates drop to a lower level). A drawback of this method is that clients have more control over a time and materials contract and might take on tasks for which they are not qualified to minimize time and material costs."[18]
- In selecting a corporate tax package, differentiate between "flash" and function. "Not everything that looks impressive is functional. For example, just because a method is suitable for spreadsheets and write-ups does not mean that it is suited for a tax program."[19]
- "Management accounting (sometimes referred to as managerial or cost accounting) is concerned primarily with financial reporting for internal users."[20]
- "Annuities are of two types: ordinary annuities (annuities in arrears) and annuities due (annuities in advance)."[21]

Establishing Context

Exercise 5-7 helps you review an explanation written *in context* for a lay audience. And Exercise 5-8 offers a checklist for reviewing a definition written in context for professionals. Defining the same term for two different audiences entails establishing a context for each audience. The trick is to choose *one* term to define two different ways: one way for a lay audience and another way for a professional audience. You must create the audience's "need to know":

1. Why would each audience need to read the definition?
2. Is it a new term to the reader?
3. Is the term frequently misunderstood?

The following table shows some approaches to working with terms in two different contexts—for a lay audience and for a professional audience:

Term	*Lay Audience*	*Professional Audience*
Barter	A bookkeeper for a funeral home offers to barter for services for certain bereaved clients.	The funeral home's accountant advises the bookkeeper on the tax implications of bartering.
Profit per share	A financial institution offers a free seminar for potential investors.	The financial institution's officers discuss what the seminar should cover.
Electronic filing	An accounting firm promotes electronic filing's quick refund feature to new clients.	The IRS promotes electronic filing to tax practitioners as a means of gaining new tax season clients by generating quick refunds.
Peer review	An accounting firm touts its recently passed peer review for promotional purposes.	An accounting firm advertises its expertise in helping other firms prepare for peer review.
Calendar year conformity	A tax practitioner writes a legislator to protest calendar year conformity as causing severe work bottleneck.	An accounting firm writes a letter to the *Practical Accountant* opposing calendar year conformity, and also asking others to write to their legislators.
Post-retirement benefits	A controller of a hardware chain explains postretirement benefits to newly retired personnel.	The controller explains the new liability (postretirement benefits) on its financial statements to a bank.

Locating Professional Sources for Accountancy

To establish credibility—to appeal to *ethos*—in your definition for a professional audience, you will have to consult professional resources, just as accountants do when they verify findings, cite relevant cases, research precedents, document sources, and investigate accounting and management problems. Exercise 5-9 will prompt you to locate and exploit numerous professional sources. Places where useful references for accountancy can be found include the following:

Libraries

- Accounting department libraries
- University and college libraries
- Interlibrary loan
- Accounting firm libraries
- Accounting organization libraries

Print Resources

- Bibliographies appended to professional articles and books
- Accounting resource sections of accounting books and journals
- Electronic bibliographical databases
- *Books in Print*
- *Readers' Guide to Periodical Literature*
- *Business Periodical Index*

USING WRITING CHECKLISTS

GOAL ◆ Adapt accounting review strategies to writing review.

KEY TERMS *Macro-editing* Rhetorical and organizational revising.
Micro-editing Sentence level revising.

Accountants develop and use specialized checklists extensively to ensure that a report meets professional requirements, that nothing is overlooked, and that the expectations of all users are met. Checklists must be adjusted periodically to satisfy constantly evolving standards of accountancy, and updated checklists appear regularly in accounting journals. For example, Michael G. Sherwood says in "Preparing Form 1120: A Checklist Approach" that by using a checklist, a staff can be trained to prepare Form 1120 efficiently, to "standardize tax workpapers and returns, reduce training and review time, and help eliminate common mistakes."[22] R. K. McCabe, in "A Quality Review Checklist," advocates reviewing a checklist *before* peer review to pinpoint potential problems.[23] And Source Finance offers a "checklist of questions to ask when checking references" in its "1990 Hiring Guide and Salary Survey."[24] Obviously, accountants have learned the value of using checklists to study criteria before an accounting task is undertaken, during an engagement, and when reviewing a completed report or return for completeness and accuracy.

So it should be with writing tasks. Since the accountant's writing situation is so complex, he or she cannot afford to miss professional criteria, to disappoint users, to send a mixed message, or to damage a professional image. Fortunately, some checklists geared to specific writing genres of accountancy are already available. For example, an AICPA Management Advisory Services Practice Aid features a fifty-six–item "Illustrative Checklist to Review Letters or Formal Reports," divided into *content* and *format* concerns.[25] Another MAS Practice Aid offers a "Sample Checklist for MAS Engagement Understandings."[26] If a writer or reviewer scrutinizes a report according to a specialized checklist designed to target the professional purpose, legal constraints, user expectations, and conventions of a writing genre, the "expectation gap" can be narrowed, and much miscommunication (not to mention legal complications) can be avoided.

Reviewing for Professional Concerns

Because accountants write within complex rhetorical and litigious situations, a generic writing checklist will not address the distinctive reviewing needs of accountancy. The reviewing process varies within accounting organizations. For example, the sole practitioner writes and reviews his or her own material from collection letters to multipage reports. Accountants in larger organizations may routinely submit their writing to peers or supervisors, especially writing that is destined for external use. Accountants in Big-Six firms will at least draft, write, and review their own internal memos. As Ken Davis, editor and publisher of *The Communications Edge* observes, "Most of us... even in large organizations—have to be our own 'writing department.' We have to take personal responsibility for the stream of writing that cross[es] our desks."[27] Obviously, it is impractical to run everything you write in the workplace by someone else. Therefore, accountant-writers must develop strategies for reviewing their own writing as well as for reviewing the writing of others. The following tips should help:

- Use authoritative models for specific accounting genres, such as the model cover letters to compilation and review reports found in *Guide to Compilation and Review Engagements*, published by Practitioners Publishing Company.[28]

- Raid the file cabinet to see how a particular writing genre has been handled in the past. As Lee Clark Johns relates, when faced with a new writing task, writers in the workplace regularly flock to the file cabinet to look "for writing models that have succeeded in the past, models they can efficiently copy, models that their supervisor will approve."[29] Of course, you must selectively choose writing samples because files are full of ineffective as well as effective writing.
- Run your writing through a spell-checker. It won't catch misspellings of proper names, or words correctly spelled but used incorrectly; however, it will locate embarrassing typographical errors and misspelled words.
- Run your text by a grammar checker, such as Grammatik 5. You can turn off the features you find annoying or unnecessary; in other words, you can tailor the checker to edit particular weaknesses such as split infinitives, subject-verb agreement, archaic diction, redundancies, and so on.
- Use or develop a review checklist to inspect your work or the work of others. Exercise 5-10 covers professional concerns, **macro-editing** concerns (content and format), and **micro-editing** concerns (paragraph and sentence style, and grammar and punctuation).
- Use or develop a specialized review checklist geared to the special requirements of certain genres of accountancy. The aforementioned "Illustrative Checklist to Review Letters or Formal Reports" exemplifies such useful resources.

The writing checklist in Exercise 5-10 will help you review your own work or the writing of others. You might also try formulating your own checklist geared to your personal writing habits, or a specialized checklist for a particular accounting genre.

Notes

1 Lloyd F. Bitzer, "The Rhetorical Situation," *Philosophy and Rhetoric* (Winter 1968): 6.

2 The MedWeCare Company case study is based on an actual situation, but the place, names, dates, and figures have been altered.

3 The Montana Electric Service, Inc. case study is based on an actual situation, but the place, names, dates, and figures have been altered.

4 The QRS Corporation case study is based on an actual situation, but the place, names, dates, and figures have been altered.

5 The material on sexist language is based partly on "Guidelines for Nonsexist Use of Language" in NCTE [National Council of Teachers of English] (Revised, 1985)" (Urbana, Ill.: NCTE, 1985).

6 "Please Check Your Account," American Institute of Certified Public Accountants (New York: AICPA, n.d.): 2–3.

7 Jay M. Smith, CPA, and K. Fred Skousen, CPA, *Intermediate Accounting*, 10th ed. (Cincinnati: South-Western, 1990), 1231.

8 Philip E. Fess, CPA, and Carl S. Warren, CPA. *Accounting Principles*, 16th ed. (Cincinnati: South-Western, 1990), "Glossary," 4.

9 Smith and Skousen, 246.

10 Fess and Warren, 70.

11 From a student paper in a business writing class, explaining a *401(k) plan* to a lay audience.

12 From a student paper in a technical writing class, explaining *nepotism* to a lay audience.

13 From a student paper in a technical writing class, explaining *very large scale integration* to a lay audience.

14 William Morris, ed. *The American Heritage Dictionary* (Boston: Houghton Mifflin Company, 1980), 355.

15 From a student paper in a technical writing class, explaining a *modem* to a lay audience.

16 Fess and Warren, 1–2.

17 Jean M. Dupree, CPA; Al H. Hartgraves, CPA; and William H. Thralls, CPA, "How Management Accountants Can Communicate Better," *Management Accounting* (February 1987): 41.

18 Robert S. Brieff, ed. *The Practical Accountant Digest 1989* (New York: Warren, Gorham & Lamont, 1989), 310.

19 Brieff, 362.

20 Smith and Skousen, 5.

21 Smith and Skousen, 223.

22 Michael G. Sherwood, CPA, "Preparing Form 1120: A Checklist Approach," *The Practical Accountant* (January 1989): 70–76.

23 R. K. McCabe, CPA, "A Quality Review Checklist," *Journal of Accountancy* (September 1990): 69–74.

[24] Source Finance advertisement, *Journal of Accountancy* (September 1990): 141.

[25] American Institute of Certified Public Accountants, "Illustrative Checklist to Review Letters or Formal Reports," in *Written Communication of Results in MAS Engagements*, Management Advisory Services Practice Aid No. 3 (New York: AICPA, 1987), 4–6.

[26] American Institute of Certified Public Accountants, "Sample Checklist for MAS Engagement Understandings," in *Communicating With Clients About MAS Engagement Understandings*, Management Advisory Services Practice Aid No. 5 (New York: AICPA, 1987), 7–9.

[27] Ken Davis, "Manage Your Writing Time," *The Communication Edge* (January/February 1991): 1.

[28] Dennis R. Meals, John R. Clay, and Dan M. Guy. *Guide to Compilation and Review Engagements*, Vol. I (Fort Worth: Practitioners, 1990), 6/51–6/111.

[29] Lee Clark Johns, "The File Cabinet Has a Sex Life: Insights of a Professional Writing Consultant," in *Worlds of Writing: Teaching and Learning in Discourse Communities of Work*, ed. Carolyn B. Matalene (New York: Random House, 1989), 153–187.

NAME

EXERCISE 5-1: ANALYZING THE MEDWECARE RHETORICAL SITUATION

Answer the following questions after reading the case study on page 119–121.

1. What was the exigence behind Mr. Schmidt's proposal to buy land and erect a building in the industrial park? ______

2. Under what constraints did he write the proposal? ______

3. Who was the audience for the proposal? ______
4. Would Mr. Schmidt expect the audience to be hostile or receptive to his idea? ______
5. What motivated Mr. Acosta to request a feasibility study from the controller? ______

6. Why did Mr. Acosta request the study instead of Mr. Schmidt? ______

7. Under what constraints did Mr. Acosta request the feasibility study? ______

8. What was the exigence for Ms. Theriault's recommendation report? ______

9. Who was the primary reader and the overhearer for the controller's report? ______

10. Under what constraints within the company did Ms. Theriault write the report? ______

11. What professional constraints affected her writing of the report? ______

12. Why did she seek the counsel of a colleague from her former accounting firm? ______

13. Would you describe her situation in writing the report as "lose-lose" or "win-win"? Justify your answer. ______

EXERCISE 5-1: ANALYZING THE MEDWECARE RHETORICAL SITUATION (CONTINUED)

14. How else could Ms. Theriault have handled the recommendation report? ______________________________

____

____

____

15. Did the bank's approval of MedWeCare's building loan affirm or contradict Ms. Theriault's conclusions? Explain.

____

____

16. If Ms. Theriault had accepted another controllership, what organizational situation do you think she would have tried to avoid? ____

____

NAME

EXERCISE 5-2: WRITER'S ANALYSIS

The following questions should be considered for any rhetorical situation:

1. What genre did the writer employ? ____________________
2. What special constraints had to be considered because of the genre? ____________________
3. Who is the writer? ____________________
4. What is the writer's overt purpose in writing? ____________________
5. Are there any covert purposes? ____________________
6. What is the writer's role? ____________________
7. By writing, what does the writer stand to gain? ____________________

   Or lose? ____________________
8. What is the writer's relation to the reader(s)? ____________________
9. How can the writer enhance his or her professional image within the communication? ____________________
10. By writing, how does the writer increase legal exposure? ____________________
11. How can the writer reduce legal exposure? ____________________

NAME

EXERCISE 5-3: READER'S ANALYSIS

The following questions should be considered for any rhetorical situation:

1. Who is the recipient of the communication? ______________________

2. Who else is likely to read the communication (one or more overhearers)? ______________________

3. What is the recipient's or overhearer's knowledge of accountancy? ______________________

4. What is the recipient's or overhearer's relation to the writer? ______________________

5. What is the recipient's or overhearer's attitude toward the subject matter? ______________________

6. Why would the recipient read the communication? ______________________

7. Why would each overhearer read the communication? ______________________

8. What should the recipient know after reading? ______________________

9. What should the recipient be able to do after reading? ______________________

10. What should the overhearer be able to do after reading? ______________________

NAME

EXERCISE 5-4: ANALYZING MR. MANDEL'S RHETORICAL SITUATION

Answer the following questions after reading the QRS case study on pages 122–126:

1. What information did the QRS Board want from Mr. Mandel? ______
2. What was Mr. Mandel's purpose in writing QRS? ______
3. What was the level of the Board's accounting knowledge compared with Mr. Mandel's? ______
4. Were Mr. Mandel's calculations correct? ______
5. If so, why was the QRS Board unable to make a decision to accept or reject TUV's first offer? ______
6. What would have happened if QRS had accepted TUV's first offer? ______
7. Why did Mr. Carter discuss the QRS situation with another CPA? ______
8. As the audience, what did QRS stand to lose or gain? ______
9. As the writer, what did Mr. Mandel stand to lose or gain? ______
10. Why was Mr. Mandel's communication ineffective? ______
11. What did Mr. Mandel lose? ______
12. Did Mr. Mandel fulfill his professional role? ______

NAME

EXERCISE 5-5: ANALYZING MR. JUNTUNEN'S RHETORICAL SITUATION

1. Why did Mr. Carter bring up the QRS situation with Mr. Juntunen during a personal tax discussion? ____________

2. What information did Mr. Carter want from Mr. Juntunen? ____________

3. Was Mr. Juntunen guilty of "soliciting" business? Why or why not? ____________

4. What was Mr. Juntunen's purpose in writing QRS? ____________

5. What was the level of the Board's accounting knowledge compared with Mr. Juntunen's? ____________

6. Were Mr. Juntunen's calculations correct? ____________

7. Why was the QRS Board able to make a decision to accept or reject TUV's first offer after reading Mr. Juntunen's letter? ____________

8. In what ways did QRS benefit from Mr. Juntunen's letter? ____________

9. As the audience, what did QRS stand to lose or gain? ____________

10. As the writer, what did Mr. Juntunen stand to lose or gain? ____________

11. Why was Mr. Juntunen's communication effective? ____________

12. What did Mr. Juntunen gain? ____________

13. How did Mr. Juntunen fulfill his professional role? ____________

NAME

EXERCISE 5-6: REVISING SEXIST AND PREJUDICIAL LANGUAGE

Revise the following sentences to eliminate sexist and prejudicial language:

1. Did each seminar participant turn in his evaluation form? ______

2. We should select the best man for the job from the qualified candidates. ______

3. If we land the county contract, we'll need to increase our manpower. ______

4. John, who is deaf, is doing a fine job as our new seminar coordinator. ______

5. Send a man over immediately to repair the copier. ______

6. Margaret will be chairman of the coordinating committee next year. ______

7. Our accounts receivable clerk seems to have exceeded our expectations. What a credit to his race! ______

8. When you survey the business executives, ask each man to rate electronic spreadsheets. ______

9. We are very proud of José, who is Hispanic, for his high score on the CPA exam. ______

10. If I'm not in, just have your girl leave a message on my recorder. ______

11. Anybody in business should strengthen his interviewing skills. ______

12. Yes, our gals from the typing pool really pulled together last tax season. ______

NAME

EXERCISE 5-7: EVALUATING A DEFINITION FOR A LAY AUDIENCE

Carefully review a paper explaining an accounting term to a lay audience. Answer the following questions:

Writer's name: ______________________________

Reviewer's name: ______________________________

1. What term is defined? ______________________________
2. Who is the audience? Why is he or she a lay audience for the accountant? ______________________________
3. What is the context for explaining the term? Why does the reader need to understand the term? ______________________________
4. What definitional techniques does the writer use? What others would aid audience comprehension? ______________________________
5. Does the writer engage the reader's attention in the first paragraph? How does the writer appeal to the reader's self-interest?
6. Does the term appear in an emphatic position within sentences (i.e., early in a sentence)? (Circle the term in the manuscript.) ______________________________
7. How has the information been geared to the understanding of the reader? ______________________________
8. Does the writer use accounting jargon that the reader might not understand? How could the writer clarify the terms?

EXERCISE 5-7: EVALUATING A DEFINITION FOR A LAY AUDIENCE (CONTINUED)

9. Are there any areas in the paper that could confuse the reader? How could the writer revise for clarity? ____________

10. Does the writer satisfy reader expectation implied by the context? If not, what is lacking? ____________

11. What should the reader know or be able to do after understanding the term? ____________

NAME

EXERCISE 5-8: EVALUATING A DEFINITION FOR A PROFESSIONAL AUDIENCE

Carefully review a paper explaining an accounting term or concept for a professional in the accounting field. Answer the following questions:

Writer's name: ____

Reviewer's name: ____

1. What term or concept is explained? ________________________________
2. Who is the audience? What is his or her relation to the writer? ________________________

   ____
3. What is the context for explaining the term? Why does the reader need to understand the term? Since the reader is a professional, why would he or she not already know the term? ________________________

   ____

   ____

   ____
4. How does the writer establish the reader's "need to know" the term? ________________________

   ____

   ____
5. How does the writer appeal to the reader's self-interest? ________________________

   ____

   ____
6. What definitional techniques does the writer use? ________________________

   ____

   ____

   ____
7. How does the writer establish credibility? ________________________

   ____

   ____
8. What sources have been documented? Are the sources credible? ________________________

   ____

NAME

EXERCISE 5-9: A PROFESSIONAL RESOURCES CHECKLIST

Your answers to the following questions can serve as a valuable checklist of resources.

1. Where are academic libraries for accountancy located? ______

2. Where are professional (practitioners') libraries for accountancy located? ______

3. What professional resources might be found in public libraries? ______

4. What electronic databases that specialize in business and accounting are available? ______

5. What print indexes to business and accounting resources are available? ______

6. What are the bibliographies for accounting resources? ______

7. What are the "guides to research" or "references guides" in accountancy? ______

8. What are the specialized encyclopedias for accountancy? ______

9. What are the specialized dictionaries for accountancy? ______

10. What are the specialized handbooks for accountancy? ______

11. What are the standard or recommended textbooks for accountancy? ______

EXERCISE 5-9: A PROFESSIONAL RESOURCES CHECKLIST (CONTINUED)

12. What are the directories to accounting organizations? ______________________________

13. Where are bibliographies to accounting books and articles located? ______________________________

14. How can I access national accounting associations? ______________________________

15. How can I access state and local accounting associations? ______________________________

16. What is the student accounting organization on campus? ______________________________

17. What are the theoretical academic journals for accountancy? ______________________________

18. What are the pedagogical academic journals for accountancy? ______________________________

19. What are the historical academic journals for accountancy? ______________________________

20. What are the major accounting journals for practitioners? ______________________________

21. What are the periodicals issued by accounting associations? ______________________________

22. What accounting-related publications are used by lay readers? ______________________________

EXERCISE 5-9: A PROFESSIONAL RESOURCES CHECKLIST (CONTINUED)

23. What is the focus of recent accounting dissertations? ______________________________

____

____

24. Do I know any academic experts in accounting (professors, graduate students)? ______________________________

____

25. Do I know any practicing professionals (in public practice, government agencies, accounting organizations, private industry)? ______________________________

____

____

____

26. Do I know any knowledgeable people who deal with accountants (bankers, bonders, salespersons)? ______________________________

____

____

27. How can I get access to accounting "junk mail" (announcements, sales catalogs, product descriptions, seminar descriptions)?

____

____

NAME

EXERCISE 5-10: AN ACCOUNTANT'S WRITING CHECKLIST

Professional Concerns

Check that the document	Yes	Needs work
1. Follows conventional formatting for the genre	______	__________
2. Adheres to professional criteria for the genre	______	__________
3. Has been reviewed according to genre checklists	______	__________
4. Follows firm/agency/company formatting conventions	______	__________
5. Fulfills engagement understandings	______	__________
6. Satisfies the client's expectations	______	__________
7. Meets the recipient's requirements	______	__________
8. Informs overhearers judiciously	______	__________
9. Enhances the writer's professional image (*ethos*)	______	__________
10. Avoids sexist and prejudicial language	______	__________
11. Serves the writer's overt purpose(s)	______	__________
12. Furthers the writer's covert purpose(s)	______	__________
13. States methodology employed	______	__________
14. Reduces the writer's legal exposure	______	__________
15. Is sent only to appropriate parties	______	__________
16. Clearly declares findings, conclusions, recommendations, and opinions (if appropriate)	______	__________
17. Explicitly disclaims or qualifies findings, conclusions, recommendations, and opinions (if appropriate)	______	__________
18. Documents sources accurately	______	__________
19. Fulfills copyright law by securing permission to use copyrighted material (if needed)	______	__________

Macro-editing Concerns

(Chapter 7 treats macro-composition elements: organization, outlining, coherence, and paragraphing.)

Content

Check that the document	Yes	Needs work
1. Bears an informative title (if used)	______	__________
2. States and fulfills its purpose	______	__________
3. Limits the scope of the discussion	______	__________
4. Presents all sides of an issue fairly	______	__________
5. Anticipates and answers user's questions and objections	______	__________
6. Gets to the point	______	__________
7. Projects objectivity and sincerity	______	__________
8. Conveys a professional tone appropriate to the message	______	__________
9. Explains technical terms	______	__________
10. Summarizes key points in an "executive summary"	______	__________

Format

Check that	Yes	Needs work
1. Margins are balanced	______	__________
2. Vertical and horizontal spacing is consistent	______	__________
3. The document is correctly paginated	______	__________
4. All sections of the document are assembled logically	______	__________
5. Extraneous matter is placed in an appendix	______	__________
6. The user can easily locate elements within the text	______	__________
7. Graphics are conveniently placed and informatively labeled	______	__________
8. The firm's image is enhanced through attractive covers and binding, quality paper, and crisp typeface	______	__________
9. Headings and subheadings are informative and follow a consistent system	______	__________
10. Bullets, underline, italics, or boldface are used sparingly for emphasis	______	__________

Micro-editing Concerns

(Chapter 7 treats micro-composition elements: transitions, readability, conciseness, sentence combining, concreteness, nominalizations, syntax, diction, grammar, spelling, and punctuation.)

Style (Paragraphs)

Check that	Yes	Needs work
1. Transitions between paragraphs aid audience understanding	______	__________
2. Dense text is broken up into short paragraphs or lists	______	__________
3. Paragraphs include more than one sentence	______	__________
4. Paragraphs signal new topics	______	__________
5. Paragraphs follow a logical sequence	______	__________
6. Subject matter is presented positively when possible	______	__________

Style (Sentences)

Check that the sentences	Yes	Needs work
1. Exclude unnecessary repetitions	______	__________
2. Present given information before new	______	__________
3. Employ the active voice where possible	______	__________
4. Are not too long	______	__________
5. Do not contain prepositional and noun strings	______	__________
6. Do not contain nominalizations	______	__________
7. Do not begin with "There are," "There is," or "It is" constructions	______	__________
8. Use active verbs rather than "be" verbs	______	__________
9. Use subject-verb-object patterns when possible	______	__________
10. Contain shorter words rather than longer, pompous-sounding words	______	__________

Grammar and Punctuation

Check that	Yes	Needs work
1. Headings and subheadings are parallel	______	__________
2. The text is spell-checked	______	__________
3. Proper names are double-checked for spelling	______	__________
4. The text has been run through a grammar checker	______	__________
5. The text is free of serious grammatical errors in syntax, diction, pronoun referents, agreement, and verb tenses	______	__________
6. Punctuation is correct	______	__________
7. The copy is proofed again when changes are inserted	______	__________
8. The company stylebook (if one exists) is followed	______	__________

CHAPTER 6
When Accountants Write

OVERVIEW When accountants perform functions vital to business and government, their findings, opinions, and other communications take the form of conventional formats familiar to their readers. The audience, purpose, and nature of the accountant's message determine the prescribed mode of communication (genre). These modes are not limited to accounting-related engagement letters, management letters, and notes to financial statements. As businesspersons, accountants utilize all types of business communication ranging from letters of inquiry to letters of complaint, from proposals to completion reports, from promotional brochures to bills, from in-house newsletters to press releases. This chapter focuses on conventions of business communication in general and writing genres of accountancy in particular. It teaches the accountant-writer to:

- Identify and analyze the writing genres of business and accounting;
- Determine the appropriate writing genres to suit the audience, the purpose, and the occasion;
- Manipulate formats and graphics to meet user expectation and to assist user understanding;
- Observe the principles of document design;
- Use consistent and tasteful formats to enhance a professional image.

GOALS

- ◆ Design and write rhetorically sound workplace documents.
- ◆ Create user-centered documents.
- ◆ Critique an accounting brochure.

KEY TERMS

Boilerplate Form letters and workplace documents, sometimes personalized.

Desktop publishing Near–typeset quality printing produced with microcomputer software and laser printers.

Exigence What spawns written or spoken discourse.

Font size Typeface size.
Format The consistent arrangement of textual and visual elements in a workplace document.
Genre Prescribed mode of communication (i.e., engagement letter, interoffice memo, promotional brochure).
Gloss Condensed explanatory text placed to the side of the larger text.
Metadiscourse Text that helps readers understand content.
Overhearer Unintended reader or user of a text.
Serifs Short finishing lines added to the main strokes that form letters. (*Sans serif*: lacking serifs.)
Typeface The style of letters, numbers, and symbols.
User Intended reader of a text.

Identifying the Writing Genres of Accountancy

Like other businesspersons, accountants employ numerous conventional genres of business, including:[1]

Acceptance letters
Acknowledgment letters
Adjustment letters
Annual reports
Application letters
Booklets
Brochures
Collection letters
Boilerplate letters
Feasibility studies
Inquiry letters
Instructions
Job descriptions
Memorandums
Minutes
Newsletters
Policy manuals
Press releases
Procedure manuals
Progress reports
Proposals
Questionnaires
Recommendation reports
Reference letters
Resignation letters
Resumes
Sales letters
Transmittal letters

Each of the aforementioned writing genres has its own conventions that satisfy writer purpose and reader expectations. For example, contrast the purpose and formatting conventions of two distinct workplace documents—the resume and the collection letter:

Resume		*Collection Letter*
Purpose:	To secure a job interview	To secure payment
Format:	1–2 pages, resume format	1 page, standard letter format
Writer:	Job applicant	Company/attorney/collection agency
Reader:	Employer/personnel officer	Debtor
Conventions:	Understood "I"	Personal pronouns
Tone:	Factual	Polite to insistent

These and other workplace documents are so distinctive in appearance that the reader can immediately differentiate between them by merely glancing at the documents.

Even though accountants employ the conventional writing genres used in business, they also use specialized writing genres that have evolved over the years, that are geared to professional requirements, and that satisfy the purpose of the writer as well as the needs of users. Documents often cluster around a workplace occasion (exigence), as the following chart illustrates:

Job-Opening Documents	*Audit Documents*
Job description	Engagement letter
Position-opening letter	Modified engagement letter
Job advertisement	Confirmation letters
Resume	Progress billing
Letter of application	Audit report cover letter
Follow-up/thank you letter	Representation letter
Rejection letter	Management letter
Acceptance letter	Client billing
Decline-offer letter	

The varied writing genres of accountancy include:

Advertisements
Appraisal reports
Audit reports
Billing statements
Brochures (accounting firms)
Business plans
Client surveys
Comfort letters
Compilation reports
Computer manuals
Disengagement letters
Employee references
Engagement letters
Forecasts
Histories (accounting firms)
Keep-well letters
Loan proposals
Management letters
Marketing plans
Newsletters (of accounting firms)
Notes to financial statements
Notices of Deficiency (IRS)
Performance reviews
Quality review reports
Representation letters
Review reports

Wherever possible, the writings of accountancy are standardized; in fact, AICPA offers the following computerized organizational documents and client and personnel correspondence that accountants can modify to suit their purpose:[2]

Billing adjustment letters
Buy-sell agreements
Client termination letters
Confirmations
Fee explanation and agreements
Independence memorandums
Letters announcing position opening
Merger agreements
Notices of new partners
Notices of partner separation
Requests to transfer client records

Accountants use these and other writing genres to report financial information and to convey information unique to the situations of accountancy. The following are examples of prescribed report modes that meet professional criteria, the writer's purposes, and the user's needs:

OTHER COMPREHENSIVE BASIS OF ACCOUNTING REPORT (OCBOA) A report that complies with the reporting provisions of a governmental agency; a report prepared with an entity's income tax accounting method, a cash receipts and disbursements statement, or a statement based on a definite set of criteria having substantial support.

COMPILATION REPORT A financial statement prepared according to GAAP, but the accountant is not necessarily independent and expresses no assurance as to its reliability.

REVIEW REPORT A financial statement prepared according to GAAP in which an independent accountant expresses limited assurance after performing certain analytical procedures.

AUDIT REPORT A financial statement prepared according to GAAP, in which the accountant has audited (verified) the information and thus expresses full assurance that it is fairly presented in accordance with GAAP. The user expects to find particular information in certain locations within the audit format. For example, the user finds the headings "Assets" and "Liabilities and Stockholders' Equity" in a prescribed order in the balance sheet, as shown in the following headings:

FRY TEXTILE MANUFACTURING, INC.
BALANCE SHEET
MARCH 31, 1993

ASSETS	LIABILITIES AND STOCKHOLDERS' EQUITY
Current Assets	Current Liabilities
Cash	Accounts Payable
Accounts Receivable	Accrued Expenses
Inventory	Notes Payable—Current
Total Current Assets	Total Current Liabilities
Fixed Assets	Notes Payable
Land	
Buildings	Total Liabilities
Equipment	Stockholders' Equity
Accumulated Depreciation	Capital Stock
Total Fixed Assets	Retained Earnings
	Total Stockholders' Equity
TOTAL ASSETS	TOTAL LIABILITIES AND STOCKHOLDERS' EQUITY

Just as accountants are careful to adhere to guidelines for professional criteria and for proper formatting, so accountants follow standard wording and formatting for writing genres of accountancy wherever possible. To ensure that professional criteria are followed for specialized accounting tasks, guides for the writings of accountancy should be consulted. Here are a few examples:

- Authoritative guidelines: *Comprehensive Engagement Manual* (AICPA)[3] and *Bank Audit Manual* (AICPA).[4]
- Volumes of illustrative letters: *Guide to Compilation and Review Engagements* (Practitioners Publishing Company);[5] *Guide to Construction Contractors* (Practitioners Publishing Company);[6] and *Accountant's Complete Model Letter Book* (Prentice Hall).[7]
- Articles on specific writing genres: "Writing Effective Management Letters," *CPA Journal*;[8] "Keep-Well Letters: The Elusive Contingency," *CPA Journal*;[9] and "Computer Consulting Engagement Letters You Can Use," *The Practical Accountant*.[10]

Incorporating the Rhetorical Appeals in the Writing Genres of Accountancy

An advertisement for a guide to preparing loan proposals, "How to Package More Effective Loan Proposals," exemplifies the accountants' concern that professional criteria accommodate writer purpose and user needs.[11] The guide helps accountants to prepare a rhetorically sound proposal by

- Determining what information is required by the lender (logical appeal)
- Obtaining specific data from the client with minimum resistance (pathetic appeal)
- Presenting the proposal in the best light (ethical appeal)
- Overcoming obstacles that might delay approval (pathetic appeal)

The criteria for effective loan proposals fall under the three rhetorical appeals:

Logos (Satisfying professional criteria)	*Ethos* (Professional presentation)	*Pathos* (Meeting client and banker needs)
• Complete information • Accurate information	• Correct format • Presentation	• Required client data • Favorable exhibits

Analyzing a Writing Genre of Accountancy

To understand how professional criteria (which implies legal considerations), writer's purpose, user's needs, and the rhetorical appeals (*logos*, *ethos*, and *pathos*) figure into the writing genres of accountancy, look at the following management letter[12] and analysis:

Ethos—Supported by correct spelling, punctuation, grammar, and a professional presentation.

Hauch, Hoke, and Hake, Chartered
20 Center Street
St. Louis, MO 63130

Jeanne Rosenmayer, President
Surge Publishing Company, Inc.
P. O. Box 3119
St. Louis, MO 63129

Writing Genre

Management Letter

Logos—Facts about the scope and period of the audit. Purpose—The writer states the purpose of the report.

As a part of our special audit for Surge Publishing Company, Inc. for the period ended March 31, 1993, we made a limited study and evaluation of internal accounting controls to determine the nature, timing, and extent of the auditing procedures.

Pathos—Meets user needs.

Our study and evaluation disclosed no condition that indicates a material weakness. This report is to be used by Surge Publishing Company, Inc. only and is not to be used by third parties.

Budget Implemented

Logos—Proposed and actual budgets are compared.

Surge Publishing Company's 1992 expenditures were very close to budgeted amounts. Overall expenses were only 6 percent over the budgeted amounts, due mostly to benefit increases.

Insurance Coverage Increased

Pathos—Positive observations are presented before the negative one.

The increased insurance coverage that we recommended now provides adequate coverage.

Improvement Needed

Surge Publishing Company, Inc. should add password protection to the computer system to assure the security of company records.

Pathos—An effort is made to maintain goodwill and to continue audit business.

We appreciate the opportunity to serve Surge Publishing Company, Inc. The staff has been very cooperative and provided the information we requested in a timely manner. We look forward to a continuing professional relationship.

Respectfully submitted,

Hauch, Hoke, and Hake, Chartered
July 21, 1993

Rhetorically aware accountants take advantage of any opportunity to incorporate the rhetorical appeals into whatever documents they write, as Mark L. Frigo and Peter F. Stone point out in "Writing Effective Management Letters."[13] For this genre (which comments to management about company procedures observed during an audit, and which also seeks to generate additional accounting services), they caution the writer not to "sour the client/auditor relationship" by incorporating "politically insensitive advisory comments." They suggest "how ordinary tact can assure a more sympathetic management review," and advise the writer to "anticipate possible objections" and "defensive reactions" to his or her recommendations. They offer this example:

Tactless	*Tactful*
Our report was qualified because the financial statements departed from generally accepted accounting principles. Computations for estimates are erroneous. Loss experience does not justify the large amounts accrued or provided. These are accrued warranty expenses and the allowance for bad debts. Excessive accruals or allowances could be used by management to generate misleading statements.	Our report was qualified because the financial statements departed from generally accepted accounting principles. Amounts for accrued warranty expenses and and the allowance for bad debts are too large. The following schedule summarizes loss experience and suggests provisions to anticipate such losses. By reducing the accrual and allowances to the recommended amounts, the Company would provide only for those losses that can be estimated. In addition, the Company would avoid a qualified opinion in the future.[14]

Each genre of the writings of accountancy has its own professional mandates and constraints. For example, the wording of the audit report cover letter is mandated by GAAP; the wise accountant follows standard wording. But other writings of accountancy require rhetorical analysis and audience accommodation on the individual accountant-writer's part. To test your sensitivity to professional criteria, to writer's purpose, to user's needs, and to the rhetorical appeals that the accountant must consider in drafting a workplace document, analyze the engagement letter for a quality review in Exercise 6-1.

Using Metadiscourse to Guide Users

Joseph M. Williams in *Style: Ten Lessons in Clarity and Grace* says that "whenever we write more than a few words, we usually have to write on two levels. We write about the subject we are addressing. . . but we also directly or indirectly tell our audience how they should take our ideas." Williams is referring to *metadiscourse*, which distinguishes "writing that guides the reader from writing that informs the reader."[15] Metadiscourse guides users of documents to the intended meaning, as this passage from an AICPA publication illustrates:[16]

Text:	*Metadiscourse:*
In our opinion, because of the effects of the matters discussed in the preceding paragraph, the financial statements referred to above do not present fairly, in conformity with generally accepted accounting principles, the financial position of RMW Company as of December 31, 1993, or the results of its operations and changes in its financial position for the year then ended.	Opinion expressed is adverse—the departures from generally accepted accounting principles are so material that the financial statements as a whole are misleading.

Users of workplace documents appreciate informative titles, forecasting paragraphs, headings and subheadings, lists, and explanatory glosses, which break up dense text and guide them to the meaning intended by the writer.

Inventing Informative Titles

A creatively written report title can intrigue, inform, and persuade prospective report users. Notice the differences among these titles:

Generic	Marketing Plan
Informative	A Five-Year Marketing Plan for Fox and Wolfe, P.A.
More informative	A Marketing Plan for Fox and Wolfe, P.A.: 1993–1998
Generic	Feasibility Study
Informative	Feasibility Study to Buy a Copier
More informative	Feasibility Study to Purchase a Full-Color Copier for the Marketing Department of Accounting Associates
Generic	Recommendation Report
Informative	Recommendation Report for Podiatry Professionals, P.A.
More informative	"CompuMedic": A Recommendation Report to Computerize Podiatry Professionals, P.A.

The writer who acquaints users with report content through a brief yet informative title gains ground in persuading them that the report contains ideas worth reading.

When creating informative titles, consider what the audience already knows. For example, a company name might not be needed for a report generated for in-house use, but would be an important factor for a widely disbursed report.

Forecasting Organization

In the article "Measuring the Effect of Training and Education," the author sets up and satisfies reader expectation by forecasting his organization (in the order of topics discussed), and then by reminding the reader of the organization and topics through the use of informative headings:

Forecasting

You can measure the outcome of training programs from at least four points of view:
- Reaction of participants,
- Knowledge gained,
- Application of new knowledge and skills on the job,
- Impact on the business.

Headings

Measuring Reaction.
Measuring Knowledge Gained.
Measuring Application.
Impact on the Business.[17]

This forecasting paragraph, followed by informative headings in "What is a Business Plan?," again illustrates how reader expectation is raised and satisfied:

Forecasting

The planner must carry out a number of very specific tasks to make sure that the end document answers [the questions raised above]. They involve various steps which can be remembered by the mnemonic: How Gainfully A Quiet Reflection Can Succeed.
- History
- Goals
- Assumptions
- Quantification
- Resource Allocation
- Checking
- Sensitivity Analysis

Headings

History—Where is the business now?
Goals—Where does the business want to be?
Assumptions—Are they correct?
Quantification—How can objectives be expressed in financial terms?

Resource Allocation—How do we achieve objectives?
Checking—Is the plan realistic?
Sensitivity Analysis—Is the plan flexible?[18]

Making Headings and Subheadings Informative

Reading long sentences and dense paragraphs tires many readers. In fact, users of the writings of accountancy tend to skip over long, densely written passages—perhaps including text they *need* to read. One way to break up thick text is to use headings and subheadings. You can guide your readers into meaning if you make the headings informative. The headings need not be elaborate as the following one-word headings from a short piece in *Management Accounting* illustrate.[19] The author structures his article according to guidelines geared to three age groups:

Title Teach Your Children the Value of Money

Headings
- Preschool
- Grade School
- High School

A "Platinum" software advertisement in *Journal of Accountancy* is structured persuasively with a play on its title:[20]

Title MULTIACCOUNTING

Headings
- MultiTasking
- MultiUser, MultiServer
- MultiSolution
- MultiService

Notice that the headings lead the prospective user to think that "Platinum" addresses and solves multiple tasks and serves multiple users simultaneously—and all in one-word headings.

A systems advertiser, EDS (Electronic Data Systems), poses a series of rhetorical questions suggesting that its products and services can meet the information technology needs of prospective users:

(The ad shows a picture of an operating-room scene.)

WHEN YOUR EMPLOYEE IS ON THE TABLE,
YOU'RE COUNTING THE MINUTES.
BUT WHO'S COUNTING THE DOLLARS?

Caring deeply about your employees and being concerned about the skyrocketing costs of health care is a conundrum for many corporations. The company that finds ways to increase the commitment they make to their people while controlling the cost of that commitment, is the company with the competitive edge. EDS has helped a variety of companies acquire this competitive edge with innovative applications of information technology.

ARE YOUR NEEDS UNIQUE?

EDS has a well-known record of developing systems and software for a business's individual needs—not off-the-shelf-, one-size-fits-all solutions. In fact, no one has as much systems development experience in as many business areas as EDS.

CAN YOUR SYSTEMS REALLY BE INTEGRATED?

For over 28 years, we've been making hardware, software, communications, process and people work together seamlessly. You won't find an information technology company with a longer or better record of results.

IS MANAGING YOUR INFORMATION MANAGING YOU?

Information that helps you achieve your business goals is valuable. Information for information's sake is not. EDS can help evaluate your information technology to make sure you get more of the former and less of the latter.

SHOULD YOU MANAGE LESS AND LEAD MORE?

We provide systems management for giant industry leaders and small companies on their way to becoming leaders. So we can help manage your information systems a little or a lot. We work closely with your people, to add resources and new technology, and to provide flexibility, so you can focus on your core business.

CAN EDS PUT INFORMATION TECHNOLOGY
TO WORK FOR YOU?

Keeping your eyes on the changing business environment has never been more important. And even though you can't control change, you can take advantage of it with EDS.[21]

Exercise 6-2 offers you practice in inventing headings for various texts from the writings of accountancy.

Creating Lists

Another way to break up dense portions of text is to sort out points, categorize them, and list them, as in this example from "Section 89: Complex and Costly," an article that warns of the consequences for failing to comply with Section 89 of the Tax Reform Act of 1986:

RED ALERTS

If you think that Section 89 may not apply to your business, here are some potential Section 89 "red alerts" to consider. I recommend that you seek professional assistance quickly if any of the following characteristics apply to your company:

- Plans that are used primarily by highly compensated employees.
- Businesses with a significant number of part-time employees who work more than 17 ½ hours per week and who are not eligible to participate in employee benefit plans.
- Businesses with significant numbers of second-wage earners who do not participate in plans.
- Different benefits for hourly and salaried employees.
- Different benefits for employees based in different geographic locations.
- Different plans or contributions for different classes of employees.[22]

The following two paragraphs are computer composing tips by Shirley Logan.[23] The first version lacks the listing technique that makes the second version more readable:

Composing Tips (Version 1)

Turn the monitor contrast down and freewrite by typing whatever comes to mind. Because you cannot see the text as you enter it, you can focus on generating content, not on how it appears. You can also enter major headings for a long document. Then insert new information as you gather it. You won't destroy the initial framework and you can add as much information as you want. In addition, you can use one color for all major headings and a contrasting color for supporting details. Later, as you scroll through the document, you can easily identify these major headings and check for parallelism. Finally, use your wordprocessor's Outline mode to generate a standard outline. Then insert new information as you gather it.

Composing Tips (Version 2)

- Turn the monitor contrast down and freewrite by typing whatever comes to mind. Because you cannot see the text as you enter it, you can focus on generating content, not on how it appears.
- Enter major headings for a long document. Then insert new information as you gather it. You won't destroy the initial framework and you can add as much information as you want.

- Use one color for all major headings and a contrasting color for supporting details. Later, as you scroll through the document, you can easily identify these major headings and check for parallelism.
- Use your wordprocessor's Outline mode to generate a standard outline. Then insert new information as you gather it.

Exercise 6-3 offers you practice in breaking up thick text to form lists.

Using Glosses

Glosses are explanatory text placed next to the main text. Glosses enable the reader to scan and grasp the text's meaning quickly. The following is an example of a gloss from AICPA's *Understanding Audits and the Auditor's Report: A Guide for Financial Statement Users*:

Text	*Gloss*
The Standard Compilation Report	Meaning
We have compiled the accompanying balance sheets of MLJ Company as of December 31, 1992 and 1991, and the related statements of income, retained earnings, and cash flows for the years then ended, in accordance with standards established by the American Institute of Certified Public Accountants. A compilation is limited to presenting in the form of financial statements information that is the representation of management. We have not audited or reviewed the accompanying financial statements and, accordingly, do not express an opinion or any other form of assurance on them.[24]	Since the CPA is not obliged to verify the underlying data, no assurance is given on the conformity of the financial statements with GAAP. Audits have value because they provide reasonable assurance that management's representations embodied in the financial statements are free of material misstatement. Reviewed financial statements offer the user a limited amount of assurance. The user of compiled financial statements should understand that the financial statements are the representation of management, and, in this case, no assurance is provided by the CPA.

To test your recognition of the techniques of metadiscourse, do Exercise 6-4. Then try your hand at incorporating metadiscourse within a text by doing Exercise 6-5.

Designing Workplace Documents: Guidelines for Readability

Each writing genre of business and accountancy has its own purpose, professional criteria, format, and tone; but just as important is its readability. Nearly everyone has grappled with workplace documents that defy comprehension: IRS tax forms, medical insurance claim forms, work policy manuals, social security regulations. Unfortunately, an inability to design readable documents hurts those for whom the document is intended—the taxpayer, the patient, the employee, and the retiree, to name a few—and often backfires against the writers. For example, by designing even the simpler tax forms that require professional help, the IRS has been criticized for thwarting its own tax collection process and for making tax collection more odious that it already is. And just as unfortunate is the fact that many workplace documents are boilerplate (standardized form), which compounds the confusion on a massive scale.

The confusion can be costly. In "Worst Forms Unearthed," the results of a survey sponsored by the American Institute for Research (5,607 *Modern Maturity* readers responded) show the devastating consequences of badly designed forms:

> More than 21 percent of respondents told us that when they encountered a bad form or notice, they didn't get the correct service or help they needed. Another 20 percent said they were forced to get help before they could complete the document. And more than 34 percent reported losing either money or benefits.

Dealing with indecipherable documents frustrates and intimidates users. One survey respondent admitted, "when I receive what I think might be a form, I postpone opening it for as long as possible."[25]

In a sense, everything that writing entails affects readability; for example, correct grammar, diction, syntax, and punctuation contribute to reader understanding (or confusion). Forecasting a document's organization, unpacking thick text by listing, and using glosses to interpret content enhances readability. The following sections discuss additional guidelines that ensure the readability of workplace documents. These guidelines relate to purpose, audience, visual elements, emphasis, highlighting, white space, typography and font size, capitalization, and common-sense designing.

Purpose

To illustrate how document design can affect reader comprehension, consider the following boilerplate letter, which acknowledges prospective clients' inquiries about an accounting firm's Estate Planning Seminar:

> Dear taxpayer:
>
> Re: Acknowledgment of Request for Estate Planning Seminar Appointment and/or Confirmation of Appointment
>
> This letter acknowledges your request for an Estate Planning Seminar appointment and/or confirms your Estate Planning Seminar appointment. We will soon be notifying you of your appointment time, date, and location of the next available Estate Planning Seminar and would like to thank you for the interest you have shown. There is no charge for the Estate Planning Seminar, but we do require that you sign up for an appointment because there is a class size limit. Please call or write if we can be of any further service.

Is the recipient supposed to sign up for an Estate Planning Seminar appointment? If a request was already made, is the recipient supposed to sign up again? Or will notice of the appointment time be forthcoming? The letter's problem? *Mixed purpose.* A registrant cannot simultaneously request and receive confirmation for an appointment. (If the registrant has already requested an appointment, that portion of the letter cannot apply to him or her.) An accounting firm that seeks to attract prospective clients through a free seminar cannot afford to confuse them by a botched form letter. Because of the confusing purpose, the writer should compose *two* form letters: the first to acknowledge requests for Estate Planning Seminar appointments, and a second to confirm appointments:

Letter 1:

> Dear taxpayer:
>
> Re: Acknowledgment of Request for Estate Planning Seminar Appointment
>
> This letter acknowledges your request for an Estate Planning Seminar appointment. We will soon be notifying you of your appointment time, date, and location of the next available Seminar. We appreciate your interest, and we look forward to seeing you soon. Please call or write if we can be of any further service.

Letter 2

Dear taxpayer:

Re: Appointment for Estate Planning Seminar

This letter confirms your Estate Planning Seminar appointment.

Time: 1:00–2:00
Date: November 10, 1993
Place: Offices of Smythe and Smith, P.A.
14 Taliaferro Street, Room 211
Iowa City, IA 52242

We appreciate your interest in our Seminar, and we look forward to seeing you soon. Please call or write if we can be of any further service.

Audience

The nature of the intended audience (or possible overhearers) for a document affects its design. If you are addressing a person or a community of people with similar backgrounds and interests, you can appeal to their common situation and needs. For example, the writer of an employee benefits manual usually knows the audience or at least the audience's situation and can adjust the wording accordingly. But the writer of a press release, a job advertisement, or a letter to the editor addresses the educated "public"—a harder task. Designing documents for the general public is the hardest, which is why the IRS, Social Security Administration, and other government agencies have so much difficulty communicating. They must operate under confusing congressional mandates and address audiences with widely varying degrees of reading ability. While they should design documents for the lowest common denominator (sixth-grade reading level), they often design incomprehensible documents due to legal constraints and attempts to protect their own interests. Whatever their constraints, if agencies and businesses followed sound principles of document design and readability, their audiences would have an easier time understanding their messages—which could lead to better compliance.

Visual Elements

Just as "clutter" or excess verbiage in writing distracts and confuses the reader, so does visual "clutter" or "busyness" in workplace documents. Although the principles of graphic design are beyond the scope of this book, certain visual elements affect the readability of documents. To ensure reader comprehension, a writer must consider several elements when designing documents: emphasis, white space, typeface, font size, and capitalization.

Emphasis

In an effort to attract prospective clients, some writers overload their business cards, creating a cluttered appearance in which the forest is lost amid the trees, as in Figure 6-1 (enlarged to show detail). Similarly, cluttered letterheads (as in Fig. 6-2) leave little space for a message.

The business card and letter are examples of too much text for the available space. Other designing mistakes involve the overuse of highlighting techniques (especially since desktop publishing and laser printers offer so many choices heretofore unavailable). The writer can choose from a dazzling array of typefaces and font sizes, underline, boldface, colors, all capitals, boxes, black or shaded backgrounds, and ornaments. If these features are not used judiciously and consistently, the results can be cluttered and garish, as this paragraph from a fundraising letter illustrates:

At year end for the past <u>ten</u> years, we have selected a **charity** for those who wish to contribute money, time, or goods. *This* year, we chose the House of Ruth. As

FIGURE 6-1
A Cluttered Business Card

```
Office: (207) 555-8302    FAX: (207) 555-8129
            Marjorie Staunton, Accountant
                40 Congress Street
                Portland, ME 04102

     Member: National Society of Public Accountants

• Personal Tax Returns Prepared  • Fully Computerized
• Payroll Tax Returns Prepared   • General Ledger
• Accounts Payable               • Financial Statements
• Accounts Receivable            • Other Accounting Services
```

you know, it is a shelter for battered women and their children. The need is especially PRESSING now because of the FIRE DAMAGE they suffered in their kitchen area. $ Cash, ¤ Canned goods, ♥ Toys, ♣ Baby clothes, and ◊ Kitchen equipment are ESPECIALLY needed. Make **checks** payable to "House of Ruth." Donated goods will be gathered on Friday and taken to the shelter in the company van. See **Janice** if you can help. *Thank you*, thank you, thank you!!!!

The problems with the preceding paragraph involve consistency and emphasis. We have all seen similar appeals with multiple exclamation points, boldface, "handwritten" color underline, and parenthesis "(( ))" in color along the sides—all fashioned to get our attention. But such tactics are ineffective. By highlighting so much, nothing is emphasized. And indiscriminate use of highlighting techniques tires and irritates the reader as well—hardly the writer's intention. The lesson: just because technology provides the opportunity to use highlighting techniques doesn't mean you have to use them *all* in a document. Use discernment for an appealing and professional presentation. To test your discrimination in selecting from available highlighting techniques, do Exercise 6-6.

White Space

When laying out elements on a page, desktop publisher Tom Lichty says to "give the same consideration—form and purpose—to white space that you would to any other item on the page."[26] In an effort to save money, office document designers try to cram too much on a page, imparting a cluttered appearance. Yet, the visual impact of text depends on white space

1. around the margins
2. between lines of texts

FIGURE 6-2
A Cluttered Letterhead

```
               Turfle, Tuttle, & Tutweiller, Chartered
                    CERTIFIED PUBLIC ACCOUNTANTS

Timothy Q. Turfle                  Member                      Phoenix Offices
W. Theodore Tuttle          American Institute of             202 Cactus Street
Thomas M. Tutweiller      Certified Public Accountants        Phoenix, AZ 85034
Timothy Q. Turfle, Jr.  Private Companies Practice Section      (602) 555-2955
Mynta U. Berry                                                FAX (602) 555-3911
      -----                 Arizona Association of
Timothy Q. Turfle, Jr.    Certified Public Accountants           Mesa Offices
Melvin X. Algonquin                                         35 Hummingbird Parkway
J. L. Johnson                                                  Mesa, AZ 85202
Kenneth S. Henderson                                           (602) 555-3955
Christina A. Gold                                            FAX (602) 555-9923
P. R. Simpson
```

3. between letters
4. around graphics

Lichty notes that "white space adds proportion to a page, placing other elements in perspective and organizing their arrangement. It is yin to black's yang: Neither can exist without the other."[27] Instead of wasting space, white space acts as a frame, separates elements, forms distinct shapes—and it highlights as well. It creates an oasis for the fatigued reader. To illustrate the importance of white space in rendering a document readable, compare the *appearance* of the text of the following letters (the text is identical):

WaySaver Bank & Trust Company 400 Main Street Salt Lake City, UT 84112 (801) 555-6181
February 4, 1993
Paul T. Trencher Trencher Construction Company 30 Winding Way Salt Lake City, UT 84116
RE: Commercial Loan - 029463
Dear Mr. Trencher:
To remain aware of your current financial situation and to update our files, we need the following information: ● Personal Financial Statement ● Personal Tax Return and Schedules for 1992 ● Fiscal year-end Business Financial Statement
Please send the information to me as soon as possible. An envelope is enclosed for your convenience. If you have any questions, please do not hesitate to call.
Yours truly,

Catherine S Baker

Catherine S. Baker Assistant Vice President
CSB:wfs Encl.

WaySaver Bank & Trust Company
400 Main Street
Salt Lake City, UT 84112
(801) 555-6181

February 4, 1993

Paul T. Trencher
Trencher Construction Company
30 Winding Way
Salt Lake City, UT 84116

RE: Commercial Loan - 029463

Dear Mr. Trencher:

To remain aware of your current financial situation and to update our files, we need the following information:

- Personal Financial Statement
- Personal Tax Return and Schedules for 1992
- Fiscal year-end Business Financial Statement

Please send the information to me as soon as possible. An envelope is enclosed for your convenience. If you have any questions, please do not hesitate to call.

Yours truly,

Catherine S Baker

Catherine S. Baker
Assistant Vice President

CSB:wfs
Encl.

Obviously, reading the second version is easier because of white space. Rather than seeing white space as a void to be filled, think of it as graphic designers do: as a visual "element on the page, equal in importance to text and graphics."[28]

". . . Maybe a little too much white space."

Joe Spitzig, *Technical Communication*[29]

White space entails *vertical* spacing between lines of text and headings and *horizontal* spacing in indenting and centering. Consistency in vertical and horizontal spacing is critical to a well-formatted, professional presentation.

Typeface

Word processing and **desktop publishing** software offer document designers choices of **typeface** (the style of the letters) and **font size** (the size of the letters). Documents use two categories of typeface:

- the body text (paragraph text)
- display text (headings, subheadings)

Typefaces, particularly in body text, "may be the single most important decision" in document design, according to Tom Lichty. Body text can make or break readability, "can whisper or shout, look old or look new, relax the reader, startle the reader, or send the reader away after two paragraphs, never to return."[30] Lichty prefers a typeface with **serifs** for body text:

> The serif makes life easier on the reader by accomplishing three things: It cuts down the reflection of light from around the letter into the reader's eye (halation), it links the letters in a word and provides a horizontal guideline, and it helps distinguish one letter from another.

Serifs "aid the eye in pattern recognition and improve the overall readability of the page." With sans serifs, however, "the eye is forced to read, rather than scan [so] efficiency suffers."[31] Sans serif typefaces should generally not be used for large blocks of type. For greater readability, however, Lichty does recommend the use of sans serif for smaller fonts such as those used for footnotes. And sans serifs are useful for headings, margin notes, captions, and quotations. The following are examples of serif and sans serif typefaces:

Serif | Writing
Sans Serif | Writing

Font Size

The most readable type size for body text is 10 point (type size is measured in points; the larger the number of points, the larger the type). Older readers appreciate a larger font size (which accounts for the popularity of large-print books and publications). Document designers observe that

> Readers will often skip over text which is printed in type that is too small. Small type strains the eye and puts too much information in too little space. It makes a document look crammed and uninviting.[32]

Large font size, conversely, takes up too much space (and thus is expensive to use) and makes the reader work harder. You can see the difference by contrasting the next two paragraphs. Neither make for easy reading.

8 point type Readers will often skip over text which is printed in type that is too small. Small type strains the eye and puts too much information in too little space. It makes a document look crammed and uninviting.

12 point type Large font size, conversely, takes up too much space (and thus is expensive to use) and makes the reader work harder.

Capitalization

The authors of *Guidelines for Document Designers* advise against using all capital letters ("caps") for extended pieces of text. They report that "research consistently supports the belief that words and phrases in all capital letters take longer to read, are hard to read, and require up to 30% more space than words set in lower case."[33] Amazingly, government agencies such as the Internal Revenue Service persist in sending out full page notices with long stretches of text in all caps. Putting *short* titles or headings in all caps, however, imparts proper emphasis; in other words, as with other highlighting techniques, use all caps sparingly.

Common-Sense Designing

Sometimes only a sharp eye and common sense can cure visual problems with documents, as this sign on a conference room door illustrates:

Reserved
Controller

The simple addition of a horizontal line corrects the impression that the controller is taciturn.

Reserved
———
Controller

Another problem is an unintended acronym arising from capitalizing letters:

Society of Institutional Controllers in Kansas

The proper use of highlighting techniques, white space, typeface, font size, and capitalization contribute to a workplace document's readability and enhances a writer's *ethos*. Try your hand at designing a commonly used tax return document in Exercise 6-7.

Using Graphics to Inform Users

In one sense, accountants have been using "graphics" for years—in the form of tabular financial statements. Unfortunately, many users have trouble understanding how financial statements "quantify and track results" of their business decisions. Hans Kasper, in "One Graph is Worth a Thousand Numbers," promotes graphics as a way of "allowing the financially unskilled user to see the big picture that streams of numerical data tend to hide."[34] With sophisticated graphics capability readily available in software packages, accounting offices are recognizing and exploiting the visual impact of graphics in financial reports and other writing genres of accountancy, including manuals, newsletters, and brochures. Besides adding visual interest, graphics or illustrations add to the readability of workplace documents by

- Clarifying data and concepts
- Emphasizing information and ideas
- Interpreting complex statistics
- Transforming abstract concepts into concrete forms
- Organizing findings
- Establishing relationships between facts
- Breaking up text

Unless the appropriate type of graphic is used, however, document users become more confused than enlightened. Larry R. Davis, in "Reporting Financial Information Graphically," cautions accountants against the imprudent use of graphic forms:

> The danger is that the accountant, who usually does not possess much training or experience in choosing among different forms of presentation, will select an inappropriate type of graph or will format the graph in such a manner that it is either inaccurate or misleading.[35]

Accountants use a variety of graphics to simplify and explain complex financial data and business-related concepts:

Graphic	*Use*	*Example*
Table	To incorporate extensive and precise financial data	Widget production, gross sales and net profits ($) per region over a 20-year period
Bar graph	To compare quantity over time	Annual company profits over 10 years
Pie chart	To illustrate how parts relate to the whole, as in percentages and dollars	Manufacturing costs by percentages for raw materials, labor, processing, packaging, and delivery
Line graph	To portray past or future trends and cycles over time	Starting salaries of junior accountants for the past 7 years and for the next 3 years
Organizational chart	To show hierarchical structure of an organization	Relative positions of personnel in an accounting firm
Flow chart	To describe overview of procedure or process	Hiring procedure of an accounting firm
Pictograph	To provide thematic interest	Widgets stacked vertically in a bar graph to illustrate widget production
Diagram	To illustrate an idea	Reference to time in a financial report

Whatever graphic form is selected to suit the writer's purpose and the user's need to know, the writer must keep some general rules in mind if the graphic is to contribute to the user's understanding of the data or concepts depicted:

1. Simplify the graphic. The user should be able to comprehend the information without too much effort.
2. Refer to the graphic in the text. Use "figure" numbers unless the graphic is part of the text as in the preceding chart.
3. Title the graphic concisely yet informatively.
4. Use instructive labeling.

5. Use parallel headings.
6. Place the graphic conveniently where the user needs to see it.
7. Wherever possible, position the graphic vertically on the page so that the user doesn't have to turn the document.
8. Use consistent logical arrangement (e.g., hierarchical, alphabetical, sequential).
9. Avoid a cluttered appearance.
10. Document data sources.

Tables

Creating a table by using a word processor is relatively easy with a software package like WordPerfect 5.1. Figure 6-3 is a simple table format that takes only six quick keystrokes to construct.[36]

The writer has only to place data within the blocks, and furnish the title and headings. Other kinds of tables use white space instead of vertical rules, as Figure 6-4 from "Ethics in the Management Accounting Curriculum" illustrates.

Here are some tips for creating readable tables:

- To avoid a cluttered appearance, use white space instead of vertical rules between columns.
- Title the table informatively.
- Use concise, informative, and parallel labels for each vertical column and horizontal row.

Bar Graphs

The bars in bar graphs may be arranged either vertically or horizontally (see Fig. 6-5).

When designing bar graphs, be careful to do the following:

- Design the bars to be of equal width.
- Make the spaces between the bars narrower than the bars.
- Use vertical bars for amounts and dollars.
- Use horizontal bars to indicate time.
- Create pictographs when possible.
- Label the bars informatively.
- Don't compare too many items.

FIGURE 6-3
Creating a Table with WordPerfect 5.1

FIGURE 6-4
Constraints on Ethics Integration[37]

	All Respondents		*Those Not Integrating Ethics*	
	Number	*%*	*Number*	*%*
Curriculum constraints	217	40.2	97	38.8
Lack of subject matter/materials	156	28.9	74	29.6
Lack of interest/desire to integrate ethics	44	8.1	31	12.4
Lack of ability/knowledge how to integrate ethics	84	15.6	44	17.6
Other constraints	39	7.2	4	1.6
Totals	540	100.0	250	100.0

FIGURE 6-5
Vertical and Horizontal Bars

Pie Charts

The pie chart with the patterned segments in Figure 6-6(a) illustrates the problem of trying to cram too much information into one chart. In addition to having a cluttered appearance, the pie chart contains labels that refer the reader inconveniently to a legend that explains the chart.

Rules for creating understandable pie charts include the following:

- Start the largest segment at the 12 o'clock position.
- Locate the other segments (largest to smallest) in clockwise order.
- Unless the pie chart is large, place the labels *outside* the segments, as in Figure 6-6(b).
- Avoid clutter by controlling the number of segments.
- Let the segment sizes indicate the percentages instead of using "busy" patterns as in Figure 6-6(a).
- Make the labels consistent.

Line Graphs

Figure 6-7 is a simple line graph that categorizes computer costs and shows their comparative annual costs over a ten-year period.

FIGURE 6-6
Cluttered and Clear Pie Charts

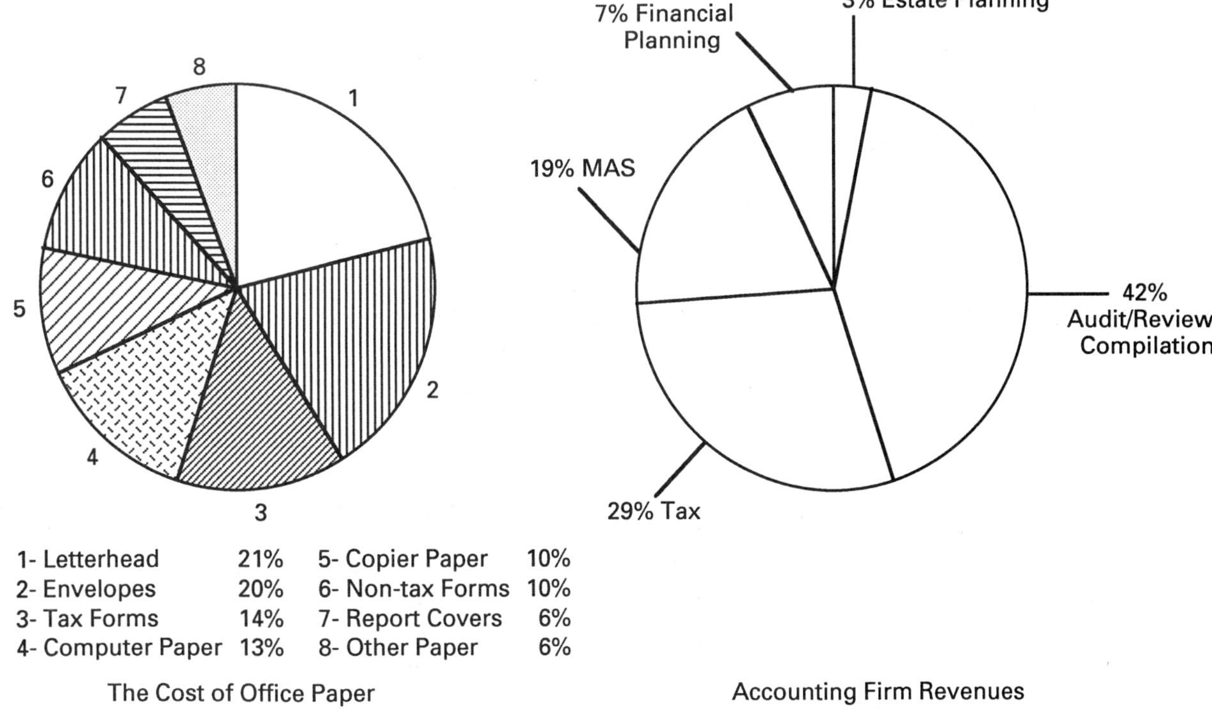

FIGURE 6-7
Computer Costs

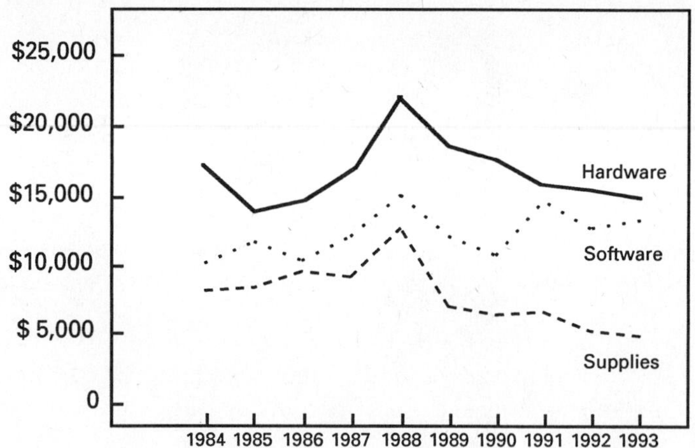

Like other graphics, excessive clutter in line graphs can cause the user to misinterpret the data. So that users can spot trends that line graphs depict, observe the following guidelines:

- Provide sufficient grid lines or tick marks to orient the user, but avoid excessive use of grid lines that tend to compete with the plotted lines.
- Use different symbols for data; label for clarity.
- Label the *x* axis (horizontal) for the independent variable (e.g., years); limit the variable to actual data (if you plot the information for 10 years, don't place 12 years on the *x* axis).
- Label the *y* axis (vertical) for the dependent variable (e.g. dollars). Limit this variable to actual data (if the dollar figures plot up to $25,000, don't place $50,000 on the *y* axis).
- Label the lines informatively, to avoid referring the user to a legend.
- To avoid clutter, don't plot too many lines. Instead, categorize the data differently or use two line graphs.

For practice in simplifying information to be plotted on a line graph, do Exercise 6-8.

Organizational Charts

Figure 6-8 gives an overview of the chain of command and areas of responsibility for Widgets Unlimited.

When designing an organizational chart,

- Lay out the chart to read from top to bottom;
- Place clear titles within rectangles;
- Don't crowd information within the rectangles; and
- Connect the rectangles to reflect the lines of authority.

FIGURE 6-8
Departmental Structure of Widgets Unlimited

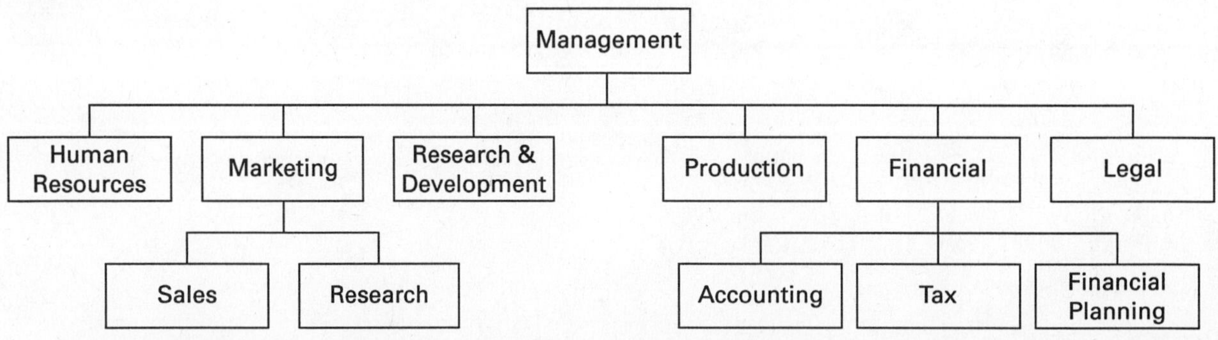

Flow Charts

Figure 6-9 is a flow chart that indicates an accounting firm's tax season procedure for dealing with clients.

When designing a flow chart, highlight the key parts of the process or procedure by following these directions:

- Sequence the information to read from top to bottom and from left to right.
- Place clear labels inside rectangles or other shapes.
- Don't overdo the number of shapes used.
- Indicate the procedure flow by connecting the rectangles with arrows.

Pictographs

Using relevant symbols to represent data, particularly in bar graphs, is a clever way to tie the graphic to the material thematically. Examples include

- Using coal cars to represent tons of coal:
- Using barrels of oil to represent oil imports:
- Using houses to represent housing starts:

While pictographs can add visual interest, the following guidelines apply:

- Avoid visual clutter by using uncomplicated symbols.
- Use only one pictograph per bar chart.
- Use a symbol appropriate to the information presented.

Diagrams

Diagrams or line drawings can illustrate almost anything that a writer wants to explain. Writers often miss the opportunity to clarify complex material, ideas, and concepts by means of simple diagrams. Figure 6-10 shows texts common to the writings of accountancy.

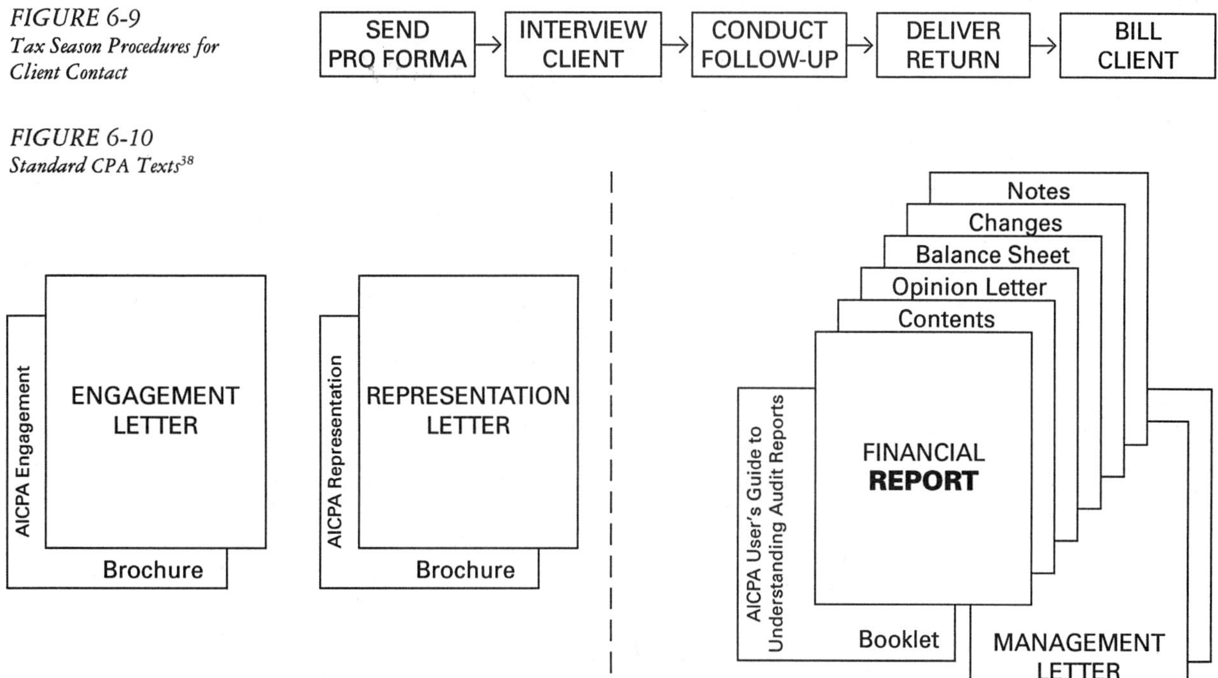

FIGURE 6-9
Tax Season Procedures for Client Contact

FIGURE 6-10
Standard CPA Texts[38]

Figure 6-11 pictures the references to points in time in a financial statement.

Figure 6-12 uses a pictograph (gears) to remind writing students that it is the actual *writing*, not the writer, that reaches the reader; in other words, the mind of the writer affects the mind of the reader through the medium of the text.

Rhetorical Considerations

The preceding discussion stresses general rules for choosing the appropriate graphic for a particular purpose and for rendering the data available to the user. The rhetorically aware accountant who wants to establish credibility and promote a professional image avoids sloppy presentations in graphics just as he or she does in writing (*ethos*). Despite the accountant's desire to cater to the client (*pathos*), particular care must be taken that information is not misconstrued by the user (*logos*). Because of the accountant's professional mission to convey complex financial data to interested users, guidelines for financial graphics press beyond readability issues:[41]

- *Distorting information* in a graphic is as dishonest as misrepresenting figures in the text, and leads to unwanted legal exposure.
- Some *complex financial graphics* are as indecipherable to the nonaccountant user as financial statements. As with any presentation destined for users, gear the graphic to the ability and interests of potential users, even if it means dumping a complex graphic in favor of traditional tabular forms.
- When *precise figures* are needed, stick to traditional tabular forms or tables. To allow users to make financial decisions on the basis of approximations inferred from graphics is risky.
- *Three-dimensional forms* should be avoided because implying volume can be misleading.
- For accuracy, all *scales* (e.g., the vertical *y* axis in a line graph) should begin with zero and contain no breaks.
- *Negative numbers* should "be shown automatically at the opposite direction of positive numbers. Pie charts, for example, do not meet this criterion."[42]

To test your ingenuity in creating interesting graphics, do Exercise 6-9.

FIGURE 6-11
Reference to Time in a Financial Statement[39]

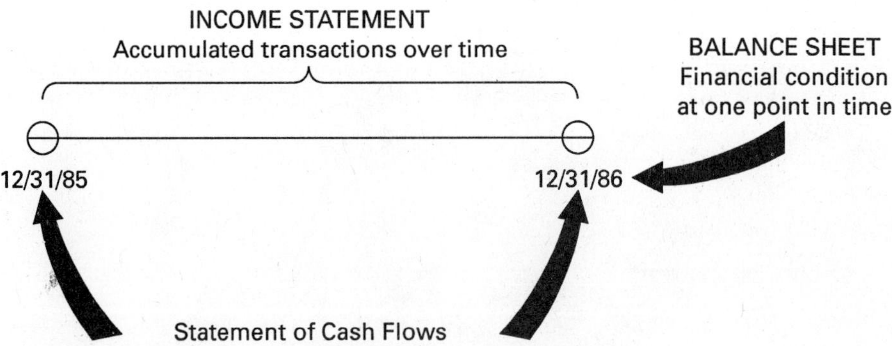

FIGURE 6-12
How Writers Reach Readers[40]

Using Brochures as a Marketing Tool

Judging from these advertisements and articles from accounting journals, CPAs are locked in fierce battle for quality clients:

"How to Market Your Consulting and Professional Services" (Book review)[43]
"Build Your Accounting Practice" (Seminar advertisement)[44]
"CPAs Increase Marketing Expenditures" (Article)[45]
"Forty-Seven Ways to Increase Your Marketing Response and Profit" (Advertisement)[46]
"Building a Consulting Practice" (Article)[47]
"The Journal of Practice Building Strategies" (Marketing advertisement)[48]
"Develop New Clients" (Advertisement)[49]
"Practices Needed" (Advertisement)[50]

One proven way of attracting clients is through a well-designed, rhetorically sound brochure to promote an accountant or an accounting firm. This effective marketing document fulfills the specific objectives of a firm:

It attracts new clients.
It introduces the firm or accountant.
It informs readers of the firm's services.
It establishes or reinforces the firm's image.
It highlights areas of the firm's expertise.
It reaches a multiple readership.
It enjoys a long shelf life.

Firm brochures come in various formats. Two of the more common are the six-panel barrelfold (8 ½" x 11" folded in thirds) and the eight-panel gatefold (8 ½" x 14" folded in fourths). See the examples in Figure 6-13.

A six-panel barrelfold allows a layout illustrated by these headings from a brochure for Dun and Donne, Chartered, a small accounting firm:

1st panel	(Title page)
2nd panel	Firm History, Partner's Profile
3rd panel	The Dun and Donne Team Approach
4th and 5th panels	Professional Services Offered: Audited Financial Statements, Review and Compilation Financial Statements, Taxes and Tax Planning, Management Advisory Services
6th panel	Other Services, Geographic Regions Served, Major Clientele Categories

The eight-panel gatefold layout is represented by the headings in this brochure from a sole practitioner, Glen M. David, CPA, MBA:

1st panel	(Title page)
2nd panel	About the Accounting Practice of Glen M. David, CPA, MBA

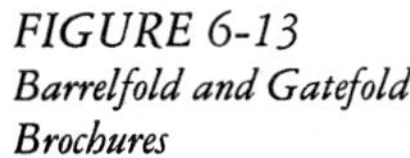
FIGURE 6-13
Barrelfold and Gatefold Brochures

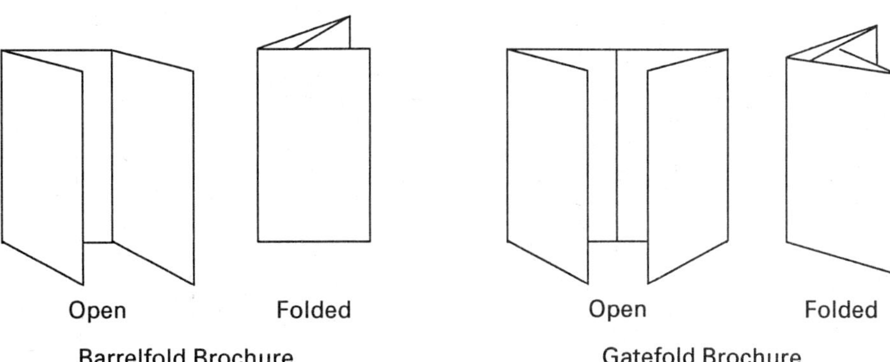

3rd panel	Education
4th panel	Experience
5th panel	Professional Affiliations and Licenses
6th panel	Continuing Professional Education
7th panel	Businesses Served
8th panel	Personal

Whatever the format and layout of the brochure, the persuasive accountant will incorporate the three rhetorical appeals when writing and designing inhouse, or verify that the appeals are included when reviewing a brochure composed outside the firm:

Ethos Because the brochure paves the way for the accountant, it must be letter-perfect, concisely written, and attractively designed so that it projects a professional image.

Logos Rather than concentrating on what you want to tell prospective clients, focus on what clients need to know about you and your firm. Include enough relevant detail about your expertise to interest a client in your particular services.

Pathos Persuading prospective clients that you can meet their accounting needs is the main reason for the expense of brochures. As one proponent of brochures as a powerful marketing tool puts it,

> Brochures are real value for every business provided they are designed to answer the one question that all potential clients ask. . . "What's in it for me if I do business with you?"[51]

Test your ability to apply rhetorical principles to the text of an accounting brochure by doing Exercise 6-10.

Notes

1 Listing based partly on Charles T. Brusaw, Gerald J. Alred, and Walter E. Oliu, *The Business Writer's Handbook* (New York: St. Martin's Press, 1987).
2 Brochure, "1991 Software Tools Catalog," (New York: AICPA, 1991), 18.
3 George Marthinuss, CPA, et al., *Comprehensive Engagement Manual* (New York: AICPA, n.d.).
4 George Marthinuss, CPA, et al., *Bank Audit Manual* (New York: AICPA, n.d.).
5 Dennis R. Meals, CPA, et al., *Guide to Compilation and Review Engagements* (Fort Worth, Tx.: Practitioners, 1990).
6 Dennis R. Meals, CPA, et al., *Guide to Construction Contractors* (Fort Worth, Tx.: Practitioners, 1990).
7 Mitchell Hakoun, CPA, and Gerald Tomlinson, *Accountant's Complete Model Letter Book* (Englewood Cliffs, N.J.: Prentice Hall, 1987).
8 Mark L. Frigo and Peter F. Stone, "Writing Effective Management Letters," *CPA Journal* (April 1989): 52–55.
9 Rene Sacasas, Kay Tatum, and Don Wiesner, "Keep-Well Letters: The Elusive Contingency," *CPA Journal* (November 1989): 45–52.
10 Robert J. Glaser, "Computer Consulting Engagement Letters You Can Use," *The Practical Accountant* (February 1989): 68–75.
11 Advertisement (flyer), "How Bankers Evaluate Your Loan Proposals," (Santa Ana, Calif.: James Publishing Group, [1988]).
12 The letter is a truncated version of a small accounting firm's management letter. Used by permission.
13 Frigo and Stone, 52–55.
14 Frigo and Stone, 52–53.
15 Joseph M. Williams, *Style: Ten Lessons in Clarity and Grace*, 2d ed., (Scott, Foresman, 1985), 81.
16 Alan J. Winters, *A User's Guide to Understanding Audits and Auditors' Reports* (New York: AICPA, 1982), 24.
17 James C. Hall, "Measuring the Effect of Training and Education," *Management Accounting* (June 1989): 32.
18 Alan West, *A Business Plan* (London: Pitman, 1988), 9–11.
19 Jonathan D. Pond, "Teach Your Children the Value of Money" in "Managing Your Money," *Management Accounting* (June 1989): 11.
20 Advertisement, "Platinum," *Journal of Accountancy* (October 1988): 13.
21 Advertisement, "EDS," *Harvard Business Review* (May-June 1991): 65. Reprinted by permission of Electronic Data Systems Corporation.
22 Arnold J. Chassen, "Section 89: Complex and Costly," *Management Accounting* (June 1989): 35.

[23] Shirley Logan, "Perfect Tips," *The Professional Writing Consultant* (Fall 1990): 3. Reprinted with permission of Shirley W. Logan.

[24] Dan M. Guy and Alan J. Winters, *Understanding Audits and the Auditor's Report: A Guide for Financial Statement Users* (New York: AICPA, 1989), 38.

[25] Carolyn Boccella Bagin and Andrew M. Rose, "Worst Forms Unearthed," *Modern Maturity* (February-March 1991), 64–66.

[26] Tom Lichty, *Design Principles of Desktop Publishers* (Glenview, Ill.: Scott, Foresman, 1989), 105.

[27] Lichty, 104.

[28] Lichty, 104.

[29] Cartoon, Joe Spitzig, *Technical Communication: Journal of the Society for Technical Communication* (First Quarter 1991): 15. Reprinted by permission of *Technical Communication* and the Society for Technical Communication.

[30] Lichty, 25.

[31] Lichty, 30–31.

[32] Daniel B. Felker, *Guidelines for Document Designers* (Washington, D.C.: American Institutes for Research, [1981]), 77.

[33] Felker, 88.

[34] Hans Kasper, CPA, "One Graph Is Worth a Thousand Numbers," *Journal of Accountancy* (November 1988): 132.

[35] Larry R. Davis, CPA, "Reporting Financial Information Graphically," *Journal of Accountancy* (December 1987): 108.

[36] Alan Simpson, *Mastering WordPerfect 5.1* (San Francisco: Sybex, 1990), 676.

[37] Steven M. Mintz, "Ethics in the Management Accounting Curriculum," *Management Accounting* (June 1990): 51.

[38] Aletha Hendrickson, "How to Appear Reliable without Being Liable: CPA Writing in Its Rhetorical Context," *Worlds of Writing: Teaching and Learning in Discourse Communities of Work* (New York: Random House, 1989): 304.

[39] Hendrickson, 310.

[40] Eugene R. Hammond, *Critical Thinking, Thoughtful Writing*, 2d. ed., (New York: McGraw-Hill, 1989), 54. Reprinted by permission of Eugene R. Hammond.

[41] Some of the material in this section is adapted from an excellent article on financial graphics: Irwin M. Jarett, CPA, and Yair Babad, "Guidelines and Standards for Accounting Graphics," *Journal of Accounting and EDP* (Summer 1988): 4–14.

[42] Jarett and Babad, 5.

[43] "How to Market Your Consulting and Professional Services," *The Practical Accountant* (June 1991): 91.

[44] "Build Your Accounting Practice," Parker, Colo.: KC, 1991.

[45] David Singband, "CPAs Increase Marketing Expenditures," *Accounting Week* (July 8, 1991): 6.

[46] "Forty-Seven Ways to Increase Your Marketing Response and Profit," *The Practical Accountant* (April 1991): 63.

[47] Fern Lentini, "Building a Consulting Practice," *Journal of Accountancy* (July 1991): 69–72.

[48] Marketing advertisement, "The Journal of Practice Building Strategies" (Fall 1991).

[49] Advertisement, "Develop New Clients," *Journal of Accountancy* (July 1991): 134.

[50] Advertisement, "Practices Needed," *Journal of Accountancy* (July 1991): 132.

[51] "The Business of Brochures," *Australian Accountant* (August 1988): 19.

NAME

EXERCISE 6-1: ANALYZING AN ENGAGEMENT LETTER

Answer the questions in the spaces provided. Take into account professional criteria and resources, the writer's purpose, the user's need, and the rhetorical appeals (*logos*), (*ethos*), and (*pathos*). The following engagement letter is sent to a sole practitioner who has asked for a quality review to comply with AICPA's peer review mandate.*

Huey, Dewey, and Louis, P.A.
100 S. Main Street
Ann Arbor, MI 48109

January 20, 1993

Godfrey B. Jarbak, CPA
1700 Andrew Place
Ann Arbor, MI 48110

Re: Quality Review

You have requested that Huey, Dewey, and Louis, P.A. provide a review team to perform a quality review of your firm's accounting and auditing practice. We are willing to perform such an engagement, subject to the terms and conditions set forth in this letter.

Stanley D. Browsky, CPA, will be the team captain. If any changes need to be made in the review team, we will notify you immediately and ask you to authorize those changes.

Scope of the Review

The review will be performed in accordance with the standards applicable to quality reviews.

If it is necessary to obtain the consent of your clients for review of files and records pertaining to them, you will assume the responsibility for obtaining such consent. In connection with the review, no review team member will have any contact with clients of your firm.

Liability and Subpoena

You agree not to take, or assist in, any action seeking to hold liable, jointly or singly, us or the review team--including any staff, assistants, committees or the review team's firms--for damages on account of any good faith act or omission or on account of any deficiency in the files overall, unless those damages arise from malice, gross negligency, or recklessness.

Also, you agree not to subpoena any of those persons or organizations, or otherwise call them to testify, in any action to which they are not a party, with respect to any of the work performed, reports made, or information acquired or developed in connection with this review.

1. What is the exigence for the letter?

____

____

2. What is the letter's purpose? ____

____

____

3. To what accounting procedure does the letter relate? ____________

____

4. Would the writer need to consult professional sources for criteria for the letter? ____________

5. What does the writer stand to gain?

____

____

To lose? ____________

____

6. How does the writer arrange the format for the reader's convenience?

____

____

____

7. How does the writer appeal to reader's self-interest (*pathos*)? ____

____

____

____

8. How does the writer protect her firm's self-interest? ____________

____

____

____

____

* The text is adapted from a small accounting firm's quality review engagement letter. Used by permission.

<u>Timing of Review and Fees</u>

We anticipate that the review will begin in May or June 1993 and take between 10 and 15 hours to complete.

Billing rates are $66 per hour for the team captain. Your firm will also pay all reviewer out-of-pocket expenses. We expect the cost to be $1,000.

Invoices are due upon presentation. Normally, fees will be billed after the report is issued on the review. However, under certain circumstances, progress billing may be rendered.

If you accept these terms and conditions, please sign and return the enclosed copy of this letter. This letter will then become a contract between you and us.

Sincerely,

AF Louis

Anne F. Louis, CPA

AFL:bf

We consent to the terms and conditions described in this letter.

____

Firm to Be Reviewed

____

By

____

Date

____

Position

9. How does the writer control legal exposure? _______________

10. How does the writer incorporate *logos*? _______________

11. How does the writer evidence credibility (*ethos*)? _______________

12. How would you describe the tone of the letter? _______________

NAME

EXERCISE 6-2: CREATING INFORMATIVE HEADINGS

The following sections of text are from the writings of accountancy. In each space provided, supply an informative heading to guide the reader.

(1) ____________________

"Students enter the work force with preconceptions of business conduct that often bear little relation to practice. Many students presuppose they have higher moral standards than do practitioners.

"A corollary assumption made by students is that those in positions of authority may have advanced on the basis of shady dealing. These assumptions are not undercut by the popular press speculating on the ethical makeup of individuals, such as Ivan Boesky or Michael Milken, who have been glamorized as antiheros. Similarly, successful managers often have been vilified by the press for having achieved success through legal business means that do not appear to conform with some nebulous norm of fair play generally held in the public mind.

"Students find it exceedingly difficult to grasp that standards of corporate behavior are established not to conform to esoteric levels of absolute propriety, but rather to approximate the behavioral expectations of prudent business people. In that regard, business ethics are absolute and not situational. But standards of ethical conduct in business evolve over time in response to changing environmental factors and public expectations.

"For instance, 40 years ago sexual harassment was tolerated to a higher degree that it is today. Only within the last decade has sexual harassment become a major focus of ethical standard setting. Behaviors that previously were tolerated may now be subject to discipline."

(From "Business and Academe: Forging an Ethics Partnership")*

(2) ____________________

"Creditors must have confidence in key executives to accept a plan that provides for future debt payments or for the exchange of stock for debt. Replacing existing top management may prove necessary to get this confidence level. In many public companies, individuals experienced in turning troubled companies around are brought in as replacements. For smaller companies where the owner is also the manager, creditors may indirectly insist that operations be turned over to another executive, or that a workout specialist—in many cases an accountant—be retained to work with the debtor.

"If the creditors are uncomfortable with existing management and the debtor refuses to make changes, the creditors may petition the court to appoint a trustee to run the business, develop their own plan, or move to have the case converted to Chapter 7 and liquidated."

(From "The Keys to Developing a Successful Chapter 11 Plan")**

(3) ____________________

"Finally there's a comprehensive library that shows you how to plan and implement every aspect of your client's major business transactions—and recognize the tax implications up front.

"RIA's Business Transactions Library gives you all the rules, plus detailed, expertly-focused guidance on major business decisions: choice of entity; business formation; acquisitions & mergers; control & ownership; financing alternatives; sale/dissolution/liquidation options; and more."

(4) ____________________

"This unique source provides specific planning and practice aids, including planning articles and more than 150 checklists of information to gather, factors to consider, and steps to follow to determine the optimum course of action. Think of them as safety nets to help avoid major errors.

"Our editorial staff of in-house tax experts provides in-depth analysis of the controlling authorities, plus observations, cautions, and illustrations—all in clear business English. So you can make recommendations with confidence."

(5) ____________________

"RIA's Business Transactions Library—it makes business less taxing for your clients. Which, in turn, should make life considerably less taxing for you."

(From a Research Institute of America advertisement)†

* Gary B. Frank, M. H. Sarhan, and Steven A. Fisher, "Business and Academe: Forging an Ethics Partnership," *Management Accounting* (June 1990): 48. Reprinted with permission of *Management Accounting* and the Institute of Management Accountants.

** Grant W. Newton, "The Keys to Developing a Successful Chapter 11 Plan," *The Practical Accountant* (June 1991): 42. Reprinted with permission of *The Practical Accountant*, Warren, Gorham & Lamont, Inc.

† Advertisement, Research Institute of American Business Transactions Library, *Journal of Accountancy* (July 1991): 16. Reprinted by permission of Research Institute of America.

(6) ______________________________

"Frierdich agreed in 1979 to act as attorney for the estate of Reeves. Mrs. Reeves gave Frierdich $100,000 in 1980, in exchange for a note at 8% interest. At the time, the prime rate was 15%. It was due when the attorney's fees due him, 'subject to the closing of the estate,' were paid. There was no definite due date, and no interest was ever paid. The estate was closed in 1990. The IRS claimed the loan was really an advance payment for legal services. *Held*: For the IRS. The $100,000 was an advance payment, taxable in 1980."

(7) ______________________________

"Owrutsky filed his returns late for several years. He was owed a refund for those years. The IRS barred him from practice before the IRS for the late filings. Owrutsky argued that because no tax was owed in those years, he should not have been disbarred. *Held*: For the IRS. Owrutsky knew of his legal duty and knowingly breached it. Under 31 CFR Section 10.50, disreputable conduct, including willfully failing to file returns in violation of the revenue laws, is grounds for disbarment from IRS practice."

(From "Tax Alert," *The Practical Accountant*)*

* "Tax Alert," *The Practical Accountant* (June 1991): 13. Reprinted with permission of *The Practical Accountant*, Warren, Gorham & Lamont, Inc.

NAME

EXERCISE 6-3: MAKING DENSE TEXT READABLE

The following passage is based on an article, "Perfect Tips," that offers computer revision tips.* Recast the passage in the space provided, using the listing technique.

Tips on Revising

To revise on computer, experiment with various sentence patterns and "cut and paste"—electronically. You can insert informal, not-to-be-printed comments at any point in a document. These comments can serve as reminds or needed changes. Try using the Replace command to identify and correct frequently misspelled or misused words. You can also use Search to locate overused words or phrases. For example, to ensure correct pronoun antecedent, you could search for each "this." In addition, you might run your spelling checker to catch errors in spelling or in typing, a step many novices forget. Finally, fine-tune word choice with the thesaurus—often a part of the word-processing program.

* Logan, 3.

NAME

EXERCISE 6-4: ANALYZING METADISCOURSE

The following is a partial MicroMash advertisement* that contains various types of metadiscourse. After listing the types in the spaces provided, comment on how the metadiscourse guides the reader.

FREE CPE DEMO!

MicroMash CPE
TOPICS!
TOPICS!
TOPICS!

Tired of the same old seminars? Bored by books? Tranquilized by tapes?

Then do something different! Try Continuing Professional Education (CPE) courses from MicroMash.

Each one is comprehensive. Each one is exciting, challenging, and rewarding. Each one is fully interactive. And each one runs on an IBM-PC (or compatible) or Apple Macintosh.

Still uncertain? Then call us and we'll send you a FREE CPE DEMO to try yourself.

ACCOUNTING & AUDITING

- Accounting for Income Taxes (FASB #96)
- Accounting for Pensions
- Audit Sampling
- Auditing Update
- Audits of State and Local Governmental Units—1
- Cash Flows (FASB #95)
- Compilation and Review
- FASB Update
- GAO Standards: Revised Yellow Book on Government Auditing Standards
- Internal Controls for Auditors and Managers—Evaluation
- Internal Controls for Auditors and Managers—Theory
- Researching Corporate Accounting and Auditing Problems on NAARS
- Using Electronic Spreadsheets in Auditing

MANAGEMENT

- Bankruptcy!
- Capital Budgeting
- Marketing Your Practice—Introduction

* Advertisement, MicroMash, *Journal of Accountancy* (July 1991): 24–25. Reprinted by permission of MicroMash.

NAME

EXERCISE 6-5: USING METADISCOURSE TO GUIDE THE READER

The following is an advertisement for the College for Financial Planning.* Insert metadiscourse (titles, forecasting, headings/ subheadings, listing, and/or glosses) to guide the reader into understanding the meaning intended by the advertiser.

Introducing Two New Measures of Tax Expertise

(1) ____________________

____

In recent years, the frequency and complexity of tax law changes have increased consumer demand for professional tax preparation and planning services. Yet, identifying a tax professional specifically equipped to offer these services hasn't always been easy. Until now.

(2) ____________________

The College for Financial Planning, in cooperation with the National Society of Public Accountants (NSPA) and the Accreditation Council for Accountancy and Taxation (ACAT), announces the establishment of two tax designations intended to serve both the public and the profession by attesting to the competency, dependability, and ethical commitment of individuals who perform tax preparation and planning services.

(3) ____________________

The Accredited Tax Preparer and Accredited Tax Advisor designations are based on educational programs available exclusively through the Institute of Tax Studies, a new division of the College for Financial Planning. The two-course Tax Preparer Program emphasizes tax return preparation and compliance issues for individuals and businesses. The Tax Advisor Program is a six-course, advanced curriculum that focuses on tax issues ranging from structuring sophisticated transactions to specialized tax planning and management.

(4) ____________________

Successful completion of each program and related requirements leads to the Accredited Tax Preparer or Accredited Tax Advisor designation, both granted by the Accreditation Council for Accountancy and Taxation.

(5) ____________________

Give your clients the tax expertise they deserve. To learn more about the College for Financial Planning's Institute for Tax Studies and the Accredited Tax Preparer and Accredited Tax Advisor designations, call 1-800-555-5343, or complete and return the coupon.

COLLEGE FOR FINANCIAL PLANNING

INSTITUTE FOR TAX STUDIES

4695 S. Monaco St. • Denver, CO • 80237-3403 • (303) 220-4200

Yes! Send me more information about:

❑ Tax Peparer Program ❑ Tax Advisor Program

Name ____________________

Company ____________________

Address (Indicate: ❑ home ❑ business) ____________________

City ____________________ State ____________________

Zip ____________________ Daytime Telephone ( ) ____________________ AD3343

Send to: College for Financial Planning
4695 South Monaco St. • Denver, CO 80237-3403

* Advertisement, College for Financial Planning, *National Public Accountant* (July 1991): 3. Reprinted by permission of College for Financial Planning.

NAME

EXERCISE 6-6: DESIGNING AN OFFICE NOTICE

The following memo is about a recycling plan that an office manager wants to start. No highlighting techniques are used. Convert the memo into a one-page notice, using metadiscourse techniques and *judiciously* using whatever highlighting techniques your computer offers.

MEMO

Snyder, Snidley, and Snodgrass, Chartered
Janet Smith, Office Manager

To: All employees
Date: May 3, 1993
Subject: Recycling

We've just received notice from Carroll County that the county must reduce its solid waste stream by 15% through recycling by January 1, 1994. Fines will be imposed on those companies who do not institute a recycling program.

To avoid the fines and to encourage conservation of our resources through recycling, we will comply by recycling the following items: (1) Newspaper should be bundled and tied, or placed in paper bags. Deposit in the third-floor storeroom. (2) Computer paper should be boxed and placed in the third-floor storeroom. (3) White office paper should be boxed and placed in the third-floor storeroom. (4) Cardboard should be flattened and placed in boxes. Take to the third-floor storeroom. (5) Glass (all colors; remove caps) should be placed in the blue receptacle in the third-floor hallway. (6) Plastic (bottles only) should be deposited in the yellow receptacle in the third-floor hallway. (7) Aluminum cans (not tin) should be placed in the red receptacle in the third-floor hallway.

Thank you for cooperating and participating in our recycling program. Incidentally, did you know that our letterhead and envelopes are now printed on recycled paper?

NAME

EXERCISE 6-7: DESIGNING A TAX RETURN COVER SHEET

A tax preparation service needs a one-page form to help its individual and business clients file their prepared taxes correctly. It should be designed so that the accountant can check blocks *manually* to indicate which of the options the client should follow. Design a form consistent with the principles of metadiscourse and document design. Incorporate the information indicated (not necessarily in the following order):

1. Letterhead information: Champion Associates, Accountants; Robert Champion; 45 Maple Street, New Windsor, MD 21776 (301) 646-2140.
2. Instruct the client to file any of the following federal forms: Individual Income Tax Form 1040; Fiduciary Income Tax Form 1041; Partnership Income Tax Form 1065; Corporation Income Tax Form 1120; Declaration of Estimated Income Tax Form 1040ES.
3. Direct the client to file any of the following Maryland forms: Individual Income Tax Form 502, Fiduciary Income Tax Form 504, Partnership Income Tax Form 501, Corporation Income Tax Form 500, Declaration of Estimated Income Tax Form 500D, Sales Tax Report Form, Unemployment Tax Return Form, Personal Property Tax Report Form, Homeowners' Property Tax Credit Application Form.
4. Indicate the amount of tax due (if any) for an April 15 filing or quarterly filings (federal and state).
5. State who should sign each form: Individual Taxpayer, Taxpayer and Spouse, Officer or Officers, Partners.
6. Instruct the client to make checks payable to "Internal Revenue Service" for the federal return and "Comptroller of the Treasury" for the Maryland return.
7. Tell the client how much refund to expect (if any).
8. Direct the client to send the signed forms to Internal Revenue Service Center, Philadelphia, PA 19255 (federal) and to Comptroller of the Treasury, Income Tax Division, Annapolis, MD 21411 (Maryland).
9. Instruct the client to keep a copy of the federal and state returns.
10. Direct the client to send the federal and state returns by certified mail.
11. Thank the client for the business, and invite him or her to call if more information is needed.

NAME

EXERCISE 6-8: REPRESENTING DATA IN GRAPHS

The office manager of Grant and Davie, P.C. analyzed the gross receipts of the firm for various categories over a 10-year period. The following line graph is to be submitted to the annual partners' meeting. State the design problem(s) in the space provided; then redesign the graphic for greater readability.

The design problems include

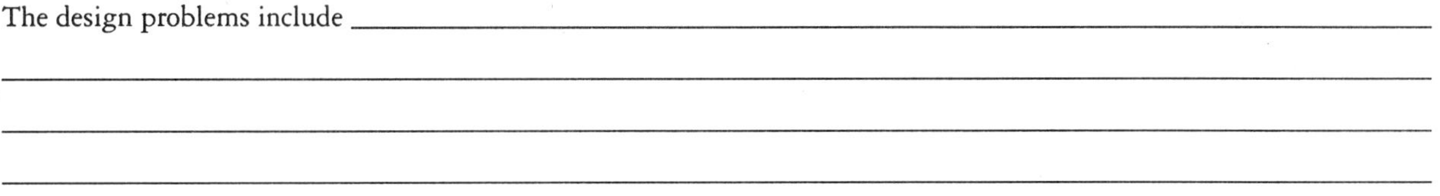

Gross Receipts per Professional Service

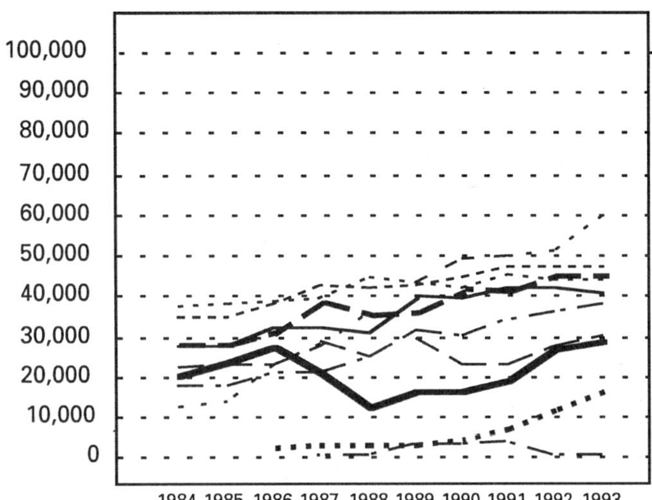

Individual Tax Returns	————————	Monthly Write-up Work	- - - - - - - - - .
Corporate Tax Returns	— — — —	MAS (noncomputer)	- - - - - - -
Audits	▬▬▬▬▬▬	Computer Services	— - — - —
Reviews	▬ ▬ ▬ ▬	Estate Planning	— - - — - -
Compilations	- - - - - - - - - -	Financial Planning	■■■■■■■■■■

NAME

EXERCISE 6-9: CONVERTING FINANCIAL DATA TO GRAPHIC FORM

For each of the following assignments, integrate the raw data into an appropriate graphic. In a sentence or two, defend your choice.

1. A partial job cost analysis for a construction company follows. Design a graphic to show the status of job completion.

Coleman Construction Group, Inc.
Analysis of Job Costs
For the Six Months Ended June 30, 1993

JOB	LABOR	MATERIAL	SUB-CONTRACT	PAYROLL OVERHEAD	TOTAL COST TO DATE	ESTIMATED TOTAL COST	PERCENT COMPLETE
Laurendale	97,024	466,218	186,936	19,404	769,582	769,582	100.00%
Rubytown	11,912	13,396	25,388	2,382	53,078	56,000	94.78%
Loganville	29,689	82,708	71,956	5,937	190,290	200,600	94.86%
Lewistown	12,666	48,197	26,810	2,533	90,206	109,407	82.45%
Faithburg	109,033	215,368	192,062	21,806	538,269	1,966,638	27.37%
CURRENT YEAR COSTS	260,324	825,887	503,152	52,062	1,641,425	3,102,227	

Type of graphic: ____________________

2. Using the preceding job cost analysis, design a graphic to show the percentages of the various job cost factors.

Type of graphic: ____________________

NAME

EXERCISE 6-10: CRITIQUING AN ACCOUNTANT'S BROCHURE

The following text is from a gatefolded (eight-panel) brochure of Glen M. David, CPA, MBA. In the space provided, explain how the three rhetorical appeals are incorporated (or not incorporated) in each panel. Comment positively (what works) and negatively (what doesn't work).

Panel 1

GLEN M. DAVID, P.C.
Certified Public Accountant

P. O. Box 1000
Milwaukee, WI 53201

Phone: (414) 555-8620
FAX: (414) 555-3954

Panel 2

ABOUT THE ACCOUNTING PRACTICE OF
GLEN M. DAVID, P.C. . . .

After 10 years with a public accounting firm and 5 years as a controller in private industry, my aim in establishing a public accounting practice is to address the financial, managerial, and tax problems of small businesses.

In limiting the number of clients I can serve on a personal basis, I can insure a close working relationship. In other words, my clients don't get handed over to inexperienced junior accountants.

In my accounting practice, I strive to help each client make the best use of his available resources, to reach his potential, and to realize his personal and business financial goals.

Panel 3

EDUCATION

B.A. in Accounting, University of Dayton, Dayton, Ohio, 1972
M.B.A., University of Michigan, Ann Arbor, Michigan, 1980

Panel 4

EXPERIENCE—Public accounting and private industry

Accounting, accounting systems, auditing, budgeting and financial planning, business financing, business sales and acquisitions, cash-flow planning, client representation before the IRS, computer system consulting, corporate merger and reorganization, estate planning, financial forecasting, lease-buy decisions, management of data processing and accounting departments, management consulting, managing partner of an accounting firm, MAS, negotiating with banks, profit center analysis, S-corporation election, tax planning, tax return preparation (corporations, partnerships, individuals, nonprofit organizations and estates).

Panel 5

PROFESSIONAL AFFILIATIONS

Member: AICPA
MAS Division of AICPA
WACPA
WACPA Committee on Accounting Standards

Past Member: WACPA Committee on
Management of an
Accounting Practice

PROFESSIONAL LICENSES HELD

CPA in Wisconsin and Michigan

Panel 6

CONTINUING PROFESSIONAL EDUCATION

As a member of the American Institute of CPAs and the Wisconsin Association of CPAs, Glen M. David participates in continuing professional education including courses, seminars and publications designed to give up-to-date training and information on all aspects if the accounting profession.

Panel 7

BUSINESSES SERVED

- Small businesses
- Contractors
- Service Industries
- Manufacturers
- Wholesalers
- Real Estate Developers
- Nonprofit organizations

Panel 8

PERSONAL

Glen M. David is married with three children and has resided in the Milwaukee area since 1982.

Glenn is active in community organizations including the Rotary Club and Kiwanis. He is also interested in home gardening projects.

CHAPTER 7

How Accountants Write

OVERVIEW Because accountants grapple with intricate accounting theories, complex rhetorical situations, professional and legal constraints, and conflictive purposes, they risk sending muddled messages to users who need information to make important financial decisions. This chapter focuses on rhetorical, stylistic, and grammatical choices available to accountants. It teaches the accountant-writer to:

- Apply the principles of accuracy and completeness expected of accounting professionals;
- Ensure reader understanding;
- Compose an organized, coherent message;
- Use correct grammar and punctuation to clarify information, and to promote and project a professional image;
- Select language appropriate to the accountant's purpose, audience, and occasion.

GOALS

◆ Cultivate a reader-based attitude.
◆ Develop strategies to improve readability.
◆ Correct common errors of grammar and punctuation.

KEY TERMS

Agreement Consistency in number, person, and gender.
Diction Usage; appropriate word choice.
Doublespeak Misleading, euphemistic, confusing, or self-contradictory language.
Grice's Maxims Four principles of effective and efficient communication.
Jargon Terms specific to a profession but not always understood by nonprofessionals.
Noun string A series of nouns that modify another noun.
Reader-based prose Writing that considers reader or user needs.
Scope The parameters of what will and will not be discussed.

Syntax The order of words, phrases, and clauses.

Writer-based prose Writing that is solely from the writer's point of view, with no regard for user needs or understanding.

Accountants: Guardians of Language

The public is used to thinking of accountants as professionals who do taxes, consult with management, evaluate computer software and hardware, analyze financial data, advise clients about financial planning—in short, accountants are those who involve themselves in anything that concerns finances. And accountants are keenly aware of the unavoidable communications gap that occurs when complex, ever-evolving theories and conflicting ever-changing tax laws are mandated by Congress, academics, the AICPA, professional societies, state boards of accountancy, and the IRS. Notwithstanding the accounting communications gap, which no single accountant can close, there is another kind of communications gap that every accountant *can* do something about: the abuse of composition principles and the misuse of language that results in **writer-based prose** (prose written without regard for user needs).

Even though accountants are considered respected guardians of financial information, they have another role in communicating that information. As transmitters of financial data and information vital to business and to individuals, their writings are characterized by a **reader-based** attitude. As guardians of language, accountants must take care to compose organized, coherent, readable messages—writing that is concrete, concise, and correct. Communicating effectively is one reason accountants must observe sound principles of composition, grammar, and punctuation. Moreover, accountants must write well to project, maintain, and protect a competent *ethos*. Users quickly lose confidence in accountants whose messages are not only incomprehensible but grammatically incompetent. Thus, guarding the English language from further deterioration preserves the language, closes the communication gap, and enhances a professional image.

Grice's Maxims: The Cooperative Principle

In analyzing communication, H. P. Grice observed a "Cooperative Principle"[1] at work that includes four maxims, known as **Grice's Maxims**. Each maxim governs communication exchanges and *assumes* that communicators want to get through to their audiences in the most effective and efficient ways possible.

The First Maxim: Quantity

1. "Make your contribution as informative as is required (for the current purposes of the exchange)."
2. "Do not make your contribution more informative than is required."

Accountants want to give users what they need to know, but not more than they need to know. Furnishing superfluous information would not only waste the user's time, but could also result in divulging more information than is prudent. By way of illustration, Mark A. Pridgeon, in "Strategies for Handling IRS Audits," advises "Do not volunteer information. A basic rule in dealing with the [Internal Revenue] Service is not to volunteer information; provide only the information the agent specifically requests."[2]

The Second Maxim: Quality

1. "Do not say what you believe to be false."
2. "Do not say that for which you lack adequate evidence."

A look at AICPA's disciplinary actions proves the wisdom of this maxim. The AICPA's "Rules of Conduct" require that the accountant report only what he or she knows to be true. Rule 102—Integrity and Objectivity states, "A member shall not knowingly misrepresent facts. . . ."[3] Members can be admonished or even expelled for lying. A case in point is the Washington, D.C., CPA who "was found guilty of violating the Institute's Acts Discreditable Rule and was admonished. The violation involved his indicating in 1982 on an internal data sheet for an employer for whom he was working part-time that he had been employed by one of the eight largest firms for two years, when, in fact, he had not."[4]

Regarding the second part of this maxim, GAAS states in its section on field work:

> Sufficient competent evidential matter is to be obtained through inspection, observation, inquiries, and confirmations to afford a reasonable basis for an opinion regarding the financial statements under examination.[5]

The Third Maxim: Relevance

1. "Be relevant."

The accountant's communication should focus on his or her purpose, user needs, professional mandates, and genre requirements. Just as a seminar on S Corporations would be expected to cover various aspects of special tax effects related to S Corporations, so all accounting communication should be pertinent and free of extraneous, irrelevant matter.

The Fourth Maxim: Manner

1. "Avoid obscurity of expression."
2. "Avoid ambiguity." Although accountants strive to avoid ambiguity when communicating, they deliberately violate this maxim in the standard wording of cover letters to compilation, review, and audit reports. Perceptions of ambiguity depend on the knowledge of the user; CPAs, bankers, and financial analysts do not find certain standard phrases ambiguous, while unknowledgable stockholders might.
3. "Be brief." Avoid unnecessary wordiness or tediousness.
4. "Be orderly."[6]

Although all four of Grice's Maxims are necessary to successful communication effort, this chapter discusses the Second, Third, and Fourth Maxims, which should characterize the writings of accountancy. Looking ahead into this chapter, you can see how the topics fall within the **scope** of the latter three maxims:

Second Maxim: Quality "Do not say what you believe to be false." (Doublespeak)
Third Maxim: Relevance "Be relevant." (Scope, Doublespeak)
Fourth Maxim: Manner
- "Avoid obscurity of expression." (Grammar, diction, syntax, concreteness, readability, logical lapses, transitions, unity, jargon, nominalizations, noun strings, prepositional strings, multiple negatives)
- "Avoid ambiguity." (Referents, transitions, coherence, modifiers)
- "Be brief." (Readability, conciseness, density, wordiness, sentence combining, editing)
- "Be orderly." (Grammar, structure, outlining, paragraphs, transitions, starting, concluding, parallelism, spelling, punctuation)

Macro-Composition: A Framework for Communication

Organized writing implies that its writer is a logical thinker, just as disorganized writing implies that its writer is a fuzzy thinker. Rather than being a jumble of random, unconnected thoughts, reader-based prose is orderly and easy to follow at the macro level. Outlining (before, during, or after writing) creates a framework for the building blocks of your composition. Forecasting your organization sets up reader expectation, and effectively concluding your document leaves your reader with more than a rehash of what you have just covered.

Paragraphs are the building blocks that fill in your framework, but to make your document coherent—to enable your reader to follow your train of thought—means to use connective techniques between paragraphing (*inter*paragraphing) and within paragraphs (*intra*paragraphing).

Readability is also improved by conciseness. The less "fat" in your text, the less the reader has to do to grasp your message.

Organization

One key to establishing well-structured writing is to create a coherent outline. As you will see from the discussion that follows, outlining isn't the same process for all writers. This section also discusses the hardest-to-write paragraphs: the first and the last.

Outlining: Detailing Structure

One sure way to stop many writers in their tracks is to ask them to create a formal outline before they actually write a paper. English handbooks give all sorts of advice: be consistent, use parallel structure, create equal elements. Some even furnish a fill-in form for the traditional outline (see Fig. 7-1):

FIGURE 7-1
The Traditional Outline Form

I. ______
    A. ______
        1. ______
            a. ______
            b. ______
        2. ______
            a. ______
            b. ______
    B. ______
        1. ______
            a. ______
            b. ______
        2. ______
            a. ______
            b. ______
II. ______
    A. ______
        1. ______
            a. ______
            b. ______
        2. ______
            a. ______
            b. ______
    B. ______
        1. ______
            a. ______
            b. ______
        2. ______
            a. ______
            b. ______

Bill is a very organized person. He completes his research, analyzes his audience, confirms his purpose, identifies his thesis, and fills in a classic outline before he starts composing. Also pressed for an outline, Daniel works quite differently. Although he too completes his research, analyzes his audience, and confirms his purpose, he cannot generate a thesis statement. He simply stares at the empty computer screen. He can think of something to fill the I-A slot, but nothing for the I-B slot. He wants to plug in four items under A-1 but only one under A-2. Because he can't create equal elements in consistent, parallel form, he turns from the screen, discouraged.

These scenarios are hardly any surprise if you understand that some people, like Bill, prefer to think out everything they want to say before they enter a keystroke or set pen to paper. But other writers who, like Daniel, are just as competent couldn't outline their own shopping lists. These writers discover what they want to say only as they move along in their writing task. They may be able to determine the structure of their message somewhere along the way, but sometimes not until they are finished. For these "process" writers, the Move Block feature of word processors are lifesavers: you can move paragraphs around at will and then outline the communication *after the fact*. Some of these writers even resort to the tried-and-true method of cut-and-paste. The point is that writers who cannot structure their writing before the fact end up with structured compositions anyway; they just generate outlines later. It makes no difference if a writer creates an outline before starting, during, or after finishing—as long as the completed product is organized, coherent, and logical. So, if you can get all your ducks in a row before you write, or if you can line them up only after you have finished, just be sure your organization aids the flow of information to your reader.

An easy way to create an outline after writing is "reverse outlining." In the margins of your composition, write a phrase that describes the gist of each paragraph. Do *not*, however, start at the beginning. Instead, start somewhere else, picking paragraphs at random. (Proceeding from the start, paragraph by paragraph, defeats the purpose.) When all your paragraphs have been summarized, start at the beginning, reading all marginalia in order. This method reveals the logical order of your paper.

You don't have to generate a *formal* outline. You can work with paragraphs, sentences, phrases, or topics. Just take the advice of the English handbooks: be sure your elements are consistent, parallel, and more or less equal.

Fortunately, many genres of accountancy provide their own structures, such as engagement letters, resumes, management letters, and personnel manuals. Harder to organize are letters to the editor, essays, and longer letters or memos.

The following is a phrase outline for a student's oral report, titled "Automating the Accounting System at Olympic Trophy Center":

I. Introduction
   A. Background of the Olympic Trophy Center
   B. Need for Automation
      1. Problems with Paperwork
      2. Benefits of Automation
II. Discussion
   A. Comparison of Software Evaluated
      1. Dac Easy Light Checkbook Accounting
      2. At Once
   B. Recommendation of Dac Easy Light Checkbook Accounting
      1. Benefits to Accounting System
      2. Cost and Feasibility to Olympic Trophy Center

As you can see, the simple outline would be enough to talk from, and it could be adapted for a written report.

Using paragraphs, sentences, phrases, or topics, outline the article from Exercise 7-1.

Starting: Taking the First Step

Beginning a letter, report, essay, or other written communication is the most difficult part of writing for many people. The first sentence just won't materialize, so writers stare at a blank computer screen or a piece of paper as if wishing hard enough could make the elusive sentence magically appear. Why is writing the first paragraph so difficult, and what can be done about it? The good news is that nowhere is it written that introductions or opening paragraphs must be composed first. In fact, many writers who write inductively (working from detail to controlling idea) can't envision a controlling idea or thesis statement until they are well into the piece. For them, writing is *heuristic* (a discovery process), and to expect them to start at the beginning and proceed paragraph by paragraph to the end works against the way they think and write. Consequently, inductive writers start anywhere they please, even at the end, knowing they will eventually construct a coherent message.

What if you can't get started at all? The cure is to get something on screen or on paper. You can always revise written text, but you can't revise a blank computer screen or piece of paper. Here are some tips to help you get going:

1. Realize you can start anywhere in your communication.
2. Think about why you are writing. Who is the audience? What do you want them to know or to do as a result of your writing? Mapping out your goals will help you focus.
3. Force yourself to get something on screen or on paper. You can always tinker with it later.

Eventually you will write your introductory paragraph(s). Your goals should be to:

1. Establish a controlling assertion or thesis statement;
2. Define the topic;
3. Specify parameters or scope: what you will and will not discuss;
4. Focus the reader's attention;
5. Pique reader interest;
6. Set up reader expectation by forecasting the organization of your communication;
7. Convince the reader that it is in his or her best interest to continue reading;
8. Secure the goodwill of your reader;
9. Get to the point; readers shouldn't have to plod through three paragraphs before they grasp what you are talking about.

Ending: Getting Out Gracefully

Many writers have as much difficulty extricating themselves from their communication as others have in getting started. Like the long-winded speaker who promises, "In conclusion. . . ," and then rambles on for another fifteen minutes, some writers don't know when to "sit down." It's one thing to end by reemphasizing your main point, by challenging your reader to consider a fresh point of view, by spurring your reader to action. It's quite another thing to rehash what you've already stated. As William Zinsser, author of *On Writing Well*, says, "Are you summarizing because you think [the reader] is too dumb to get the point?"[7] Why not give the reader credit and end gracefully, or to put it in Richard D. Altick's terms, "Say what you have to say, and when you've said it, quit."[8]

Coherence

Most writers worry about the "flow" of their text, and rightly so. Like jumbled paragraphs, disorderly sentences perplex the reader. This section discusses connective and transitional techniques to aid coherence between and within paragraphs.

Paragraphs: Ordering Sentences

Imagine trying to read a five-hundred page book without chapter divisions, or a twenty-page report without sections. How far would you get before feeling fatigued?

Books are divided into chapters, and reports are sectioned off for the same reasons that texts are broken up into paragraphs:

1. Smaller portions are easier to comprehend than the whole.
2. Smaller portions reveal the structure of the whole.
3. A smaller portion can confine itself to one dominant idea.
4. A smaller portion can contain a developed idea.

Paragraphs constitute units of thoughts that relate to and build upon one another. Indenting paragraphs or double-spacing between paragraphs signals readers that a new idea or topic will be discussed. Once so prompted, the reader expects new, relevant information.

When paragraphing, you must consider connections between paragraphs (*inter*paragraphing) as well as links between the sentences within paragraphs (*intra*paragraphing).

Interparagraphing. Even though a paragraph is a *discrete* group of sentences, it isn't necessarily interchangeable with other paragraphs within a text. There must be a certain continuity or flow from one to topic to another. You can help your reader follow your train of thought by providing bridges or links between paragraphs. Some connecting strategies you can use include the following:

1. Use transitions between paragraphs (see pp. 198–199 for a list of transitions).
2. Repeat key words from the previous paragraph.
3. Use alternate words (e.g., pronouns or synonyms) in place of key words from the previous paragraph.
4. Refer to information from the previous paragraph.
5. State "given" or old information first in the new paragraph.
6. Present new information after the old information.

In Exercise 7-2 you will have a chance to break up text into paragraphs. Then, to test your ability to order scrambled paragraphs, do Exercise 7-3. When deciding which paragraph should follow another, look for transitions, repetition of key terms and alternate words, referrals to previous information, and old/new information, which provide clues to the ordering of the paragraphs.

Intraparagraphing. Paragraphs are composed of related sentences that build on one another to form a unit of thought, just as paragraphs together constitute a whole text. To aid the reader in comprehending the gist of each paragraph, each one should contain:

- Connectives to the previous paragraph;
- A topic sentence or mini-thesis or assertion that can be placed anywhere within the paragraph;
- Details, information, and/or examples that provide evidence to support the topic statement; and
- Sentences that focus on the paragraph topic.

In keeping with Grice's Third Maxim, "Be relevant," each sentence within the paragraph should contribute to the development of the topic or dominant idea. Consequently, a paragraph composed of only a single sentence generally cannot meet the criteria for a developed paragraph. In addition, one-sentence paragraphs strung together (as in much journalistic writing) makes for choppy reading. Conversely, overlong paragraphs can also violate paragraphing criteria. Readers find wading through dense text tiring.

To ensure coherence or flow within the paragraph, observe the following strategies:

1. Maintain consistency in person, verb tense, and number. Sudden shifts throw the reader off balance.

2. Use parallel grammatical structure.
3. Repeat key words.
4. Substitute pronouns or synonyms for previously used key words.
5. Use transitions.
6. Present old or given information before discussing new material.
7. If you set up reader expectation with an initial topic sentence, supply the expected information.
8. Discuss events in chronological order.

As you do Exercise 7-4, consider the eight tips for paragraph coherence just discussed as clues to arranging the sentences.

Transitions: Aids to Understanding

Users of financial information need guidance to follow the accountant's arguments, ideas, methodologies, evidence, and details. In short, users need everything that is involved in written communication. Informative titles, headings and subheadings, introductions, forecasting, summaries, restatement—all these help the reader apprehend the message. Even so, readers need additional guidance in negotiating the text, so that they understand the full meaning intended by the writer. Transitional devices (words and phrases) guide the reader into understanding by indicating connections occurring in sections, paragraphs, sentences, phrases, and words of a text. For example, you just now read a paragraph containing six transitional devices:

> Users of financial information need guidance to follow the accountant's arguments, ideas, methodologies, evidence, and details. *In short*, users need everything that is involved in written communication. Informative titles, headings and subheadings, introductions, forecasting, summaries, restatement—*all these* help the reader apprehend the message. *Even so*, readers need *additional* guidance in negotiating the text, so that they understand the full meaning intended by the writer. Transitional devices (words and phrases) guide the reader into understanding by indicating connections occurring in sections, paragraphs, sentences, phrases, and words of a text. *For example*, you *just now* read a paragraph containing six transitional devices.

(summing up)
(summing up)
(contrasting previous point)
(adding information)
(giving an example)
(indicating time)

Transitional devices can be categorized according to the relationship you are indicating:[9]

TO SHOW TIME After, afterward, always, as soon as, at last, before, briefly, eventually, finally, first (second, third, fourth, etc.), immediately, just now, later, next, now, often, presently, promptly, sometimes, soon, then.

TO SHOW PLACE Above, among, around, behind, below, beside, beyond, down, forward, here, in front of, inside, nearby, next to, on, on the other side, opposite, outside, over, through, under.

TO ADD AN IDEA Additionally, again, also, and, as well as, besides, for one thing, further, furthermore, in addition, lastly, likewise, more, moreover, next, plus, too.

TO EXPLAIN AN IDEA For example, for instance, in other words, in particular, namely, specifically, such as, that is, to illustrate.

TO COMPARE Analogous to, correspondingly, in like manner, in the same way, similarly, to compare.

TO CONTRAST But, conversely, despite the fact, even so, however, in contrast, nevertheless, on the contrary, on the one hand/on the other hand, otherwise, still, yet.

TO SHOW A RESULT Accordingly, as a result, consequently, for that reason, hence, then, therefore, thus.

TO EMPHASIZE AN IDEA Above all, especially, indeed, in fact, most important, most of all.

TO SUMMARIZE Finally, in brief, in other words, in short, on the whole, to sum up.[10]

For practice with transitional devices, do Exercise 7-5.

Readability

Readability researchers have long observed that rendering complex, technical reports understandable to users is a losing battle. Many readability formulas have been advanced, including Flesch, Fry, Cloze, and Fog, but such efforts, even when incorporated into computerized grammar checkers like Grammatik 5, are not as successful in ensuring readability as writers would like. The reasons? Readability formulas fail to account for

- The reader's level of interest and knowledge;
- Multiple audiences;
- The reader's trust in the accountant; and
- The particular accounting genre involved.

Revising by cutting wordiness and by combining sentences are two important ways to assure readability.

Conciseness: Pruning Verbiage

Like an orchardist who mercilessly prunes twigs and branches from trees to produce more fruit, so the writer "prunes" syllables, words, phrases, and clauses to produce more effective communication. This pruning or editing or revision is no easy task. To strip every sentence of words that do no useful work,[11] as William Zinsser recommends, is to recognize that not every word you place on screen or set to paper is sacred. Writers naturally resist striking any portion of their composition that took so much effort. And yet, revision is the key to better writing. If professional writers spend as much time editing their work as composing it, shouldn't the writer in the workplace spend time pruning as well?

The following are some problem twigs and branches that need to be cut for more concise, readable prose:

1. Use a short word instead of a long word if it can serve the same purpose.

Wordy We are experiencing a precipitation event at this point in time.

Concise It is raining today.

2. Cut passive constructions.

Less Concise The tax package was evaluated by the tax partner.

Concise The tax partner evaluated the tax package.

3. Use a word instead of a phrase.

Wordy James verified cash in an accurate and speedy manner.

Concise James verified cash accurately and speedily.

4. Avoid prepositional strings.

Wordy | Set the counter of the copier back to "0" so we can obtain an accurate count of the exact number of copies for the XYZ Corporation audit.

Concise | Set the copy counter back to "0" to get an accurate count for the XYZ Corporation audit.

5. Halve coupled words that say the same thing.

Wordy | Betty is willing and able to sit for the CPA exam at the present time.

Concise | Betty is able to take the CPA exam now.

6. Don't state the obvious.

Wordy | Attached you will find the interim financial statement which gives the current monthly operating profit.

Concise | Attached is the interim financial statement.

7. Cut empty fillers.

Wordy | <u>It is</u> apparent that the Taxpayer's Bill of Rights has been of assistance to certain aggrieved clients.

Concise | The Taxpayer's Bill of Rights has apparently helped aggrieved clients.

Wordy | <u>There seems to be</u> an infinite number of accounting packages, so <u>it is important</u> that we discover some way to decide which of them are worth taking the time to evaluate.

Concise | With innumerable accounting packages available, we must decide which are worth evaluating.

8. Make positive statements.

Wordy | We have no reason to believe that we should not consult a marketing specialist.

Concise | We should consult a marketing specialist.

9. Avoid multiple negatives.

Wordy | There is no justification for your lack of consideration in not reviewing Kathryn's salary history.

Concise | How can you justify failing to review Kathryn's salary history?

10. Cut adverbs that duplicate a verb's meaning.

Wordy | We should completely stop employee pilfering.

Concise | We should stop employee theft.

11. Cut adjectives that duplicate a noun's meaning.

Wordy | We have an immediate emergency: a disk crash.

Concise | We have an emergency: a disk crash.

12. Convert clauses into phrases.

Wordy | The copier, which was on its last legs, was replaced.

Concise | The copier, on it last legs, was replaced.

13. Convert clauses into adverbs.

Wordy | We finished the market analysis with such speed that it amazed everybody.

Concise | We finished the market analysis quickly.

14. Convert verbs into nouns.

Wordy | The pressure of tax season seems to be caused by those who come in at the last minute.

Concise | Tax season pressure seems to be caused by latecomers.

15. Convert adjectives into nouns.

Wordy | That he is prompt is one of his strengths.

Concise | His promptness is one of his strengths.

16. Avoid excessive **noun strings.**

Unclear

The consulting group promised a state-of-the-art multiuser accounting, individual and corporation tax software package.

Concise and Clear

The consulting group promised an updated accounting and tax package that can accommodate all of our users.

Obviously, pruning is an integral part of writing clear prose. And pruning, like writing, takes effort. As William Zinsser says,

> Writing is hard work. A clear sentence is no accident. Very few sentences come out right the first time, or even the third time. Remember this as a consolation in moments of despair. If you find that writing is hard, it's because it *is* hard. It's one of the hardest things that people do.[12]

Using the sixteen ways of simplifying prose, do Exercise 7-6.

Sentence Combining: Tinkering with Text

This section covers sentence combining. Sentence combining helps you correct choppy sentences. Sentence combining helps you reduce redundant information. Sentence combining helps you enhance the readability of your text. Sentence combining helps you improve reader comprehension of your text.

Did you find the preceding paragraph choppy and tedious? Sentence-combining strategies can improve readability of the passage as follows:

> In this section, you will learn sentence-combining strategies that correct choppiness and reduce redundant information, and improve the readability of the text for easier reader comprehension.

Besides improving the "flow" of the passage, the revised version reduces the text by 30.76 percent *without* losing any meaning or emphasis.

According to the writers of *Style and Readability in Technical Writing: A Sentence-Combining Approach*, "sentence combining works because it taps the innate ability of language users to tinker with expression until they get it right."[13] The authors show how writers can choose from several sentence-combining strategies to "tinker" with their prose:[14]

1. Combine by deleting material from one sentence and adding it to another:

Original

The report points out the advantages of computerizing a building contractor's business. The report also points out the disadvantage of computerizing a building contractor's business.

Revise by Deleting and Adding

The report points out the advantages and disadvantages of computerizing a building contractor's business.

2. Combine by using relative pronouns such as *that*, *which*, *who*, and *whose*:

Original

The "Basic Builder" software performs cost accounting. Cost accounting is an important feature of "Basic Builder." Cost accounting helps the company monitor its costs by the job. Cost accounting also helps the company monitor its profits by the job.

Combine by Using Relative Pronouns

The "Basic Builder" software performs cost accounting, <u>which</u> is an important feature. Cost accounting helps the company monitor its costs and profits by the job.

3. Combine by using appositives:

Original

"Drawbase 5000" is an architectural-design computer program. "Drawbase 5000" calculates planning estimates. "Drawbase 5000" also calculates cost estimates.

Combine by Using Appositives

"Drawbase 5000," <u>an architectural-design computer program</u>, performs planning and cost estimates.

4. Combine by converting verbs to *-ing* and *-ed* forms (participles):

Original

The software costs $1,695. The software keeps track of job costs. The software keeps records of phase costs. The software provides spreadsheets. The spreadsheets are used for cost estimating. The spreadsheets are also used for referencing.

Combine by Using Participles

Costing $1,695, the software keeps records of job and phase costs, and also provides spreadsheets for cost estimates and referencing.

5. Combine by using *and*, *but*, *for*, *nor*, and *or* (coordinating conjunctions).

Original

Scheduling a construction job requires breaking the job into a number of phases. Scheduling a construction job requires determining which phases precede other phases. Scheduling a construction job also requires linking timed phases in a chronological order.

Combine by Using Coordinating Conjunctions

Scheduling a construction job requires breaking the job into a number of phases, determining which phases precede other phases, and linking timed phases into a chronological order.

6. Combine by using subordinate clauses:

Original

The construction management division uses the software. The accounting department also uses the software. Number codes are needed for each job.

Combine by Using Subordinate Clauses

Because both the construction management and the accounting division use the software, number codes are needed for each job.

Obviously, not all the strategies will work in every case where you want to combine sentences to make them more readable and efficient. Fortunately, you have many options from which to choose. Try your hand at tinkering with sentences by using sentence-combining strategies in Exercise 7-8.

Micro-Composition: The Particulars of Communication

Grice's Maxims govern the particulars of communication. To communicate honestly involves the Second Maxim, "Do not say what you believe to be false." Accountants who hide behind doublespeak not only confuse their readers but risk damaging their own reputations as well. Accountants who don't translate accounting jargon for lay users violate Grice's First Maxim and will find themselves losing clients to accountants who do care about effective communication. Accountants violate the Fourth Maxim when they indulge in excessive nominalizations, sloppy syntax, poor grammar, illogical writing, misspelling, and inaccurate punctuation at the micro level. Such dense, obscure prose baffles and sometimes annoys readers. It also undermines the image of a competent professional.

Concreteness

Your readers are generally interested in your message. Why else would they take the time and effort to read it? Take advantage of their receptiveness by writing what you really mean, by adapting the level of technical discourse to your audience, by being precise in the words you choose, by reducing the density of the text they must negotiate. When writing, assume your readers are as interested in the communication effort as you are, and use all possible means to promote effective communication.

Doublespeak: Saying What You Mean and Meaning What You Say

Doublespeak—misleading, euphemistic, confusing, or self-contradictory language—violates two of Grice's Maxims: quality and relevance. Did anyone really believe the financially beleaguered Donald Trump, who pooh-poohed any notion that he was cornered by bankers and insisted that he had "a great relationship with the banks"? He rationalized his difficulty by saying, "the 1990s are a decade of deleveraging. I'm doing it too."[15] And what employee, when faced with being laid off, appreciates a company calling the dismissals "a career change opportunity"? Doublespeak is so pervasive in our society that a journal titled *Quarterly Review of Doublespeak* collects and publishes pages and pages of examples from business, government, education, medicine, the military, and advertising.

William Zinsser accuses American corporations of using "clutter," a form of doublespeak, "to hide its mistakes."[16] For example, IBM asks for "voluntary resignations" from its "population."[17] And Kodak's disposable camera is called instead a "single-use" camera to avoid offending environmentalists who oppose disposable products.[18]

Obviously, the motivations behind doublespeak go beyond glorifying a bank teller as a "Financial Services Specialist" or a watchmaker as an "Architect of Time." Doublespeak attempts to sidestep issues and responsibility by calling a jet engine explosion an "uncontained engine failure" and medical malpractice a "therapeutic misadventure."

Mark Patinkin, in "Making a Bad Situation Look Good," maintains that doublespeak abounds because "business people, these days, have a lot of explaining to do":[19]

> You are the bank that just took that $300 million pretax write-off. That was last quarter. Now you've lost another $300 million. Do not admit you're sinking into a sea of bad loans. Try this phrase instead: You're only having temporary "asset quality problems." As for those 1,000 employees you had to pink-slip because of massive losses? They were not laid off at all. Only "involuntarily separated."[20]

The point to this discussion is, what should an accountant do when faced with conflicting pressures to convey financial information that users may or may not want to hear? How is an accountant supposed to meet the demands of GAAP, GAAS, clients, bankers, bonders, stockholders, and his or her own self-interest—all within the same text? The answer isn't easy. Sometimes, accountants, like other people in business, must put the best face on bad situations by resorting to euphemisms, as Lee Iacocca did when confronted with Chrysler Corporation's $664 million fourth-quarter loss in 1989. He said, "I'm not in the least bit disappointed. It's called restructuring to compete in the long term."[21] Thus, accountants use terms like "negative net worth," "write-downs," and IRS's notorious "we are here to help you."

Obviously, accountants would like to be in the happy position of saying what they mean and meaning what they say. But, realities of business and accountancy being what they are, raw honesty isn't always possible or advisable.

Doublespeak works two ways: accountants need to determine when employing a euphemism serves a valid professional purpose, and when doublespeak crosses the line into outright deceit. Accountants also need to see through the doublespeak thrown at them daily. To test your ability to "translate" doublespeak into plain English, try Exercise 7-9. The terms are culled from various publications as reported in *Quarterly Review of Doublespeak*.

Jargon: Keeping It Simple

Schema, *Burke's pentad*, *Socratic dialogue*, and *doxa*—these are everyday terms to rhetoricians, but unfamiliar "academese" to most accountants. In like manner, few rhetoricians understand the specialized **jargon** of accountancy: *FASB statements*, *GAAS*, *present value*, or *cost-or-less principle*. Even more confusing to the uninitiated is accounting jargon that seems like ordinary, understandable English, but in reality denotes quite opposite meanings: *chunk*, *identity*, *lag*, or *marshall*.

To communicate effectively with users who are nonaccountants, the accountant must take pains to write, using as little jargon as possible. Because accountants often address a mixed audience (e.g., accountants, bankers, clients, stockholders), jargon must be used; nevertheless, the accountant has several options in accommodating the nonaccountant portion of the audience:

1. Use parenthetical expression.

   We use the *chunk* method of sampling (not based on probability) rather than a random method of sampling.

2. Set the explanation off as an appositive.

   The *lag*, the time between the receipt and the deposit of cash, needs to be shortened.

3. Use definitional techniques geared to a general audience (see pp. 129–131).

Diction: Choosing the Appropriate Word

With well over 155,000 words to choose from,[22] it is no small wonder that writers agonize over **diction**—the selection of just the right words that convey the exact meaning intended. Since accountants are noted for their precision, an educated reader would be surprised if an accountant wrote,

> "I ensure you that this procedure insures that internal control measures are initiated."

Insures is appropriate only when discussing insurance. The writer should have said,

> "I *assure* you that this procedure *ensures* that internal control measures are initiated."

While no one except Samuel Johnson could be expected to read a dictionary cover to cover, you can ensure better English usage if you take the time to master the distinctions between often confused words in Exercise 7-10.

Nominalizations: Increasing Density

When you first began writing in elementary school, and long into high school and even college, you probably favored the English teacher who gave assignments by page count rather than by word count. Why? Because you stumbled onto nominalizations, ways of making short words longer with minimal effort. By converting enough verbs and adjectives into nouns, you could write longer assignments using fewer words.

By adding suffixes such as *-ance*, *-ence*, *-ion*, *-ment*, *-ness*, or *-ancy* to verbs you can increase the letter count by 22 percent, 50 percent, even a whopping 100 percent, automatically increasing the density of your text (see Fig. 7-2a).

Adding certain suffixes such as *-ness*, *-ence*, *-ity*, *-cy*, or *-ism* to adjectives also creates nominalizations (see Fig. 7-2b).

FIGURE 7-2
Increasing Text Density with Nominalizations

Verb	*Nominalization*	*% Increase*
act	act*ion*	100%
astonish	astonish*ment*	50%
manage	manage*ment*	66%
contain	contain*ment*	57%
reduce	reduct*ion*	50%
exist	exist*ence*	80%
transport	transport*ation*	55%
produce	product*ion*	66%
alert	alert*ness*	80%
account	account*ancy*	57%
maintain	mainten*ance*	50%
appear	appear*ance*	66%

(a)

Adjectives	*Nominalizations*	*% Increase*
great	great*ness*	80%
quick	quick*ness*	80%
professional	professional*ism*	25%
brief	brev*ity*	75%
sweet	sweet*ness*	80%
probable	probabil*ity*	37%
specific	specific*ity*	37%
convenient	conveni*ence*	22%

(b)

But the percentage of increased letters due to nominalizations is nothing compared with the wordiness many nominalizations create. Because you transform verbs and adjectives into noun forms, they can no longer function as verbs and adjectives in their sentences:

(verb) (adjective)
To impress your clients, you should cultivate a professional image. (10 words)

(nominalization)
To make an impression on your client, you should cultivate an image that exudes professionalism. (15 words)
(nominalization)

Notice that the two nominalizations cause a 42 percent and 25 percent increase in *letters* plus a 50 percent increase in *words*. The word count increases because any time you use a nominalization you create extra words needlessly. Why? Because nominalizations are nouns that function less effectively in sentences than verbs and adjectives do. Nominalizations cause the following changes in the preceding example:

- Converting *impress* into *impression* forces the nominalization to become a direct object for a new verb, *make*.
- *Client* can no longer be the direct object of *impress*. Instead, *client* becomes the object of the newly created preposition, *on*.
- *Professional* can no longer modify *image*. Instead, a clause is created with *professionalism* as its direct object.

You can see by this example that nominalizations tend to beget more nominalizations, not to mention prepositional phrases. So now you know why nominalizations are so highly prized by students who are worried about word and page counts.

The point is that active verbs are more efficient and can carry more of the meaning and weight of the sentence than inert nominalizations can. And adjectives do a better job of describing and modifying things than wooden nominalizations can. Converting nominalizations back to verb forms and adjectives in the following example shows how verbs and adjectives do their jobs effectively, thereby reducing density and increasing readability:

Ms. Philips finally came to the realization about the sensibleness and the necessity to make an incorporation of new time and billing software. (23 words)

Ms. Philips finally realized that incorporating new time and billing software was sensible and necessary. (15 words)

Getting rid of the nominalizations makes the sentence more readable, puts the emphasis where it belongs, and reduces verbiage by 65 percent.

In Exercise 7-11, try your hand at reducing wordiness while increasing readability.

Correctness

As mentioned previously, Grice's Fourth Maxim advocates avoiding obscurity and ambiguity, and recommends brief, orderly communication. This section focuses on the particulars of writing that contribute to correct, clear communication. Garbled syntax, lack of agreement between verbs and their subjects or between pronouns and their antecedents, sentence fragments, unclear referents, misplaced and dangling modifiers, logical lapses, unparallel construction, doublespeak, specialized jargon, inappropriate word choice, nominalizations, misspelled words, and erroneous punctuation tend to confuse the reader. Such errors also tend to weaken the reader's confidence in the accountant. Thus, accountants, long known for the integrity and accuracy of their financial communication, can hardly afford mistakes and confusion in their written communication. By observing common-sense rules of grammar and punctuation, you will be following Grice's Fourth Maxim for clear, concise, and orderly communication.

Syntax: Ordering Words

Clearly, computers have revolutionized the day-to-day operations of accountancy. Who fills out tax returns by hand or typewriter anymore? Who generates letters on a typewriter? But with the manifold blessings of tax, accounting, and word processing software comes the specter of **syntax** errors, or garbled word order. Such computer-generated errors happen something like this:

The writer enters the original sentence:

> The project will be completed by the due date of September 11, just one week later than the due date of September 4, the date I agreed to originally.

The writer decides to change the sentence to read:

> I will complete the project by September 11, just one week later than planned.

Unfortunately, by manipulating the text on a word processor (inserting words and closing up the sentence), the writer inadvertently creates a syntax error:

> I will be complete the project by September 11, just one week later than originally planned.

Consequently, what looks like a grammatical error is really a word processing error. However, the reader doesn't know that. He or she sees only ungrammatical construction, which reflects badly on the writer.

This is not to say that writers aren't capable of generating syntax errors all by themselves, without the aid of word processors. One common cause of confused word order that careful editing should catch is misspelled words and typos:

> White skimming through *Barron's*, I found and ad for Republic Bank of Long Island which touted a strong industrial rating.

Neither word processing errors, nor misspellings, nor typos account for the baffling word order in this student example:

> How much sales were increased by this ad is too new for any marketing researcher to have actual percentage of increase.

To be charitable, you can assume the student knew what she was talking about. Regrettably, she was unable to convey her message to her readers. In rereading the passage, you get the idea that an ad hadn't been out long enough for market researchers to assess its effectiveness, but the reader has to work hard to ferret out that meaning.

The student writers of the following passages weren't able to communicate clearly either:

> With diagrams and steps drawn, almost anyone can set up a system that is comparable and capable of broadcasting any multimedia presentation.

> If he doesn't get very excited or seen to say anything that stirs the viewer or listener, than he isn't doing a very good job.

> If the U.S. lowered its capital gains tax, we to could increase are market share.

> Giving competitive advantages, lower capital gains countries invest in technology, research and development, and their labor force with these advantages other countries can achieve economies of scale.

In a classroom situation, students who are unable to communicate (or edit) effectively get a lower-than-desired grade, numerous rewrite "opportunities," and trips to the writing lab. But in the workplace, writers who can't communicate clearly find themselves receiving few job offers, being passed over for promotion, or losing clients.

Whether syntax errors are caused by word processing, misspelling, typing, or hasty composing, how do you catch muddled word order before your professor or employer or client does? These self-editing tips should help:

1. Run your text by a grammar checker and a spell-checker to catch mechanical and typographical errors. Understand, however, that checkers can spot only the errors they are programmed to check. Nothing can take the place of a human editor.
2. Read your work *out loud*, preferably to someone else, or at least to yourself.[23] Read slowly enough to enunciate each word clearly. Often, your ear will catch syntax errors as you read aloud. Your ear tends to hear what your eyes can't see.
3. Let some time pass before you review your text.
4. Review lengthy passages in shorter segments.
5. Read sentences and paragraphs out of order.
6. Allow sufficient time for revision, even for short correspondence.

Develop a reviewing procedure and stick to it, whether for a lengthy report or a short memo. Accountants can no more afford syntax errors in their writing than they can afford mathematical errors in their financial statements.

Agreement: Being Consistent in Number

Agreement involves consistency in number between verbs and their subjects, and between pronouns and their antecedents.

Verbs and Their Subjects. Plural verbs—such as *are*, *were*, *speak*, and *count*—follow plural subjects; singular verbs—such as *is*, *was*, *speaks*, and *counts*—follow singular subjects, regardless of modifying words or phrases. Notice that the subjects agree in number with their verbs in the following examples:

1. The Big-Six accounting firms command a majority of the market for accounting services.
2. The benefits of growth affect all members of small accounting firms.
3. Traditionally, a professional—such as a physician, lawyer, or accountant—discourages blatant advertising, but *Bates v. State Bar of Arizona* confirms a professional's right to advertise.
4. Either the cost accounting course or the business ethics seminar counts as an upper-level requirement.
5. Both accounting professors assign weekly case studies.
6. Neither the senior accountant nor the junior partners want electronic tax filing at this time.
7. The partnership agrees to the audit provisions.
8. There are numerous seminars that grant CPE credits.
9. Some former partners who were once with Big-Six firms are striking out on their own; they still find that accounting is an ever-changing, challenging profession.
10. $1,000 is the cost of the software update.
11. *Accounting Principles* by Fess and Warren is in its 17th edition.

Pronouns and Their Antecedents. A plural pronoun such as *their* refers to a plural antecedent (a word to which the pronoun refers); singular pronouns such as *his*, *her*, and *its* refer to a singular antecedent. Notice in the following examples that the pronouns agree not only in number but also in gender:

1. The accounting firm must determine the message it wants prospective clients to hear.
2. If the firm has members adept at public speaking, they should be encouraged to represent the firm by speaking before outside groups.

3. The conscientious accountant ensures that his or her communication can be understood by the user.
4. The partner-in-charge, Mr. Striker, will hold a meeting in his office this coming Thursday.
5. Neither the junior partner nor the senior partner agree on his proposed strategies.
6. All who favored the new proposal signed their names to it.
7. Anyone could warm up to the idea, once it was explained to him or her.
8. Parrott, Finch, and Dove, PA will host a tax update seminar for its clients in December.

To test your command of subject-verb agreement and pronoun-antecedent agreement, do Exercise 7-12.

Sentence Fragments: Avoiding Nonsentences

Phrases lacking a subject and/or a verb, and certain types of clauses (containing a subject and a verb) constitute nonsentences called sentence fragments. If you read a sentence fragment out loud, it usually *sounds* like a nonsentence, as in this fragment: "Since I struggled with an advanced cost accounting course." Sentence fragments are unacceptable in most professional writing. However, there is one major exception; sentence fragments are acceptable when answering a question posed for rhetorical effect:

> Why should taxpayers be aware of the Taxpayer's Bill of Rights? Because taxpayers need to know when the Internal Revenue Service has overstepped its authority.

The underlined portion is a sentence fragment. It can't stand alone because it opens with a subordinating conjunction ("because") and contains no *main* subject or verb. Even though answering the question by means of a fragment is acceptable, it can be corrected by simply deleting "because":

> Taxpayers need to know when the Internal Revenue Service has overstepped its authority.

The following sentences in the imperative mood (commands) may look like sentence fragments because they lack subjects. Nevertheless, they are true sentences because the subjects are "understood":

> (You) Secure the clamp before engaging the paper feed.
> (You) Push button "A" before starting the fax transmission.

Resume job descriptions also contain sentences that look like fragments, but which also contain "understood" subjects:

> (I) Performed job costing analysis.
> (I was) Promoted to supervisor of thirty junior accountants.

In the left-hand column of Figure 7-3 are sentence fragments. The middle column states the reasons for the nonsentences, and the right-hand column illustrates a corrected version.

From these examples, you can see several ways of correcting sentence fragments:

- Eliminate the introductory relative pronouns (*that*, *what*, *which*, *who*, *whose*, *whomever*).
- Delete the introductory subordinating conjunctions (*after*, *although*, *as*, *because*, *before*, *if*, *once*, *since*, *that*, *though*, *till*, *unless*, *until*, *when*, *whenever*, *where*, *wherever*, *while*).
- Recast the sentence to insert subject and/or verb.
- Add words before or after the fragment to make a complete sentence.
- Hook the fragment to the preceding sentence by means of a dash, comma, parentheses.

Sentence Fragments	*Reason*	*Correction*
That supporting information comes mostly from Government Accounting Office reports.	Relative pronoun introduces subordinate clause.	Supporting information mostly comes from Government Accounting Office Reports.
Submitting the accompanying report, titled "An Improved Tax Collection System."	No main subject or verb.	I submit the accompanying report, titled "An Improved Tax Collection System."
That is, to reduce the rapidly increasing rate of noncompliance.	No main subject: infinitive phrase.	A possible solution is to reduce the rapidly increasing rate of noncompliance.
Electronic filing being the best solution possible.	No main verb.	Electronic filing is the best solution possible.
And to shut down the system prematurely.	No subject; infinitive phrase.	Budget cuts force us to reduce power usage and to shut down the system prematurely.
Integrating the new software package with the old hardware.	Participial phrase; no subject or verb.	Integrating the new software package with the old hardware seems the only sensible solution.

FIGURE 7-3
Correcting Sentence Fragments

To practice identifying and repairing sentence fragments, do Exercise 7-13.

Referents: Clarifying Who and What

One cause of communication gaps is misuse of the pronoun, a word that substitutes for a noun. Obscure and unclear reference to the pronoun's antecedent causes confusion, as in these passages:

Unclear The drainage system can be repaired by replacing the pipe and by rebuilding the floor so that it is at a slant, and at the bottom of this, place a new drain.

Problems What is the antecedent for "it"? The pipe or the floor? Does "this" refer to the bottom of the pipe, or of the floor?

Unclear This report focuses on racism, affirmative action, and reverse discrimination in the workplace. It has become a controversial topic.

Problem Does "it" refer to the report, to racism, to affirmative action, or to reverse discrimination?

Unclear The completion report for this project needs revision; I now know exactly what needs mending. I felt this was important to bring up due to time pressures.

Problem Does "this" refer to the report, the project, the revision, or what needs mending?

Unclear The comptroller informed the auditor that he had yet to sign the confirmation letters.

Problem Which "he" needs to sign the letters? The comptroller or the auditor?

You must be certain that the antecedent is clear, especially when using the following referents:

PRONOUNS he, she, it
RELATIVE PRONOUNS who, that, whom, whose, which, whichever, whatever, what, such
DEMONSTRATIVE PRONOUNS that, this, these, those

To test your ability to determine referent problems, do Exercise 7-14.

Modifiers: Changing Meaning

In written communication, placement of phrases, implied clauses, and other modifying expressions can make all the difference in meaning:

The folders should be filed in the cabinets with green labels.

In this case, the folders, not the cabinets, have green labels. Thus, the prepositional phrase, "with green labels," should be moved nearer to the word it modifies, "folders":

The folders with green labels should be filed in the cabinets.

Another example of a misplaced modifier involves fire fighters' oxygen masks:

Do not wear breathing apparatus with a beard, sideburns, or glasses.

Obviously, oxygen masks do not wear beards, sideburns, or glasses. Therefore, the sentence should be recast to read:

Do not wear breathing apparatus if you have a beard, sideburns, or glasses.

Even one misplaced word can change meaning:

Booting up the system can damage the computer repeatedly.

Actually, booting up the system is repeated, not damage to the computer. (Presumably, the computer can be damaged only once.) Hence, the modifier should be moved closer to the word it modifies:

Booting up the system repeatedly can damage the computer.

If a long modifier is placed between the subject and predicate, the reader can lose track of the gist of the sentence:

Management feels, despite budget cutbacks, loss of two key clients, and an expensive computer system overhaul, that we will weather the current financial crisis.

Relocating the phrases that separate the subject and predicate aids reader understanding:

Despite budget cutbacks, loss of two key clients, and an expensive computer system overhaul, management feels that we will weather the current financial crisis.

When participial, gerund, and infinitive phrases, or implied clauses lack something to modify, they are said to "dangle":

DANGLING PARTICIPLE	Booting up the system, the program was reactivated.
DANGLING GERUND	By booting up the system, the program was reactivated.
DANGLING INFINITIVE	Unable to boot up the system, the program couldn't be activated.
DANGLING IMPLIED CLAUSE	Although faced with a cursor in the "stuck" position, booting up reactivated the program.

In the four preceding examples, *who* booted up the system? Jack did, so the sentences should be recast as follows:

PARTICIPLE	Booting up the system, Jack reactivated the program.
GERUND	By booting up the system, Jack reactivated the program.
INFINITIVE	Able to boot up the system, Jack reactivated the program.
IMPLIED CLAUSE	Although faced with a cursor in the "stuck" position, Jack was able to reactivate the program.

To hone your ability to identify and correct misplaced and dangling modifiers, do Exercise 7-15.

Logical Lapses: Making Sense

One of the more amusing examples of writer-based prose is the logical lapse. The sentence can be grammatical and can make perfect sense to the writer, but to the user it can be cause for hilarity. But what is funny to the user is not so funny to the embarrassed writer. Sometimes the cause for such gaffes is faulty translation into English, such as these signs in English from foreign countries:[24]

For your convenience, we recommend courteous, efficient self-service. (Hong Kong supermarket)

If this is your first visit to the USSR you are welcome to it. (Moscow hotel room)

Ladies are requested not to have children in the bar. (Norwegian cocktail lounge)

Please do not feed the animals. If you have suitable food, give it to the guard on duty. (Budapest zoo)

Other times the cause is the dangling modifier:

DANGLING	Unable to accept the audit engagement, a letter of regret was sent to the client.
CORRECTED	Because we were unable to accept the audit engagement, we sent a letter of regret to the client.
	OR
	We sent a letter of regret to the client because we were unable to accept the audit engagement.

Whatever the cause, logical lapses find their way into print, into the media (remember J. Danforth Quayle's famous "What a waste it is to lose one's mind or not to have one," or his "I didn't live in this century"?), and more commonly into writing instructors' hands, as evidenced in these logical lapses culled from student papers:

Silence in the artery is heard through the stethoscope before inflation of the cuff. (Can "silence" be heard?)

The word "on" should appear in Area A of Diagram 1. The word "off" should disappear. (Shouldn't "off" disappear before "on" can appear?)

Use food coloring (one drop at a time) and mix before adding. (Quite a trick if you can pull it off.)

Remove the metal canister (detector) from the box without removing anything from it. (Say again?)

If a string is damaged or broken, a new one should be replaced. (The string manufacturers would be pleased.)

A holder approaches the calf from its rear backside. (As opposed to its front backside?)

As is the case many times, your records are always different from the bank's records. (Implies a new meaning for "always.")

Given human frailty for slips of the tongue in speech and slips of the pen (or computer keys) in writing, how can logical lapses be avoided? Try these suggestions:

1. If possible, have someone else read the manuscript before you hand it in or mail it. The reader need not be an English major to catch logical lapses.
2. Get away from your text, preferably overnight. You will more likely catch logical lapses when you return to the manuscript refreshed.
3. Read the paragraphs out of order. (e.g., read paragraph 3, then 6, then 1, etc.).
4. Proofread lengthy manuscripts in sections.
5. Never attempt to proofread your work just after writing it. Students who start, complete, and proof a writing assignment the night before a paper is due are likely to contribute to the instructor's collection of logical lapses.

Parallel Construction: Being Consistent with Structure

Whether it involves words or sentences, subheadings or headings, infinitive phrases or entire clauses, parallel construction means being consistent when using equivalent elements. But parallelism involves more than merely balancing grammatical elements within sentences or paragraphs:

1. Parallel construction pleases the "ear" rhetorically.
2. Information is more easily remembered because of parallel construction.
3. Unity of ideas is improved.
4. Also helping coherence, tying ideas from one sentence to another.
5. Indicates equal emphasis.
6. Also to contrast ideas.

Of course, the preceding list is anything but parallel in construction, as the corresponding sentence patterns for the above sentences and phrases illustrate:

1. subject–verb–direct object
2. subject–verb–subject complement–prepositional phrase
3. subject–verb–subject complement
4. verb phrase–verb phrase–prepositional phrases
5. verb–direct object
6. infinitive phrase (*to* + verb + object)

One option in revising the list for parallelism is to use a subject–verb–direct object sentence pattern:

> But parallel construction goes beyond merely balancing grammatical elements within sentences or paragraphs. Parallelism also
> (subject)
>
> (verb) (direct object)
> 1. pleases the "ear" rhetorically;
>
> (verb) (direct object)
> 2. renders information more easily remembered;
>
> (verb) (direct object)
> 3. improves unity of ideas;
>
> (verb) (direct object)
> 4. helps coherence by tying ideas from one sentence to another;
>
> (verb) (direct object)
> 5. indicates equal emphasis; and
>
> (verb) (direct object)
> 6. contrasts ideas.

Parallel construction involves elements within sentences, paragraphs, and entire texts. Starting at the sentence level, look at the balanced, parallel elements in these examples:

VERBS Rather, we think the profession should work to <u>seek</u> uniformity in state regulation, <u>eliminate</u> the differences that exist and <u>promote</u> the mobility of CPAs and the services they provide to the public.[25]

All CPAs are <u>examined</u>, <u>licensed</u> and <u>regulated</u> under state accountancy laws.[26]

PREPOSITIONS Particular attention should be paid to the existing state structure and current heirs. Inappropriate selection of heirs could have a disastrous impact <u>on</u> the estate—and <u>on</u> the family business.[27]

RELATIVE PRONOUNS The new code of ethics should be reviewed by <u>those who</u> will enforce the policies as well as by <u>those who</u> will be subject to the policies.

SUBORDINATE CONJUNCTIONS In addition, the edit program provides an audit trail, so if an error is discovered later, or even if there is the suspicion of an error, an accounting clerk can track down the source.[28]

INFINITIVE PHRASES XYZ Corporation must try to distribute the new policies and to explain them to all affected parties.

PREPOSITIONAL PHRASES For the "tone at the top" to pervade the ethics initiative, it is important for the code to be endorsed by executives near the top of the organizational chart and by employees throughout the organization.[29]

SUBORDINATE CLAUSES Because the software program failed, and because we couldn't diagnose the problem ourselves, we were forced to call in a consultant.

CORRELATIVES Top management must not only strongly support the ethical thrust, but it should also ensure that customers, suppliers, and employees are aware of the company's emphasis on and support for an ethical environment.[30]

SENTENCES The simple truth is, the business of business is to grow. The sad truth is, most accounting software can't handle that.[31]

SERIES Recognize staff members who made outstanding contributions, including those who met tight turn-around demands, preparers with the fewest review points and managers who identified additional client service opportunities.[32]

LISTS
- Service and supply sources
  1. Review performance and responsiveness of suppliers and tax processing service staff during the crunch.
  2. Investigate alternatives to improve service or reduce cost.
  3. Send thank you letters to helpful suppliers. This can help improve response time next year.[33]

HEADINGS AND SUBHEADINGS (from IRS's "Instructions for Form 1120S"[34])

Interest and Penalties
  Late Filing of Return
  Late Payment of Tax
  Underpayment of Estimated Tax
  Failure to Furnish Information Timely

OUTLINES (Sentence outline derived from "How to Evaluate Audit Risk and Materiality"[35])

I. Introduction
II. How Audit Risk and Materiality Affect the Extent of Substantive Testing
  A. How to Quantify Audit Risk
    1. Inherent Risk
    2. Control Risk
    3. Detection Risk
    4. Measurement Model
  B. How to Make Preliminary Judgments about Materiality and Allocate Them to Financial Statement Accounts
  C. How to Evaluate Audit Findings in Light of Risk and Materiality Concepts
III. Conclusion

CHAPTERS (Chapter titles from *The Bottom Line: Inside Accounting Today*[36])

Introduction
1. Accountants and Accountability: An Overview
2. CPAs Today: Auditors, Tax Planners, Management Consultants, and More
3. Competing for Business: Marketing of Services
4. Onward and Upward: Education and Career Paths
5. Rules of the Road: Standards and Codes
6. The Auditor's Role: Expectation and Reality
7. We the People: Accounting for Government

8. A Global Economy and Technological Change
   Summary: Where Do We Go from Here
   Index

Exercise 7-16 offers you a chance to spot and correct passages containing examples of faulty parallelism.

Spelling: Getting It Letter-Perfect

Spelling errors used to be the bane of writers, publishers, and typists until spell-checkers rescued those whose brains invariably worked faster than their fingers. Since accountants are computer literate, letting writing leave the office with typographical errors (typos) announces to the reader that the accountant was either too lazy to run the spell-checker or just doesn't care about his or her work. Either way, misspellings affect an accountant's image and hence, his or her credibility.

Some writers, who fancy they can spell, wince at the thought of a spell-checker: "*I* know how to spell," they sniff, or they may say, "Spell-checkers keep you from learning how to spell." But even the best of spellers grow fatigued if poofreading a twenty-page report. As for entertaining the thought that a spell-checker keeps a writer from learning how to spell, consider that every time you run a document through the program, you are reviewing how to spell each word the checker displays as misspelled. (Incidentally, did you catch the misspelled word in this paragraph? It is "poofreading.")

Given the obvious benefits of spell-checkers, you should still be aware of some disadvantages:

1. Spell-checkers won't catch correctly spelled words used incorrectly:

   There will be a software demonstration at 2:00.
   Their will be a software demonstration at 2:00.

2. Running a spell-checker becomes tedious if you have many specialized terms or proper names not in its memory. You can add frequently used terms and names, but do so *carefully*. You wouldn't want to enter a misspelled word into your system.
3. A spell-checker works only if you remember to run it. One of Murphy's Laws has to be:

   The day you neglect to run a document past your spell-checker is the day you send out a letter that begins, "Thenk you for sending teh Jume financal statements."

4. Reviewers ordinarily proofread paper copy and are thus not able to spell-check. Copy that has already been spell-checked eases the reviewer's proofing task.
5. Spell-checkers won't distinguish between British and American spellings. Look at the following examples:

American	*British*
acknowledgment	acknowledgement
center	centre
color	colour
connection	connexion
humor	humour
judgment	judgement
offense	offence
realize	realise
theater	theatre
traveled	travelled

6. If your word processing program doesn't automatically hyphenate, you need to consult a dictionary to determine how to divide words at the end of a line. (Ragged

right margins, preferred in business correspondence, eliminate much end-of-line hyphenation.)

7. You can't assume typos in your writing will be attributed to typists. After all, your correspondence, reports, and other documents go to readers in *your* name.

In addition to owning *and running* a spell-checker, what else can you do to ensure that your copy is letter-perfect? First, own and consult a good dictionary. Second, get someone to proofread the finished document for you. You wouldn't let a tax return out of the office without being reviewed, would you? Third, remind yourself that misspelled words in your letters, memos, and other documents are analogous to presenting yourself to your audience with ketchup on your tie or shirt front.

To review your spelling, do Exercise 7-17a and Exercise 7-17b.

Punctuation: Observing GAPP (Generally Accepted Punctuation Practices)[37]

Punctuating sentences serves the same function as incorporating symbols in accounting. Without conventional symbols, financial statements would read as in the following excerpt:

Other Income and Deductions			
Interest Income		8992	dollars and 57 cents
Other Income		0	dollars and 0 cents
Interest Expense	minus	16332	dollars and 52 cents
			subtotal line
Net Income before Taxes	minus	216577	dollars and 0 cents
Provision for Income Taxes		84744	dollars and 46 cents
			subtotal line
Net Income after Taxes	minus	131832	dollars and 54 cents
BEGINNING RETAINED EARNINGS		786667	dollars and 64 cents
			subtotal line
ENDING RETAINED EARNINGS		654835	dollars and 10 cents
			totals line
Earnings (Loss) Per Share	minus	329	dollars and 58 cents
			totals line

Reading such a statement would be a tedious chore, to say the least. Therefore, accountants use the following symbols to guide users to the meaning of their communication:

$	dollar sign	========	total
.	decimal point	#	amount (as opposed to dollars)
- or ( )	negative amount	@	at
________	subtotal	%	percentage

Such symbols facilitate a more readable format for the preceding column:

Other Income and Deductions		
Interest Income	$	8,992.57
Other Income		0.00
Interest Expense		–16,332.52
		________
Net Income before Taxes		–216,577.00
Provision for Income Taxes		84,744.46
		________
Net Income after Taxes		–131,832.54
BEGINNING RETAINED EARNINGS		786,667.64
		________
ENDING RETAINED EARNINGS	$	654,835.10
		=========
Earnings (Loss) Per Share	$	–329.58
		=========

So too, writers employ conventional symbols or marks within their texts to help readers decipher their communications. To mispunctuate is to ignore the Generally Accepted Punctuation Practices (GAPP) and possibly to misguide the reader. Readers expect the same preciseness of accountants in writing that they do in accounting. Accountants who want to communicate clearly, therefore, will not punctuate with a semicolon when a comma is indicated, nor will they use an exclamation point when a period is appropriate.

Confusion reigns if the GAPP are not observed as in the preceding paragraph, deliberately mispunctuated here:

> So too! writers employ conventional symbols or marks within their texts to help readers decipher their communications? To mispunctuate is to ignore Generally Accepted Punctuation Practices ¿GAPP? and possibly to misguide the reader, Readers expect the same preciseness of accountants in writing that they do in accounting' Accountants who want to communicate clearly: therefore; will not punctuate with a semicolon when a comma is indicated! nor will they [use an exclamation point when a period is appropriate:

Like other writers, accountant-writers use suitable punctuation to imitate the emphasis of the human voice in speech, so as to clearly communicate. Some punctuation marks are straightforward and cause few problems. For example:

Periods (.) indicate a "full stop" at the end of statements, declarations, commands, and indirect quotations.
Exclamation points (!) denote strong emotion and are rarely, if ever, used in the writings of accountancy.
Question marks (?) end direct questions.
Colons (:) signal lists, clarifications, and quotations.
Dashes (—) mark parenthetical information, are used in conjunction with commas, and also indicate interruptions in thought. Dashes are often mistakenly used in place of commas.
Hyphens (-) divide syllables at the end of a line, compound words, and some suffixes and prefixes.
Parentheses ( ) signify parenthetical information.
Brackets ([ ]) indicate alterations in directly quoted text and also are used to place parenthetical information within parentheses.
Ellipsis points (. . .) mean omissions in direct quotes. Ellipsis points are rarely used in accountants' writing.
Apostrophes (') show possession in words (e.g., accountants') and take the place of letters in contractions (e.g., can't).

Commas. Most writers either overpunctuate or mispunctuate commas. As a general rule, GAPP states that you should use commas only when you have reason to do so. Some of the reasons are as follows:

1. Commas are used to separate at least three items in a series.

   Determine the limits of cost, time, space, and personnel.

   The proposal advocated selecting one overall cost driver, calculating direct labor hours, and allocating the overhead.

   Informal and journalistic writers omit the comma before the conjunction in a series (serial comma):

   Determine the limits of cost, time, space and personnel.

   Omitting the serial comma, however, often leads to confusion, which the precise accountant cannot afford. For example, suppose you recommend splitting profits three ways among partners:

Split $15,000 among Mr. Brown, Ms. White and Mr. Green.

Because the serial comma is omitted, the directive could result in this distribution:

Mr. Brown	$7,500
Ms. White	$3,750
Mr. Green	$3,750

Add the serial comma:

Split $15,000 among Mr. Brown, Ms. White, and Mr. Green.

Now the distribution is as intended:

Mr. Brown	$5,000
Ms. White	$5,000
Mr. Green	$5,000

Of course, items that ordinarily go together are not separated, even in a series:

Please put decaffeinated coffee, herbal teas, and cream and sugar on the shopping list.

2. A comma is used to separate sentence patterns (independent clauses) in a compound sentence, except for very short sentences:

   (independent clause)
   The accounting system has no work in process inventory, and the finished goods inventory value can be constructed only at year end.
   (independent clause)

   Notice that the comma precedes "and," a coordinating conjunction in this sentence. The comma also precedes any other coordinating conjunction that joins a compound sentence:

   and, but, for, nor, for, so, yet

3. A comma is used to set off introductory subordinate clauses in complex and compound-complex sentences:

   <u>Although management needs inventory figures throughout the year,</u> the accounting system has no work in process inventory, and the finished goods inventory value can be constructed only at year end.

   Such subordinate clauses begin with these typical introductory words or phrases:

   after, although, as long as, because, before, if, now that, since, though, unless, until, when, whenever, where, whether or not, while

4. A comma is used to set off nonrestrictive information. Restrictive and nonrestrictive clauses cause much confusion over punctuation. An easy way to remember that a clause needs to be set off by commas is to ask, is it relevant to the meaning of the sentence? In other words, if the sentence reads the same with or without the clause, the clause is considered *nonrestrictive* and must be set off with commas. Consider this sentence containing a nonrestrictive clause:

   Barry, who is an accounting major with an economics minor, has been accepted to the MBA program at Columbia.

   The sentence's meaning is not dependent upon the nonrestrictive clause:

   Barry has been accepted to the MBA program at Columbia.

   Since the clause is not necessary to the meaning of the sentence, it must be set off with commas as shown.

   Conversely, consider this sentence containing a *restrictive* clause:

Graduating seniors who are accounting majors will preregister for classes in room 102 of the new business building.

Not *all* seniors should preregister in room 102, only accounting majors; therefore, the clause is restrictive. That is, the meaning is *restricted* to accounting majors and requires no commas.

5. A comma is used to set off a long introductory phrase, but should be omitted after a short introductory phrase:

   By implementing a cost accounting system now, we can solve our process inventory and finished goods inventory problems.

   By now we should have had a reply to our inquiry.

6. A comma is used to set off introductory expressions used as transitional devices:

   For example, see the chart showing income variations at Sunburst Milling.

   In fact, data shows that Sunburst needs a better cost accounting system.

7. A comma is used to set off an appositive (a word, phrase, or clause placed beside a noun to explain it):

   A cost-flow assumption, one of the most important parts of any inventory valuation system, provides costs in valuing raw materials inventory.

Semicolons. Semicolons separate two or more sentence patterns (independent clauses) within a sentence:

(independent clause)
A finished goods inventory is easy to update and monitor;
it will provide a cost-of-goods-sold figure.
(independent clause)

If a comma replaced the semicolon in the preceding sentence, it would be a *comma splice*.

To avoid reader confusion, you must use semicolons in conjunction with commas when constructing lists containing commas, as in this billing statement excerpt:

> Accounting services performed during the month of February 1993 including completion of audit; preparation of financial statements for the years ended December 31, 1992 and 1991; preparation of 1992 corporate income tax returns; and 1993 Maryland personal property returns.

Because a comma is necessary to separate the date from the years, other elements that would ordinarily be separated by commas are instead separated by semicolons as shown.

For practice in punctuation, do Exercises 7-18 and 7-19.

Putting It All Together

As difficult as writing is for many people, revision is a task even more dreaded because it takes an immense amount of expertise, experience, and hard work. The list of things to consider when reviewing or editing is breathtaking:

Rhetorical Concerns	Macro Concerns	
Audience	Organization	Paragraphing
Purpose	Introduction	Transitions
Genre	Conclusion	Readability
Style	Coherence	Conciseness

Micro Concerns
- Concreteness
- Doublespeak
- Jargon
- Diction
- Usage
- Nominalizations
- Correctness
- Grammar
- Syntax
- Agreement
- Sentence fragments
- Referents
- Modifiers
- Verb tenses
- Logical lapses
- Parallelism
- Spelling
- Punctuation

As you advance in the accounting profession, you will review more and more peer and subordinate writing. Since it is easier to edit someone else's work, apply the writing skills you have learned in this chapter by editing the student paper provided in Exercise 7-21. Use the appropriate proofreading symbols shown in the Appendix. For practice in interpreting proofreading symbols, do Exercise 7-20.

Notes

[1] H. P. Grice, "Logic and Conversation," in *The Logic of Grammar*, eds. Donald Davidson and Gilbert Harman (Encino, Calif.: Dickenson, 1975), 64–75.

[2] Mark A. Pridgeon, "Strategies for Handling IRS Audits," *The Practical Accountant* (April 1987): 26.

[3] "Rule 102—Integrity and Objectivity," in "Bylaws and Implementing Resolutions of Council as amended October 15, 1981" and "Rules of Conduct of the Code of Professional Ethics as amended March 31, 1979," (New York: AICPA, 1981), 39.

[4] "AICPA Disciplinary Actions," *The CPA Letter* (April 19, 1990): 2.

[5] "Generally Accepted Auditing Standards," in "Bylaws" and "Rules of Conduct," 43.

[6] For a comprehensive discussion of the "Cooperative Principle" at work in financial statements, see Aletha Hendrickson, "How to Appear Reliable without Being Liable: CPA Writing in Its Rhetorical Context," in *Worlds of Writing: Teaching and Learning in Discourse Communities of Work*, ed. Carolyn B. Matalene (New York: Random House, 1989), 302–331.

[7] William Zinsser, *On Writing Well*, 3d ed. (New York: Harper & Row, 1985): 78.

[8] Richard D. Altick, *The Art of Literary Research*, 3d ed. (New York: W. W. Norton, 1981): 210.

[9] Only the most common of the hundreds of transitional devices are mentioned. See Victor C. Pellegrino, *A Writer's Guide to Transitional Words and Expressions* (Maui, Hawaii: Maui Arthoughts Company, [P.O. Box 967, Wailuku, Hawaii 96793], 1989) for an exhaustive yet compact listing of over one thousand transitional words and expressions.

[10] Adapted from "Transitional Expressions," Writing Center, (College Park: University of Maryland, n.d.).

[11] Zinsser, 7.

[12] Zinsser, 12.

[13] James DeGeorge, Gary A. Olson, and Richard Ray, *Style and Readability in Technical Writing: A Sentence-Combining Approach* (New York: Random House, 1984), v.

[14] The sentence-combining strategies are adapted from DeGeorge et al. *Style and Readability in Technical Writing: A Sentence-Combining Approach*. The examples are adapted from a student paper on selecting software for a building contractor.

[15] Janice Castro, "Trump Trips Up," *Time* (May 6, 1991): 46.

[16] Zinsser, 15.

[17] "Business Doublespeak," *Quarterly Review of Doublespeak* (October 1990): 1.

[18] "Business Doublespeak," 1.

[19] Mark Patinkin, "Making a Bad Situation Look Good," *Quarterly Review of Doublespeak* (January 1991): 11.

[20] Patinkin, 12.

[21] *The Champaign-Urbana News-Gazette* (14 February 1990): B-8, quoted in *Quarterly Review of Doublespeak* (April 1990): 1.

[22] *The American Heritage Dictionary of the English Language* (1980 ed.).

[23] The entire manuscript for *Writing for Accountants* was read aloud to an indefatigable CPA before it was sent to an editor. Numerous errors were caught by both the author and the hearer as a result of the oral reading.

[24] J.L.D., Ann Landers column, *Carroll County Times* (May 15, 1991): C-4.

[25] Thomas W. Rimerman, CPA, and Jerome P. Solomon, CPA, "Uniformity of Regulation—The Time Is Now," *Journal of Accountancy* (April 1991): 69.

[26] Rimerman and Solomon, 69.

[27] Barton C. Francis, CP, CFP, "Succession Planning for Closely Held Businesses," *Journal of Accountancy* (April 1991): 83.

[28] J. L. Boockholdt, CPA, "Protecting Mainframe Data from PCs," *Journal of Accountancy* (April 1991): 88.

[29] Robert B. Sweeney and Howard L. Siers, Survey: "Ethics in Corporate America," *Management Accounting* (June 1990): 35.

[30] Sweeney and Siers, 34.

[31] Computer Associates advertisement, *Computers in Accounting: 1990 Buyer's Guide and Directory* (New York: Warren, Gorham & Lamont, 1990), back cover.

[32] J. E. Osborne, "The Best Time to Plan for Next Tax Season Is Now," *Journal of Accountancy* (April 1991): 94.

[33] Osborne, 94.

[34] Internal Revenue Service, "Instructions for Form 1120S," *1990 S Corporation Income Tax Package* (n.p.: Internal Revenue Service, 1990).

[35] H. James Williams, CPA, and David N. Ricchiute, CPA, "How to Evaluate Audit Risk and Materiality," *The Practical Accountant* (October 1987): 75-89.

[36] Grace W. Weinstein, *The Bottom Line: Inside Accounting Today* (New York: New American Library, 1987): n.p.

[37] Because most writers understand conventional uses of periods, exclamation points, question marks, dashes, hyphens, parentheses, brackets, ellipsis points, and apostrophes, this section concentrates on the most misused punctuation marks: commas and semicolons. Students should refer to a good English-language handbook for rules and examples of punctuation.

NAME

EXERCISE 7-1: OUTLINING AN ARTICLE

Outline the following article from *Management Accounting*.*

KPMG Peat Marwick's "Code of Conduct"
By Larry D. Horner

Every business that develops a code of conduct has to work out what best suits its own history, operations, and needs, so I do not offer my firm's experience as a model for others to copy. Certainly large public accounting firms are very different from other businesses and differ from one another, as well. Nevertheless, there are common problems that each business faces in putting together a code, and I want to share how we coped with those we faced.

The first problem was to define our objectives. One of the strongest reasons a business organization could have for adopting a code is to make obvious and explicit what employees need to know to avoid mistakes. But in light of the extensive manuals governing employee behavior that KPMG Peat Marwick already had, in addition to the AICPA's code of ethics and the AICPA's professional standards on how to perform services, our professionals did not lack rules on appropriate conduct.

We defined three objectives:

- First, we wanted to facilitate understanding and observance of our requirements by reducing them to a brief, generalized set that covered all behavior. A concise set of rules can be internalized more easily than lengthy, elaborate directives and would complement the manuals already in place.
- Second, we wanted to have a code that also served a symbolic function—to convey what we stand for. That meant the code would have to contain some type of philosophical statement.
- Third, we wanted a code that would promote firm unity. Although this unity also would result from successfully stating what we stand for, we felt it was important to define it as a separate objective.

We started by synthesizing the ethical and behavioral directives from professional sources and our manuals to a set of very brief statements. The basic theme was the relationship between assumed responsibilities and the fundamentals that ensure quality performance in fulfilling those responsibilities. That meant our professionals had to act with integrity, obey relevant rules and regulations, be committed to developing their skills, be objective in making judgments, and give their best to their work. The set of statements we came up with was the precursor of the 12 principles in our code.

The initial draft of behavioral principles enabled us to see something that helped shape our philosophical statement. We realized that the clarity and brevity of behavioral directives could never alone be enough to achieve our goals of facilitating understanding and observance. We needed to express the rationale for the principles, meaning that our philosophical statement had to supply the rationale as well as be the primary element expressing what we stand for.

For this reason, we chose as the format for our philosophical statement/rationale a preamble that would be an integral part of our code. The idea behind the preamble was to state several truths about what we stand for that, if accepted, would make adherence to the principles necessary. The truths are:

- Our firm serves the public interest by providing our clients with the highest quality of services.
- Both the usefulness of our services and the viability of our practice depend on our credibility with those who rely on our work.
- High-quality work is the most important factor in achieving and maintaining credibility.
- Anything that undermines our reputation for dedication to the public interest diminishes our credibility.

The principles follow from the preamble because they are necessary to ensure our ethical purpose (serving the public interest), providing high-quality service to our clients, our credibility, and our economic success.

When we stepped back to examine what we had drafted, it became clear that some of the obligations in the principles applied to the firm. We also saw that for almost every obligation we had defined for individuals, there was a parallel obligation for the firm to fulfill to ensure that we were going to live up to the preamble's four truths. For example, if individuals were to be obligated to fulfill their responsibilities in accordance with applicable regulations, KPMG Peat Marwick had an obligation to adopt the policies necessary to achieve the objectives of those regulations. And if no one in the firm could act in a way that damaged the firm's credibility, KPMG Peat Marwick should not tolerate such actions.

We concluded that we needed two parallel sets of principles, one for individuals and one for KPMG Peat Marwick. Moreover, the parallel sets emphasized that those with any authority over others had to exercise that authority in a way that furthered the same principles their subordinates were supporting.

* Larry D. Horner, "KPMG Peat Marwick's 'Code of Conduct,'" *Management Accounting* (June 1990): 16–17. Reprinted by permission of *Management Accounting*, published by the Institute of Management Accountants (formerly National Association of Accountants).

Of course, the principles for individuals apply to superiors as well as to subordinates. And the obligations specified for the KPMG Peat Marwick obviously apply to those individuals with authority to set firm policy, commit firm's name, hire, and supervise others, and so forth.

One may think of individuals with such authority as management, but we deliberately chose to avoid this term. We wanted every member of the firm to be aware that KPMG Peat Marwick is an institution with vastly greater significance and performance than its management and that management members are bound by that institution's obligations.

The counterpart to our decision to use KPMG Peat Marwick was to refer to the individuals covered by the other principles as KPMG Peat Marwick people. This inclusive term applies to every person in our firm. When administrative personnel are newly hired, they are told in orientation sessions that they, too, by supporting the provision of our professional services are covered by the code. They must understand it, uphold it, and be conscious of the ways it applies to their particular responsibilities.

Other firms that set out to develop a code must define their own objectives and determine the relationship between the behavioral directives they have already communicated and those they wish to express. However, I believe everyone who pursues these endeavors gains a rewarding sense of renewed links with his or her firm's traditions and the satisfaction of reaching into the future to assure the continuity of these traditions.

NAME

EXERCISE 7-2: PARAGRAPH BREAKS AND CONNECTING STRATEGIES

The following text is an editorial from the *National Public Accountant*.* The text is exactly as published except that all paragraph breaks have been deleted. Indicate proper paragraph breaks by using the paragraph symbol (¶). In the spaces provided, identify connecting strategies.

Practice Pointers—Let Us Hear From You

Recent NPA readership surveys have indicated the Practice Pointers column to be one of the most "looked for" standard features in each issue. According to our readers, its usefulness seems to stem from the practitioner-to-practitioner forum the pages offer for sharing practice information and ideas. The tips are tried and true, practitioner-tested tools for making life a little easier. From the input we have received, the column has proved to be enormously popular with NPA readers across the country, and the demand for this type of information remains strong. Now that tax season is all but over, why not consider submitting a form or idea that helped you make it through? Keep in mind that it need not be revolutionary to help another reader in managing his or her time or practice, or in saving money. Practitioners experience many of the same day-to-day concerns in terms of practice management, promotion, client relations, organization, handling employees or sorting through the changing requirements of the tax laws. If you've developed a special technique or short-cut in any of these areas, you can be sure another reader would like to hear about it. Think over the Practice Pointers you've found most useful in the past. Chances are they were useful not because they were particularly unique but because they addressed a common problem from a fresh perspective. The item may have explained how one firm streamlined its billing procedures or organized client information, or it may have offered marketing ideas that were especially effective or a summary of complex tax information in one handy reference sheet. In publishing the material, the practitioner is not saying, "Here's an idea nobody has thought of before," but rather, "Here's something that has worked for me." Don't hesitate to share your insights and experience with your colleagues. As the 1991 tax filing season comes to a close, now may be the best time to reflect on your operation these past months and submit a practice management tip. Any and all management techniques are welcome—forms, checklists, schedules, outlines and practice aids are but a few possibilities. We are also seeking any suggestions related to running a business such as energy-saving tips, applying for loans, office procedures or equipment, etc. For your convenience this month, we've provided a handy tear-out, postage paid form. If you have a technique or idea which benefits you in your day-to-day operations, you can be sure it will benefit someone else as well. Take advantage of the postage paid form on page 44 and send in your ideas today. More than 23,000 NPA readers will be glad you did. ■

* Susan Brown Cappitelli, "Practice Pointers—Let Us Hear From You," *The National Public Accountant* (May 1991): 4. Reprinted by permission of *National Public Accountant*.

NAME

EXERCISE 7-3: ORDERING PARAGRAPHS

The following text is an advertisement from Pencil Pushers Tax Software.* The paragraphs (identified by letter) are out of order. Order the paragraphs by noting the letter in the numbered space provided at the top. Then, in the right-hand column, indicate what in the text prompted you to order each paragraph.

1-_____ 2-_____ 3-_____ 4-_____ 5-_____ 6-_____ 7-_____ 8-_____ 9-_____ 10-_____

(A) To order your free trial 1040 tax software program, call us toll free at 1-800- 333-8297. Or fax (617) 273-0575. Or write Pencil Pushers, 3 New England Executive Park, Burlington, MA 01803.

(B) You Don't Have To Be A Rocket Scientist To Try Pencil Pushers Tax Software.

(C) In effect you get the 1990 program FREE.

(D) Pencil Pushers will send you the complete 1990 1040 program free for 30 days. If you are not completely satisfied, return the program and pay nothing. If you decide to keep the package, pay us $100 which will be applied to the purchase of the 1991 program.

(E) PENCIL PUSHERS Tax Software

A Division of the Damirus Corporation

(F) So if you're serious about tax software, check out Pencil Pushers. It may be the best experiment you've ever performed.

(G) Experimenting with evaluation copies of tax programs can be a hair raising experience. With over 80 tax programs available, how do you know which program will have the chemistry that's right for you?

(H) The complete 1040 program features:

- Over 50 Federal forms and schedules
- Programs for ALL states with a tax
- Year round toll-free telephone support
- New on-line "Pick-A-State" program
- Low cost Federal and State programs:

  Federal 1040: $900; renewal: $450

  State: $200–$400; renewal: $100–$200

  Laser software additional.

* Pencil Pushers Tax Software advertisement, *EA Journal* (Spring 1991): 33. Reprinted by permission of Ken Gray, Pencil Pushers Tax Software, and the Damirus Corporation.

(I) At Pencil Pushers we believe that the best way to test a program is to use it. That's why we offer a FREE trial of our complete 1990 1040 program. It works like this.

(J)
- Other programs available include: 1120, 1120S, 1065, 1041, Fixed Assets, Tax Planning, Electronic Filing and more.
- Compatible with Nelco Inc. overlay print format.

NAME

EXERCISE 7-4: ORDERING SENTENCES INTO PARAGRAPHS

The following sentences are from the National Association of Enrolled Agents (NAEA) president's memo in the *EA Journal*—in random order.* Rearrange the sentences into coherent paragraphs. Then place the sentence letters in the spaces provided. Reordering the sentences will be easier if you first photocopy the exercise and then cut the sentences into slips of paper. After you have reassembled the sentences, indicate the paragraph breaks by placing the paragraph symbol (¶) between the appropriate sentences.

1-______ 2-______ 3-______ 4-______ 5-______ 6-______ 7-______ 8-______ 9-______

10-______ 11-______ 12-______ 13-______ 14-______ 15-______ 16-______ 17-______ 18-______

(A) I urge all of our members to be constantly alert for violations of the Taxpayer's Bill of Rights, and to advise NAEA if any are occurring in their district.

(B) The GAO has been requested by the Senate Subcommittee on Oversight of the IRS to report to Senator David Pryor, chairman, with a review of the implementation by the Internal Revenue Service.

(C) Like our Constitution's Bill of Rights, we must remain vigilant to see that all are protected.

(D) While the reason for the phone call was to set up an appointment within a reasonable time (thereby avoiding a delay of some 30 days or longer in finally hearing from the taxpayer, which frequently happened when the contact was originated by writing), the practice of obtaining information without providing the rights is contrary to the new rules.

(E) This practice imposes a severe hardship on taxpayers, whereby they may never look ahead to living any kind of a satisfactory life.

(F) However, I did point out to the representative of the GAO two areas which we had brought to the attention of the IRS at our annual liaison meeting in December.

(G) We will be certain to call these to the attention of the Internal Revenue Service National Office.

(H) In some cases, the amount of the installment payment being imposed was not even enough to pay the interest on the liability.

(I) I am positive that Commissioner Goldberg is as interested in enforcing this bill of rights as are we Enrolled Agents.

(J) I was glad to be able to advise that from all reports I had received the consensus was, as a general practice, the IRS was, in the main, following the rules contained in this bill.

(K) The IRS representatives at the liaison meeting assured us that these areas would be addressed with advice going out to the districts in due course.

(L) The Taxpayers' Bill of Rights—It's Working

(M) A recent telephone call from the General Accounting Office brought to my attention the fact that Congress is following this legislation closely to see that the Internal Revenue Service is abiding by the rules of conduct laid down therein, and seeing if further safeguards of the public should be added.

(N) One was the practice in some districts of tax auditors and revenue agents making their first contact with a taxpayer selected for audit by telephone in order to set up an appointment, and using that call to solicit information about the taxpayer, his activities, etc., without first providing the taxpayer with his rights, as provided in the Taxpayer Bill of Rights.

(O) NAEA feels that a telephone contact is permissible to set up an appointment, but only after sending by mail official notice of the pending examination together with the required notice of their rights, including the right of representation.

(P) In addition, the citizen has no way of knowing who the caller is, and if, in fact, the caller is even a representative of the IRS.

(Q) By Howard J. Sobelman, EA

(R) The other item concerned the practice in some districts of requiring taxpayers to sign waivers of the statute for collection of up to 25 years in order to execute a payment agreement.

* Howard J. Sobelman, EA, "The Taxpayers' Bill of Rights—It's Working," *EA Journal* (Spring 1991): 2. Reprinted by permission of Howard J. Sobelman, and Deborah B. Vieder, Managing Editor, *EA Journal*.

NAME

EXERCISE 7-5: INCORPORATING TRANSITIONAL DEVICES

Assume that the following passage (about Total Quality Management) needs transitional devices to aid reader understanding. Selecting from the transitional devices listed on pages 198–199, or inventing your own, insert transitional words or phrases in the spaces provided.

In a presentation to XYZ Corporation in February 1993, the head of operations, John Wallace, identified problem areas that Total Quality Management could address. ______________________(1), he cited a lack of communication between management and employees, ______________________(2) a lack of recognition for employees. Implementing Total Quality Management, ______________________(3), can solve these problems and help XYZ Corporation improve employee production and satisfaction.

Although Total Quality Management is a relatively new concept as a whole, its components have been around for many years. ______________________(4), employee training is an area that has been emphasized at Smith and Company. Continuing education has ______________________(5) been offered to employees at Jones Corporation. Their employees receive paid tuition ______________________(6) excused time off from work. ______________________(7) is strategic planning, which calls for goal setting. As you know, we've just recently announced a ten-year plan at XYZ Corporation.

One of the goal-setting ideas underlying Total Quality Management is to examine the efficiency of current procedures and to propose sensible improvements. ______________________(8), it may not be possible to set goals for certain areas past next year for all our divisions. ______________________(9), I've been able to mention only a few of the main areas that Total Quality Management addresses. It is an innovative program because it provides a comprehensive way to achieve high performance and to improve quality of work by examining all of the current individual methods and by improving them when necessary.

NAME

EXERCISE 7-6: SIMPLIFYING PROSE

Simplify the following phrases and words.

past experience ____________________

right now ____________________

at this point in time ____________________

completely stopped ____________________

after that point in time ____________________

in light of the fact that ____________________

in the month of June ____________________

attached herewith ____________________

attempted to ____________________

each and every one ____________________

completely destroy ____________________

fewer than ten in number ____________________

the amount of $400 ____________________

subsequent to ____________________

coarse feel ____________________

grainy consistency ____________________

active runner ____________________

15 ounces in weight ____________________

3 ½" size diskette ____________________

spicy taste ____________________

terminate ____________________

cognizant of ____________________

made a determination ____________________

compensation ____________________

hereinafter ____________________

rectangular in shape ____________________

my personal opinion ____________________

innumerable ____________________

facilitate ____________________

we are of the opinion that ____________________

a total of $300 ____________________

be so kind to ____________________

as soon as possible ____________________

fill up ____________________

past memories ____________________

red in color ____________________

mottled appearance ____________________

for the length of one year ____________________

repudiate ____________________

smooth surface ____________________

working employee ____________________

at that point in time ____________________

settled down ____________________

acrid smell ____________________

4 hours duration ____________________

initialize ____________________

amusing and humorous ____________________

necessitated ____________________

initiatives ____________________

the sum of $25 ____________________

NAME

EXERCISE 7-7: PRUNING VERBIAGE

Simplify the following sentences.

1. It is important to note that this computer terminal is not hooked up to a modem.

2. At the present time we are experiencing a rain event.

3. He proceeded to insert the diskette in the slot provided for the purpose.

4. Due to the fact that we are in the middle of a heat wave with humidity that is oppressive, we must think about the possibility of an overhaul of our air conditioning system.

5. It is important for me to point out that your vacation schedule is in conflict with Susan's.

6. One finds that most people experience a slow-down in energy after they eat a heavy lunch.

7. It is imperative that all the rules be followed in a conscientious manner.

8. Enclosed is my resume, which summarizes my education and job experience.

9. There is a possibility that we might try electronic tax filing next tax season.

10. In light of the fact that PDQ Company was unresponsive to our emergency crises during the past tax season, we are proceeding to look for another tax service bureau to employ for the next tax season.

11. It is incumbent upon us to remember that our profession is governed by a strict and stringent code of ethics.

12. We are in receipt of your resume and accompanying letter of application for the vacant position of senior accountant.

13. In my personal opinion, it is apparent that appropriate internal control measures regarding the petty cash account are not in place.

14. Your account is past due in that our records show that an old balance is still due of a total of $350, which should be paid as soon as possible.

15. Various alternative methods may be required to keep the backup diskettes in storage in a safe manner.

16. In your computer manual you will note that there is a Reveal Codes feature that facilitates a determination of formatting problems.

____

17. All of the partners concurred in their disagreement about the necessity for establishing a newly created branch office.

____

NAME

EXERCISE 7-8: COMBINING SENTENCES

To reduce choppiness and to improve the "flow," rewrite the following passages by using the sentence-combining approach:

1. Please accept the accompanying report. The report is called "Total Quality Management—A Recommendation for XYZ Corporation."

2. The report discusses the need for quality improvement. Quality improvement is needed at XYZ Corporation. The report gives the history of Total Quality Management. The report discusses Total Quality Management's success. The report discusses Total Quality Management's failures.

3. I would like to thank Mr. John Wallace for his expertise. I would like to thank Mr. John Wallace for his assistance with this report.

4. Taxpayers should be able to receive tax refunds promptly. For taxpayers to be able to receive tax refunds promptly, IRS must collect payroll taxes. The payroll taxes must be collected in a timely manner. If IRS collects payroll taxes in a timely manner, taxpayers should be able to receive refunds promptly. Artificial Intelligence can expedite IRS collection of payroll taxes. Artificial Intelligence can expedite tax refunds.

5. Some taxpayers report less income than they really earn. An example is farm sales for cash. Some farmers sell produce for cash without recording the sale. Some farmers sell other farm products for cash without recording the sale. Other workers must pay taxes on every penny they earn. Workers whose total income is reported resent those who evade taxes. Taxes can be avoided by unreported cash sales.

NAME

*EXERCISE 7-9: TRANSLATING DOUBLESPEAK**

In the spaces provided, translate the following examples of doublespeak.

1. career change opportunity ____________________
2. 7406D Voice Terminal ____________________
3. unstaffing an office ____________________
4. entry systems ____________________
5. experiencing no electricity ____________________
6. nonperforming real estate assets ____________________
7. space relief center ____________________
8. criminal defense and trial boutique ____________________
9. excess over expenses ____________________
10. rightsizing the bank ____________________
11. mild market correction ____________________
12. mistruth ____________________
13. seek new revenues ____________________
14. personnel schedule adjustments ____________________
15. negative net worth ____________________
16. write-down ____________________
17. long-distance copier ____________________
18. restructurings ____________________
19. pretax write-off ____________________
20. misconnect rate ____________________
21. portable hand-held communications inscriber ____________________
22. packaging agents ____________________
23. contingent deferred sales load ____________________
24. low-income circumstances ____________________
25. receipts proposal ____________________

* Examples of doublespeak are culled from *Quarterly Review of Doublespeak* (January 1990, April 1990, October 1990, and January 1991). Used by permission of the *Quarterly Review of Doublespeak* and the National Council of Teachers of English.

NAME

EXERCISE 7-10: PROPER ENGLISH USAGE

In the spaces provided, construct sentences of the following confused words to illustrate proper usage.

1. accept ______

   except ______
2. advice ______

   advise ______
3. affect ______

   effect ______
4. aggravate ______

   annoy ______

   irritate ______
5. ain't ______

   are not ______

   aren't ______
6. all ready ______

   already ______
7. all right ______

   "alright" ______
8. altogether ______

   all together ______
9. among ______

   between ______
10. amount ______

    number ______
11. apt ______

    liable ______

    likely ______
12. a while ______

    awhile ______
13. beside ______

    besides ______
14. biannual ______

    biennial ______
15. biweekly ______

    every two weeks ______

    every other week ______
16. can ______

    may ______

EXERCISE 7-10: PROPER ENGLISH USAGE (CONTINUED)

17. capital ____________________

capitol ____________________

18. compare to ____________________

compare with ____________________

19. compliment ____________________

complement ____________________

20. continuous ____________________

continual ____________________

21. damage ____________________

damages ____________________

22. differ from ____________________

differ with ____________________

23. disinterested ____________________

uninterested ____________________

24. disperse ____________________

disburse ____________________

25. every day ____________________

everyday ____________________

26. farther ____________________

further ____________________

27. fewer ____________________

less ____________________

28. foreword ____________________

forward ____________________

29. good ____________________

well ____________________

30. hopeful ____________________

"hopefully" ____________________

31. imply ____________________

infer ____________________

32. in ____________________

into ____________________

33. ensure ____________________

insure ____________________

34. irrespective ____________________

regardless ____________________

"irregardless" ____________________

EXERCISE 7-10: PROPER ENGLISH USAGE (CONTINUED)

35. its ______________________________

    it's ______________________________

36. mean ______________________________

    median ______________________________

37. moral ______________________________

    morale ______________________________

38. off ______________________________

    off of ______________________________

39. oral ______________________________

    verbal ______________________________

40. principal ______________________________

    principle ______________________________

41. raise ______________________________

    rise ______________________________

42. respectfully ______________________________

    respectively ______________________________

43. set ______________________________

    sit ______________________________

44. stationary ______________________________

    stationery ______________________________

45. that ______________________________

    which ______________________________

46. their ______________________________

    there ______________________________

    they're ______________________________

47. than ______________________________

    then ______________________________

48. to ______________________________

    too ______________________________

    two ______________________________

49. if I was ______________________________

    if I were ______________________________

50. who's ______________________________

    whose ______________________________

51. your ______________________________

    you're ______________________________

NAME

EXERCISE 7-11: CONVERTING NOMINALIZATIONS TO READABLE PROSE

In each of the following sentences, reduce wordiness and increase readability by converting the nominalizations to verb forms and adjectives. Circling the nominalizations first will help.

1. Our productivity for the second quarter showed negativity as a result of the disruption that was caused by the installation of a new computer system.

2. The failure of the copier was the result of a faulty paper feed.

3. If an introduction to the new software is conducted with accommodation to the user in mind, the result will be greater productivity when the firm experiences a time of great difficulty in tax season.

4. We perform calculations each month that yield a detailed job cost analysis.

5. There was a continual insistence on the part of Mr. Brinker to redo calculations on the validity of his investment strategy.

6. If we plan on an implementation of the new plan for weekly assessment, we should see an early resolution to the bottleneck problem in Phase 3.

7. An improvement of our hiring practices is needed.

8. An expansion of the accounts payable unit might be a complication to our cash-flow projections.

9. The senior partner's motivation to make provision for an expansion of professional education opportunities was a result of the promptings of AICPA to mandate an increase of academic credit hours for all members.

10. The office manager made identification of a need for greater efficiency in the collation of tax returns.

EXERCISE 7-11: CONVERTING NOMINALIZATIONS TO READABLE PROSE (CONTINUED)

11. After the ad hoc committee held a discussion about the phenomena of the spring purge that seemed to be in evidence during the past few years, a recommendation was made to conduct a thorough review of the situation and to write a report for the partners.

    ____

    ____

    ____

    ____

12. An extensive review of our firm's library holdings gave indication that we need to conduct an analysis of what we actually see as useless, and what we actually find need for.

    ____

    ____

NAME

EXERCISE 7-12: AGREEMENT: BEING CONSISTENT IN NUMBER

A. In each of the following sentences, indicate agreement in number between subject and verb by underlining the subject and circling its correct verb.

1. As a result of *Bates v. State Bar of Arizona* and increased competition in the accounting field, many members of AICPA (advertise/advertises).
2. Before AICPA's ruling in 1978, advertisements—those in the Yellow Pages in particular—(were/was) scarce.
3. In the 1990s we are already seeing competition and marketing for accounting services (increases/increase).
4. Apparently, *Bates v. State Bar of Arizona* (have/has) revolutionized the marketing efforts of accountancy.
5. Among some accountants (is/are) the cherished notion that there (are/is) only one effective way to market services: by unsolicited referrals.
6. Each accounting firm (make/makes) its own decision about advertising.
7. Building a good reputation and building a successful accounting practice (are/is) synonymous.
8. Everybody, it seems, (have/has) strong opinions on advertising.
9. The problems for some accounting firms (are/is) keen competition for clients and aggressive marketing practices.

B. In each of the following sentences, circle the correct pronoun and underline its antecedent:

1. A novice speaker might unconsciously reveal (her/his/his or her/their) nervousness by verbal or physical mannerisms.
2. The IRS requested copies of (its/it's/their) recent correspondence.
3. Judy or Audrey (I can't remember which) lost (their/her) contact lens.
4. Anyone who applies for a job with a public accounting firm had better gear (herself/himself/themselves/ herself or himself) for tax season.
5. David and Robert both want (his/their) vacation schedules changed.

NAME

EXERCISE 7-13: CORRECTING SENTENCE FRAGMENTS

In the following passages taken from student papers, underline the sentence fragments and then correct them to form complete sentences.

1. Recommending research on artificial intelligence be pursued by the IRS.

2. Based on the cost/benefit analysis and the criteria of simplicity and fiscal economy. The plan proves to be the best available to us.

3. Total Quality Management has been offered as a means to solve the problem. Founded on the principles of interactive management practices.

4. Large outstanding balances not only require time to collect but also represent the probable loss of future government revenue. A fact which is of major concern to the IRS.

5. Older, more serious delinquencies being processed in Taxpayer Delinquent Account status.

6. Applying the economists' marginal cost theory, when marginal cost increases more than the average cost. Total cost will be pulled up by the additional expenditures.

7. Unless the IRS has no effective means to detect the true payments that are less than $600 or payments that are not results of a trade or business. Therefore, the underpayment and delay in deposits become major factors contributing to the failure of the current system.

8. Electronically Cooperative Tax Collection Network defined as an improved tax collection system that relies on modern electronic technology and full cooperation from taxpayers.

EXERCISE 7-13: CORRECTING SENTENCE FRAGMENTS (CONTINUED)

9. If human beings can depend on computer technology to travel in the galaxy, why can't the IRS use modern computer technology to collect taxes? Because taxpayers pressure Congress to keep collection costs down.

____

____

____

____

10. The process, similar to the "electronic mailing" currently used by many firms to communicate within the company.

____

____

NAME

EXERCISE 7-14: CLARIFYING REFERENTS

In the following passages, underline the unclear referents. List the possible antecedents for the pronouns in the space provided.

1. When the owners expanded the warehouse, they never bothered to install siding or to insulate the walls. This causes condensation to build up on the floor.
2. Although not much can be done with the cramped space, the manager should have the copier moved out of the way of traffic so they can't hurt themselves.
3. Shelves need to be installed above the copier and heavy-duty electrical wiring should be installed also, which would make the copier area safer.
4. The copier table is wet because the water cooler drips onto it. The only solution is to move it.
5. The accounts receivable clerk will be taking maternity leave and will be temporarily replaced by the accounts payable clerk, who is pregnant.
6. If Ms. Butler's division needs more staff, will they be able to hire from within the company?
7. In the seminar on merger and acquisitions, we learned that it requires caution, foresight, and planning.
8. The Kipper Computer Consortium and our programmers do always respond to our emergencies promptly, especially in tax season, but they usually solve the problems.
9. The division manager furnished a history of the account to the client. He felt it wasn't detailed enough.

NAME

EXERCISE 7-15: MISPLACED AND DANGLING MODIFIERS

Underline the misplaced and dangling modifiers in the following sentences. Then recast the sentences to avoid confusion.

1. The impending corporate restructuring, although it will result in numerous layoffs and hardships for some, is necessary to put the corporation's enterprises on a paying basis.

2. Sparking electricity all over the terminal, the technician shut off the power to the console.

3. Using needle-nosed pliers, the copier feed was fixed, at least until a qualified technician could arrive.

4. My interviewer told me, during the employment interview when I was very nervous, to relax and take my time in answering her questions.

5. By recording client charges promptly, billing will reflect work actually performed.

6. To write an audit report cover letter, AICPA's guidelines should be consulted.

7. Frantically looking around all over the office, the glasses were found on Stan's head.

8. Before leaving the office, the console should be shut down according to the procedures outlined in the computer manual.

9. To operate the copier efficiently, the machine should be left on during office hours.

10. Balking at the size of the bill, a breakdown of charges was requested.

11. An open modem line, assuming someone wants to access your data, is an invitation to breach security.

EXERCISE 7-15: MISPLACED AND DANGLING MODIFIERS (CONTINUED)

12. To ensure a well-attended seminar on recent tax changes, scheduling should be planned near the end of the year.

13. Experiencing phenomenal growth, a revised chart of accounts should be constructed as soon as possible.

NAME

EXERCISE 7-16: PARALLEL CONSTRUCTION

Correct faulty parallelism in the following passages. (Passages are adapted from a student recommendation report.)

1. Myers Management Incorporated (MMI) specializes in phone systems installations, consulting for Local Area Network (LAN) installations, and manufactures custom LAN hardware.

2. The outdated inventory system creates a problem for our salespeople, putting a strain on our purchasing agents, and taking many months to restock a specific item.

3. MMI is left with the dilemma of needing to keep inventory levels nearly constant to complete orders efficiently, competing successfully in the ferocious computer hardware field.

4. The inventory system is outdated, ineffective, and a paper system.

5. Discussing current inventory problems and to recommend a possible solution are the focuses of my recommendation report.

6. Table of Contents

Executive Summary
Introduction
Background of the MMI Inventory System
How the MMI Inventory System Works
Current Inventory Problems
Upgrading Hardware
Software Upgrade Solutions
    Bar-coding Hardware and Software
    Nonintegrated Software
    Integrated Software
Recommendations

EXERCISE 7-16: PARALLEL CONSTRUCTION (CONTINUED)

7. The current system is too unwieldy to be workable, causes customer dissatisfaction, and is too complicated for everyone to understand.

8. The warehouse area measures 90,000 cubic feet, is seriously understaffed, needing an efficient, computerized system.

9. The inventory list, created with a word processor, is never up-to-date, posted all over the warehouse, seldom checked by anyone, and costing us sales.

10. What we promise to do and what is actually accomplished are two different things at MMI.

11. When MMI is out of stock, sales suffer; excess inventory hinders our cash flow.

12. Can we imagine an efficient system? A system that frustrates everyone who must cope with it?

13. Benefits of Computerized Inventory

(1) Customers can count on firm delivery dates.
(2) Products shipped sooner.
(3) Fewer incorrect orders.
(4) Fewei items will have to be back-ordered.

14. (Resume job description)
Handled over $10,000 cash daily; reconciling accounts receivable; supervise three employees; trained two summer interns.

15. The benefits include not only satisfied customers and less frustrated employees.

EXERCISE 7-16: PARALLEL CONSTRUCTION (CONTINUED)

16. We are considering two types of bar code readers: In one, the hand-held wands must be dragged across the bar codes. Stationary readers read an entire code at once.

17. MMI will either continue to lose sales, or we have the option to select from available inventory systems.

18. The wand model, with a numeric keypad and alphanumeric display, could be carried about the warehouse, scan a bar code, receive input, and communicate with the network to change the inventory list.

NAME

EXERCISE 7-17A: FREQUENTLY MISSPELLED WORDS

Circle the correct *American* spellings of the following words:

1. thier	their				
2. grammar	grammer				
3. surprize	surprise				
4. alot	a lot				
5. its (possessive)	it's (possessive)				
6. achieve	acheive				
7. liason	liaison				
8. judgment	judgement				
9. vacuum	vaccuum				
10. develop	develope				
11. developement	development				
12. occassion	ocassion	occasion			
13. buisness	business				
14. existance	existence				
15. acknowledge	acknowlege				
16. priviledge	privilege				
17. acknowledgement	acknowledgment				
18. consensus	concensus				
19. acommodate	accommodate	accomodate			
20. embarrass	embarass				
21. benefited	benefitted				
22. occurr	ocur	ocurr	occur		
23. occurrence	occurrance	occurence	occurance	ocurrance	ocurrence
24. definately	definitely				

NAME

EXERCISE 7-17B: ADDITIONAL FREQUENTLY MISSPELLED WORDS

Circle the correct *American* spellings of the following words:

1. wierd	weird
2. supersede	supercede
3. useage	usage
4. acheivement	achievement
5. till	til
6. Febuary	February
7. address	adress
8. parallelism	parrallelism
9. challange	challenge
10. absence	absense
11. sponser	sponsor
12. calender	calendar
13. harass	harrass
14. solely	soley
15. wherever	whereever
16. conscientous	conscientious
17. incalculable	incalcuable
18. competant	competent
19. sophmore	sophomore
20. forty	fourty
21. accross	across
22. publicly	publically
23. resistence	resistance
24. arguing	argueing
25. resemblance	resemblence

NAME

EXERCISE 7-18: PUNCTUATION

The following paragraphs are the opening passages from a student paper recommending a computer system for British Passage.* All punctuation has been removed. Using standard proofreading symbols (see Appendix), supply the appropriate punctuation. (The lines are numbered for easy reference.)

Introduction

British Passage is a womens retail chain that specializes in handknit sweaters and coordinating sportswear British Passage owns seventeen stores all controlled by the home office in Houston Texas For a business that focuses on keeping up with the latest trends British Passage is missing out on one trend that has modernized almost every type of business in the world that is to use computers to cut time spent on paperwork accounting procedures inventory and improving cash flow Currently all work done at British Passage from daily bookkeeping to company inventory is done by hand The chain must update its ancient bookkeeping methods

This report considers various hardware systems and software packages that would best suit the needs of British Passage

British Passage Philosophy

In 1972 James Metz began British Passage with the philosophy of creating a shopping experience for the customer The shopping experience included selling one of a kind handknit sweaters and coordinating sportswear with very personalized service An article in The Houston Post Success Story Retailer Follows Instinct to Stay Ahead of Latest Trends called Metz a strong believer in service setting a store apart from competitors[1] Personal service includes handwritten tickets handwritten thank you notes and salespeople who act as personal shoppers for each individual customer British Passage salespeople thoroughly know the store merchandise so they can fulfill customer needs

One aspect of the personalized service philosophy at British Passage is the follow up to the sale it may include writing a note to a customer to let him or her know that a particular item is in stock Another type of follow up might be a phone call to a customer about an upcoming sale Follow ups are a major part of the British Passage philosophy of personal service they help to create and maintain loyal customers Couldn t this service be improved by an updated computer system

Need for Computerization

The British Passage philosophy of personal service created the difference needed to be successful For continued growth and success it is necessary not only to keep up with the latest trends in fashion but also to keep up with the latest trends in technology According to U S News & World Reports 1990 Guide to Small Business the key to successful growing within a company is to be able to identify the right expansion signs[2] Now is the time to update the entire internal systems by computerization At this crucial time in British Passages growth computerization will help ease transitions and allow for greater productivity in all areas of the company

Currently all daily procedures at British Passage are done by hand The bookkeeping methods are very time consuming with tickets written by hand there is a greater chance for error Can a striving company afford errors in simple calculations With computerization the current system of bookkeeping stock counts payroll etc can be accomplished with much less time and effort and with more accuracy

[1] Beverly Narum Success Story Retailer Follows Instinct to Stay Ahead of Latest Trends The Houston Post March 19 1990 Section E 12

[2] Lisa J Moore with Sharon F Golden The 1990 Guide to Small Business U S News & World Report Vol 107 No 16 October 23 1989 72 73

* Student paper by Catherine Maselka. Used by permission.

NAME

EXERCISE 7-19: ELIMINATING UNNECESSARY PUNCTUATION

The following excerpt from a student recommendation report for an inventory system is erroneously punctuated or overpunctuated. Correct and/or eliminate unnecessary punctuation.

Sunburst Milling Co., Ltd., is a food manufacturing, and processing company in Jamaica, which packages a range of products, including sugar, flour, peas, and corn meal; but their main product is rice. . . The foodstuffs are packaged in a factory, which employs about eighty people, and stores its' own inventory. All three types of manufacturing inventories are present in this factory; raw materials, work in progress and finished goods. However—the cost accounting system is rudimentary, at best, and no one knows exactly how much product is in each inventory: or what it costs to manufacture it. In the past, the present system was adequate but lack of control and information is causing increasing management problems, which are reflected in inconsistent profits.

For financial accounting purposes, Sunbursts accounting system is excellent; but for internal control purposes, it is inadequate. An extensive, cost accounting system does not exist due to the physical, and logistical difficulty of designing one that works. In the financial accounting system the expenses and revenues are recorded correctly, but there is no way to know exactly where these costs are going. For example where does the $30,000 that is paid in wages every week go. To loading vehicles, milling rice or sweeping the floor? No one knows exactly; so precise product cost information cannot be calculated! This lack of information has caused erratic profits because of unpredictable operating expenses, and inaccurate capital investment planning, long term breakeven analysis and strategic planning. Bad capital investment planning has also generated lower depreciation expenses, which have led to higher taxes.

NAME

EXERCISE 7-20: INTERPRETING PROOFREADING SYMBOLS

Below is a letter marked with proofreading symbols. Reformat and retype the letter according to the symbols.

KENNETH N. DONOHUE, P.C.
Certified Public Accountant
1 Court Place
Cranbury, NJ 08512

Member
American Institute of
Certified Public Accountants

(609) 555-4185

SEptember 12, 1991

Deportment of the Treasury
Internal Revenue Service
Philadelphia, PA 19255

RE: The XYZ Corporation
42-8834502
435 Enterprise Street
New Brunswick, NJ 08903

I am enclosing two (2) United States Treasury checks made payable to the above reference taxpayer. The two checks, dated 6/3/90 in the amounts of $4289.51 and $1208.04 reflect tax deposits for the 1st quarter 1990 form 941 tax liabilities.

The forms 8109 for the deposits were erronously coded for 940 tax liabilities.

The 941 tax deposits were made as follows

2/5/89 $ 4,289.51
4/14/89 $1,208.04

Please process the enclosed returned checks to reflect the 941 deposits.

Thankyou.

Very Truly Yours,

Kenneth N. Donohue, CPA

Enclosures

cc: The XYZ Corporation

NAME

EXERCISE 7-21: EDITING A STUDENT PAPER

The following text is adapted from a student paper. Edit mercilessly, looking at both macro and micro concerns.

The Impact of CFAs, CFPs, PAs and Enrolled Agents on CPAs

Introduction

Certified financial analysts (CFAs), Certified financial planners (CFPs), Public Accountants (PAs) and enrolled agents now perform many of the services that used to be performed by Certified Public Accountants (CPA's). More specifically financial planning which used to be done by CPAs. Will CPA fees be affected by this new competition? By showing that CFAs, CFPs, PAs and enrolled agents are all competing with CPAs for financial planning dollars.

Discussion

Let me start out by explaining exactly what CFAs, CFPs, PAs and enrolled agents are. CFAs are financial planners certified by Financial Analysts Federation.(1) CFPs are financial planners who are certified by the institute of Certified Financial Planners. CFPs must either pass courses in financial planning or take tests to be certified CFPs.(2) Enrolled agents have either worked for the IRS or have passed a test given by the IRS.(3) Enrolled agents can represent a client at an IRS audit.(4) Public Accounts (PAs) are uncertified accountants. They can not perform CPA audits.

One can be a CPA and CFP. Infact, just be looking in the phone book, one sees several financial planners with the designation, CPA, CFP. "The accountant who chooses to be a financial planner plays many roles."(5) This quote from John Day's article is very true.

Certified Financial Analysts

The Financial Analysts Federation (FAF) and other organizations are developing performance standards.(6) The Rosenberg Committee, commissioned by the FAF to develop standards, gave CFAs greater legitimacy. The FAF Corporate Infornation Committee has begun giving corporations awards for excellence in annual reporting.(7) For example, in 1986, it gave 28 awards to companies for excellence in annual reporting.(8)

Certified Financial Planners

"The International Association of Financial Planners and the Institute of Certified Financial Planners are the professional associations for certified financial planners."(9) To a large degree these organisations have given CFPs legitimacy to the general public. All of the articles I have read indicate that CFP is becoming the main designation of financial planners because their standards are higher than those for other designations. In fact, most of the articles I read reported that it is preferable to have either a CFP or a CPA do your financial planning.

The most important thing going for CFPs is that they will only certify people who have demonstated that they know alot about all aspects of financial planning.(10) As a result of this I believe that the CFP designation is going to the greatest competition for CPAs. It is my opinion that when consumers see that CPAs are also CFPs, this gives even greater credibility to the CFP designation. It would lead them to believe that CFPs are more qualified to perform certain duties than CPAs. In fact CPAs are unquestionably more qualified to perform most of these services.

CFPs are being encouraged to use that designation only, to avoid confusing the consumer.(11) According to the International Board of Standards and Practices for Cerified Financial Planners there are currently 14,000 financial planners.(12) In order to become a CFP one must pass six national examinations. These examinations cover such things as risk management, estate planning, and investment management. The candidate must recieve at least a seventy-five percent on each examination.(13)

EXERCISE 7-21: EDITING A STUDENT PAPER (CONTINUED)

Enrolled Agents

The advantage that enrolled agents have over CFAs, CFPs, and PAs is that they can represent a client before the IRS.(14) Also, enrolled agents have either worked for the IRS for five years or more o have passed a fairly tough examination.(15) The main area where enrolled agents compete with CPAs is in representing clients before the IRS. Continuing education should be a must for enrolled agents, because of the "dynamic" nature of tax laws.

Financial Planning Duties

First let us discuss the duties of a financial planner. "A financial planner helps people assess financial goals and develope plans to achieve them."(16) Financial planning services include:

Balance sheet preparation and analysis
Preparing income taxes
Cash flow projecting
Long term income accumulation planning
Insurance analyses
Estate planning (17)

These duties are traditionally performed by CPAs. I talked with an AICPA member named Robert Matthews. He said he was not sure how much CFAs, CFPs, PAs, and enrolled agents were effecting CPAs. Mr. Matthews seemed sure that the impact was substantial. Mr. Matthews was unsure (as I am sure other CPAs are) as to whether or not CPA fees are greatly affected by this increased competition.

To my knowledge, a study to estimate the impact of CFAs, CFPs, PAs, and enrolled agents has never been done. However *Business Horizons* magazine has done a study to measure different responses from CFAs and CPAs.(18) CFAs and/CPAs see the issue of materiality differently. Materiality being the amount of money considered significant enough to make a note on a financial statement. CPAs obviously think that larger amounts are necessary for materiality. This illustrates how CPAs and other financial planners see things differently and how this affects the way that they do their jobs.

Conclusions

AICPA has done a good job of representing CPAs. It has been instrumental in the upgrading of the accounting profession. AICPA's high standards and tough educational requirements have greatly improved the way the profession is viewed. In my opinion, CFAs, PAs, enrolled agents, and especially CFPs represent significant problems to the CPA.

Endnotes

(1) Nancy Bolliveau, "Can Phony Performance Numbers be Policed", *Institutional Investor*, June,1989, p. 8o.

(2) Maria Crawfrod,"Selecting A Financial Planner", *Business*, January-March, 1987, p. 13.

(3) Denise M. Topolnicki, "How to find a Tax Pro Who's right for You", *Working Woman*, March 1988, ppgs. 130–132.

(4) Topolnicki, p. 130.

(5) John K. Day, "Financial Planning: Opportunities and challenges", The CPA Journal, September, 1987, p. 104.

(6) Boliveau, p. 81.

(7) Peter C. Lincoln, "The corporate information Committee Reports", *Financial Analysts Journal*, January-February 1986, p. 78.

EXERCISE 7-21: EDITING A STUDENT PAPER (CONTINUED)

)8) Lincoln, p. 78.

(9) Crawford, p. 13.

(10) Carole King, "Planning 'Turf battle gets rougher", *National Underwriters*, May, 1988,p. 2.

(11) Lyles, Gray, "Becoming a Certified Financial Planner", *Bottomline*, November 1987, p.65.

(12) Lyles, Gray, p. 65.

(13) Lyles, Gray, p. 66.

(14) Leslie S. Shapiro, Continuing education for Enrolled Agents: Director of practice Discusses New Proposal", *National Public Accountant*, November 1985, p. 18.

(15) Denise Lamaute, "Finding Help Before the Tax Man Comes", *Black Enterprise*, April 1987, p.30.

(15) Crawford, p. 13.

(17) Crawford, p. 13.

(18) Dan C. Kneer and Phillip M. Rickers, "Just How much Should Financial stasements realy disclose?", *BUsiness Horizons*, November-December, 1985, p. 67.

Part Three

Accountants Listen and Speak to Their Audiences

CHAPTER 8

Accountants and Oral Communication

OVERVIEW Accountants convey their messages not only in writing, but orally to diverse audiences. Accountants orally instruct, report, persuade, coax, inform, advise, dissuade, and caution audiences from one person to hundreds of listeners. The same rhetorical strategies that make *written* communication effective should be used when preparing for oral communication. This chapter focuses on the accountant as oral communicator of financial information as well as active listener. It teaches the accountant-communicator to:

- Receive messages effectively;
- Analyze the speaker's and listener's rhetorical situation;
- Recognize and exploit individual strengths;
- Compensate for individual weaknesses;
- Accommodate an oral audience;
- Develop rhetorical strategies geared to an oral presentation.

GOALS

- ◆ Listen to others effectively.
- ◆ Prepare and deliver an effective oral presentation.
- ◆ Evaluate oral presentations.

Key Terms

Logos The logical argument; incorporating evidence to interest the listener.
Ethos The character of the speaker as perceived by the hearer.
Pathos An appeal to the self-interest of the listener.
Rhetorical Situation The exigence, audience, and constraints affecting the speaker and listener.
Mannerisms A speaker's peculiar behavioral habits.
Schemes The alteration of words to change their sounds for rhetorical effect.
Tropes The manipulation of words to affect ways of thinking.

Introduction: Oral Communication and the Accountant

Accountants, although familiar with GAAP (Generally Accepted Accounting Principles) and GAAS (Generally Accepted Auditing Standards), constantly wrestle with the communications *gap* in conveying those applied principles and standards to users who need accounting information. Principles and standards must be understood before they can be *generally accepted*; what is understood and accepted by accountants is more often than not a mystery to nonaccountant users. After four years on the job, one young accountant acknowledged, "Communicating skills are important, at least as important as accounting skills."[1]

Scan employment notices and you will find that many call for "effective written and oral communication skills" or "strong communication skills." The effective oral communication and listening skills so necessary to entering, advancing, and surviving in the workplace entail more than standing up before an audience and giving a speech, or passively listening. The workplace needs accountants who can communicate orally with internal colleagues, superiors, and subordinates; external colleagues, and other personnel; clients; and the public in diverse forums, as both speaker and listener:

Speaker	*Listener*
1. Giving managerial instruction	1. Receiving managerial instruction
2. Interviewing for a job	2. Interviewing job candidates
3. Conducting meetings	3. Contributing to meetings
4. Teaching colleagues, clients, students	4. Learning from colleagues
5. Chairing panels	5. Participating in panels
6. Conferring via telephone	6. Conferring via telephone
7. Giving expert testimony	7. Receiving expert advice
8. Responding to questions	8. Asking questions
9. Delivering formal speeches	9. Hearing formal speeches
10. Interacting with colleagues, co-workers, clients, the public	10. Interacting with colleagues, co-workers, clients, the public
11. Giving formal presentations	11. Receiving formal presentations
12. Dictating correspondence	

In a 1987 study involving 305 Big-Eight accountants' perceptions of 32 oral communication tasks that contributed to success on the job, respondents ranked the following as the top four tasks:[2]

1. Answering questions with clients
2. Asking questions with clients
3. Giving supervisory instruction
4. Receiving supervisory instruction

Judging from the preceding lists, there is ample room for communication gaps when speaking or listening. Just as GAAP and GAAS state established accounting and auditing principles and standards, so GALP (Generally Accepted Listening Principles) and GASP (Generally Accepted Speaking Principles)[3] state rhetorically sound listening and speaking principles. Effective oral communication starts with active *listening*, since every speaker interacts with an audience and since you will listen more than you speak in your accounting career.

Listening: An Acquired Skill

Speakers can be described as "aggravating," "boring," "challenging," "entertaining," and "eloquent." But so can listeners. A co-worker who sits with arms folded, with a foot tapping impatiently, is clearly aggravated—and unlikely to contribute constructively to the conversation. A conference attendee who doodles, looks around the room, and flips through reading material is obviously bored, and neglects the speaker. In contrast, a seminar participant who sits slightly forward in the chair, attending either to the speaker or to note-taking, is challenged—and motivates the seminar leader. An employee who chuckles at a manager's joke is entertained, and contributes to a relaxed atmosphere. And a listener who provides "feedback cues"—those nods of the head signifying agreement, or glances at the ceiling indicating analytical thought—is an active, participatory listener. Listening skills are considered so important that failure to communicate is attributed more to the listener than to the speaker, or as William Parkhurst puts it in "The Eloquence of the Good Listener," "we don't know how to listen."[4]

Failure to understand what is really intended by a speaker, especially in face-to-face encounters, results in miscommunication, defensiveness, and hurt feelings. For example, consider the chart below that shows the speaker's objectives, the means of attaining them, and listener's possible responses. Notice the listener's options to react negatively or positively, to question, or to restate to clarify:

Speaker's Objectives[5]	*Means*	*Listener's Responses*
1. Ease social interaction.	Greetings Jokes Anecdotes Small talk	*Negative:* Ignore overtures. *Positive:* Respond appreciatively.
2. Ventilate feelings.	*Overt:* "Are we getting a 401-K plan?" *Covert:* "Will our company survive the economic downturn?"	*Negative:* "No, most of our employees already have IRAs." *Positive:* "No, not now. But we're planning on a retirement plan after the economic crunch."
3. Ask for information.	"Will the report be ready this Friday?"	*Defensive:* I'm working as fast as I can!" *Positive:* "Yes, I believe we'll meet the deadline."
4. Discuss.	"We need to cut department expenditures by seven percent."	*Defensive:* "Are you saying I can't manage a budget?" *Restate to clarify:* "You mean seven percent cuts across the board." *Positive:* "Yes, I heard about a less expensive tax service, and we could buy office supplies from a wholesaler, also."
5. Negotiate.	"What if we hired you over the summer as an intern until a permanent slot opened up in September?"	*Negative:* "I need a permanent position now." *Restate to clarify:* "Are you saying the permanent position is certain?" *Positive:* "I'd prefer a permanent position, of course, but I'd accept the internship if the permanent position were guaranteed."
6. Counsel.	"For internal control, you should hire a cash receipts clerk."	*Negative:* "All our employees are honest." *Restate to clarify:* "You mean that Bill shouldn't be writing checks *and* handling cash receipts?" *Positive:* "Perhaps we could reassign cash receipts duties to Marge."

The Rhetorical Principle: Relate to the Situation

To listen is to enter into a rhetorical situation—that is, a situation in which speaker and listener have reason (exigence) to engage in discourse; in which an audience is "capable of being influenced by discourse"; and in which a set of constraints influences the delivery and reception of the discourse, including "beliefs, attitudes, documents, facts, traditions, images, interests, motives and the like. . . ."[6] Understanding how the exigence, audience, and constraints affect the speaker's situation will help you analyze your purpose in hearing the speaker, as well as your attitude toward listening to the content of the discourse. The following "Listener's Attitude Assessment" will help you identify and adjust your attitudes toward the speaker, the topic, and the purpose of the discourse:

Listener's Attitude Assessment

The Speaker

As a listener, how do you feel that the speaker relates to you? Before hearing the speaker, can you identify some affinity because of professional background, shared interests, or common goals? How does the speaker relate to the topic? Do you feel that the speaker has expert knowledge and extensive experience about the topic?

Does your nonverbal behavior (body language) signal your interest to the speaker? Do you lean forward slightly, try to look pleasant, maintain eye contact?

If you are in a small-group or one-to-one situation, what do you know of the speaker's attitude toward you personally? Do you share a common frame of reference? Can you speculate on the speaker's attitude toward the topic? What does the speaker stand to gain or lose by addressing the topic?

Purpose

Why is the speaker addressing you specifically? Could there be covert as well as overt purposes? Why is the speaker dealing with the topic? Can you think of reasons why you should listen to the speaker? Are you under constraints such as needing information to pass an exam, or preparing yourself for an engagement, or earning Continuing Professional Education credit? What do you stand to gain or lose by paying attention to the speaker?

Content

How knowledgeable are you about the topic? Can you identify your strengths and weaknesses on the topic? Were you able to formulate questions ahead of time, looking for answers in the presentation? Did you go into the situation with preconceived notions, tuning out what does not fit your tacit assumptions?

What is the bottom line of the message? What are the main points? What evidence is offered to support the points? Is the evidence credible? Did the speaker omit anything you need to know? Should you ask clarifying questions? How can you apply the information? Have you noted what you should do as a result of the talk?

The Logical Principle: Listen for the Bottom Line

As Ronald E. Dulek and John S. Fielden point out in *Principles of Business Communication*, "Always listen for the real bottom line of what someone is saying."[7] This requires preparation, focus, and follow-up:

1. Before hearing the speaker, review what you already know about the topic, and think about what you would like to learn. If the speaker is published in the topic to be discussed, bone up on his or her point of view.
2. Prepare to listen by eliminating foreseeable distractions. Select a seat away from diversions that interfere with your concentration. Take notes, not only of facts, but of conclusions and questions prompted by the information presented.

3. Concentrate on the main thrust of the message, including main points. Evaluate the evidence, weighing its credibility and relevance to the speaker's ideas.
4. Because "the rate of most speech is between 125 and 150 words a minute," you tend to listen at least four times faster than most people speak.[8] The time left over is called "lag" time and accounts for daydreaming and other distracting behavior. Make good use of lag time by taking notes, making reminders of spinoff ideas for future reference, and drafting questions to be asked if unanswered by the presentation.
5. Refrain from interrupting. An interruption might distract others, and your question may be covered later in the talk or in a question-answer session. Listen for answers to your questions.
6. Resist the urge to work on your rebuttal during the presentation. You could miss relevant points that render your opinions invalid.
7. Critically evaluate the message, but try to avoid reaching conclusions until the speaker has finished. If you jump to the bottom line prematurely, you might miss information that strengthens the speaker's position, thus weakening your own.
8. In question-answer sessions, ask open-ended questions rather than closed questions that stifle full response:

   OPEN: How would you implement a change to LIFO inventory? (invites a substantive informative response).

   CLOSED: Do you agree with our switching to LIFO inventory? (can be answered with a "yes" or "no").

The Ethical Principle: Establish Credibility

1. During most talks you can be seen by the speaker as well as by others. If you fidget or otherwise act bored, you run the risk of damaging your reputation by distracting others who might be interested, or by appearing to waste company time.
2. If you have appeared antagonistic to the speaker, an opportunity for rapport and cooperation may be hampered because you have already demonstrated your negative attitude by your behavior.
3. Keep "The Golden Rule" in mind: you will want attentive listeners when it is your turn to speak.

The Pathetic Principle: Appeal to Self-Interest

1. Effective speakers try to appeal to your best interests. As an active listener, you will separate what is said for effect from information, and the points being made from supporting evidence.
2. In group meetings, support your speaker's efforts by maintaining eye contact and by generally looking interested.
3. In face-to-face conversations, indicate agreement or interest by providing feedback such as nodding or verbal cues:

   "I see."
   "Hmmmm."
   "Of course."
   "Really?"
   "Yes."

4. If you benefitted from the speaker's message, say so. Seminar and workshop leaders and speakers appreciate positive as well as negative feedback.

To test your skills as an active listener of an oral presentation or talk, complete Exercise 8-1.

Listening: The Art of Job Interviewing

Listening, as a critical skill, affects interpersonal relations with audiences inside and outside the company. And it is a pivotal factor in deciding who, among several qualified and promising candidates, should join a company. Robert Half, author of *Robert Half on Hiring*, feels that "apart from conveying basic information about the job, everything you say should be directed toward getting the candidate to talk." He feels "the interviewer should do no more than 30 percent of the talking."[9] And Richard T. Case, in "How to Conduct an Effective Interview," maintains that you should "let the candidate do 80–90% of the talking." Listening carefully thus allows you to "focus on the candidate's *behavior* rather than on what he says."[10]

Since so much effort is devoted to getting the candidate to open up, concentrate on providing opportunity for full discussion:

1. SCREEN CANDIDATES. If you evaluate resumes, letters of recommendation, and personal referrals carefully, you can screen out unsuitable applicants, thus leaving time for lengthier interviews with more promising applicants.
2. RESERVE AMPLE TIME. Rushing the interview will throw the candidate off balance. Since you both get only one shot at the interview, provide enough time to elicit the information you need to appraise the candidate fairly. Begin on time, just as you expect the applicant to arrive on time.
3. PROVIDE AN APPROPRIATE SETTING. Attend to comfortable room temperature, lighting (it shouldn't shine in the applicant's eyes), and privacy. Avoid a deep couch that is difficult to rise from. Arrange furniture according to the authoritarian stance you want to assume:

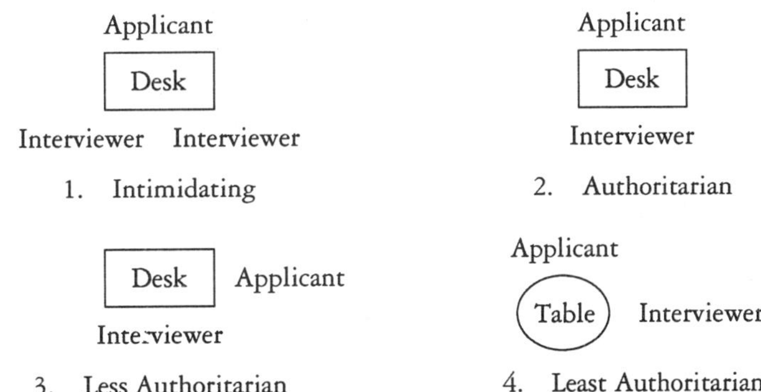

4. CREATE A NONTHREATENING ATMOSPHERE. Don't overwhelm the candidate by standing or pacing while the applicant is seated, by giving an oral version of the CPA exam, by recording the interview, or by having more than one interviewer.
5. PUT THE APPLICANT AT EASE. Introduce yourself (in the waiting area, if possible), extend a hand of welcome, smile, escort the candidate to the interview area, offer a chair, mention that you have reviewed the applicant's resume (be sure that you do). Let the applicant get seated comfortably.
6. INITIATE SMALL TALK. Get the conversation flowing by referring to something personal in the applicant's resume, school, or previous job:

   RESUME "I see you like gardening. What do you think of the new intensive planting methods?"

   SCHOOL "You financed one hundred percent of your education and living expenses. How on earth did you manage to work full-time and still achieve a 3.9 GPA?"

   JOB "We haven't had much experience with Multiplan. How does it differ from Lotus 1-2-3?"

7. AVOID UNFAIR QUESTIONS. Virginia L. Davis notes two rules consistent with Equal Employment Opportunity laws and regulations "about what constitutes discrimination in hiring practices": (1) "All questions and qualifications for individuals must be job-related," and (2) "Don't ask questions or qualifications of a minority group member (women, racial minorities, disabled, Vietnam veterans, individuals between 40 and 70, etc.) that you wouldn't ask of a majority member (i.e., white males)."[11] Asking loaded, inappropriate, and other unfairly phrased questions forces the applicant to take a defensive stance, and hampers the interview process. Here are some examples:
   - DEAD-END: "Are you interested in MAS work?" (Can be answered "yes" or "no.")
   - SCATTER GUN: "Did you know most firms nowadays have MAS departments? Would you like to specialize in MAS work? Will you be pursuing an MBA? What do you think of AICPA's new education requirement? How did you like your classes in management?"
   - PRESUMPTUOUS: "What did you think of the Dysert article in last month's *Harvard Business Review*?"
   - CONJECTURAL: "What if we had openings in the MAS or tax department? What advantage would you see in specializing in MAS?"
   - PROMPTING: "Is working with small businesses what attracts you to MAS work?"
   - UNFAIR: "Is MAS work too diversified for you?"
   - SEXIST: "MAS work entails developing close relationships with a variety of small business clients. Would you be willing to plan your maternity leaves to accommodate your clients?"
   - PATRONIZING: "We usually hire candidates with a 3.7 GPA or better. However, we need to hire more women, so we're willing to dip down to 3.5 in your case."
   - RACIST: "Would you be interested in being our liaison with the mayor's office of minority affairs?"
   - INTIMIDATING: "If you were hired, you would be on probation until the end of tax season. I assume you'll be free to travel on most weekends this spring?"
   - ILLEGAL: "You must have been a returning student. So, what year exactly did you graduate from high school?"
8. ASK APPROPRIATE QUESTIONS. The aforementioned questions tend to stifle applicant response and to put the applicant on edge. However, once the conversation is under way, you should pose pertinent questions about matters important to your firm and to the applicant's career:
   "Why does MAS work interest you?" (Open-ended; allows full response.)
   "Why did you leave your last job?"
   "What about the two-year gap between jobs?"
   "How do you feel about drug tests?"
   "Are you willing to travel thirty to forty percent of the time?"
   "Do you smoke on the job?"
   "Are you afraid of flying?"
   "How do you feel about working Saturdays during tax season?"
   "May I contact your present employer?"
   "What specialty areas interest you?"
   "What sections of the CPA exam have you passed?"
   "When do you intend to sit for the CPA exam?"
   "How do you plan to meet the MBA requirement?"
   "How would you characterize your management style?"

9. POSE SPECIFIC QUESTIONS. Phrase your questions to elicit examples and detail:
   VAGUE: "Tell me about yourself."
   SPECIFIC: "What do you want to be doing careerwise ten years from now?"
   VAGUE: "Are you computer literate?"
   SPECIFIC: "Have you used Open Systems software?"
   VAGUE: "Do you feel you have supervisory potential?"
   SPECIFIC: "How many employees have you supervised or trained?"
   VAGUE: "What interested you in accounting?"
   SPECIFIC: "Why are you applying for an accounting position in our firm?"
10. SHOW INTEREST.
    - If you take notes, maintain eye contact. Lean slightly forward in your chair.
    - Offer positive feedback cues as the applicant talks:
      "I see."
      "Hmmmm."
      "That's interesting."
      "Yes."
      "I know what you mean."
      Nod your head.
    - If you must check your watch or clock to keep track of the time, do so surreptitiously. Also, don't set an alarm clock to indicate that the interview is over. If an alarm should ring, the applicant is likely to bolt out of the chair.
11. ASK CLARIFYING QUESTIONS. Get the applicant to elaborate a point:
    "I can see you have an interest in accounting systems. Which ones have you worked with? Are there any you prefer?"
12. DON'T WASTE TIME. Demonstrating your superior knowledge of the latest FASB exposure drafts, or bragging about your latest client acquisition takes up time the applicant could be using to reveal something about himself or herself.

Maintaining an appropriate climate to foster the interview process takes effort. Applicants who sense you are truly interested in what they think, and in what they have to offer, are more likely to be frank and open about their qualifications, interests, and expectations. The art of listening, then, enables you to take full advantage of interviewing time.

Speaking: An Acquired Skill

Like writing and listening, speaking is an art that can be studied and perfected. The same rhetorical principles that enable an accountant to communicate effectively in writing and by listening also empower an accountant to communicate orally. Peter F. Stone describes ten techniques in GASP (Generally Accepted Speaking Principles):[12]

1. Memory jogging (Remember what to say.)
2. Humor (Use humor appropriately.)
3. You-better-believe-it (Believe in what you say.)
4. Eye contact (Maintain rapport with your audience.)
5. Persuasion (Convince your listeners.)
6. Anxiety (Overcome your fear of speaking.)
7. Conversation (Speak clearly.)
8. Preparation and practice (Practice your delivery.)
9. Volume (Be sure you can be heard.)
10. Brevity (Stick to your time limit.)

Useful as these practices are, effective speaking actually starts with rhetorically sound principles that consider the speaker's and the audience's situation, and logical, ethical, and pathetic principles.

The Rhetorical Principle: Analyze the Situation

The Speaking Occasion

Analyzing the rhetorical situation involves the occasion for speaking, the motivation to speak, the listener or the audience, and the constraints on the speaker and the audience. Accountants speak in all sorts of informal and formal situations, ranging from conferring by telephone to presiding over meetings; from leading seminars to giving formal speeches. Each occasion involves strategies and techniques appropriate to the circumstance. The effective accountant-speaker tailors both content and delivery to the occasion.

The Motivation for Speaking

Each speaking occasion entails its own exigence. An accountant calls a client in response to a query, presides at a staff meeting to plan new marketing strategy, holds a seminar on coping with the IRS's assaults on independent contractors, delivers a talk on estate planning options to local Rotarians. And underlying all motivation to speak, of course, is the accountant's self-interest. Speaking earns the accountant CPE credit, initiates new business contacts, publicizes his or her (and the firm's) expertise, and serves the public interest. According to Jeffrey P. Davidson in "Speaking Your Way to the Top," speaking effectively advances careers:

> First, you will be perceived as bold and dynamic. . . .Public speaking is such a valuable asset to your career [in] that it gives you visibility. You'll build a following not only within your organization, but also in your profession or industry.[13]

Exercise 8-2 helps you to assess the speaker's motivation as well as to analyze his or her situation.

Audience Analysis

Tailoring oral presentation to an audience's interests, needs, understanding, and expectations is critical to effective communication. Ignoring the audience when planning any oral communication is tantamount to sending out generic resume cover letters. C. Mike Merz reminds accountants that considering audience, or

> developing a good bedside manner—the ability to communicate accounting information to nonaccountants—is critical to achieving success. . . .This means considering both the technical content of what you say and the way that you say it.[14]

Exercise 8-3 ensures that you as a speaker incorporate content and delivery technique to accommodate the audience.

The Speaker's and Audience's Constraints

Speakers and audiences enter into speaking situations with certain assumptions. If the speaker thoroughly analyzes the situation and the audience, he or she can then adjust the presentation to whatever beliefs, traditions, and motives are likely to constrain the message's effectiveness. For example, an enrolled agent, explaining the latest restrictions on depreciation allowances to a beleaguered group of farmers, is likely to receive a frosty reception. The farmers already *believe* the IRS taxes them mercilessly, which colors their attitude toward enrolled agents—victims of "blame the messenger" syndrome. CPAs who prefer the tradition of attracting quality clients by way of satisfied-client referrals rather than by aggressive marketing campaigns are likely to give a hostile reception to the partner who proposes TV ads *à la* H & R Block. And an audience of clients who senses that a CPA touts investments in which he or she has an interest may spurn sound investment advice from the same accountant. Speakers, then, must consider constraints affecting them and their audiences when constructing oral arguments.

The charts in Figures 8-1 and 8-2 illustrate the components of the rhetorical situation involved in speaking occasions for accountants. The components apply to both in-house and external situations.

The Logical Principle: Incorporate Evidence

Everything you have learned about constructing a logical argument for written communication holds true for oral communication. Differences between written and oral communication, however, necessitate special accommodations for an oral audience. Consider the similarities and differences in the two modes of communication:

Similarities between Written and Oral Communication
Arguments are planned, structured, and forecasted.
Evidence supports points.
Audiences are generally interested in the topic.

FIGURE 8-1
In-house Occasions for Speaking

Occasion	*Exigence*	*Audience*	*Constraints*
Telephone call	Respond to client query.	Client	Client questions billing. As a nonaccountant, the client doesn't understand level of expertise involved in certain engagement complications that justify value-added billing.
Training session on new computer system	Train employees on new hardware and software.	Staff and senior accountants	Accountants had enough trouble learning current system.
Chair, tax season planning meeting	Ensure smoothly run tax season.	Tax partner, office manager, staff accountants, clerical workers, per diem preparers and reviewers	Per diem accountants unfamiliar with company procedures. New hires unfamiliar with tax season demands.
Chair, audit committee	Outline audit procedures.	Staff accountants	New client: previous audit must be reviewed.
Post–tax season performance review	Perform "spring purge."	Tax partner, senior accountants	40% of new hires must be cut.
Demonstration of new software	Select new client accounting system.	Administrative partner, data processing manager	Hardware lacks adequate expansion capability.
Electronic filing update	Stay competitive with other firms that have electronic filing.	Tax partner, senior tax preparers	Electronic filing is not cost-effective for eligible clients.
Seminar on IRS treatment of independent contractors	Earn CPE credit.	Senior accountants	30% of client base either serve as or hire independent contractors.
Client update on estate planning	Build goodwill; inform clients; promote firm.	Clients	Levels of expertise are mixed.

Occasion	*Exigence*	*Audience*	*Constraints*
Speech on tax update for local Rotary	Provide update; secure clients; build goodwill; serve community.	Rotarians and guests	Levels of expertise are mixed.
Teaching accounting course at a community college	Earn CPE credit; increase income; build goodwill.	Undergraduate students	Many students are not accounting majors.
Seminar on marketing	Build practices.	Local CPAs	Local CPAs are competitors; firms employ different advertising standards.
Talk on CPA profession for 8th-grade class.	Daughter wanted parent to partipate in "Career Day."	8th-graders, teacher	Other parents include airline pilot, veterinarian, and mortician.
Conference call	Discuss deferred compensation plan with tax attorneys.	Tax attorneys	Tax attorneys have expertise firm can't offer.
Chair, accounting standards committee for state CPA society	Provide professional service; earn CPE credit.	CPAs	Levels of expertise are mixed; professional experience is varied.
Guest speaker for college Business Communication class	Perform public service; promote firm.	Undergraduate students, professor	Students are not all accounting majors.
Recruiting at university job fair	Recruit employees.	Graduating seniors	Must consider Equal Employment Opportunity rules, competition from other firms, and hectic atmosphere.

FIGURE 8-2
External Occasions for Speaking

Audiences expect to be informed.
Audiences like to be entertained.
Audiences can take notes.
Audiences can be persuaded to share another person's point of view.
Audiences can be urged to take action.
Writers or speakers can employ visual aids.
Audiences are easily distracted.

Differences between Written and Oral Communication

Written	*Oral*
Readers can start, pause, stop reading at will without hurting comprehension.	Tuned-out hearers cannot easily catch up on missed content.
Only one sense is involved: sight.	More than one sense is involved: sight and hearing.
Writers can augment message with graphic aids.	Speakers can use both visual and audio aids.
Visual aids are generally limited to two-dimensional, flat images.	Speakers can use many types of visuals: still photos and slides, film, live presentations, handouts, etc.
Readers do not always feel the full force of the writer's personality.	Hearers can see the speaker and hear vocal inflections.

Feedback, if any, is delayed; writers cannot gauge or adjust to audience reaction.	Speakers experience immediate audience feedback and can adjust the talk accordingly.
Writers cannot interact with audience.	Speakers can interact with audience.
Writers cannot immediately respond to audience questions.	Speakers can offer immediate response to audience questions.
Writers cannot retract errors without considerable effort and embarrassment.	Speakers can correct errors immediately with no bad effects.
Writers do not have to work around a short attention span.	Speakers have to consider the audience's short attention span.

Obviously, a speaker must take special care to construct a sound argument that can be understood by an oral audience. This audience cannot go back to the text to recover a missed point or detail. The oral audience must listen intently, so as not to miss anything, whereas the reader can pause, leave the work, and return to it at leisure.

As a speaker you must observe the conventions of the speaking occasion. For example, a small audience could easily participate in a seminar or discussion; a large group would have to be addressed more formally. If you are a panelist, you will have to pay close attention to time constraints, as well as understand how your material complements the other speakers' presentations.

Before you can accommodate the oral audience, you need to learn as much about the audience as possible (see Exercise 8-3). Determining what the audience already knows, what they need to know, their constraints as hearers, and their motivation for attending the talk is critical to constructing a coherent, persuasive message. Be sure to consider your audience in every detail as you plan your presentation.

You should also determine your purpose in speaking (see Exercise 8-2). What can *you* contribute that another speaker cannot? What are your goals? What should the audience understand as a result of hearing you? What action do you want the audience to take? Only after considering the occasion, the audience, and the purpose of the talk can you actually start constructing the argument.

Incorporating Evidence to Create a Sound Argument

The Introduction: Hooking the Fish. Although the introduction to the talk is what we will discuss first, speakers as well as writers often construct their material out of order, taking care later to incorporate transitions between parts and to assemble the pieces into a coherent whole. The purpose of the introduction is to put the audience into a receptive frame of mind—to set up hearer expectation about the topic, the purpose of the talk, and the points to be made. You can capture your audience's interest in one of several ways:

1. If you follow another speaker, play off his or her topic:

   My colleague, Jerry Conrad, just detailed what is involved in defending accountants who are being sued. I'm here to show how the opposition *prosecutes* accountants.

2. Use a relevant anecdote (real or fictitious) or a hypothetical case or a scenario to whet the appetite of your audience for what is to follow. Besides using persons and situations the audience can identify with, you also establish a situation to which you can return during the talk and during your conclusion to make your point:

   One of my clients just received his eighth IRS notice threatening to seize everything except his firstborn. They keep sending the notices to the wrong address, causing delays well over the time allotted to pay the IRS claims. Can IRS hold him liable for notices he received after the due dates?

Your opening example can compare or contrast the points you cover in your talk:

COMPARISON The IRS has finally done it. They've put the fox in charge of the henhouse. If a client gets in trouble, he or she can file a 911 form with the IRS that temporarily halts seizure.

CONTRAST We all know how beleaguered and frustrated our clients feel when they're notified for an in-office audit. As inconvenient as audits are for them (and lucrative for us), they haven't really known true exasperation until they've been hauled in for the granddaddy of all tax audits, the Taxpayer Compliance Measurement Program.

You can also begin with consequences, thus suggesting that your presentation will deal with the root causes and remedies:

We've all seen ads for local bookkeeping outfits that tout accounting services, tax preparation, financial statements, monthly and quarterly write-up work. What percentage of *your* public accounting and tax practice involves those same services? And how is it that you must study and pass professional exams, while your competitors for certain services need only to buy an ordinary business license?

You might try projecting into the future:

Before we discuss practice-building strategies, I'd like to jump ahead to the year 2010. Are you willing today to invest in hardware to meet the demands of increasingly sophisticated software, or do you plan to wait for more efficient hardware? Are your hiring practices geared to obtaining the kind of accountants needed in the next century? Are you gearing your education programs to meet the new criteria?

3. Stir up audience emotion with a question:

   Should our clients be required to pay penalties and interest for failing to pay claims on time, even when their notices were sent to the wrong address?

4. Refer to a recent event well known to the audience:

   Amid all the scrambling for Laventhol and Horwath's clients, there is a problem: how will the new accountant satisfy SEC's requirements to furnish a letter from the former accountant commenting on the reason for the change in auditors? Who will write the letter?

5. Outline the benefits of the presentation to the audience:

   You will leave here today knowing how to evaluate investment portfolios and how to assist clients in choosing the best investment vehicle to achieve their goals.

6. Start with a joke or a funny story. But unless you possess the talent of a Jay Leno, it is best to let the humor flow naturally from the material. Starting a talk with a stand-up comic's routine might leave you doing Johnny Carson's famous tap dance should your jokes fall flat.

7. Open with a quote. This is one of the riskier approaches. If your quote is fresh and unknown to the audience, it can work—if not, it won't be an auspicious beginning:

   Taxing is an easy business. Any projector can contrive new impositions; any bungler can add to the old.

   Edmund Burke

   Taxes are the price we pay for a civilized society.

   Oliver Wendell Holmes, Jr.

Taxation under every form presents but a choice of evils.

David Ricardo

The income tax has made more liars out of the American people than gold has.

Will Rogers

There is one difference between a tax collector and a taxidermist—the taxidermist leaves the hide.

Mortimer Caplin[15]

Show me someone who doesn't think accounting is a creative profession and I will show you someone who does their own taxes.

Anonymous[16]

8. Start by talking about yourself. The audience should already know, through promotional material and the moderator's introduction, who you are and why you are qualified to speak about the topic. You can refer to your experiences throughout your talk, of course, but by beginning your talk with an extended introduction to yourself, you risk diverting the focus to yourself rather than to your subject matter.

Try identifying the components of effective introductions by making notes from televised sermons and political speeches, or from workplace presentations and talks, or from academic addresses. Record your observations in Exercise 8-4.

The Content: Reeling Them In

Creating Listener Expectation. Part of retaining your audience's attention entails setting up and meeting their expectations. Programs and agenda often provide the audience with an overview of the presentation. And forecasting what you will talk about is a good way to let your audience preview your subject matter. The following text is a transcribed excerpt from the "Accounting and Tax Highlights" tapes, produced by Warren, Gorham & Lamont, and used by accountants to earn CPE credit. The speaker, Deborah Silverstein, illustrates effective forecasting for an oral audience:

> On taxation, we'll review some more important provisions of the Revenue Reconciliation Act of 1990; we'll discuss a case in which the doctrine of tax only on an increase in economic wealth seemingly was violated by the IRS; we'll clarify some rules about employee reimbursements and other expense allowance arrangements; and we'll answer some frequently asked questions about the tax status of military reservists on active duty in Operation Desert Shield.[17]

Because of Silverstein's forecasting, the listener expects discussion along specified lines. When the topics come up in turn, the listener recognizes the subject matter. Notice the active verbs that are designed to attract the busy accountant's attention: "review," "discuss," "clarify," and "answer."

Here is another example, this time from a talk delivered at the 1988 Penn State Conference on Rhetoric and Composition:

> Perhaps no example of writing in the workplace rattles the recipient more than a communication from the Internal Revenue Service. One type of IRS writing that particularly affects its readers is the "Notice of Deficiency," sent by the IRS to serve notice to a taxpayer that it intends to seize property because taxes, penalties, or interest have not been paid. I will discuss a typical IRS notice of deficiency sent to a Maryland excavating contractor who has operated a small family-oriented business for fifteen years. I focus on IRS communication with small business

because their owners must make far-reaching and costly decisions based on their reading of the text.

The five points I will discuss involve questions about the writing strategies and rhetorical situation of a government forced to exact taxes from a resistant, often hostile audience. My first question is, why does IRS deliberately send a mixed, if not downright confusing, message to its readers? Second, even though the apparent purpose of the notice is to get the business to forward its tax payment, what are other purposes of the notice? Third, how does the rhetorical situation that spawns the notice of deficiency account for its ambiguity? Fourth, why is any contact with the IRS usually costly even if the business owes no taxes? And fifth, what wanted and unwanted response has the IRS notice invited from the small business community?[18]

Because of this forecasting, the audience expects discussion of the IRS Notice of Deficiency, the story of the Maryland contractor, and answers to the five points raised.

Structuring the Oral Presentation. Forecasting the organization of your oral presentation is analogous to providing an outline or headings for written communication. Once the points to be covered are established, you have only to discuss each in turn. Structuring your presentation might involve one or more of the following configurations:

- SOLVE A PROBLEM Present a problem by using anecdotes, examples, scenarios, or case studies; then suggest feasible solutions:

  Assertion: Noncertified practicing accountants are encroaching on territory previously held by certified public accountants.

  Proofs

  1. Ad by noncertified accountants for accounting services.
  2. Publications for noncertified accountants discussing accounting services.
  3. Testimony of noncertified accountants' clients disappointed at the level of accounting services available.

  Solutions

  1. Educate the public (via AICPA, other professional association ad campaigns).
  2. Educate clients (brochures, newsletters, seminars).
  3. Pressure state legislatures to restrict licensing to certified accountants.
- COMPARE AND CONTRAST For a state tax update seminar, compare and contrast old and new tax laws.
- EXPLAIN COMPONENTS OF TOPIC: Passive activity losses are now severely limited. After defining passive activity, use case studies to discuss
  1. Nonrental business activity
  2. Interest expense allocation
  3. Transfer of rental property
  4. Gifts and death transfers
- SHOW CONSEQUENCES OF ACTION Detail a situation in which an action is taken; then describe the results and implications of the action:

  Situation: IRS no longer accepts completed-contract status reporting for long-term construction contracts.

  Result: Percentage of completion accounting is now required.

  Implications:

  1. Contractor can no longer defer payment of taxes until contract is completed.
  2. The percentage of completion contract requires more complex accounting (more client paperwork, increased accounting fees).

Using Transitions to Aid Audience Comprehension. In written communication you help the audience follow your train of thought by providing transitions (see "Transitions:

Aids to Understanding," pp. 198–199). So too should you aid audience understanding by using words or phrases:

- To indicate sequence
- To add a point
- To connect points
- To summarize
- To conclude

You can also indicate divisions by these verbal and nonverbal cues:

- Between points, recap and forecast your next point.
- Look down deliberately, pause, and continue to next point.
- Shift your position physically.
- If the occasion is a lengthy seminar or presentation, plan breaks between major sections.

Using Handouts to Complement Your Message. Handouts can complicate the speaker's task if they detract from the speaker's presentation. If you want to refer to material in a handout during your talk, distribute it beforehand; otherwise, explain what material will be available and distribute it after the talk. Handouts can contain auxiliary material too cumbersome to cover verbally:

- STATISTICS A sure way to overwhelm your listeners is to throw strings of statistics at them. Instead, provide tables and charts in a handout.
- BIBIOGRAPHIES Seminar participants and other oral audiences appreciate annotated bibliographies for later reference. Bibliographies incorporating standard works and unique sources add to your credibility.
- ILLUSTRATIONS Cartoons, drawings, photographs, and other graphics add visual appeal and can be referenced in the talk.
- QUOTATIONS Lengthy passages from relevant sources can be reproduced for future reference.
- CASE STUDY EXAMPLES Accounting problems, background of the case study, and results of the study can be detailed in a handout.
- OUTLINE A bare outline of the talk with space to add notes helps the listener follow the structure and main points of the talk.

Be sure you plan for a sufficient number of handouts so that each member of your audience has one. If you run short, offer to supply them by fax or mail as soon as possible.

Exercise 8-5 offers you practice in providing material that helps audiences comprehend an oral message.

Concluding: Asking "So What?" In summarizing your points, you only partially conclude your oral presentation. Eugene R. Hammond recommends that writers induce the reader to go beyond the information presented, to see the significance of what is said, to answer the question, "so what?"[19] The speaker can also encourage the listener to supply the "so what?" by adjusting attitudes, proposing solutions, considering alternatives, giving approval, applying the information, or taking action in some way.

Also useful in concluding an oral presentation is a reference to your opening scenario, example, anecdote, or case study, as in this conclusion to the Maryland excavating contractor's hassle with the IRS, previously mentioned:

> The CPA who handled the Maryland contractor's notices wrote seventeen letters and made innumerable phone calls before the matter was settled. Incidentally, the contractor eventually received IRS *refund* checks totaling over $700. It seems that he had overpaid his taxes after all, but that did little to compensate him for his

expenses in contending with the IRS's computers. At least he was able to deduct the accounting fees.[20]

The Ethical Principle: Establish Credibility

One of your speaking objectives may be to build your firm's image, but you must first work on your own image. The most important message delivered in a riveting style falls on deaf ears *if* the listeners question the believability of the messenger. Sometimes credibility is affected by a disjunction between the topic and the speaker. For example, would the Veterans of Foreign Wars be likely to ask Jane Fonda to deliver a keynote address? And what sort of reception would Jesse Helms receive if he addressed a meeting of the National Organization of Women? Jane Fonda, however, is entirely credible in her role as aerobic exercise maven, and Jesse Helms would receive an enthusiastic welcome at a meeting of conservatives.

Assuming no conflict between you and your topic, you can take the following measures to establish your credibility, thus enhancing your image:

Believe Your Message

How can you expect listeners to consider the validity of your claims if you appear less than sincere? How can you expect an audience to take action on your ideas if you evidence a ho-hum attitude? You can't expect to generate enthusiasm for your subject matter if you aren't already sold on it yourself.

Appear Professional

Wearing appropriate business attire sets a professional tone for your presentation and supports your credibility. Appearing disheveled plants seeds of skepticism in your listeners. They invest considerable time, effort, and expense in meetings, seminars, talks, and presentations—for a professional purpose. The speaker's appearance and grooming either complements or clashes with a professional image.

Move Confidently

Slouching and leaning over the podium signals the wrong message to your audience. You want them to listen to you with interest. The least you can do is to use body language that projects enthusiasm and professionalism. If you plant yourself solidly behind the podium, you will seem to have chosen a barrier between you and your audience. If possible, move around a bit; consider planning your movement to signal transitions between points or report sections. Don't betray your nervousness, however, by restlessly circling around the podium or by crisscrossing the room.

Use Your Own Voice

Think about effective speakers you know: lecturers, people in the media, seminar leaders, religious and political figures. Why are they effective? They have a message, they are comfortable with their material, they are interested in people. They are confident enough in themselves and their message to let their true personalities show through and even to laugh at their mistakes. Effective speakers use their own "voices"; they are uniquely themselves rather than an imitation of someone else. In short, you can convey your message best by being yourself.

Recover Flaws Gracefully

One rule of thumb in any speaking situation is to expect the unexpected. You lose your place or drop your notecards; you spill your water or trip over cords; the mike collapses or buzzes intermittently; a talkative participant manipulates or dominates the discussion. If possible, turn the disaster into humor, recover yourself, and move along:

If you lose your place: I see my mouth is running ahead of my notes—I need to find my place.

If you drop your notes: Hold on while I collect my thoughts.
If you spill water: The table needed cleaning anyway.
If you trip: I really was voted "most graceful" in my high school senior class.
If the mike falls: I'm not really that short.
If the mike buzzes: I promised the mike equal time.
If a participant competes: We'll cover that point this afternoon, Ms. Jones. Just now, we need to concentrate on fiduciary accounting.

Deliver Your Message with Poise

If you are enthusiastic about your topic, if you have carefully researched credible sources, and if you want to convince your listeners to act, you don't want to sabotage your goals and efforts by calling attention to your failings as a speaker. Your audience will discover your shortcomings soon enough. If you begin your talk by apologizing for your delivery technique or lack of preparation, you send the wrong message to your expectant listeners:

> I'm just filling in for the seminar leader. I'm not very good at this. . . .
>
> I really needed more time to prepare. We'll just have to make do with what I have. . . .
>
> I'm told I'm a lousy speaker. . . .
>
> I guess you can tell I'm really nervous. . . .

If you approach the podium purposefully and unhurriedly, and you take a breath and pause before you speak, you will appear more confident and less nervous.

Field Questions Honestly

You may encounter a questioner who knows more than you do about an aspect of your topic, or who poses a question you can't answer. Rather than spout a phoney answer, say you don't know and promise follow-up:

> I don't really have an opinion on SFAS No. 95. What do you think?
>
> I haven't had time to review that particular FASB announcement, but I'll get back to you. Can we talk later?

Exploit the Introduction

Seminars generally feature brief, written summations of the leader's qualifications and experience, as in this write-up for a faculty member of a one-day Seminar for Accountants and Key Restaurant Personnel:

> Edward M. Hynes, CPA, speaker and author on financial systems and controls for restaurants, has presented this highly rated seminar to more than 30,000 CPAs and Restaurant Owners. As Accounting Manager for Universal Services, an international food service consulting firm, Mr. Hynes developed feasibility studies and evaluated financial systems and controls for hundreds of restaurants in the United States, South America, and Canada. Mr. Hynes has had his own accounting and tax practice for over 16 years, specializing in the field of restaurant accounting.[21]

If no such biographical statement is furnished for you, have someone highlight your expertise to indicate that you are qualified to speak on your topic. Rather than tout your own expertise, the person who introduces you can furnish information to enhance your credibility and image. Valuable biographical information may include:

Consulting in the subject area
Leadership positions in professional organizations
Relevant publications
Advanced degrees

Experience in leading similar seminars
High positions in government
Partnerships in firms
Professional awards or academic honors

Use Credible Sources
Audiences appreciate authoritative, updated information. Material endorsed by prestigious or governmental organizations such as the AICPA or the IRS are more likely to be believed than material from less authoritative entities. Take care that your bibliographies and references feature the latest information about your topic.

Use Attractive Audio/Visual Aids
Sloppy handouts, worn overhead masters, and scratchy audio- or videotapes do nothing to enhance your image. Be sure that audio and video material can be heard and seen clearly, and that your handouts and other visuals are well designed and readable.

Efforts at establishing credibility involve more than putting Generally Accepted Speaking Principles into practice during the actual presentation. You convey a positive or negative impression long before you open your mouth to speak. You are "on," in a sense, when you are first contacted to speak, when you confirm arrangements, and as you chat with listeners afterward. In other words, your *ethos* is enhanced or diminished with any communication connected with your presentation: written or spoken, formal or informal.

The Pathetic Principle: Appeal to Self-Interest

A businessperson's time is usually so committed that he or she can barely keep up with professional journal reading. Consequently, time and expense are carefully invested in professional education and personal development. The accountant who addresses an audience of peers, clients, or business associates should painstakingly gear messages to satisfy audience demands as to time, content, and professionalism. In addition, the successful speaker uses proven delivery techniques and rhetorical devices that tend to delight the audience and please the "ear." In short, the speaker seeks the goodwill of the audience by meeting its needs, by crafting a pleasing presentation, and by avoiding anything that would distract from the speaker's purpose and message.

Meeting Audience Expectations
Whether you are asked to "say a few words" with no notice or to plan an elaborate two-day seminar months in advance, your audience will listen with certain expectations. The AICPA's *CPE Seminar Catalog* for 1991–1992 thoroughly sets up audience expectation which seminar participants expect to be fulfilled. AICPA specifies the following criteria for all its seminars, so that prospective participants know exactly why they are committing time, money, and energy. For example, consider the offering "Today's Controller: The Total Manager":[22]

SUBJECT CATEGORY: Industry
WHO SHOULD ATTEND: Accountants in industry, MAS specialists
REQUISITE KNOWLEDGE AND EXPERIENCE: None
LEVEL: Basic.
LENGTH: 1 day.
ADVANCE PREPARATION: None.
RECOMMENDED CPE CREDIT: 8 hours.
WHEN AND WHERE: [dates and locations given]
DESCRIPTION: Today's controller must be an organizer, a policymaker, a financial analyst, and a strategic planner—that is, the total manager. This course uses case studies and discussion questions to emphasize the organizational role of the controller whose effective management of technological, economic, and human factors affects the success of a business.

OBJECTIVES:

- Use management tools that, combined with their technical skills, facilitate effective controllership.
- Advise clients in this specialized management area.

COURSE HIGHLIGHTS:

- The controller's job.
- Organizing the controller's department.
- Controller's oversight role.
- Management Information Systems.
- Business planning and financial forecasting.
- Communicating financial information.

Because of AICPA's comprehensive detail, participants know what to expect. But imagine the uproar if the seminar leader switches topics to "Professional Recruiting and Retention" or "Corporate Tax Saving Techniques." The title and other information furnished to your audience in advance *must* accurately reflect what you will actually talk about. To deviate from what was promised would disappoint listener expectation and fail to consider the self-interest of your audience.

Choosing the Type of Delivery

For presentations from the most formal to the informal, you have four choices of deliveries: memorization, impromptu, reading from a manuscript, and extemporaneous. Many speakers use a combination of one or more types.

Speaking from Memory. The most formal type of presentation is the memorized speech. Although the wise speaker works from some sort of prepared notes, memorizing an entire manuscript can be a terrifying experience for all but trained actors; it also has other disadvantages:

- A memory lapse could derail your whole effort.
- By sticking to a memorized script, you cannot adjust yourself to audience feedback.
- In relying on memory, you might alter important technical material.

Speaking Spontaneously. The opposite of a formal, memorized speech is the impromptu talk, created by exigencies of the moment. If you are asked to "say a few words," with little time to prepare, at least list a few main points to keep yourself on track. The advantages of spontaneous remarks, given mostly in small, informal groups, are brevity, low audience expectation, and natural interaction with the audience. The disadvantages are several:

- You have no time to structure your remarks.
- "Off the cuff" speakers have a tendency to ramble.
- Time doesn't permit garnering evidence to support your points.

Reading the Speech. While some authorities maintain that speakers who read speeches are boring, the response needn't be boredom—if the speaker is properly prepared and rehearsed. If you are an inexperienced speaker, reading your speech may be the only way for you to get through it. Advantages:

- You can structure your talk to suit your purpose and audience needs.
- You can deviate from your text in accord with audience feedback.
- The talk can be crafted to fit time constraints.
- You can annotate your script with reminders to yourself.
- You can rehearse the speech, reading for expression and emphasis.

Reading the speech entails disadvantages as well:

- Unless you practice, practice, practice, you will come across as stilted and unnatural.

- Maintaining eye contact with your audience while you read is difficult. Again, practice is the key: the more familiar you are with your material, the less you are forced to glue your eyes to the text.

Myles Martel, in *Before You Say a Word: The Executive Guide to Effective Communication*,[23] offers some advice for typing a manuscript:

1. Number the pages at both top and bottom.
2. Don't break sentences, paragraphs, or ideas between pages.
3. Clip rather than staple your pages together.
4. Begin each sentence at the left-hand margin. Indicate paragraphs or breaks in thought by starting a new page.
5. Type closely to the top of the page, but stop six inches from the bottom. This enables you to maintain eye contact, and to refrain from holding your head down.
6. Highlight key words and phrases in yellow.

If you read your speech, prepare *two* copies of your manuscript; keep one on your person and the other in an accessible place. What if you were to lose your only manuscript copy?

Speaking Extemporaneously. Religious speakers, teachers, and seminar and workshop leaders usually organize a message but stop at the outline stage. They speak from carefully prepared notes. This type of delivery allows for eye contact, interaction with the audience, and a conversational style. Disadvantages:

- Unless you stick to your outline and keep an eye on the clock, you can ramble into digressions that cause you to go over the alotted time, crowd the ending, or eliminate important points.
- Extemporaneous talks are difficult to rehearse.

Myles Martel recommends a hybrid approach for many speaking situations:

> The body of your speech is researched and prepared in outline form to enable you speak *extemporaneously*.
>
> You *memorize* the first few opening lines and a stirring conclusion to enable you to present them with full force and conviction.
>
> You may *read* short passages (as naturally as possible!) when it is necessary to quote someone precisely, to use specific numbers, or if you are concerned that you might be misquoted on a sensitive element of your presentation, or if you're simply uncomfortable presenting the idea extemporaneously.
>
> You allow for *impromptu* adaptation during your remarks based on audience feedback or in reaction to the comments of a previous reader.[24]

Achieving a Professional Delivery

A prelude to appealing to the self-interest of audiences is securing their goodwill. After all, how can you expect to persuade or inform listeners if they are embarrassed, uncomfortable, confused, or downright annoyed by your delivery technique? Since most people are uncomfortable in speaking situations, you already have their sympathy, especially if you are an inexperienced speaker. Even so, an audience's patience and understanding can be pressed only so far. If an unprofessional delivery style hinders the transmission of your message, your purpose will be thwarted, and everyone's time will be wasted. Therefore, study the following "do's and don'ts" of oral presentation so that you put the audience in a receptive mood for your ideas and material.

Delivery Do's.

- Do signify friendliness by smiling and maintaining eye contact.
- Do try to appear relaxed. If you start your talk by confessing your nervousness, you set up expectations that detract from your goal and your message.

- Do approach the podium or speaking area confidently. And remember that you are "on" even before you utter a word.
- Do take a sip of water before you begin speaking. Otherwise your mouth will feel like it's stuffed with cotton.
- Do stand erect. Slouching conveys a negative impression of your competence. If you talk from a seated position, sit up straight.
- Do dress appropriately for the occasion. The wrong attire can send a negative message.
- Do manage your body language. Pacing frenetically around the room causes your listeners to follow you much as spectators at a tennis match, with heads snapping back and forth.
- Do control your hands. Jamming them deep into the recesses of your pockets is as distracting as waving them around like you are swatting pesky gnats. Remember that your audience can't feel your itch or see the fly coming in for a landing on your nose. All they see is a person apparently suffering from a seizure.
- Do keep your hands away from your face. Scratching your nose, head, or neck—and twirling your hair, mustache, or beard—leads to distracting (and sometimes amusing) **mannerisms**. Some men come to the platform with full beards, but leave with Vandykes due to incessantly twirling them. And some women appear to rearrange their hairstyles during their presentations due to constantly patting their hair.
- Do enunciate your words clearly. Some speakers slur their words together so that they soundlikethisreads.
- Do speak loudly enough to be heard, but not so loud that you imply that your audience suffers from a collective hearing problem. Arrange for someone from the back of the room to signal you in case you can't be heard.
- Do speak slowly enough that everyone can grasp your message. Nervous speakers tend to talk fast; however, don't speak so deliberately that you appear to be t-a-l-k-i-n-g i-n s-l-o-w m-o-t-i-o-n. Speaking at a conversational rate is about right.
- Do speak expressively, especially if you read portions of your talk. Vary your inflections (the rise and fall of your voice).
- Do speak in your lower vocal range.
- Do maintain eye contact, sweeping the entire audience as you speak. If you try to look at everyone, however, *you* will end up looking like a tennis match spectator.
- Do observe your time limits scrupulously. Better to leave your listeners wanting a little more than to cause the audience to wish you would sit down. Also, if other speakers follow you, it is unconscionable to intrude upon their allotted time.
- Do act as if you believe in your own message. Your audience will be interested in what you have to say if *you* evidence enthusiasm.
- Do rehearse your presentation.
- Do tape yourself so you can improve your technique.
- Do be yourself.

Delivery Don'ts.

- Don't approach the podium as if you are preaching at your own funeral. There *is* life after speaking.
- Don't dwell on your nervousness. Instead, concentrate on breathing deeply, on communicating your message, on meeting your audience's needs and expectations.
- Don't eat beforehand if you have a nervous stomach.
- Don't announce your shortcomings. If you have any, the audience will sense them soon enough.

- Don't slouch or hang over the podium.
- Don't talk with your chin cupped in your hand if you are seated. This tends to cover one side of your mouth so that one side of the room can't hear you.
- Don't bang your notecards on the podium.
- Don't tap your pen on the table. Even though Johnny Carson has made millions drumming his pencil, it won't work for you.
- Don't overdress or underdress for the occasion.
- Don't rock back and forth or sway to and fro. Your audience will wonder what inner tune you are keeping time with. One accounting professor, the renowned William Paton of the University of Michigan, used to keep his three hundred students at rapt attention during his lectures by rocking backward and forward—with his feet just touching the edge of a raised platform. His students were partly interested in his accounting theories, but mostly interested in when he would lose his balance. A preacher tried the same technique to capture the attention of his congregation. It didn't quite work for him:—as he rocked forward one Sunday morning, he fell and broke his leg.
- Don't fidget with car keys, loose change, pens, pencils, jewelry, hair, or clothing.
- Don't slur your words or speak too fast. Remember that you are addressing an *oral* audience. They can't turn back to the previous page to pick up what they missed.
- Don't shout or mumble.
- Don't speak in the upper ranges of your voice. Sustained high-pitched tones sound shrill and cost at least one vice-presidential candidate an election.
- Don't speak in a monotone. Only a Henry Kissinger can get away with it.
- Don't pepper your speech with distracting verbal mannerisms such as "you know," "um," "er," "ah," or "like." Because verbal mannerisms are difficult to detect in your own speech, have someone critique you, or tape yourself to determine if you use these empty and annoying expressions.
- Don't lose your audience by avoiding eye contact. Even if you must read your talk, maintain eye contact.
- Don't run over your allotted time. You can tell when the audience is getting restless: chairs will creak as listeners change position; you will lose eye contact; people will glance at their watches; and your moderator will gesticulate wildly to indicate that your time is up.
- Don't ramble on after you have indicated that you are about to conclude your talk.
- Don't act bored with your own material. If you can't work up a little enthusiasm, no one else will either.

Pleasing the Ear

If used sparingly, as when an experienced cook adds just enough spices to enhance a recipe, rhetorical devices can increase a listener's pleasure in hearing a presentation as well as increase a listener's understanding and acceptance of the message. The rhetorical devices that follow are **schemes** which alter how words sound for rhetorical effect, and **tropes**, which manipulate words to affect ways of thinking.[25] To see the effectiveness of schemes and tropes on understanding and remembering ideas, consider the following pairs:

> My feet are sore, but I have peace in my spirit.
> *My feets is tired, but my soul's at rest.* (Rosa Parks)
>
> Fish rot by the third day; company tends to outstay its welcome by the third day also.
> *Fish and visitors stink in three days.* (Benjamin Franklin)
>
> If the pressure gets too intense, leave the situation.
> *If you can't stand the heat, get out of the kitchen.* (Harry Truman)

Mail carriers attempt to deliver the mail regardless of inclement weather or time of day.

Neither rain, nor snow, nor sleet, nor hail, nor dark of night can stay these messengers from their appointed rounds.

When things seem too much to bear, those who draw on their inner resources are the ones who cope with the situation.

When the going gets tough, the tough get going.

Why is the second sentence in each pair so much more memorable than the first? After all, both sentences express the same idea. The answer lies in the artful use of schemes and tropes, those rhetorical devices that appeal to the ear and impress the mind.

Schemes: Altering Word Sounds. Schemes alter how words sound to the ear. One of the more useful schemes for speakers is *parallelism*, any similar structure in a series of words, phrases, clauses, or sentences, as in this passage from Lincoln's *Gettysburg Address* and an article from the *Journal of Accountancy*, respectively:

> It is rather for us to be here dedicated to the great task remaining before us—that from those honored dead we take increased devotion to that cause for which they gave the last full measure of devotion; that we here highly resolve that these dead shall not have died in vain; that this nation, under God, shall have a new birth of freedom; and that government of the people, by the people, for the people, shall not perish from the earth.
>
> In summary then, we find ourselves in a profession that has become extremely competitive, that must live with a skewed year because of congressional caprice and that faces a limited supply of individuals able to commit to achieving entrepreneurial ownership status.[26]
>
> *Donald F. Istvan, "Coming Full Circle in Practice Management"*

Another effective scheme for an oral audience is *antithesis*, which works contraries to say the same thing:

A man should be mourned at his birth, not at his death. (Montesquieu)

That's one small step for a man, one giant leap for mankind. (Neil Armstrong)

Some businesspeople are trying anything to beat the recession. Smart businesspeople are trying nothing. Right now, when you buy any Konica copier or fax, you'll pay nothing in interest or finance charges. (Konica advertisement)[27]

Often-used schemes involve rhyming sounds, *alliteration* (repeated consonant sounds) and *assonance* (repeated vowel sounds):

Alliteration.

No example of writing in the workplace rattles the recipient more than the IRS Notice of Deficiency which warns a taxpayer that it intends to seize property because taxes, penalties, and/or interest have not been paid.[28]

Intuitive systems, higher levels of integration, faster, more flexible software. (Prentice Hall advertisement)[29]

Tired of the same old seminars? Bored by books? Tranquilized by tapes? (MicroMash advertisement)[30]

Each course is current and complete, created by authors prominent in their field today. (MicroMash advertisement)[31]

Assonance.

We've got what's HOT! (E. F. Haskell advertisement)[32]

Oral audiences also appreciate *anaphora* (the use of similar beginnings for successive sentences, clauses, or phrases) and *epistrophe* (the use of similar endings for successive sentences, clauses, or phrases):

Anaphora.

We shall fight on the beaches, we shall fight on the landing-grounds, we shall fight in the fields and in the streets, we shall fight in the hills. (Winston Churchill)

The voice of the LORD is powerful; the voice of the LORD is full of majesty. The voice of the LORD breaketh the cedars. . . . (Psalm 29:4, 5a [KJV])

All the features, all the training options, all the support of DacEasy Accounting is available in a powerful, multiple-user version. (DacEasy advertisement)[33]

Epistrophe.

. . . And that government of the people, by the people, for the people, shall not perish from the earth. (Abraham Lincoln)

The call is FREE, the catalog is FREE, and the DEMO is FREE! (MicroMash advertisement)[34]

Tropes: Manipulating Thought. Obviously, schemes work on the ear; tropes effectively work on the mind and are especially useful in conveying complex messages to oral audiences. Unfamiliar concepts can be compared with familiar ones by means of *metaphors* (implied comparisons) and *similes* (explicit comparisons). For example, did you notice that this chapter section, "Pleasing the Ear," opened with a simile?

If used sparingly, as when an experienced cook adds just enough spices to enhance a recipe, rhetorical devices can increase a listener's pleasure in hearing a presentation as well as increase a listener's understanding and acceptance of the message.

Here are some examples of metaphor:

For every shot, golf professionals must carefully choose the right club based on many factors. . . terrain, wind, distance and angle of approach. Successful golfers consider all the variables before they reach the green. Lacerte Software looks at tax preparation much the same way. (Lacerte Software advertisement)[35]

TKR-R Lifts You Above the Time & Billing Jungle (E. F. Haskell Software advertisement)[36]

The demise of Laventhol & Horwath has also opened the doors for accounting firms on the hospitality front.[37]

Plays on words, or *puns*, inject humor while making a serious point:

Your argument is sound, nothing but sound. (Benjamin Franklin)

"Polishing the Apple" (heading for article on Macintosh computers)[38]

"Nibbling at Composition Problems Byte by Byte" (title of article on teaching writing with the use of computers)[39]

Hyperbole exaggerates for effect:

We stand to lose our shirts if the merger doesn't go through.

I was under the gun to get my clients' returns out the door, and some of the tax changes really had me confused. (Tax Partner advertisement)[40]

Rhetorical questions prompt the hearer to supply a predetermined answer:

How can we have a great university without great teachers?

Hast thou an arm like God? (Job 40:9 [KJV])

We also offer extensive continuing professional educational seminars through our Accountants Education Services—*another way Computax keeps you in command of your practice. Isn't it time you take command?* (CCH Computax advertisement)[41]

Sometimes, *irony* causes readers to infer the opposite of what is meant, as in the "Paperwork Reduction Act Notice" (from IRS tax forms).

Oxymorons yoke two contradictory terms:

Tax simplification.

We conducted a simple audit.

They managed to pull off an amicable divorce.

Obviously, it takes imagination and facility with words to incorporate schemes and tropes in an oral presentation. But as you can see from the preceding examples, pleasing the ear and challenging the mind of the listener are worth the trouble. To test your recognition of rhetorical devices, try identifying schemes and tropes used in articles and advertisements from an accounting journal, transcribed speeches, or other oral presentations. Use Exercise 8-6 as a guide.

Delivering a Short Talk

To test your understanding of GASP (Generally Accepted Speaking Principles), and to put the rhetorical, logical, ethical, and pathetic principles you have learned in this chapter into practice, prepare and deliver a short talk or presentation based on a class project. Base your rhetorical and delivery decisions on the purpose of your talk, time constraints, your audience's interests, and your professor's direction. Consider also what types of audio/visual aids are available to you and which would augment your presentation. Most classrooms accommodate the following audio/visual possibilities:

Handouts
Chalkboard
Posters
Flip charts
Audiotape
Videotape
Overhead projector

As your professor directs, fill in the "Presenter" and "Topic" sections of Exercise 8-7 or Exercise 8-8. Then, make photocopies so that your classmates can critique your content and technique. Hand out the evaluation forms just prior to your presentation.

Notes

1 Garth A. Hanson, Ph.D., "The Importance of Oral Communication in Accounting Practice," in "Management of an Accounting Practice," *CPA Journal* (December 1987): 118.

2 Hanson, 119.

3 Peter F. Stone, "GASP: Generally Accepted Speaking Principles," *Management Accounting* (September 1989): 34–36.

4 William Parkhurst, *The Eloquent Executive* (New York: Times Books), 1988, 121–123.

5 Caroline L. Bloomfield and Irene R. Fairley, *Business Communication: A Process Approach* (New York: Harcourt Brace Jovanovich, 1991), 450–451.

6 Lloyd F. Bitzer, "The Rhetorical Situation," *Philosophy and Rhetoric* (Winter 1968): 6–8.

7 Ronald E. Dulek and John S. Fielden, *Principles of Business Communication* (New York: Macmillan, 1990), 397.

8 Raymond A. Dumont and John M. Lannon, *Business Communications*, 3d ed. (Glenview, Ill.: Scott, Foresman/Little, Brown Higher Education, 1990), 648.

9 Robert Half, "How to Conduct a Successful Interview," *The Practical Accountant* (September 1988): 96–102.

10 Richard T. Case, "How to Conduct an Effective Interview," *The Practical Accountant* (April 1986): 65–70.

[11] Virginia L. Davis, "Selecting the Best Candidate Starts with Good Interviewing Skills," *The CPA Journal* (February 1986): 73–74.
[12] Stone, 34.
[13] Jeffrey P. Davidson, "Speaking Your Way to the Top," *The National Public Accountant* (July 1986): 36.
[14] C. Mike Merz, "Accountants: Mind Your Bedside Manner," *Management Accounting* (July 1989): 38.
[15] Quotes taken from section on "Tax," comp. John P. Bradley, Leo F. Daniels, and Thomas C. Jones, *The International Dictionary of Thoughts* (Chicago: J.G. Ferguson, 1969), 708–709.
[16] Anonymous, taken from a ceramic mug, "Accountant," Art 101 Limited, Atlanta, Georgia, 1984.
[17] Deborah Silverstein, "Accounting and Tax Highlights," (CPE Cassette Program), February 1991 (New York: Warren, Gorham & Lamont, 1990): Side 1.
[18] Aletha Hendrickson, "The IRS Notice: Intimidation by Design," presented at the Penn State Conference on Rhetoric and Composition, State College, Pennsylvania, July 6–8, 1988.
[19] Eugene R. Hammond, *Critical Thinking, Thoughtful Writing*, 2d ed. (New York: McGraw-Hill, 1989), 119.
[20] Hendrickson, July 6–8, 1988.
[21] Flyer for "Restaurant and Accounting Controls," (Seattle: Restaurant Seminar Institute, n.d. [1991]): 2.
[22] "Today's Controller: The Total Manager," in *CPE Seminar Catalog* (New York: American Institute of Certified Public Accountants, 1991), 85.
[23] Myles Martel, *Before You Say a Word: The Executive Guide to Effective Communication*. (Englewood Cliffs, N.J.: Prentice Hall, 1984), 88.
[24] Martel, 84.
[25] Edward P. J. Corbett. *Classical Rhetoric for the Modern Student*, 2d ed. (New York: Oxford University Press, 1971), 462–495.
[26] Donald F. Istvan, "Coming Full Circle in Practice Management," *Journal of Accountancy* (May 1991): 42.
[27] Konica advertisement, *Journal of Accountancy* (May 1991): 98.
[28] Aletha Hendrickson, "Putting the IRS on Notice: A Lesson in the Tactics of Intimidation," in *Constructing Rhetorical Education: From the Classroom to the Community* (Carbondale, Ill.: Southern Illinois University Press, 1991), 403–422.
[29] Prentice Hall software advertisement, *Journal of Accountancy* (May 1991): 23.
[30] MicroMash advertisement, *Accounting Today* (May 29, 1991): 16.
[31] MicroMash, 16.
[32] E. F. Haskell software advertisement, *Journal of Accountancy* (May 1991): 19.
[33] DacEasy, Inc. advertisement, *Accounting Today* (April 29, 1991): 5.
[34] MicroMash, 16.
[35] Lacerte Software Corporation advertisement, *Accounting Today* (May 29, 1991): 42.
[36] E. F. Haskell software advertisement, *Journal of Accountancy* (May 1991): 19.
[37] Bob Okell, "Firms Chart New Growth Plans," *Accounting Today* (April 29, 1991): 3.
[38] "News Digest," *Accounting Today* (April 29, 1991): 1.
[39] Aletha Hendrickson, "Advantages and Limitations of CAT in Writing Classes: Nibbling at Composition Problems Byte by Byte," *The Computer-Assisted Composition Journal* (Winter 1987): 88.
[40] Tax Partner advertisement, *Accounting Today* (April 29, 1991): 17.
[41] CCH Computax advertisement, *Journal of Accountancy* (May 1991): 105.

NAME

EXERCISE 8-1: LISTENING EVALUATION

After attending an oral presentation or talk, complete the following listening evaluation.

Title of presentation: ______________________________

Presenter/speaker: ______________________________

Occasion or forum: ______________________________

Why did you attend the talk? ______________________________

Were the accommodations appropriate? ______________________________

Would you classify the audience as hostile, friendly, or indifferent? ______________________________

Did you find the presentation informative and useful? ______________________________

Give three reasons why. ______________________________

____

____

____

____

If you found the presentation uninformative, give three reasons why. ______________________________

____

____

____

Did you think about the topic beforehand? ______________________________

Were you interested in the topic? _______ Why or why not? ______________________________

____

____

How did the speaker attempt to capture your interest? ______________________________

____

How did the speaker keep your interest? ______________________________

____

During the talk, did you indicate interest? _______ If so, how? ______________________________

____

List three things about the speaker's style that appealed to you. ______________________________

____

____

____

List three things about the speaker's style or presentation that you would like to see improved. ______________________________

____

____

Did you daydream? _______ What distracted you? ______________________________

Did other members of the audience seem interested? ______________________________

What was the bottom line of the message? ______________________________

EXERCISE 8-1: LISTENING EVALUATION (CONTINUED)

List some main points covered. ____

____

____

____

Did you find the supporting evidence credible? ______ Why or why not? ____________________

____

Was your mind changed by the message? ______ Why or why not? ________________________

____

____

Did you take notes? ______ Can you understand them now? ______________________________

NAME

EXERCISE 8-2: SPEAKER ANALYSIS

Occasion: ____________________

Topic: ____________________

Date of talk __________ How much preparation time do you have? __________

How large is the audience? ____________________

If you supply handouts, will you have enough for the participants? __________

Other speakers, moderator, leader: ____________________

What is your level of expertise compared to theirs? __________

What is your role in the program (e.g., featured speaker, chair, panelist)? __________

____

Why were you asked to speak? ____________________

What do you have to gain? __________ To lose? __________

What are the conventions of speaking for this occasion? __________

____

What are your time constraints? ____________________

Will you be fielding questions from the audience? __________

What audio/visual aids would be appropriate? __________

Can you check out the facilities ahead of time? __________

Is the physical layout conducive to oral presentation? __________

If not, what can you do to improve it? __________

How will you be introduced? ____________________

Can you supply biographical information to enhance your credibility? __________

Are you comfortable before an audience? __________

How can you control nervousness? __________

How can you rehearse your presentation? __________

If your presentation has been taped beforehand, what distracting verbal and visual mannerisms can you spot? __________

____

How can you control them? ____________________

NAME

EXERCISE 8-3: AUDIENCE ANALYSIS

Occasion: ____________________

Organization: ____________________

Topic: ____________________

Why is the audience attending your talk? ____________________

What is in it for them? ____________________

What do they expect to learn from you? ____________________

How will they apply what they learn? ____________________

What is the audience's relation to you? ____________________

Are they likely to be indifferent, interested, or hostile to your topic? ____________________

Why? ____________________

Are they likely to be indifferent, interested, or hostile to you? ____________________

Why? ____________________

What is the audience's level of expertise compared to yours? ____________________

Education? ____________________ Experience? ____________________

Will you need to define terms for this audience? ____________________

What background and culture do you share with the audience? ____________________

____

____

What are the audience's biases and opinions on the topic? ____________________

____

____

What values and goals do you share with the audience? ____________________

____

What is the demographic composition of the audience? ____________________

____

NAME

EXERCISE 8-4: ANALYZING ORAL INTRODUCTIONS

Observe three different televised sermons and political speeches, or workplace presentations and talks, or academic addresses. Analyze what makes the introductions effective:

Occasion for talk #1: ____________________

Speaker: ____________________ Date: ____________________

Title: ____________________

Purpose of talk: ____________________

Audience: ____________________

Was the speaker introduced? _______ If so, how was the speaker's image enhanced? ____________________

What was the gist of the talk? ____________________

Which of the following introductory tactics were used? Provide details.

1. Playing off previous speaker: ____________________
2. Opening example, anecdote, case, scenario: ____________________

   Did the speaker return to the opening example? ____________________

   In the opening example, did the speaker compare and/or contrast, suggest cause and effect, or project into the future?
   ____
3. Recent event: ____________________
4. Benefits: ____________________
5. Humor: ____________________
6. Quotation: ____________________
7. Self-reference: ____________________

8. Other introductory tactics: ______________________________

____

____

After you heard the introduction, did you want to hear the rest of the talk? ______ Why or why not? ____________

____

How would you have improved the introduction? ______________________________

____

* * * * *

Occasion for talk #2: ______________________________

Speaker: ______________________________ Date: ______________

Title: ______________________________

Purpose of talk: ______________________________

Audience: ______________________________

Was the speaker introduced? ______ If so, how was the speaker's image enhanced? ______________

____

What was the gist of the talk? ______________________________

____

Which of the following introductory tactics were used? Provide details.

1. Playing off previous speaker: ______________________________

   ____

2. Opening example, anecdote, case, scenario: ______________________________

   ____

   ____

   Did the speaker return to the opening example? ______________________________

   In the opening example, did the speaker compare and/or contrast, suggest cause and effect, or project into the future?

   ____

3. Recent event: ______________________________

   ____

   ____

4. Benefits: ______________________________

   ____

   ____

5. Humor: ______________________________

   ____

   ____

6. Quotation: ______________________________

____

____

7. Self-reference: ______________________________

____

____

8. Other introductory tactics: ______________________________

____

____

After you heard the introduction, did you want to hear the rest of the talk? ______ Why or why not? ______

____

How would you have improved the introduction? ______________________________

____

* * * * *

Occasion for talk #3: ______________________________

Speaker: ______________________________ Date: ______________

Title: ______________________________

Purpose of talk: ______________________________

Audience: ______________________________

Was the speaker introduced? ______ If so, how was the speaker's image enhanced? ______________

____

What was the gist of the talk? ______________________________

____

Which of the following introductory tactics were used? Provide details.

1. Playing off previous speaker: ______________________________

____

2. Opening example, anecdote, case, scenario: ______________________________

____

____

Did the speaker return to the opening example? ______________________________

In the opening example, did the speaker compare and/or contrast, suggest cause and effect, or project into the future?

____

3. Recent event: ______________________________

____

____

EXERCISE 8-4: ANALYZING ORAL INTRODUCTIONS (CONTINUED)

4. Benefits: ____

____

____

5. Humor: ____

____

____

6. Quotation: ____

____

____

7. Self-reference: ____

____

____

8. Other introductory tactics: ____

____

____

After you heard the introduction, did you want to hear the rest of the talk? ______ Why or why not? ____________

____

How would you have improved the introduction? ____

____

NAME

EXERCISE 8-5: DESIGNING AN ORAL REPORT HANDOUT

Occasion: ______________________ Topic: ______________________

Title of Presentation: ______________________

Select components appropriate for a handout. Describe each component and justify its inclusion. Then create the handout for the oral report.

Handout Component	How Component Aids Audience Understanding
______________________	______________________
	______________________
	______________________
	______________________
	______________________
______________________	______________________
	______________________
	______________________
	______________________
	______________________
______________________	______________________
	______________________
	______________________
	______________________
	______________________
______________________	______________________
	______________________
	______________________
	______________________
	______________________

NAME

EXERCISE 8-6: IDENTIFYING SCHEMES AND TROPES

Identify schemes and tropes in articles, ads, and transcribed speeches.

Parallelism ______________________________

____

Antithesis ______________________________

____

Alliteration ______________________________

____

Assonance ______________________________

____

Anaphora ______________________________

____

Epistrophe ______________________________

____

Metaphor ______________________________

____

Simile ______________________________

____

Pun ______________________________

____

Hyperbole ______________________________

____

Rhetorical question ______________________________

____

Irony ______________________________

____

Oxymoron ______________________________

____

NAME

EXERCISE 8-7: ORAL PRESENTATION EVALUATION (LONG FORM)*

Presenter: ______________________________

Evaluator: ______________________________

Occasion: ______________________________ Date: ____________

Topic: ______________________________

Rate content and delivery on a scale of 1 (lowest) to 5 (highest) by circling the appropriate number.

Content

1. The introduction included a clear statement of the subject and purpose of the report.	1	2	3	4	5
2. The speaker outlined the report's plan of development and provided transitions between sections.	1	2	3	4	5
3. The report contained adequate and relevant information.	1	2	3	4	5
4. The speaker supported the content with facts and credible evidence and anecdotes.	1	2	3	4	5
5. The speaker covered a manageable number of points.	1	2	3	4	5
6. The speaker adapted the content to the needs and understanding of the audience.	1	2	3	4	5
7. The speaker avoided digressions.	1	2	3	4	5
8. Audiovisuals (if used) complemented the talk.	1	2	3	4	5
9. The conclusion pulled together the material.	1	2	3	4	5
10. The talk achieved its purpose.	1	2	3	4	5
11. The speaker fielded questions knowledgeably.	1	2	3	4	5
12. The speaker seemed well prepared and knowledgeable.	1	2	3	4	5

What was the report's bottom line? ______________________________

List three points made by the speaker: ______________________________

____

____

Delivery

13. The speaker seemed friendly.	1	2	3	4	5
14. The speaker seemed relaxed.	1	2	3	4	5
15. The speaker exuded confidence.	1	2	3	4	5
16. The speaker's posture was professional.	1	2	3	4	5
17. The speaker was professionally attired.	1	2	3	4	5
18. The speaker avoided distracting body mannerisms.	1	2	3	4	5

* I am grateful to Louise Predoehl, Professional Writing Program instructor at the University of Maryland, for helping to design the "Oral Presentation Evaluation" forms used in Exercises 8-7 and 8-8.

EXERCISE 8-7: ORAL PRESENTATION EVALUATION (LONG FORM) (CONTINUED)*

19. Enunciation was clear.	1	2	3	4	5
20. The speaker could be heard.	1	2	3	4	5
21. The speaker spoke at a normal speed.	1	2	3	4	5
22. The speaker avoided distracting verbal mannerisms.	1	2	3	4	5
23. The speaker maintained eye contact with the entire audience.	1	2	3	4	5
24. The speaker kept within time constraints.	1	2	3	4	5
25. The speaker evidenced enthusiasm.	1	2	3	4	5

BOTTOM LINE: Do you feel that the speaker is an effective communicator? ______________________

List three things you liked about the delivery. ______________________

____

____

____

____

List three things you would like to see improved in the speaker's delivery. ______________________

____

____

____

NAME

EXERCISE 8-8: ORAL PRESENTATION EVALUATION (SHORT FORM)

Presenter: ______________________ Evaluator: ______________________

Topic: ______________________________________ Date: ______________

Rate on a scale of 1 (lowest) to 5 (highest) by circling the appropriate number.

Content

The introduction included a clear statement of the subject and purpose of the report.	1	2	3	4	5
The speaker outlined the report and signaled its sections with transitions.	1	2	3	4	5
The report made a convincing, logical case with credible evidence.	1	2	3	4	5
The conclusion pulled together the material.	1	2	3	4	5
Audiovisuals (if used) enhanced the presentation.	1	2	3	4	5
The speaker seemed well prepared and knowledgeable.	1	2	3	4	5

Delivery

The speaker appeared relaxed and comfortable.	1	2	3	4	5
Attire and posture were professional.	1	2	3	4	5
The speaker avoided distracting body mannerisms.	1	2	3	4	5
Pronunciation was clear, correct, and unrushed.	1	2	3	4	5
The speaker could be heard.	1	2	3	4	5
The speaker avoided distracting verbal mannerisms.	1	2	3	4	5
Eye contact was effective.	1	2	3	4	5
Timing was appropriate.	1	2	3	4	5

Why did the speaker find the topic significant? ______________________________

____

What were the main points of the report? ______________________________

____

____

How could the speaker improve his or her delivery style? ______________________________

APPENDIX

Proofreading Symbols

When editing your own work or the work of others, or when revising an edited manuscript (e.g., one from your instructor), you will find that it saves time to observe standard proofreading symbols. The following proofreading symbols are geared to standard academic practice and are compiled and adapted from Floyd K. Baskette, Jack Z. Sissors, and Brian S. Brooks, *The Art of Editing*, 4th ed. (New York: Macmillan, 1986), 501–502; Kenneth W. Houp and Thomas E. Pearsall, *Reporting Technical Information*, 6th ed. (New York: Macmillan, 1988), inside back cover; and William Morris, ed., "Proofreaders' Marks," *The American Heritage Dictionary of the English Language* (Boston: Houghton Mifflin, 1980), 1048. Instructors sometimes develop their own adaptations of proofreading symbols.

Symbol	*Instruction*	*Example*
∧	Insert.	Acountancy (c inserted: Accountancy)
∧	Insert.	Doing business in the∧market. . . . (commercial inserted)
℘ (with loop)	Delete, take out.	Doing business in the commmercial market. . . .
℘	Delete.	Doing business in the ~~commercial~~ market. . . .
. . . (stet)	Let stand.	Doing business in the ~~commercial~~ market. . . . (stet)
. . .	Let matter stand above dots.	Doing business in the ~~commercial~~ market. . . .
≡	Change to a capital letter.	CPa
/	Change to a lowercase letter.	APple
○	Spell out.	Start with (1) comprehensive accounting program.
1/N	Use en dash,	mortgaged 1/N backed securities
=	(or hyphen).	mortgaged=backed securities
1/M	Use em dash.	Our series helps you pass peer review 1/M and helps you make money.

Symbol	Instruction	Example
¶	Begin paragraph.	¶The new accounting standards. . . .
⌐	No paragraph.	⌐ The new accounting standards. . . .
⊃⊂	Run in or connect.	At XYZ Corporation, we're satisfied with nothing but the best.
⊙	Insert period.	We believe you share our commitment⊙
^	Insert comma.	compilations, reviews^and audits
(:)	Insert colon.	We have a choice of three printers(:)matrix, daisy wheel, and laser.
(;)	Insert semicolon.	You can rely on our review material(;)these guides undergo annual scrutiny.
∨	Insert single quote or apostrophe.	independent contractor its
∨∨	Insert quotation marks.	The paper reduction act.
~~	Set in boldface type.	Our copiers deliver unsurpassed service.
___	Set in italics.	Our copiers deliver unsurpassed service.
∩∪	Transpose letters.	managemnet
∩∪	Transpose words.	assets fixed
⌐]	Move right.	We deliver!
[	Move left.	[We deliver!
] [	Center.	]We deliver![
⁀‿	Close up.	non leveraged
ℓ	Delete and close up.	C.P.A.
#	Insert horizontal space.	fixedassets
	Marginal question to writer.	*au: edit okay?*
└┘	Lower.	Our copiers deliver unsurpassed service.
┌┐	Raise.	Our copiers deliver unsurpassed service.

Glossary

A

Agreement (Ch. 7) Consistency in number, person, and gender.

Attributor (Ch. 4) The source for a writer's ideas, facts, and information.

B

"Be" verbs (Ch. 7) Eight irregular verbs indicating "state of being": *be*, *being*, *been*, *am*, *are*, *is*, *was*, *were*.

Bibliography (Ch. 3) A list of written and oral sources.

Boilerplate (Chs. 1, 6) Form letters and workplace documents, sometimes personalized.

C

Citation (Ch. 3) An acknowledgment of a written or oral source.

Constraints (Ch. 5) The components of a writer's or reader's situation that affect the writing or reading.

D

Deduction (Ch. 2) The process of reasoning from the general to the specific.

Desktop Publishing (Ch. 6) Near–typeset quality printing produced in-house with software and laser printers.

Diction (Ch. 7) Usage; appropriate word choice.

Doublespeak (Ch. 7) Misleading, euphemistic, confusing, or self-contradictory language.

E

Emphatic (Ch. 4) Expressive of confidence in an assertion.

Ethos (Chs. 1, 2, 3, 4, 8) The character of the writer or speaker as perceived by the reader or hearer.

Exigence (Chs. 3, 6) That which spawns written or spoken discourse.

Expectation gap (Ch. 2) The difference between what was meant by the accountant and what was understood by the user.

F

Font size (Ch. 6) Typeface size.

Format (Ch. 6) The consistent arrangement of textual and visual elements in a workplace document.

G

GAAG (Ch. 6) Generally Accepted Graphic Principles.

GALP (Ch. 8) Generally Accepted Listening Principles.

GAPP (Ch. 7) Generally Accepted Punctuation Practices.

GARP (Ch. 1) Generally Accepted Rhetorical Principles.

GASP (Ch. 8) Generally Accepted Speaking Principles.

Genre (Chs. 1, 2, 6) A prescribed mode of communication (e.g., engagement letter, resume, interoffice memo, letter of complaint, or promotional brochure).

Gloss (Ch. 6) Condensed explanatory text placed to the side of the larger text.

Grice's Maxims (Ch. 7) Four principles of effective and efficient communication.

H

Hedge (Ch. 4) To pull back from an assertion.

I

Induction (Ch. 2) The process of reasoning from the specific to the general.

Invention (Ch. 3) The discovery and development of materials for argument.

J

Jargon (Ch. 7) Terms specific to a profession but not always understood by nonprofessionals.

L

Logos (Chs. 1, 2, 3, 4, 8) A logical argument; incorporating evidence to satisfy the reader or listener.

M

Macro-editing (Ch. 5) Rhetorical and organizational revising.

Mannerisms (Ch. 8) A speaker's peculiar behavioral habits.

Metadiscourse (Chs. 2, 6) User-centered devices that guide reader understanding.

Micro-editing (Ch. 5) Sentence level revising.

N

Nominalizations (Ch. 4) Nouns formed from active verbs.

Noun string (Ch. 7) A series of nouns that modify another noun.

O

Overhearer (Chs. 1, 2, 5, 6) An unintended reader or user of a text (a third party).

P

Paper trail (Ch. 4) Filed or circulating writing often forgotten by the writer.

Pathos (Chs. 1, 2, 3, 4, 8) An appeal to the self-interest of the reader or listener.

Plagiarism (Ch. 3) The use of someone else's words or ideas without giving credit.

Presentation (Ch. 4) A display aimed at influencing the reader.

R

Reader-based prose (Ch. 7) Writing that considers reader or user needs.

Reader expectation (Ch. 2) That which the reader expects to learn from a document.

Rhetorical situation (Chs. 1, 5, 8) The exigence, audience, and constraints affecting the writer/speaker and reader/listener.

S

Schema (Chs. 2, 4) Knowledge about a situation, concept, or procedure stored in long-term memory, the result of prior exposure (*shcemata* is the plural form).

Scheme (Ch. 8) The alteration of words to change their sounds for rhetorical effect.

Scope (Ch. 7) The parameters of what will and will not be discussed.

Serifs (Ch. 6) Short finishing lines added to the main strokes that form letters. (**Sans Serif**: Lacking serifs.)

Sexist language (Ch. 5) Gender-specific language that assumes a male or female bias.

Stasis (Ch. 3) The status of an argument, the issue in dispute (*stases* is the plural form).

Syntax (Ch. 7) The order of words, phrases, and clauses.

T

Telling facts (Ch. 4) Relevant details from which the reader draws inferences.

Telling verbs (Ch. 4) Active verbs from which the reader draws inferences.

Thesis statement (Ch. 3) The point of an argument, a supportable assertion.

Tone (Ch. 4) The writer's attitude conveyed in the text, which affects reader reaction.

Toulmin's Warrants (Ch. 3) A model for argument; an appeal to *logos*.

Tropes (Ch. 8) The manipulation of words to affect ways of thinking.

Typeface (Ch. 6) The style of letters, numbers, and symbols.

U

User-centered (Chs. 1, 2) Written with user needs in mind.

Users (Chs. 2, 6) Intended readers or audience of a text.

V

Voice (Ch. 4) The role, persona, or stance assumed by a writer.

W

Writer-based prose (Ch. 7) Writing that is solely from the writer's point of view, with no regard for user needs or understanding.

Writer-centered (Chs. 1, 2) Written from the writer's point of view, and failing to consider the needs of users.

Writer's block (Ch. 1) The inability to start or continue a writing task.

Writing anxiety (Ch. 1) Dread of the writing task.

Name Index

Subject Index

A

N

O

P

Q

R

S

T

U

V

W

Y